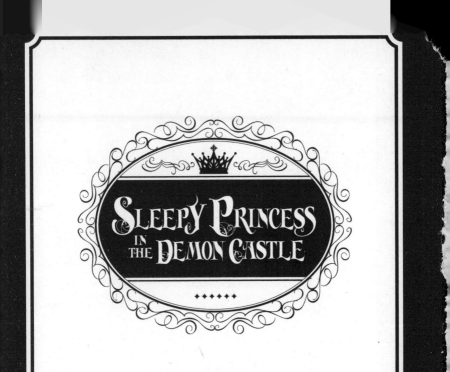

SLEEPY PRINCESS IN THE DEMON CASTLE

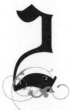

Story & Art by
KAGIJI KUMANOMATA

NIGHTS

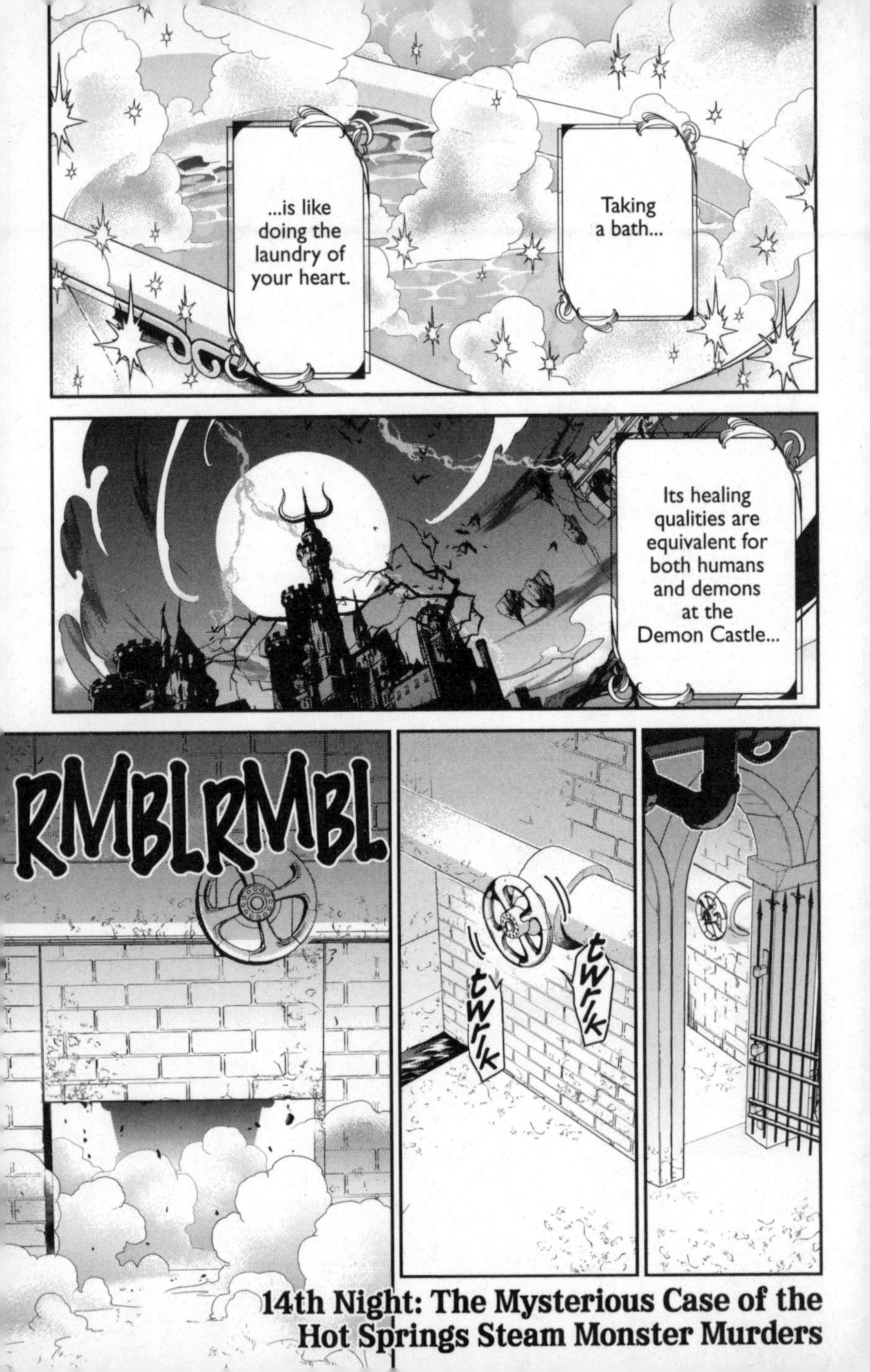
Taking a bath...
...is like doing the laundry of your heart.
Its healing qualities are equivalent for both humans and demons at the Demon Castle...
twrik
twrik
RMBLRMBL

14th Night: The Mysterious Case of the Hot Springs Steam Monster Murders

14th Night: The Mysterious Case of the Hot Springs Steam Monster Murders

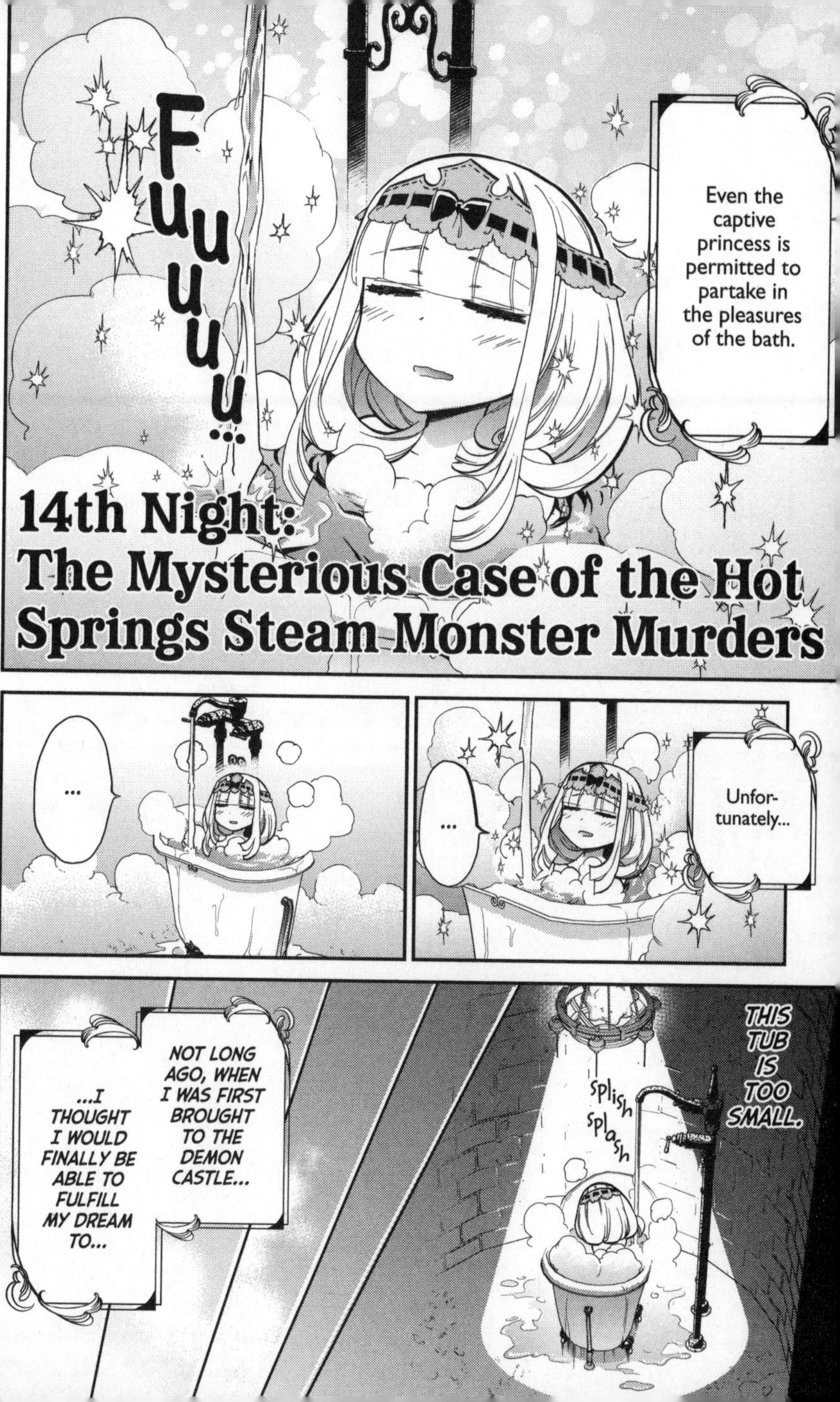
Even the captive princess is permitted to partake in the pleasures of the bath.
Fuuuuu...
Unfor-tunately...
...
...
THIS TUB IS TOO SMALL.
splish splash
NOT LONG AGO, WHEN I WAS FIRST BROUGHT TO THE DEMON CASTLE...
...I THOUGHT I WOULD FINALLY BE ABLE TO FULFILL MY DREAM TO...

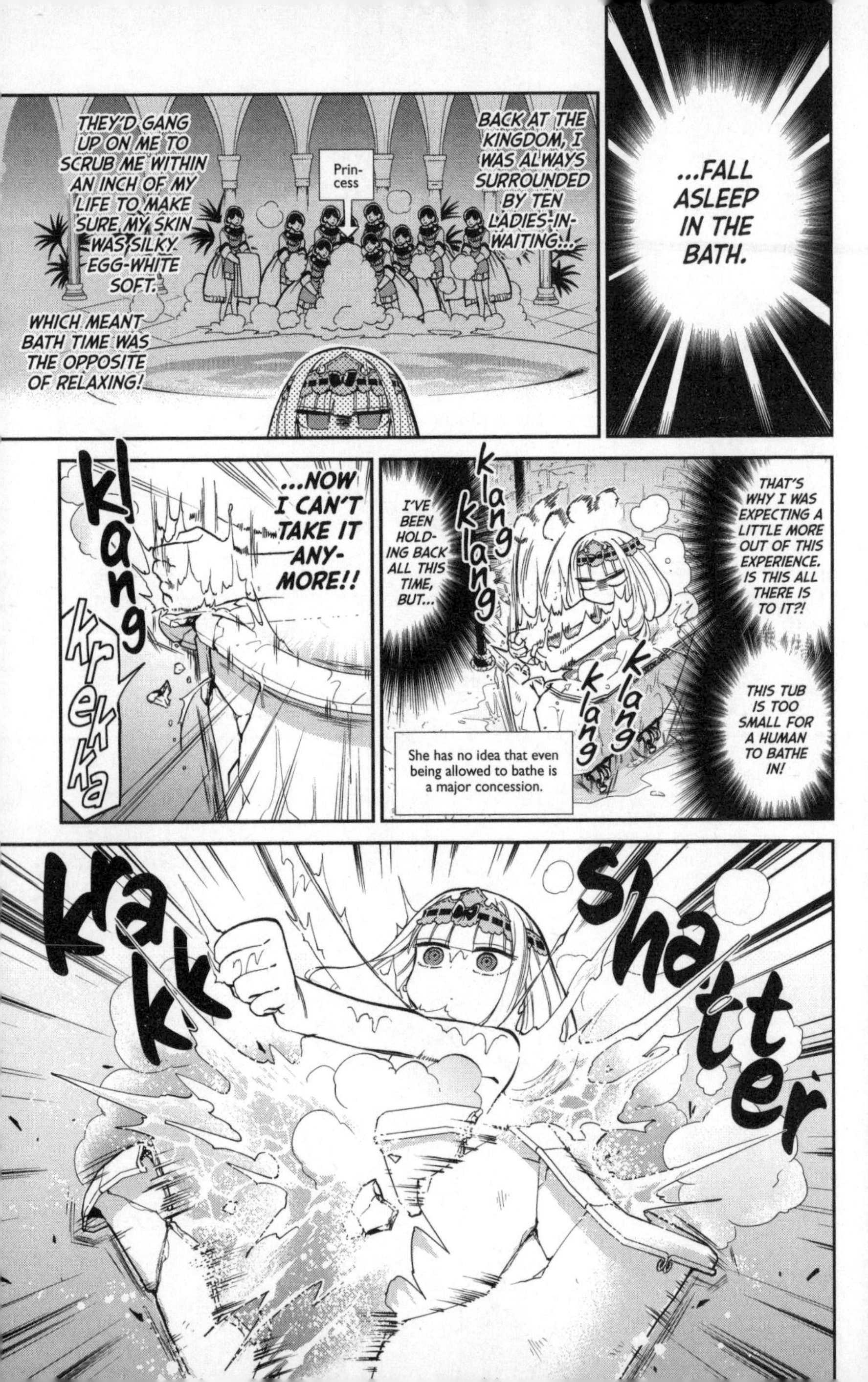
...FALL ASLEEP IN THE BATH.
BACK AT THE KINGDOM, I WAS ALWAYS SURROUNDED BY TEN LADIES-IN-WAITING...
Princess
THEY'D GANG UP ON ME TO SCRUB ME WITHIN AN INCH OF MY LIFE TO MAKE SURE MY SKIN WAS SILKY EGG-WHITE SOFT.
WHICH MEANT BATH TIME WAS THE OPPOSITE OF RELAXING!
THAT'S WHY I WAS EXPECTING A LITTLE MORE OUT OF THIS EXPERIENCE. IS THIS ALL THERE IS TO IT?!
THIS TUB IS TOO SMALL FOR A HUMAN TO BATHE IN!
klang klang
klang klang
I'VE BEEN HOLDING BACK ALL THIS TIME, BUT...
She has no idea that even being allowed to bathe is a major concession.
...NOW I CAN'T TAKE IT ANY-MORE!!
klang
krekka
shatter
krakk

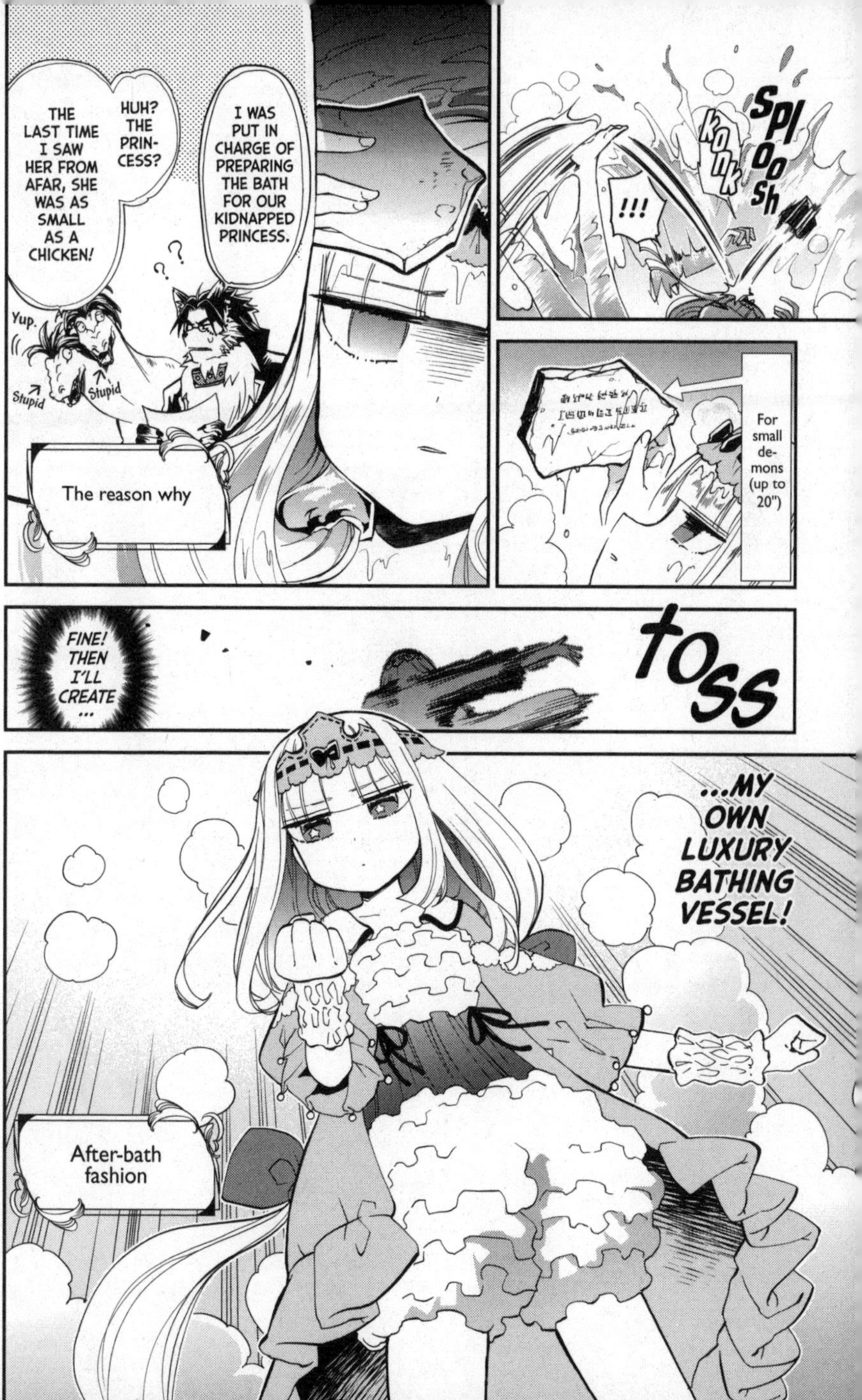
SPLOOSH
KONK
!!!
For small demons (up to 20")
I WAS PUT IN CHARGE OF PREPARING THE BATH FOR OUR KIDNAPPED PRINCESS.
HUH? THE PRINCESS?
THE LAST TIME I SAW HER FROM AFAR, SHE WAS AS SMALL AS A CHICKEN!
Yup.
Stupid
Stupid
The reason why
toss
FINE! THEN I'LL CREATE...
...MY OWN LUXURY BATHING VESSEL!
After-bath fashion

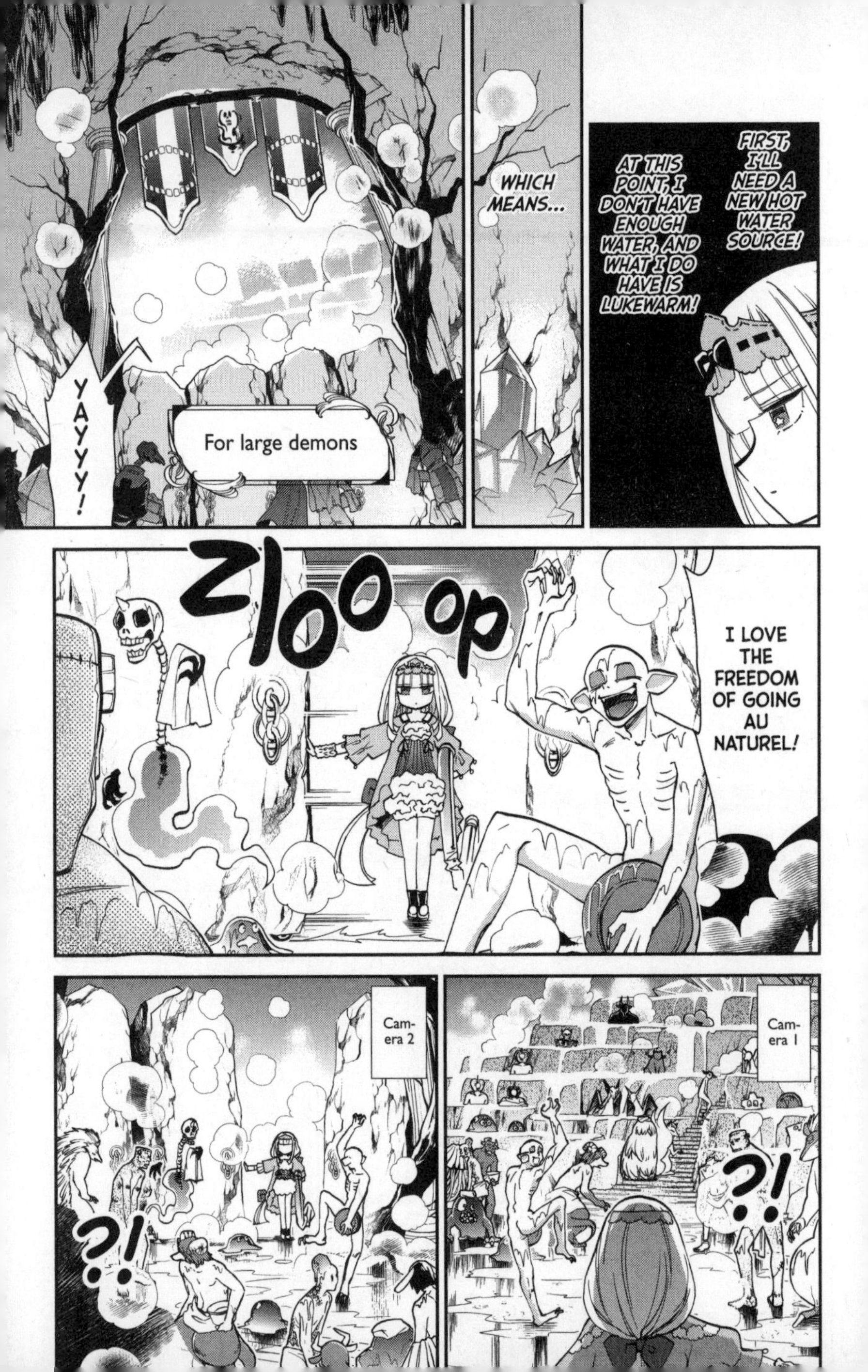
FIRST, I'LL NEED A NEW HOT WATER SOURCE!
AT THIS POINT, I DON'T HAVE ENOUGH WATER, AND WHAT I DO HAVE IS LUKEWARM!
WHICH MEANS...
YAYYY!
For large demons
I LOVE THE FREEDOM OF GOING AU NATUREL!
ZLOOOP
Cam-
era 1
?!
Cam-
era 2
?!

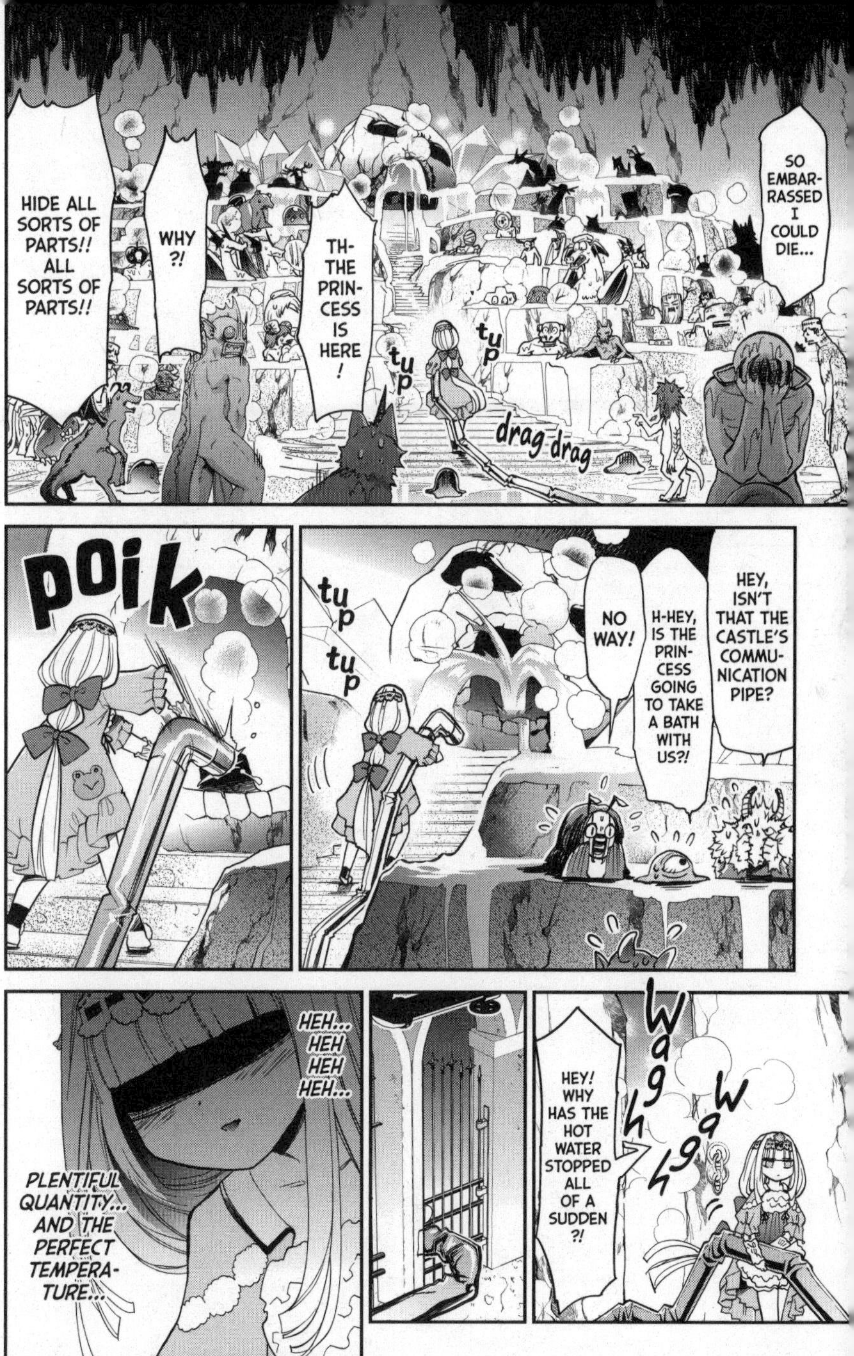
SO EMBAR-RASSED I COULD DIE...
tup
tup
drag drag
TH-THE PRIN-CESS IS HERE!
WHY?!
HIDE ALL SORTS OF PARTS!! ALL SORTS OF PARTS!!
HEY, ISN'T THAT THE CASTLE'S COMMU-NICATION PIPE?
H-HEY, IS THE PRIN-CESS GOING TO TAKE A BATH WITH US?!
NO WAY!
tup tup
poik
Wagh
Wagh
HEY! WHY HAS THE HOT WATER STOPPED ALL OF A SUDDEN?!
HEH... HEH HEH HEH...
PLENTIFUL QUANTITY... AND THE PERFECT TEMPERA-TURE...

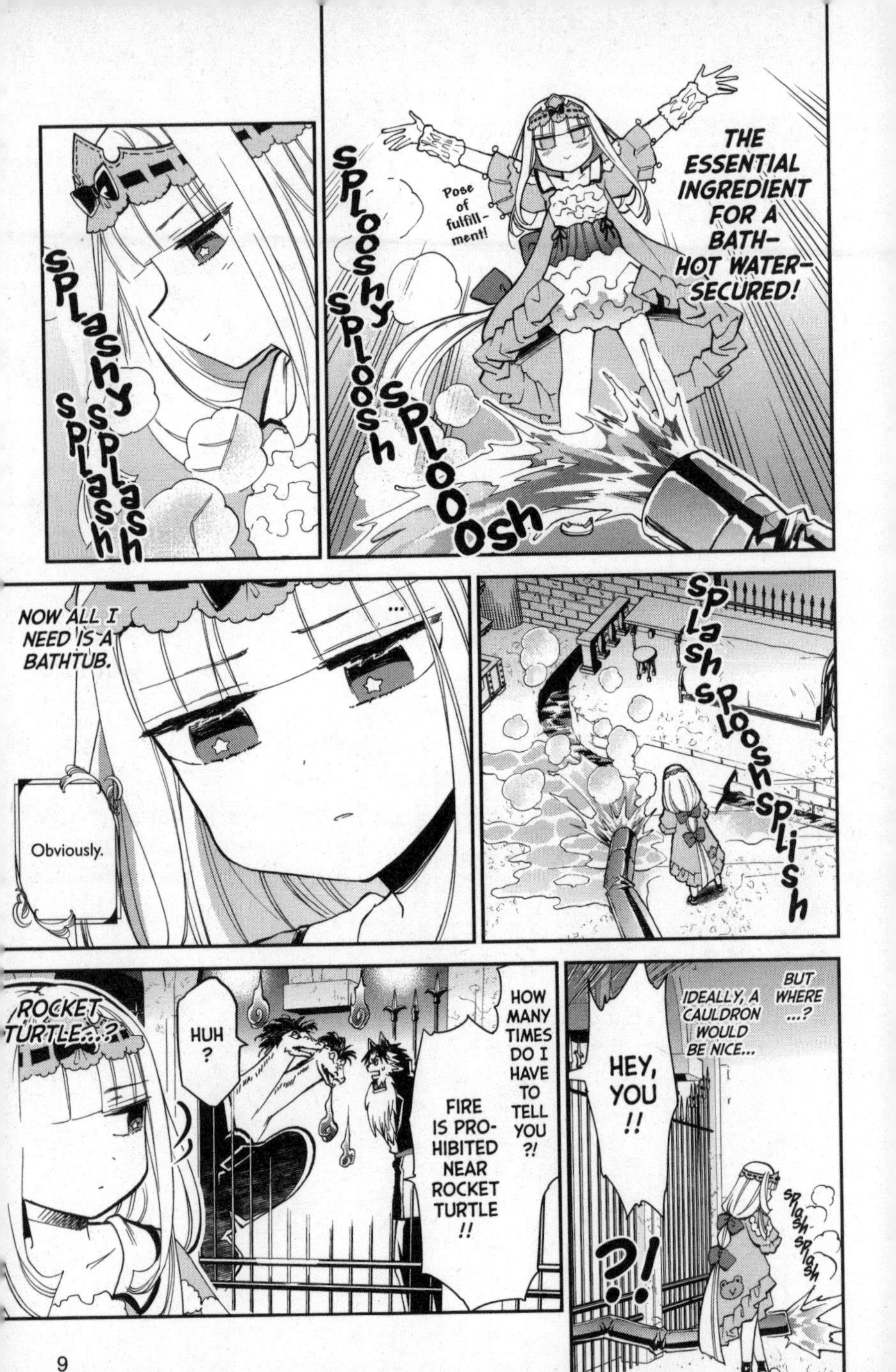
THE ESSENTIAL INGREDIENT FOR A BATH—HOT WATER—SECURED!
Pose of fulfillment!
SPLOOSHY SPLOOSH SPLOOOOSH
SPLASHY SPLASH SPLASH
SPLASH SPLOOSH SPLISH
NOW ALL I NEED IS A BATHTUB.
...
Obviously.
BUT WHERE ...?
IDEALLY, A CAULDRON WOULD BE NICE...
HEY, YOU!!
?!
SPLASH SPLASH
HOW MANY TIMES DO I HAVE TO TELL YOU?!
FIRE IS PROHIBITED NEAR ROCKET TURTLE!!
HUH?
ROCKET TURTLE...?

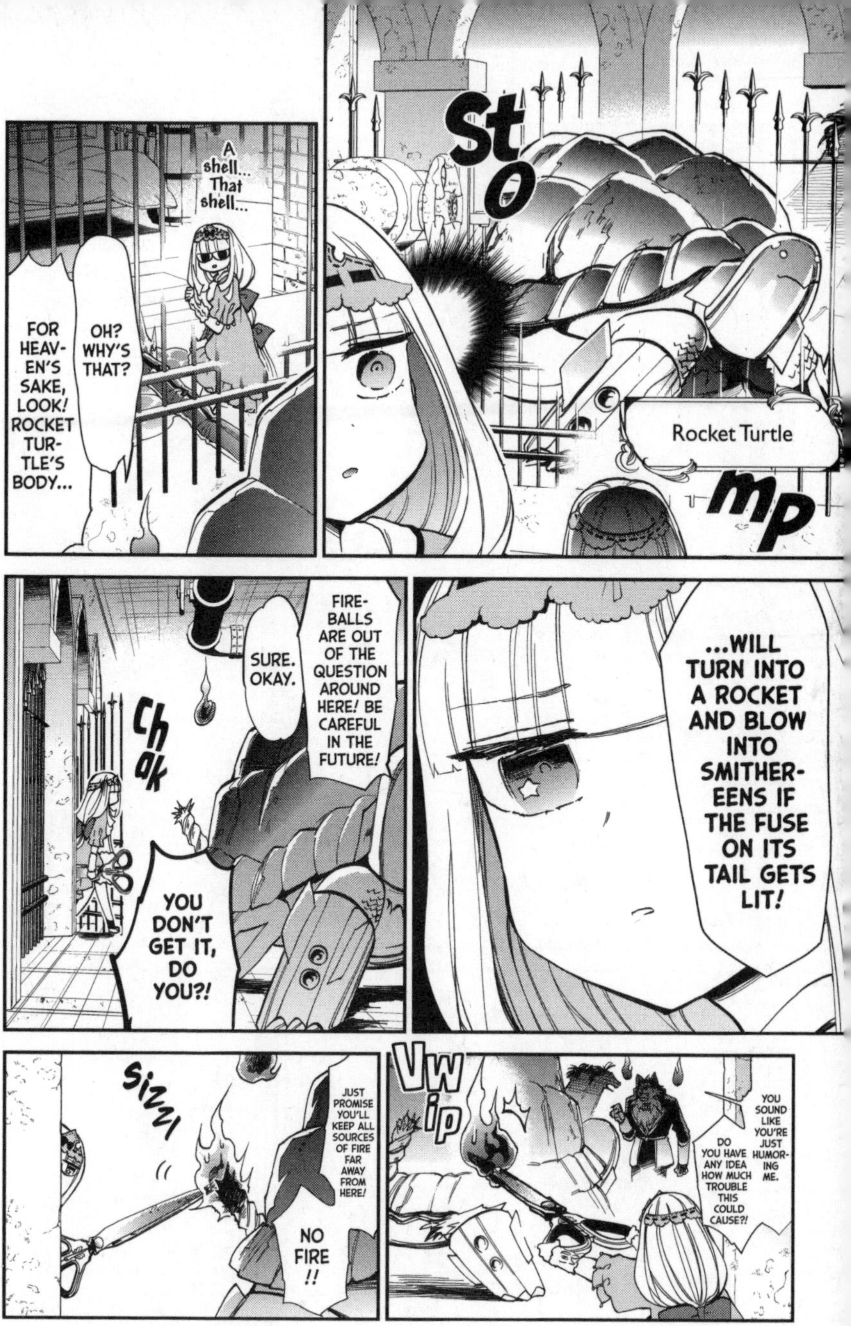
Sto
mp
Rocket Turtle
A shell... That shell...
OH? WHY'S THAT?
FOR HEAVEN'S SAKE, LOOK! ROCKET TURTLE'S BODY...
...WILL TURN INTO A ROCKET AND BLOW INTO SMITHEREENS IF THE FUSE ON ITS TAIL GETS LIT!
FIREBALLS ARE OUT OF THE QUESTION AROUND HERE! BE CAREFUL IN THE FUTURE!
SURE. OKAY.
Chak
YOU DON'T GET IT, DO YOU?!
Vwip
YOU SOUND LIKE YOU'RE JUST HUMORING ME.
DO YOU HAVE ANY IDEA HOW MUCH TROUBLE THIS COULD CAUSE?!
JUST PROMISE YOU'LL KEEP ALL SOURCES OF FIRE FAR AWAY FROM HERE!
Sizzl
NO FIRE!!

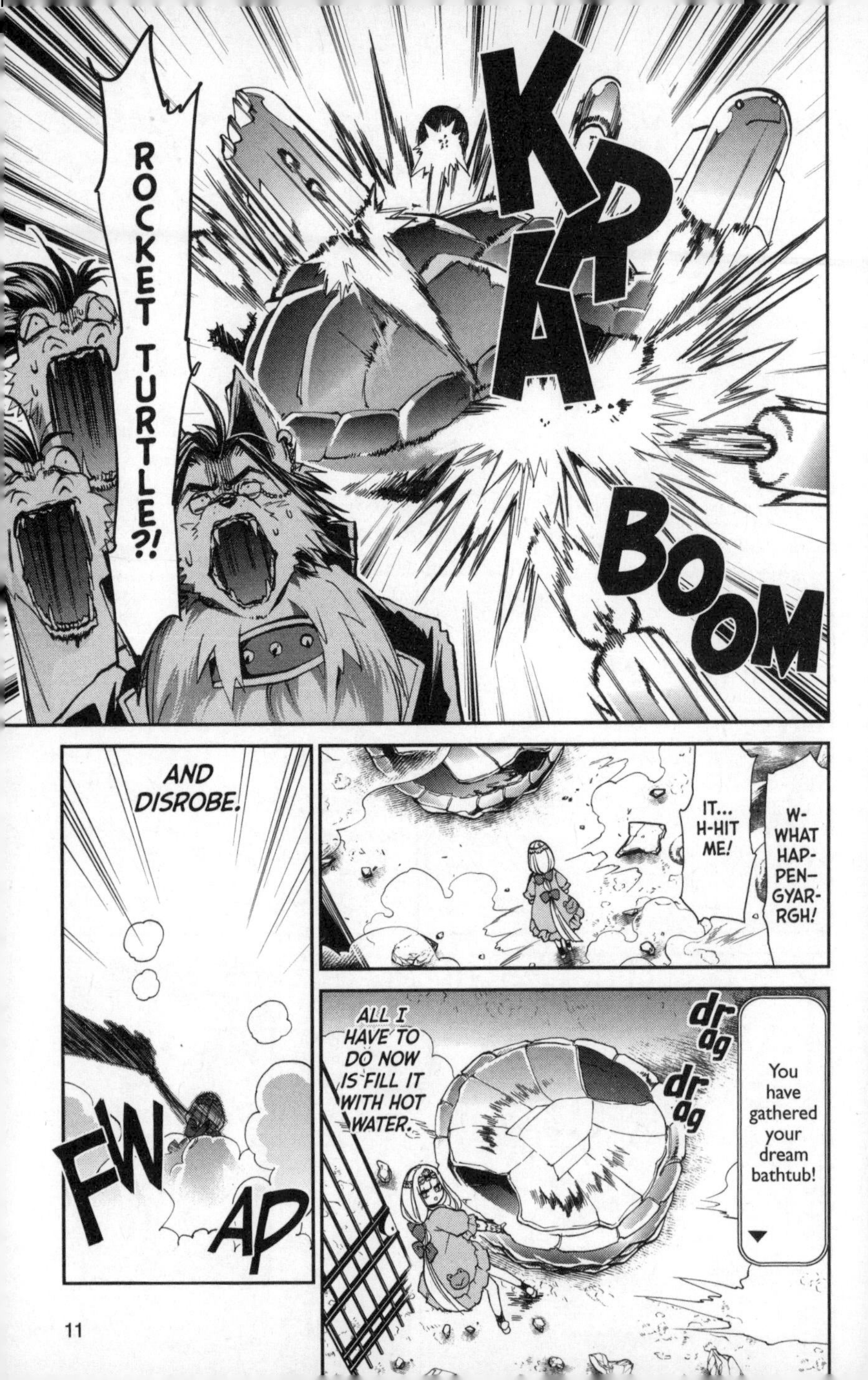
KRAKA
BOOM
ROCKET TURTLE?!
W-WHAT HAPPEN-GYARRGH!
IT... H-HIT ME!
You have gathered your dream bathtub!
drag drag
ALL I HAVE TO DO NOW IS FILL IT WITH HOT WATER.
AND DISROBE.
FWAP

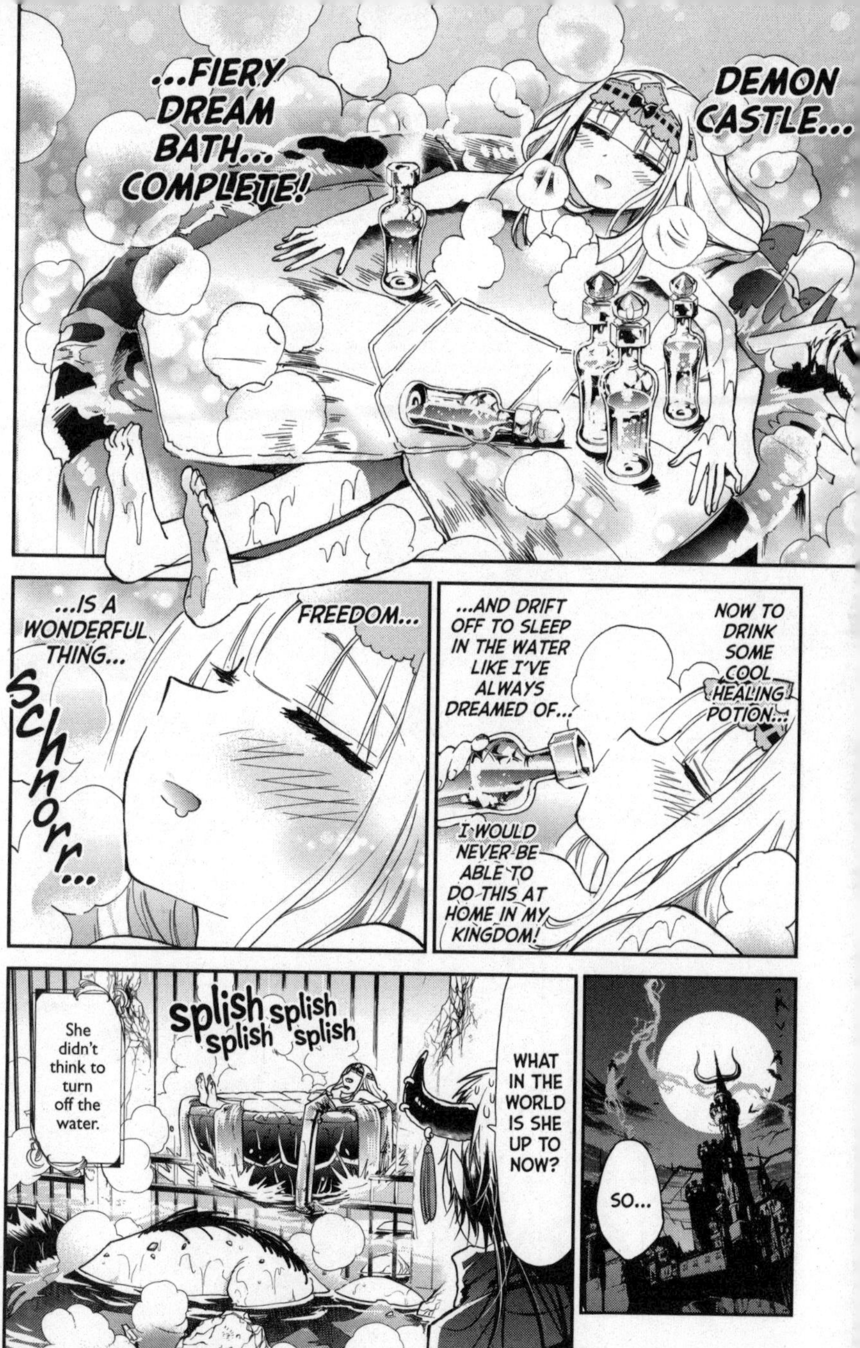
DEMON CASTLE...
...FIERY DREAM BATH... COMPLETE!
NOW TO DRINK SOME COOL HEALING POTION...
...AND DRIFT OFF TO SLEEP IN THE WATER LIKE I'VE ALWAYS DREAMED OF...
I WOULD NEVER BE ABLE TO DO THIS AT HOME IN MY KINGDOM!
FREEDOM...
...IS A WONDERFUL THING...
Schnorr...
SO...
WHAT IN THE WORLD IS SHE UP TO NOW?
splish splish splish splish
She didn't think to turn off the water.

Rocket Turtle

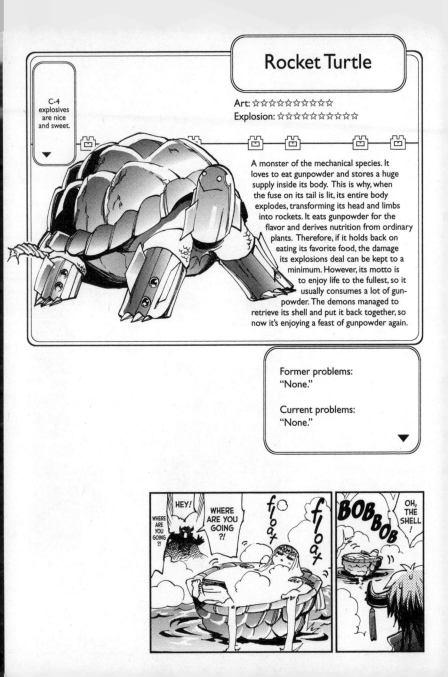

C-4 explosives are nice and sweet.

▼

Art: ☆☆☆☆☆☆☆☆☆
Explosion: ☆☆☆☆☆☆☆☆☆

A monster of the mechanical species. It loves to eat gunpowder and stores a huge supply inside its body. This is why, when the fuse on its tail is lit, its entire body explodes, transforming its head and limbs into rockets. It eats gunpowder for the flavor and derives nutrition from ordinary plants. Therefore, if it holds back on eating its favorite food, the damage its explosions deal can be kept to a minimum. However, its motto is to enjoy life to the fullest, so it usually consumes a lot of gunpowder. The demons managed to retrieve its shell and put it back together, so now it's enjoying a feast of gunpowder again.

Former problems:
"None."

Current problems:
"None."

▼

WHERE ARE YOU GOING ?!

HEY!

WHERE ARE YOU GOING ?!

float

float

BOB BOB

OH, THE SHELL !

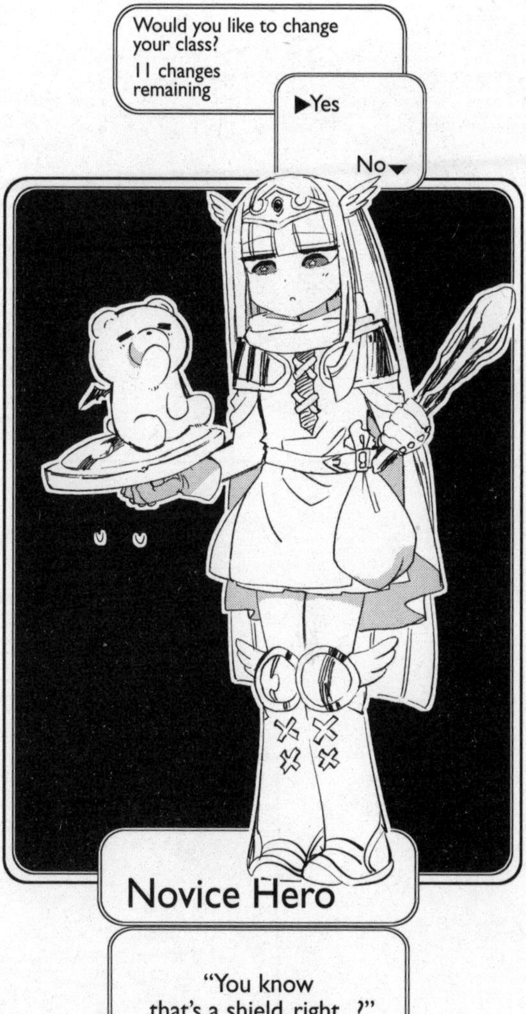
Would you like to change your class?
11 changes remaining
▶Yes
No
Novice Hero
"You know that's a shield, right...?"

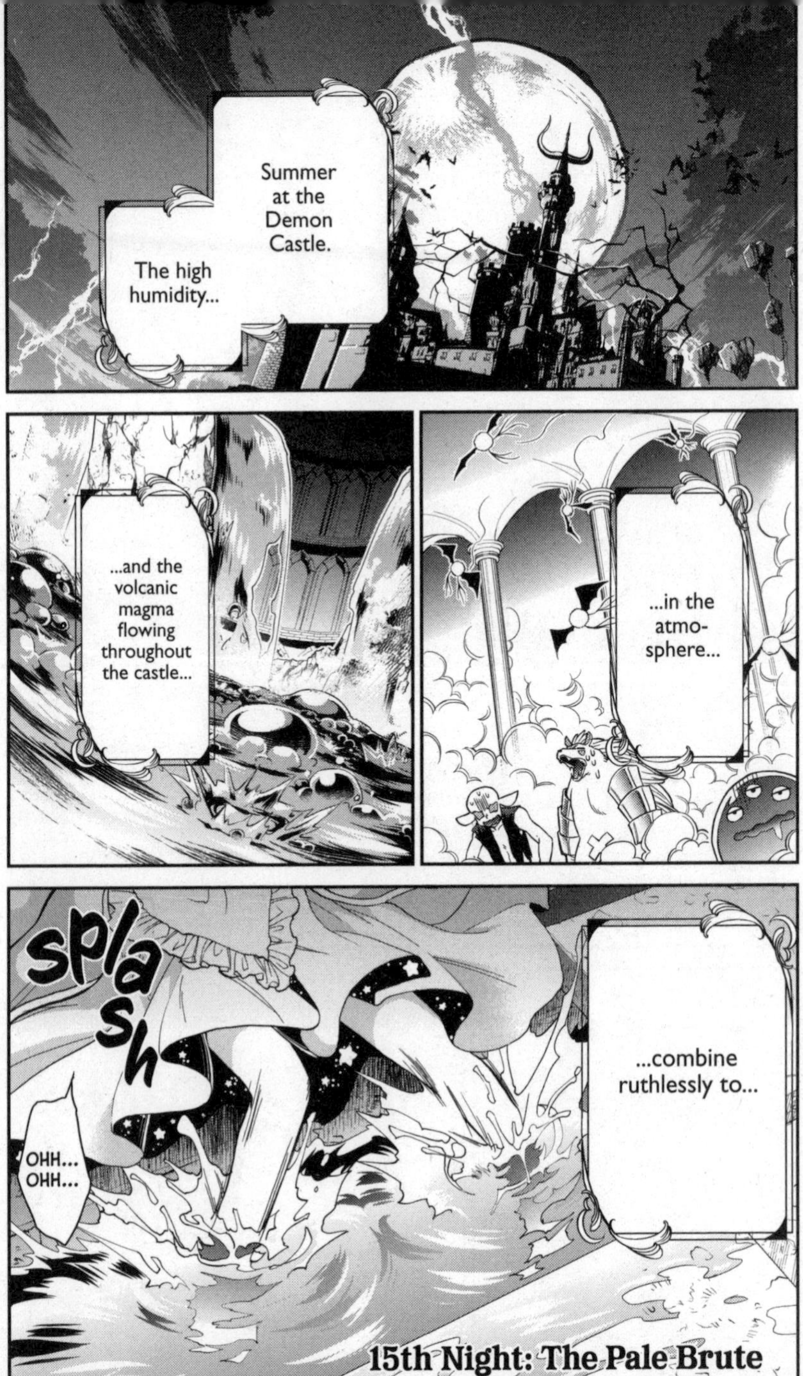
Summer at the Demon Castle.
The high humidity...
...in the atmosphere...
...and the volcanic magma flowing throughout the castle...
...combine ruthlessly to...
splash
OHH... OHH...
15th Night: The Pale Brute

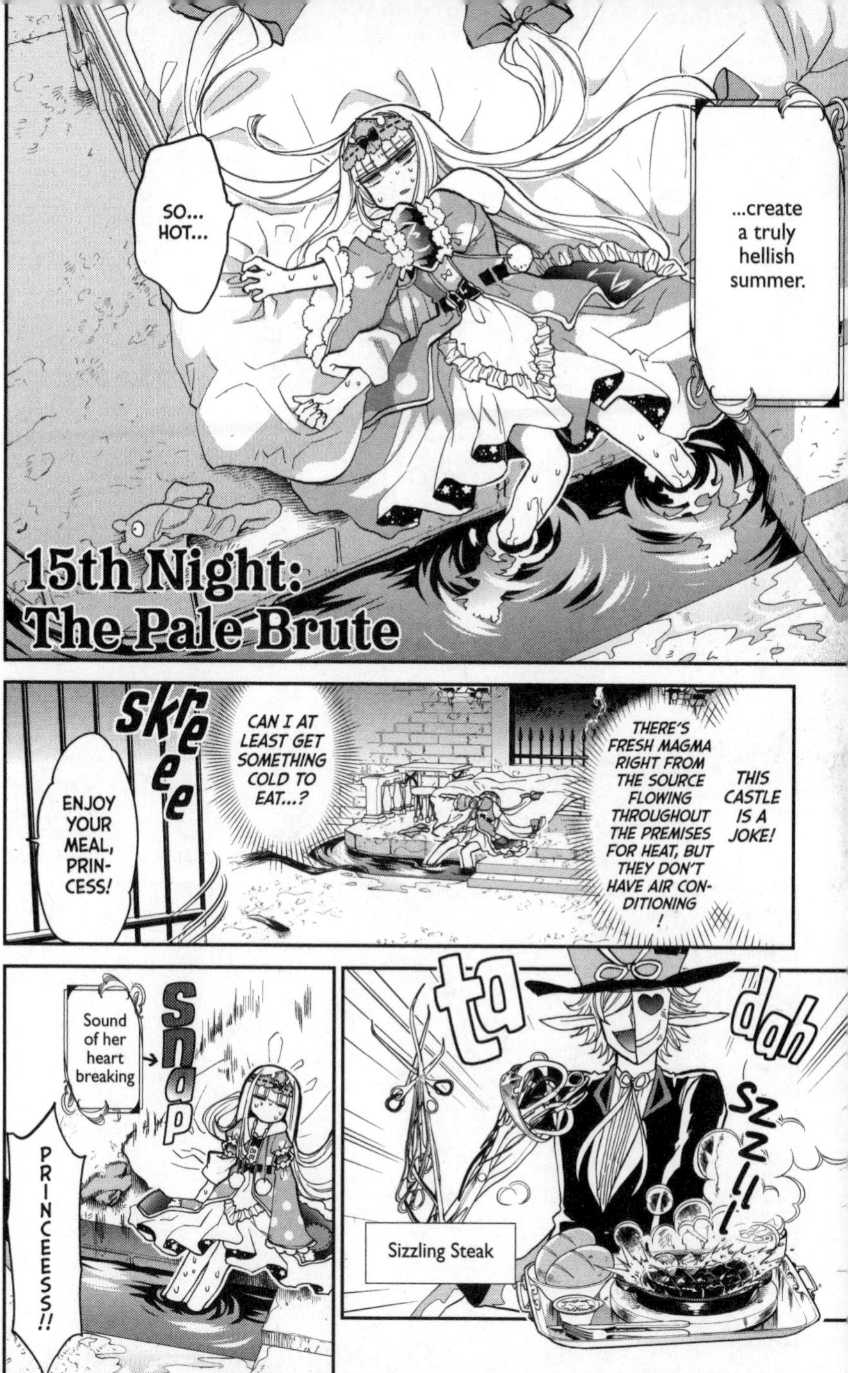
...create a truly hellish summer.
SO... HOT...
15th Night: The Pale Brute
THIS CASTLE IS A JOKE!
THERE'S FRESH MAGMA RIGHT FROM THE SOURCE FLOWING THROUGHOUT THE PREMISES FOR HEAT, BUT THEY DON'T HAVE AIR CONDITIONING!
CAN I AT LEAST GET SOMETHING COLD TO EAT...?
skreeee
ENJOY YOUR MEAL, PRINCESS!
ta dah
SZZZ!!
Sizzling Steak
snap
Sound of her heart breaking
PRINCEESS!!

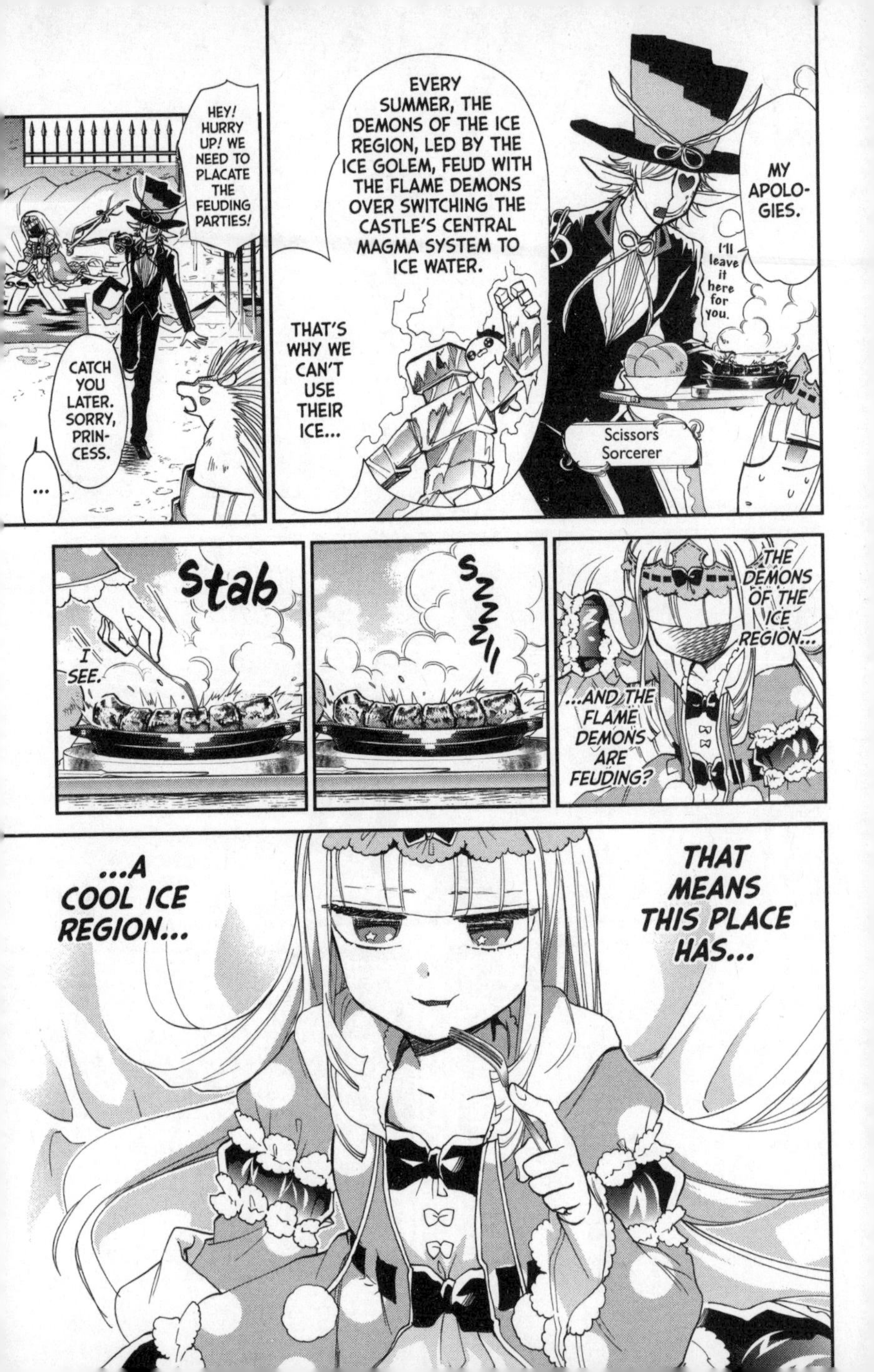
MY APOLOGIES.
I'll leave it here for you.
Scissors Sorcerer
EVERY SUMMER, THE DEMONS OF THE ICE REGION, LED BY THE ICE GOLEM, FEUD WITH THE FLAME DEMONS OVER SWITCHING THE CASTLE'S CENTRAL MAGMA SYSTEM TO ICE WATER.
THAT'S WHY WE CAN'T USE THEIR ICE...
HEY! HURRY UP! WE NEED TO PLACATE THE FEUDING PARTIES!
CATCH YOU LATER. SORRY, PRINCESS.
...
THE DEMONS OF THE ICE REGION...
...AND THE FLAME DEMONS ARE FEUDING?
SZZZ
Stab
I SEE.
THAT MEANS THIS PLACE HAS...
...A COOL ICE REGION...

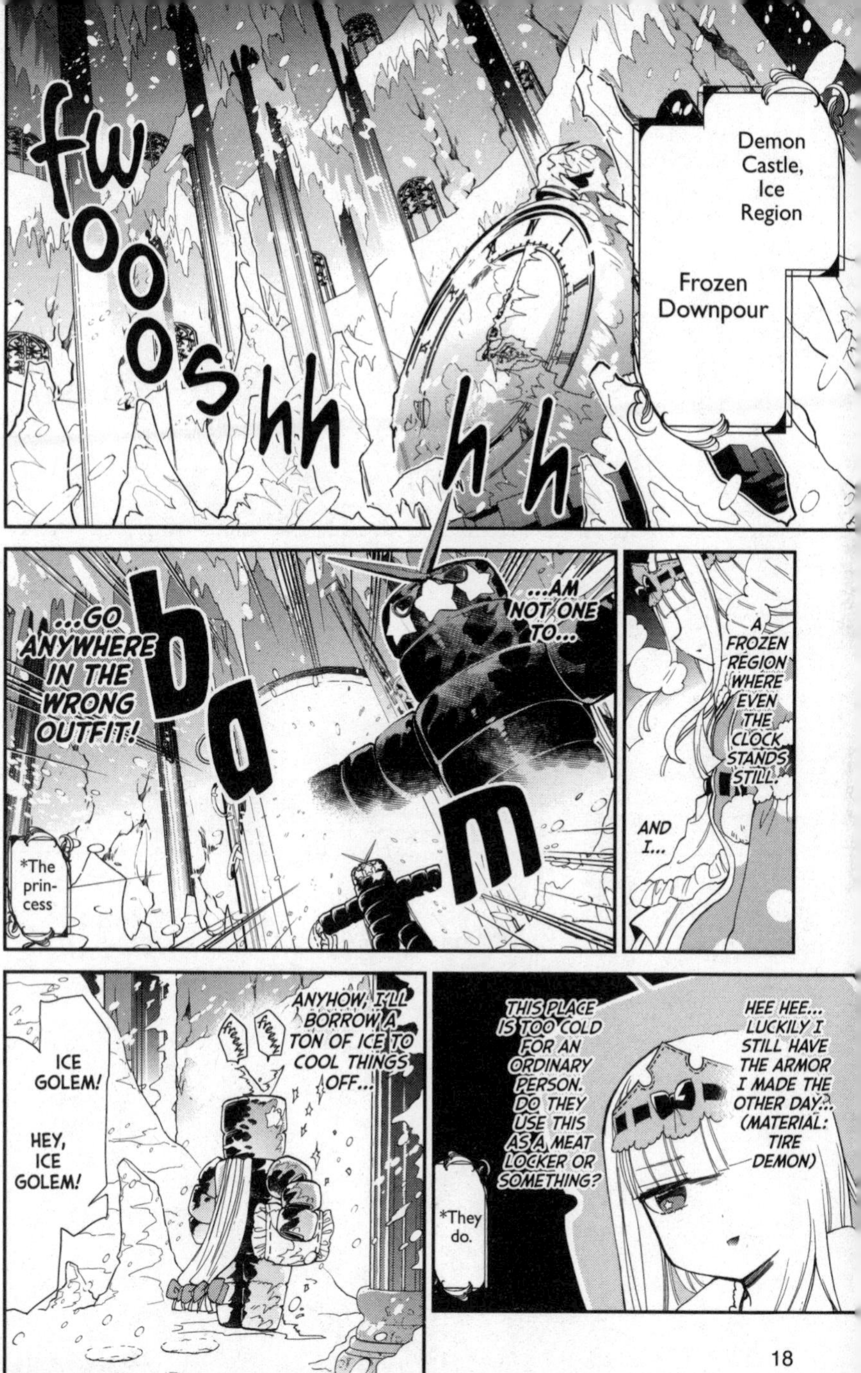
Demon Castle, Ice Region
Frozen Downpour
fwoooshhhhh
A FROZEN REGION WHERE EVEN THE CLOCK STANDS STILL.
AND I...
...AM NOT ONE TO...
...GO ANYWHERE IN THE WRONG OUTFIT!
bam
*The princess
HEE HEE... LUCKILY I STILL HAVE THE ARMOR I MADE THE OTHER DAY... (MATERIAL: TIRE DEMON)
THIS PLACE IS TOO COLD FOR AN ORDINARY PERSON. DO THEY USE THIS AS A MEAT LOCKER OR SOMETHING?
*They do.
ANYHOW, I'LL BORROW A TON OF ICE TO COOL THINGS OFF...
ICE GOLEM!
HEY, ICE GOLEM!

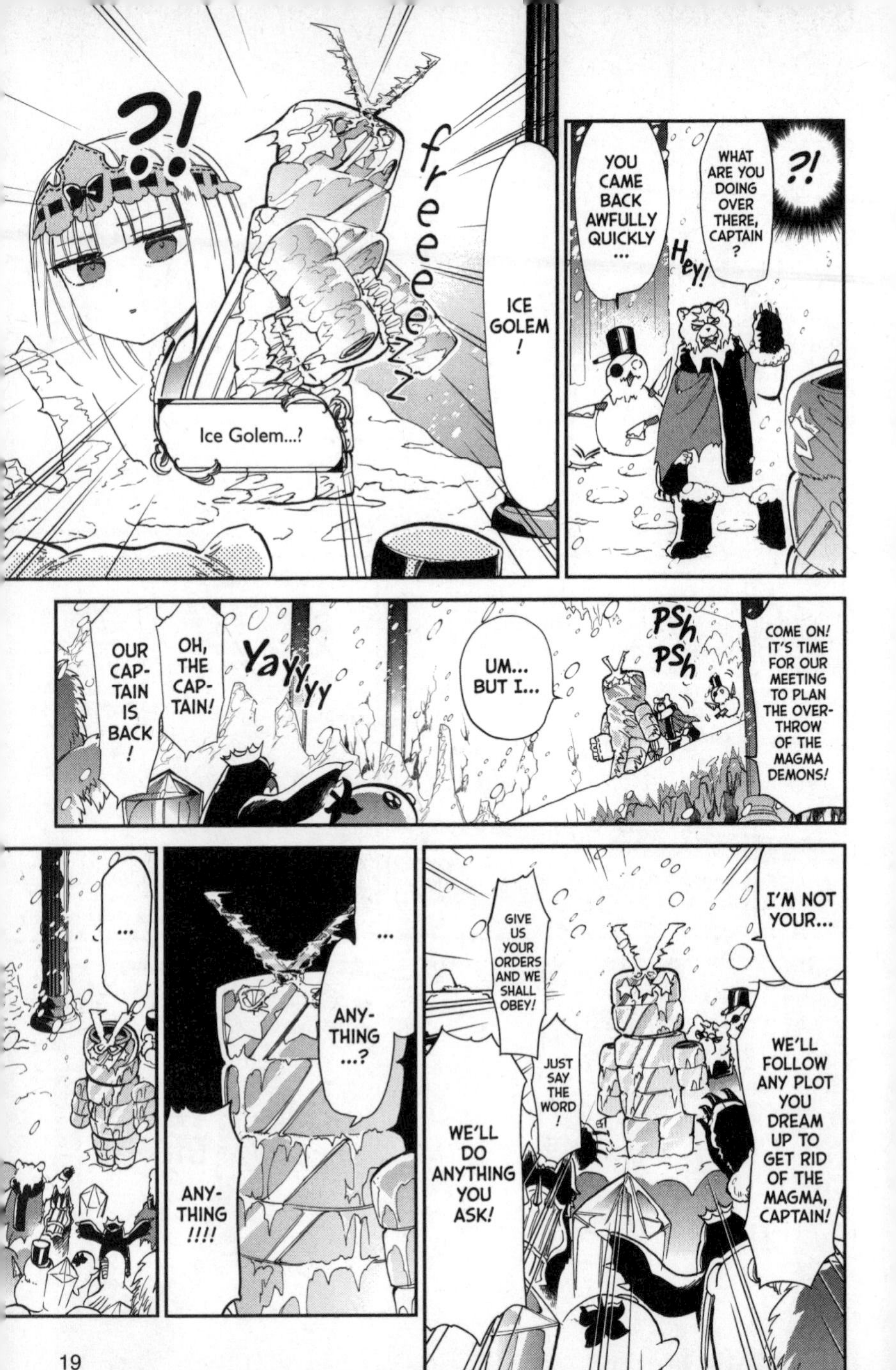
?!
WHAT ARE YOU DOING OVER THERE, CAPTAIN?
Hey!
YOU CAME BACK AWFULLY QUICKLY...
ICE GOLEM!
freeeeezzz
?!
Ice Golem...?
COME ON! IT'S TIME FOR OUR MEETING TO PLAN THE OVERTHROW OF THE MAGMA DEMONS!
PSh PSh
UM... BUT I...
Yayyyy
OH, THE CAPTAIN!
OUR CAPTAIN IS BACK!
I'M NOT YOUR...
WE'LL FOLLOW ANY PLOT YOU DREAM UP TO GET RID OF THE MAGMA, CAPTAIN!
GIVE US YOUR ORDERS AND WE SHALL OBEY!
JUST SAY THE WORD!
WE'LL DO ANYTHING YOU ASK!
...
ANYTHING...?
ANYTHING!!!!
...

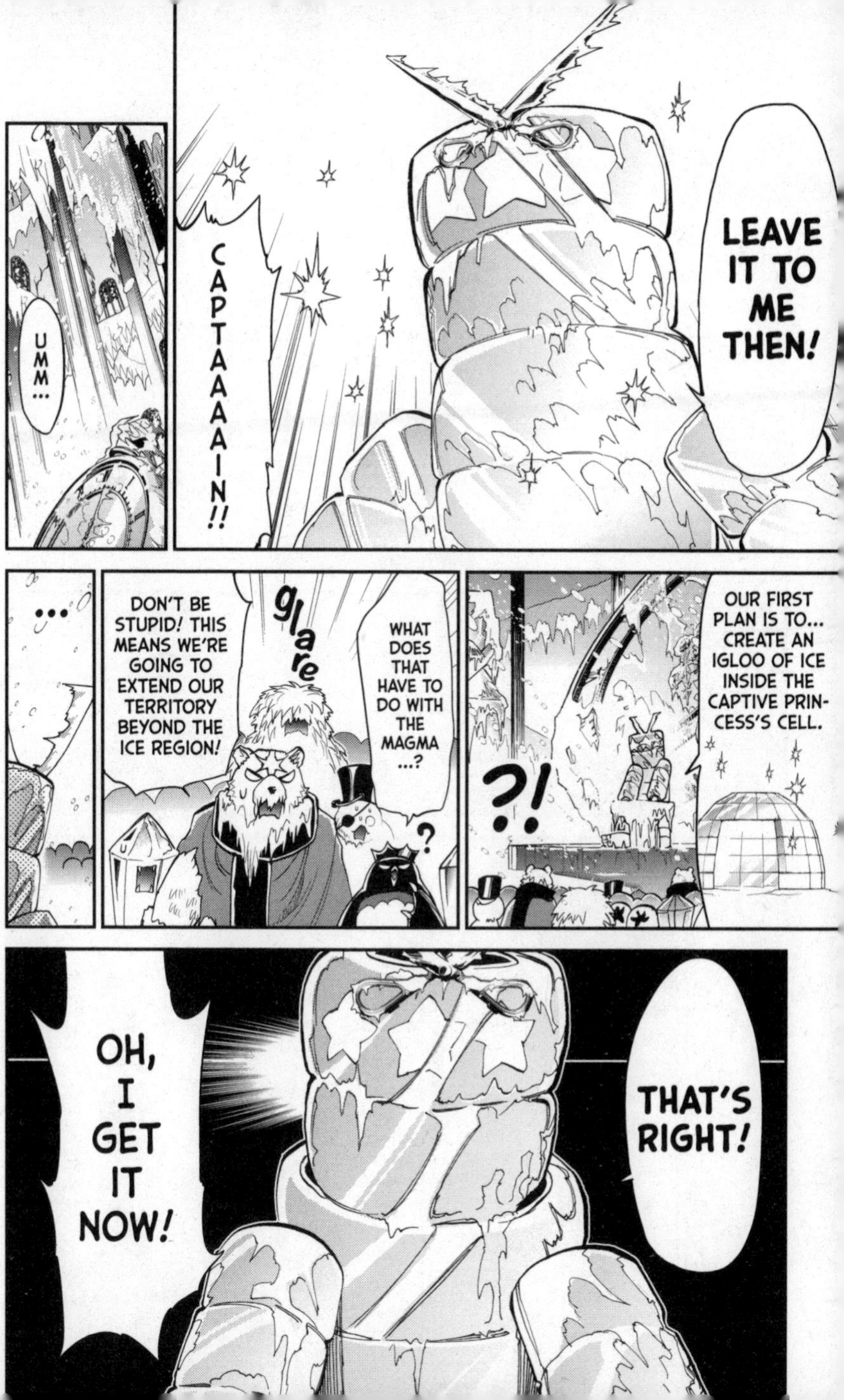
LEAVE IT TO ME THEN!
CAPTAAAAAIN!!
UMM...
OUR FIRST PLAN IS TO... CREATE AN IGLOO OF ICE INSIDE THE CAPTIVE PRINCESS'S CELL.
?!
WHAT DOES THAT HAVE TO DO WITH THE MAGMA ...?
glare
DON'T BE STUPID! THIS MEANS WE'RE GOING TO EXTEND OUR TERRITORY BEYOND THE ICE REGION!
?
...
THAT'S RIGHT!
OH, I GET IT NOW!

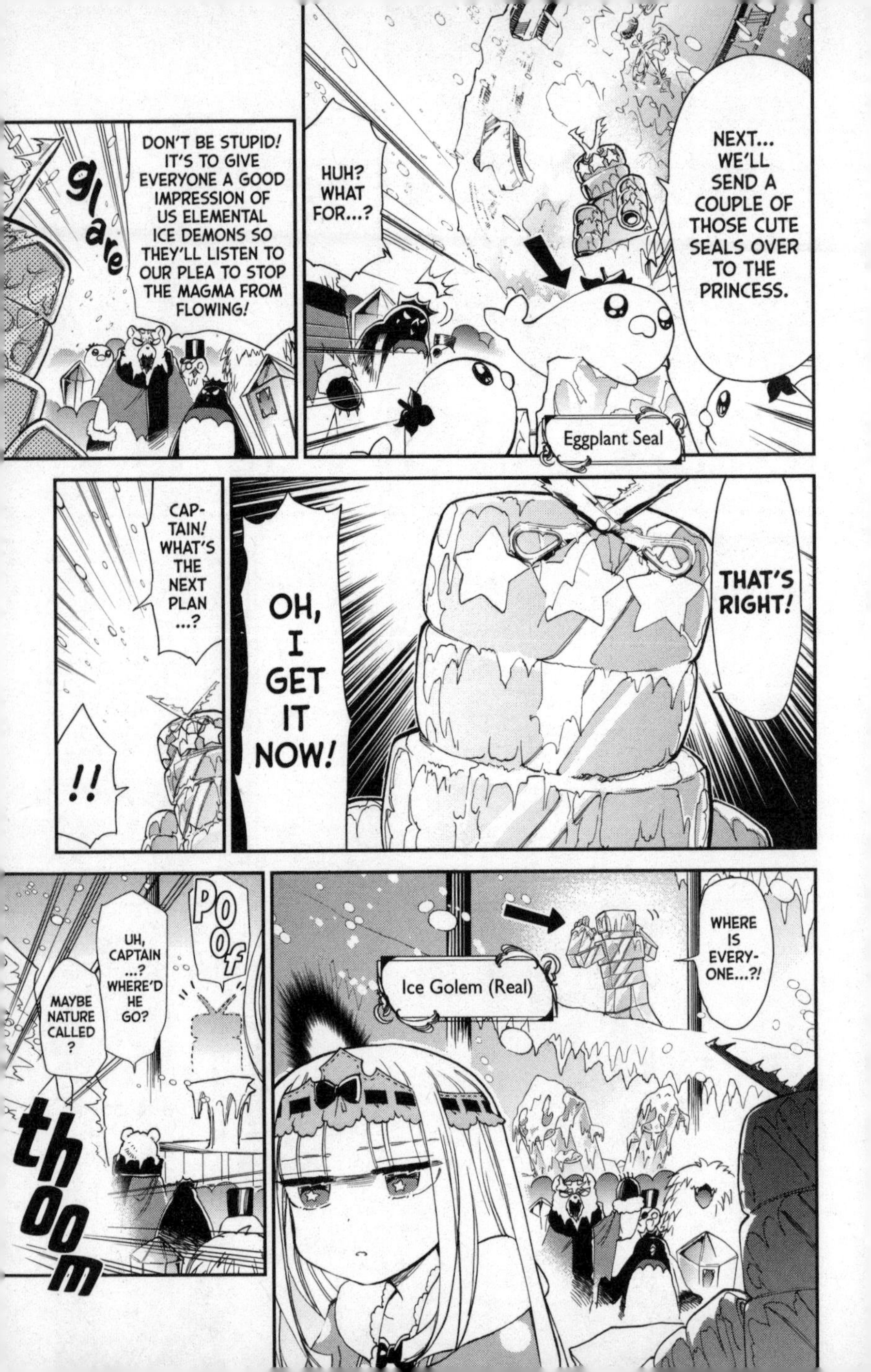

NEXT... WE'LL SEND A COUPLE OF THOSE CUTE SEALS OVER TO THE PRINCESS.
HUH? WHAT FOR...?
Eggplant Seal
DON'T BE STUPID! IT'S TO GIVE EVERYONE A GOOD IMPRESSION OF US ELEMENTAL ICE DEMONS SO THEY'LL LISTEN TO OUR PLEA TO STOP THE MAGMA FROM FLOWING!
glare
THAT'S RIGHT!
OH, I GET IT NOW!
CAPTAIN! WHAT'S THE NEXT PLAN...?
!!
WHERE IS EVERYONE...?!
Ice Golem (Real)
Poof
UH, CAPTAIN...? WHERE'D HE GO?
MAYBE NATURE CALLED?
thoom

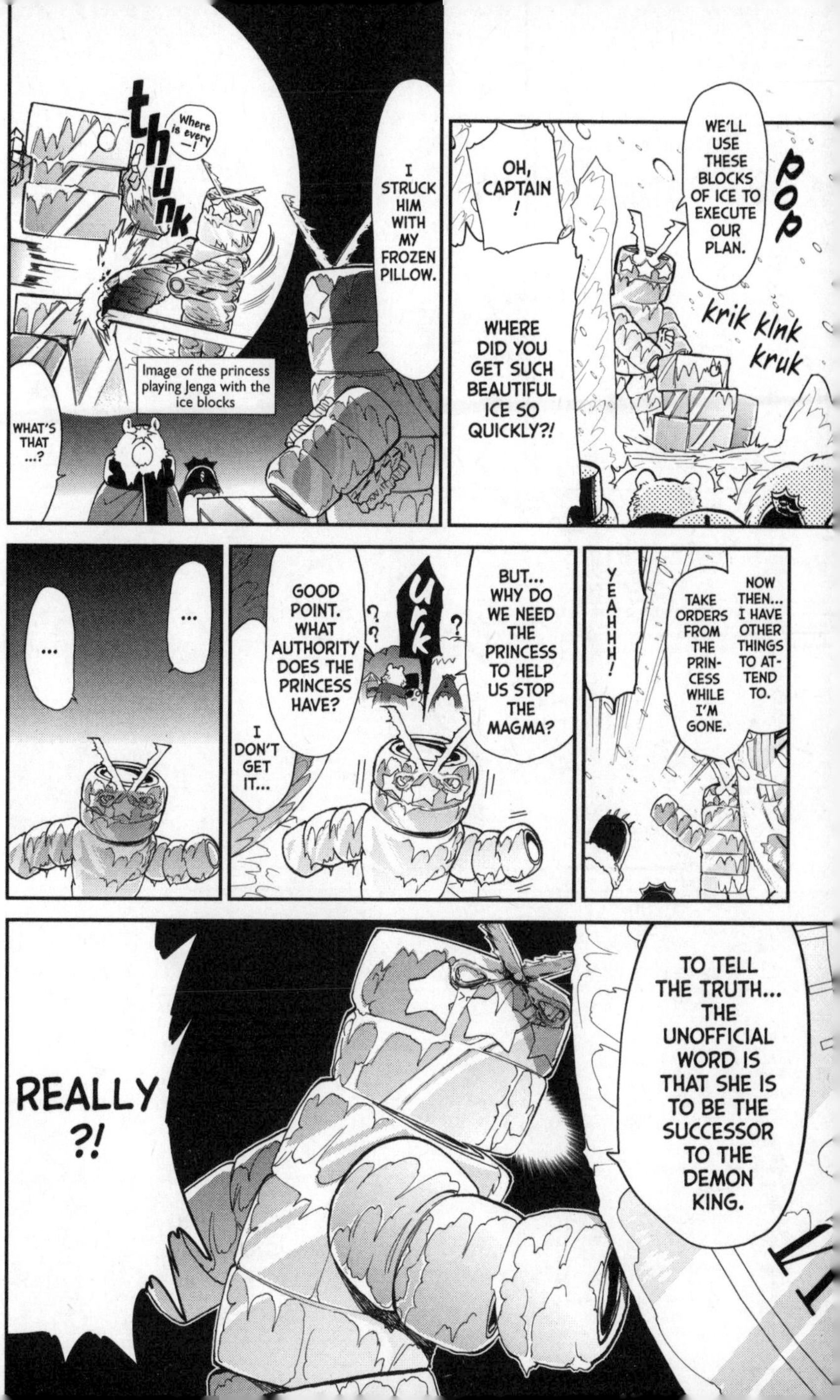
WE'LL USE THESE BLOCKS OF ICE TO EXECUTE OUR PLAN.
POP
OH, CAPTAIN!
krik klnk kruk
WHERE DID YOU GET SUCH BEAUTIFUL ICE SO QUICKLY?!
I STRUCK HIM WITH MY FROZEN PILLOW.
Where is every—!
thunk
Image of the princess playing Jenga with the ice blocks
WHAT'S THAT ...?
NOW THEN... I HAVE OTHER THINGS TO ATTEND TO.
TAKE ORDERS FROM THE PRINCESS WHILE I'M GONE.
YEAHHH!
BUT... WHY DO WE NEED THE PRINCESS TO HELP US STOP THE MAGMA?
?
urk
??
GOOD POINT. WHAT AUTHORITY DOES THE PRINCESS HAVE?
I DON'T GET IT...
...
...
TO TELL THE TRUTH... THE UNOFFICIAL WORD IS THAT SHE IS TO BE THE SUCCESSOR TO THE DEMON KING.
REALLY?!

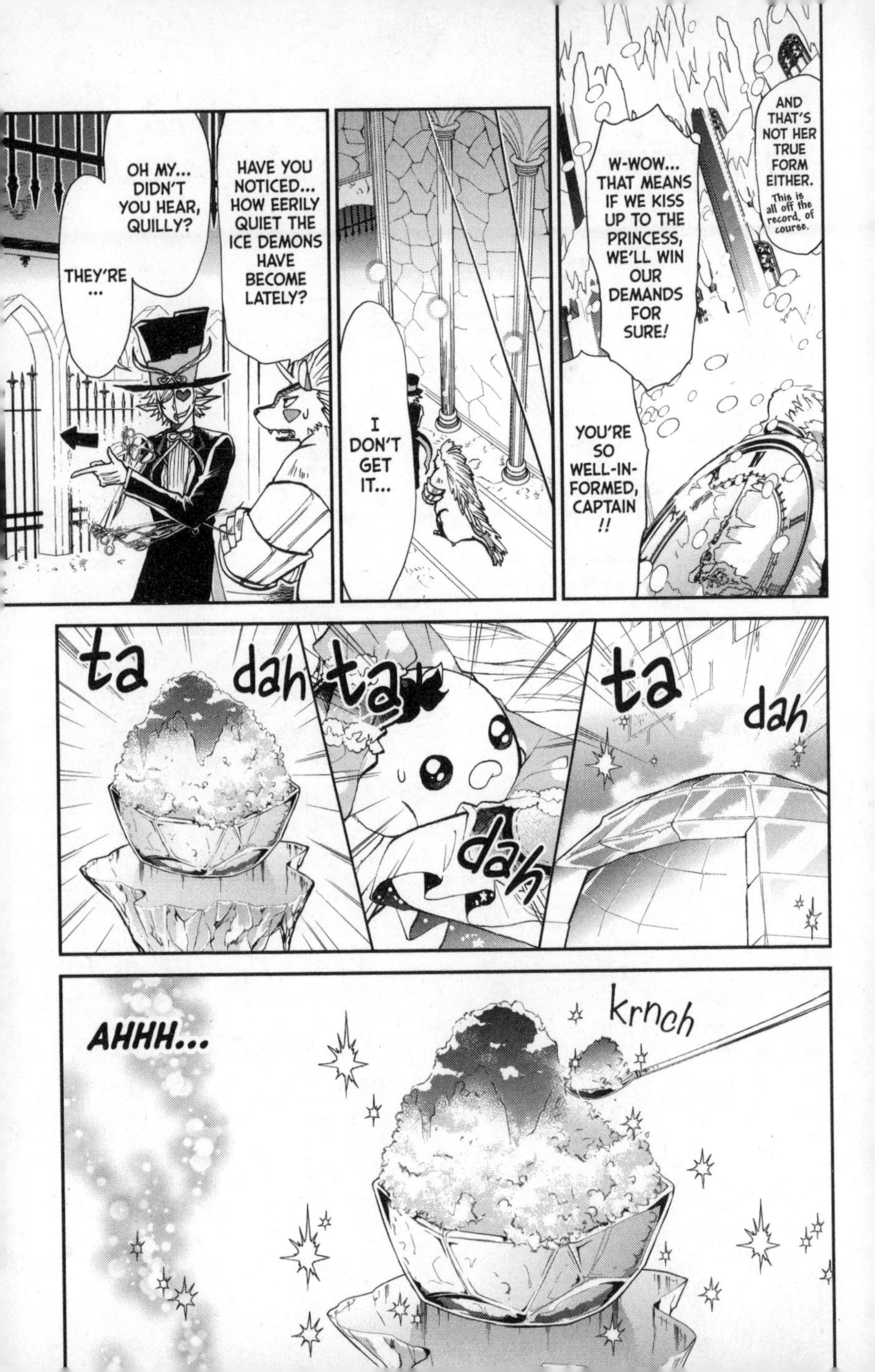
AND THAT'S NOT HER TRUE FORM EITHER.
This is all off the record, of course.
W-WOW... THAT MEANS IF WE KISS UP TO THE PRINCESS, WE'LL WIN OUR DEMANDS FOR SURE!
YOU'RE SO WELL-INFORMED, CAPTAIN!!
I DON'T GET IT...
HAVE YOU NOTICED... HOW EERILY QUIET THE ICE DEMONS HAVE BECOME LATELY?
OH MY... DIDN'T YOU HEAR, QUILLY?
THEY'RE ...
ta dah
ta dah
ta dah
krnch
AHHH...

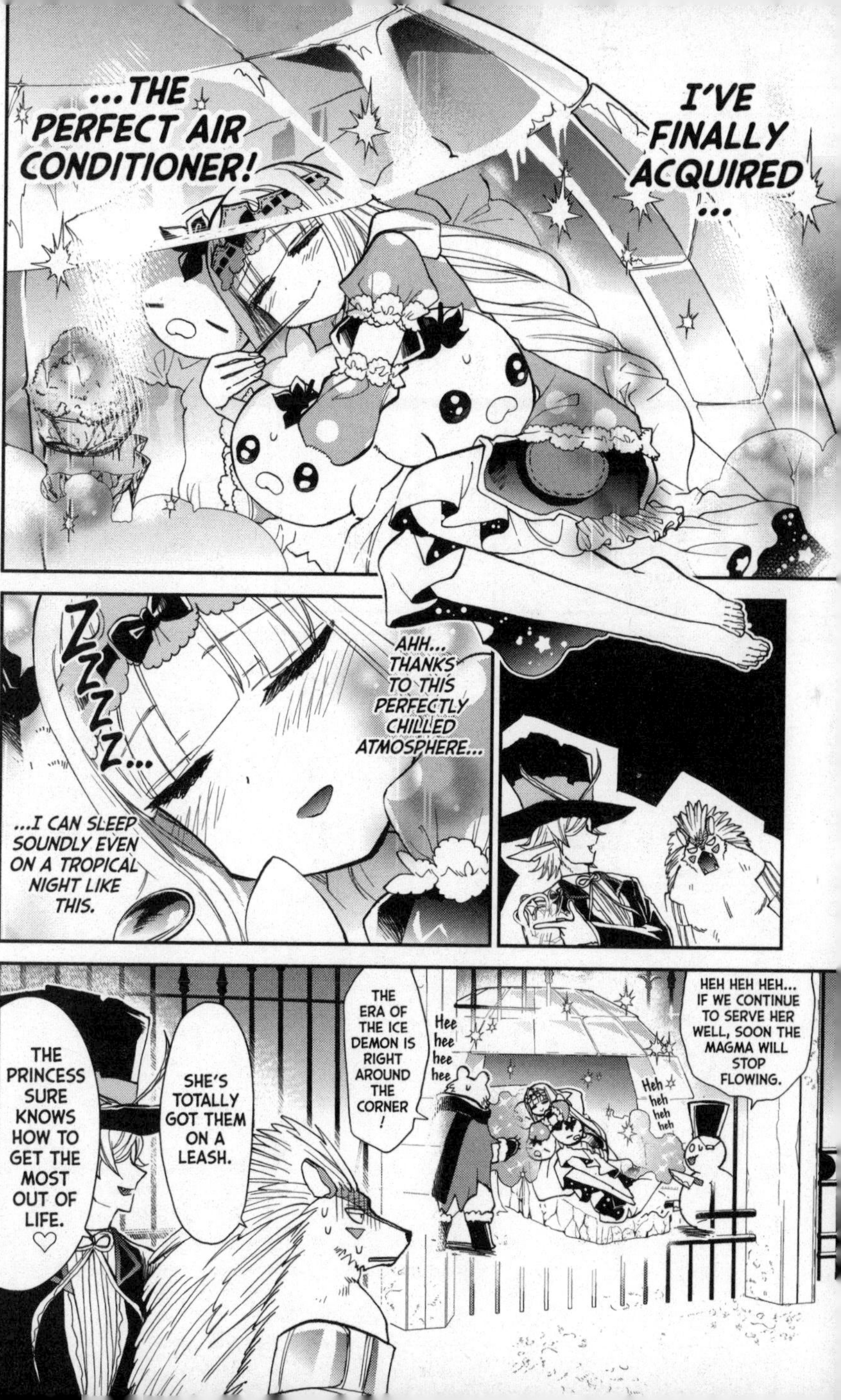
I'VE FINALLY ACQUIRED...
...THE PERFECT AIR CONDITIONER!
AHH... THANKS TO THIS PERFECTLY CHILLED ATMOSPHERE...
ZZZZ...
...I CAN SLEEP SOUNDLY EVEN ON A TROPICAL NIGHT LIKE THIS.
HEH HEH HEH... IF WE CONTINUE TO SERVE HER WELL, SOON THE MAGMA WILL STOP FLOWING.
Heh heh heh heh
THE ERA OF THE ICE DEMON IS RIGHT AROUND THE CORNER!
Hee hee hee hee
SHE'S TOTALLY GOT THEM ON A LEASH.
THE PRINCESS SURE KNOWS HOW TO GET THE MOST OUT OF LIFE. ♡

Eggplant Seal

Favorite food: Egg-plants and sesame seeds.

Roundness: ☆☆☆☆☆☆☆☆☆☆

Coolness: ☆☆☆☆☆☆

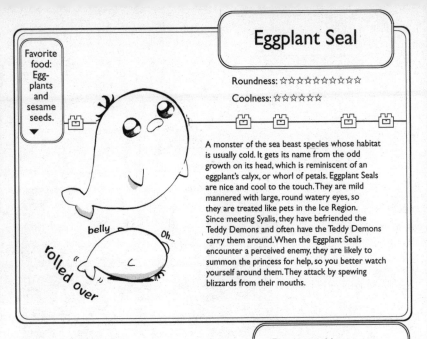

belly
Oh...
rolled over

A monster of the sea beast species whose habitat is usually cold. It gets its name from the odd growth on its head, which is reminiscent of an eggplant's calyx, or whorl of petals. Eggplant Seals are nice and cool to the touch. They are mild mannered with large, round watery eyes, so they are treated like pets in the Ice Region. Since meeting Syalis, they have befriended the Teddy Demons and often have the Teddy Demons carry them around. When the Eggplant Seals encounter a perceived enemy, they are likely to summon the princess for help, so you better watch yourself around them. They attack by spewing blizzards from their mouths.

Former problem:
"(Watery-eyed stare.)"

Current problem:
"(Watery-eyed stare.)"

You have re-cruited Egg-plant Seal.
Will you give it a name?
Yes
No
WHAT SHOULD I NAME YOU ...?
WHAT...? YOU LIKE SESAME SEEDS?
poke
THEN I'LL CALL YOU SPOT.
Even though it doesn't have any.

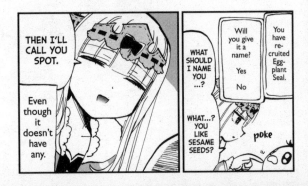

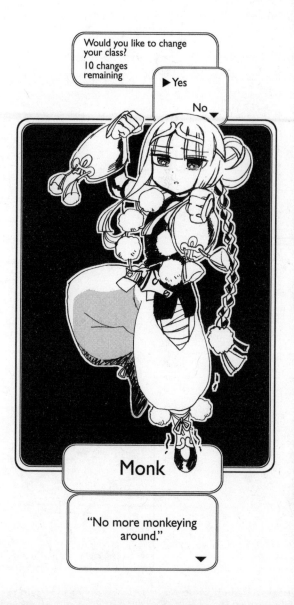

Would you like to change your class?

10 changes remaining

▶Yes

No ▼

Monk

"No more monkeying around."

▼

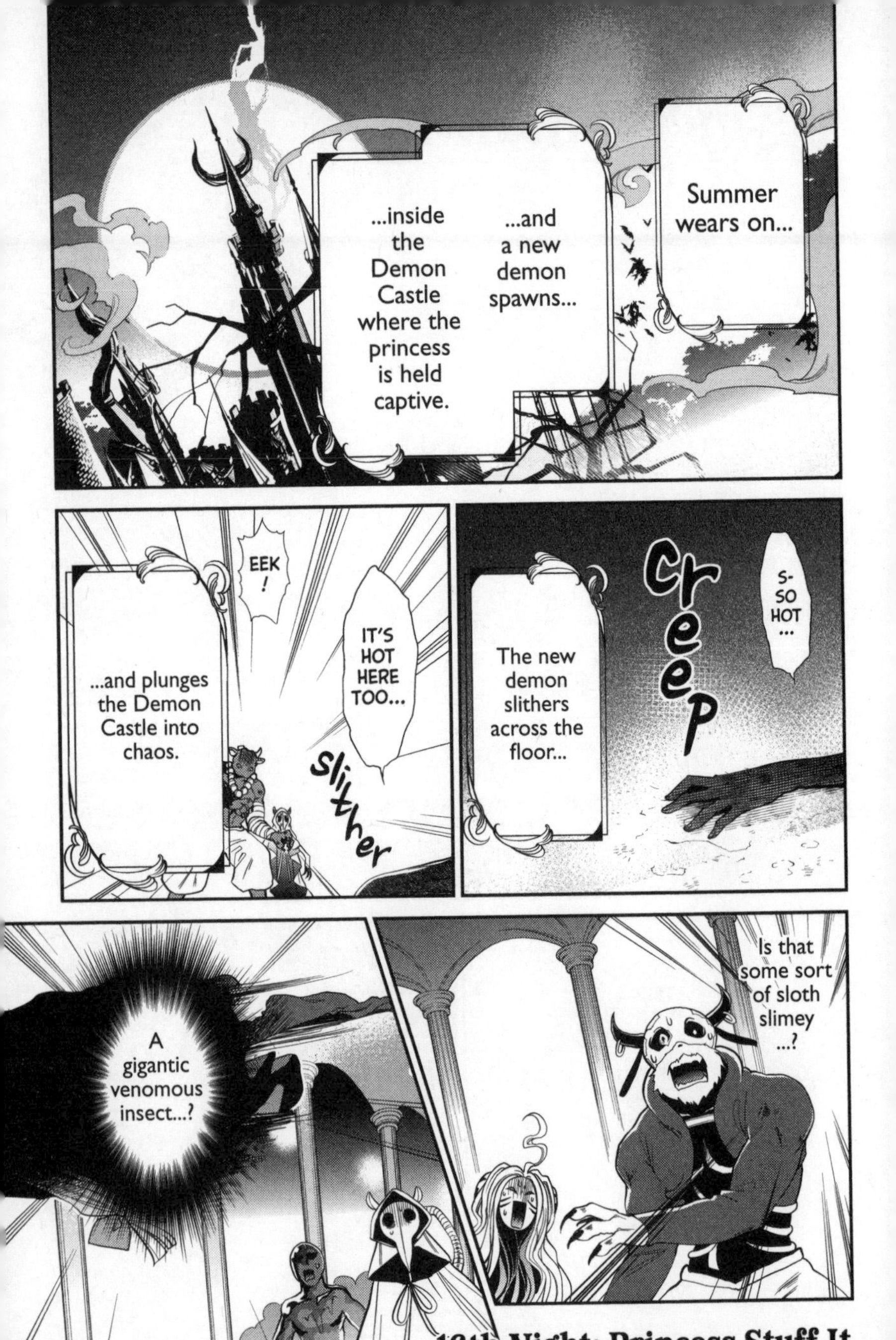
Summer wears on...
...and a new demon spawns...
...inside the Demon Castle where the princess is held captive.
S-SO HOT...
creep
The new demon slithers across the floor...
EEK!
IT'S HOT HERE TOO...
...and plunges the Demon Castle into chaos.
slither
Is that some sort of sloth slimey ...?
A gigantic venomous insect...?

16th Night: Princess Stuff It

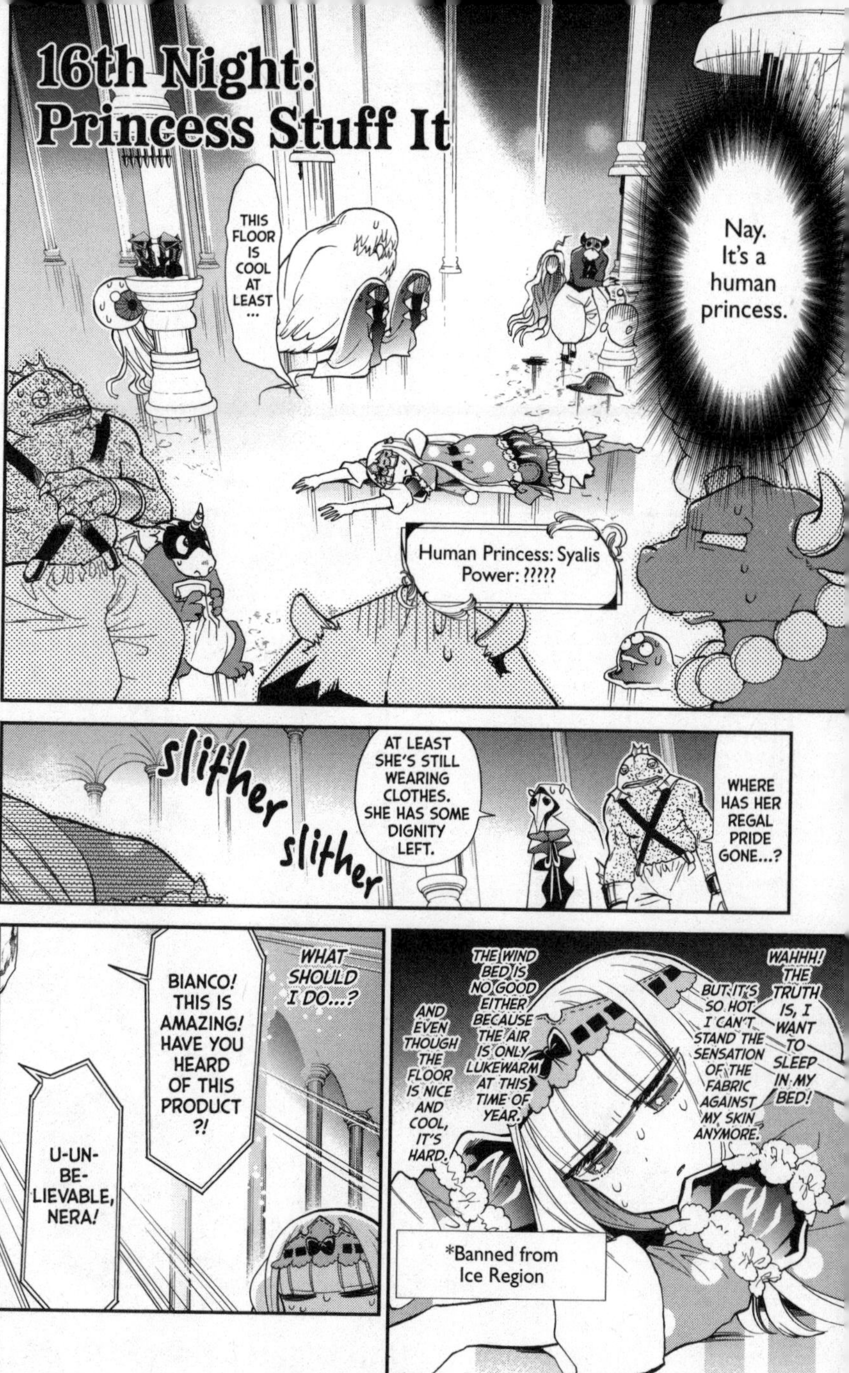
16th Night: Princess Stuff It
Nay. It's a human princess.
THIS FLOOR IS COOL AT LEAST...
Human Princess: Syalis Power: ?????
WHERE HAS HER REGAL PRIDE GONE...?
AT LEAST SHE'S STILL WEARING CLOTHES. SHE HAS SOME DIGNITY LEFT.
slither
slither
WAHHH! THE TRUTH IS, I WANT TO SLEEP IN MY BED!
BUT IT'S SO HOT I CAN'T STAND THE SENSATION OF THE FABRIC AGAINST MY SKIN ANYMORE.
THE WIND BED IS NO GOOD EITHER BECAUSE THE AIR IS ONLY LUKEWARM AT THIS TIME OF YEAR.
AND EVEN THOUGH THE FLOOR IS NICE AND COOL, IT'S HARD.
*Banned from Ice Region
WHAT SHOULD I DO...?
BIANCO! THIS IS AMAZING! HAVE YOU HEARD OF THIS PRODUCT?!
U-UN-BE-LIEVABLE, NERA!

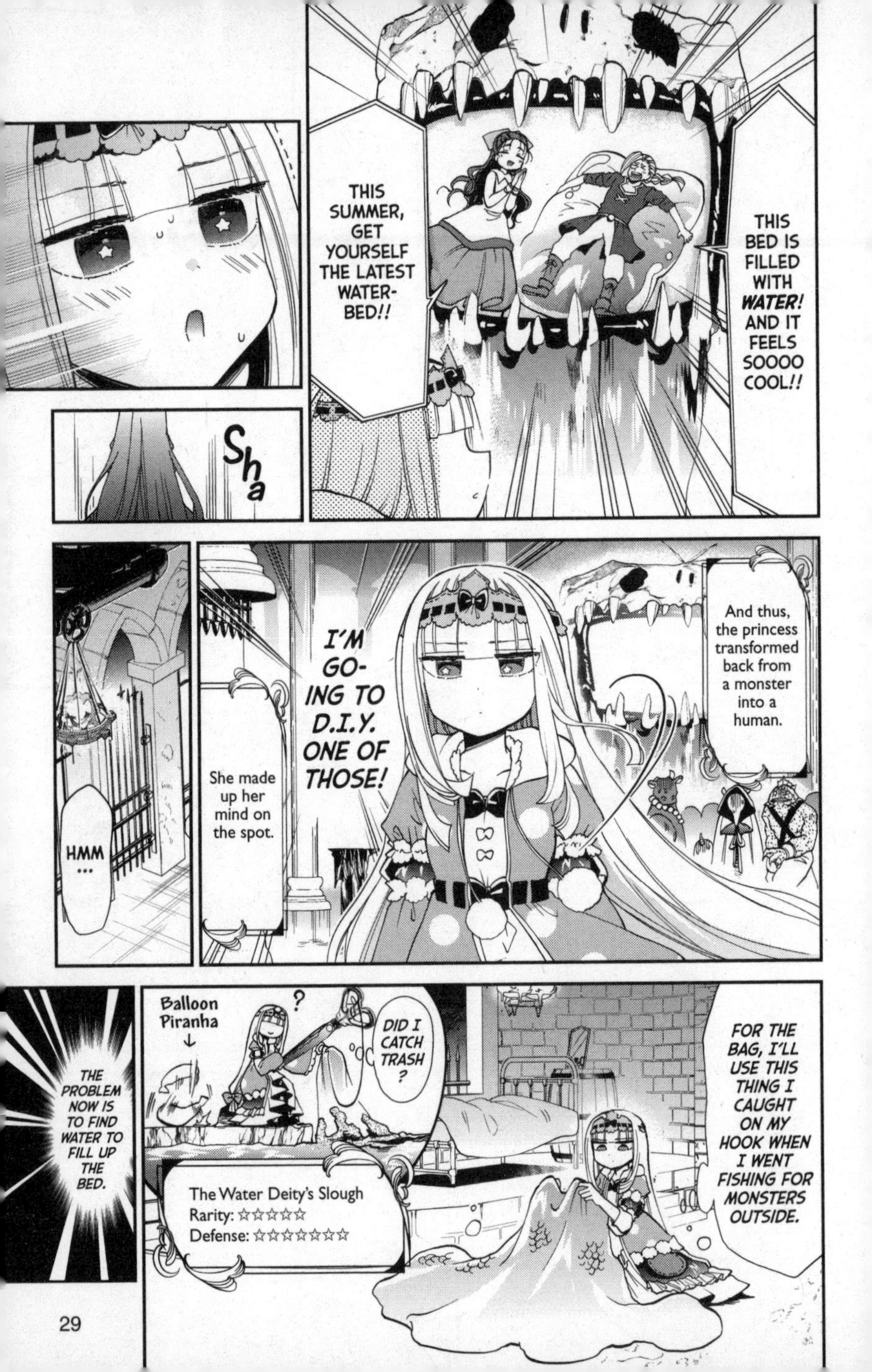
THIS BED IS FILLED WITH WATER! AND IT FEELS SOOOO COOL!!
THIS SUMMER, GET YOURSELF THE LATEST WATER-BED!!
Sha
And thus, the princess transformed back from a monster into a human.
I'M GO-ING TO D.I.Y. ONE OF THOSE!
She made up her mind on the spot.
HMM...
FOR THE BAG, I'LL USE THIS THING I CAUGHT ON MY HOOK WHEN I WENT FISHING FOR MONSTERS OUTSIDE.
DID I CATCH TRASH?
?
Balloon Piranha
The Water Deity's Slough
Rarity: ☆☆☆☆☆
Defense: ☆☆☆☆☆☆☆
THE PROBLEM NOW IS TO FIND WATER TO FILL UP THE BED.

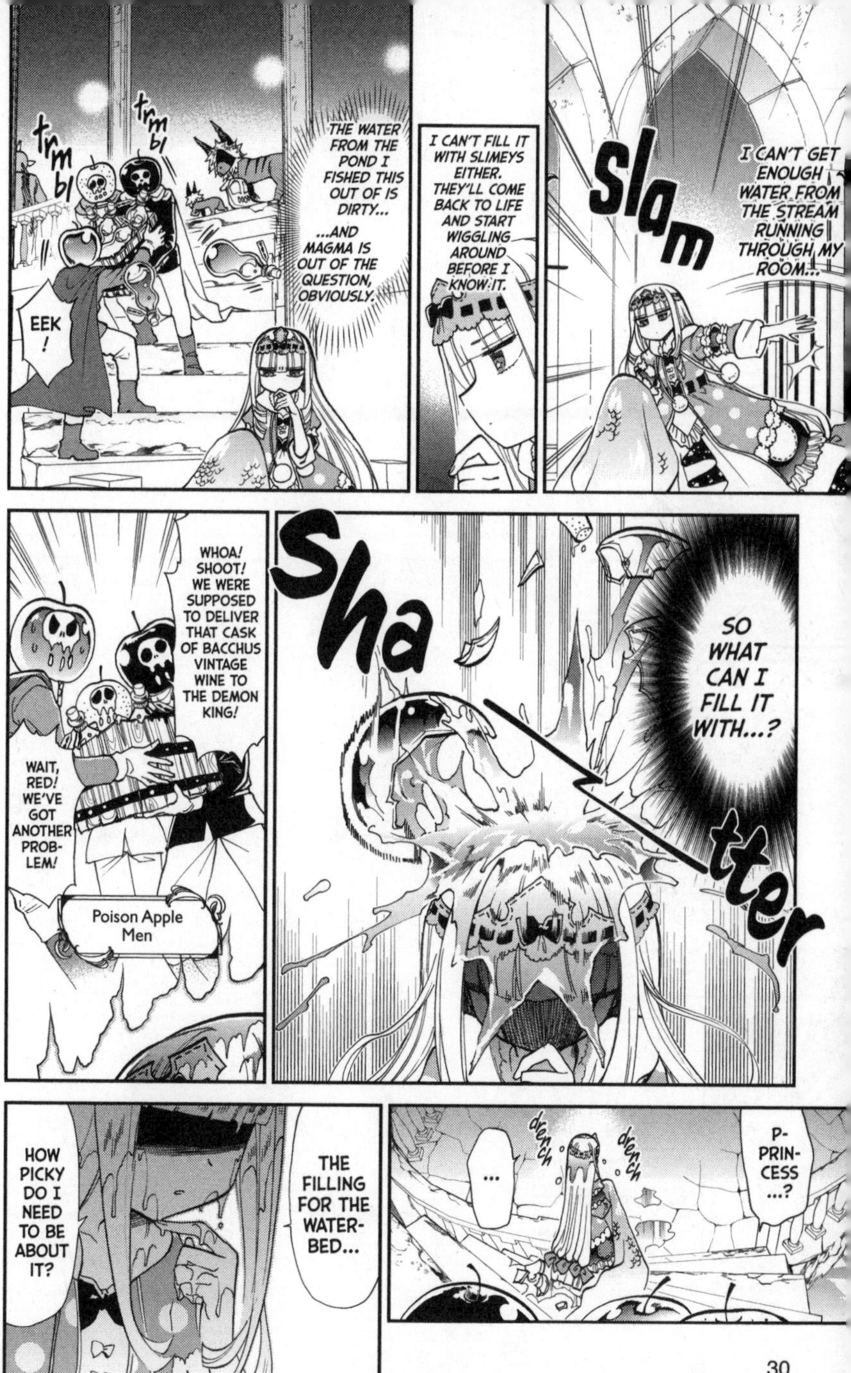
slam
I CAN'T GET ENOUGH WATER FROM THE STREAM RUNNING THROUGH MY ROOM...
I CAN'T FILL IT WITH SLIMEYS EITHER. THEY'LL COME BACK TO LIFE AND START WIGGLING AROUND BEFORE I KNOW IT.
THE WATER FROM THE POND I FISHED THIS OUT OF IS DIRTY...
...AND MAGMA IS OUT OF THE QUESTION, OBVIOUSLY.
trmbl
trmbl
EEK!
SO WHAT CAN I FILL IT WITH...?
Shatter
WHOA! SHOOT! WE WERE SUPPOSED TO DELIVER THAT CASK OF BACCHUS VINTAGE WINE TO THE DEMON KING!
WAIT, RED! WE'VE GOT ANOTHER PROB-LEM!
Poison Apple Men
P-PRIN-CESS...?
drench
drench
...
THE FILLING FOR THE WATER-BED...
HOW PICKY DO I NEED TO BE ABOUT IT?

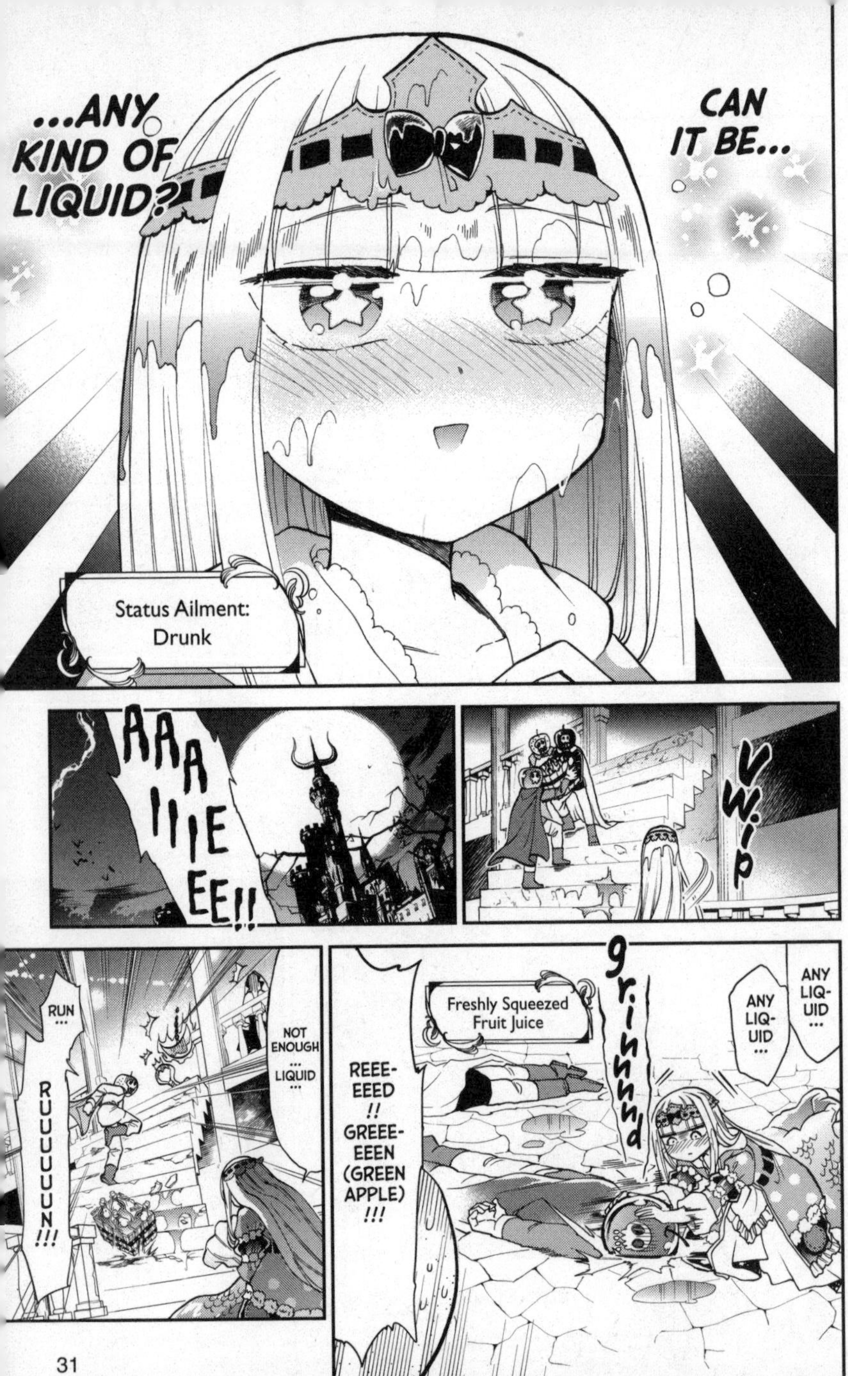
CAN IT BE...
...ANY KIND OF LIQUID?
Status Ailment: Drunk
VWip
AAAIIIEEE!!
ANY LIQ-UID...
ANY LIQ-UID...
grinnnd
Freshly Squeezed Fruit Juice
REEE-EEED!! GREEE-EEEN (GREEN APPLE)!!!
NOT ENOUGH... LIQUID...
RUN...
RUUUUUUN!!!

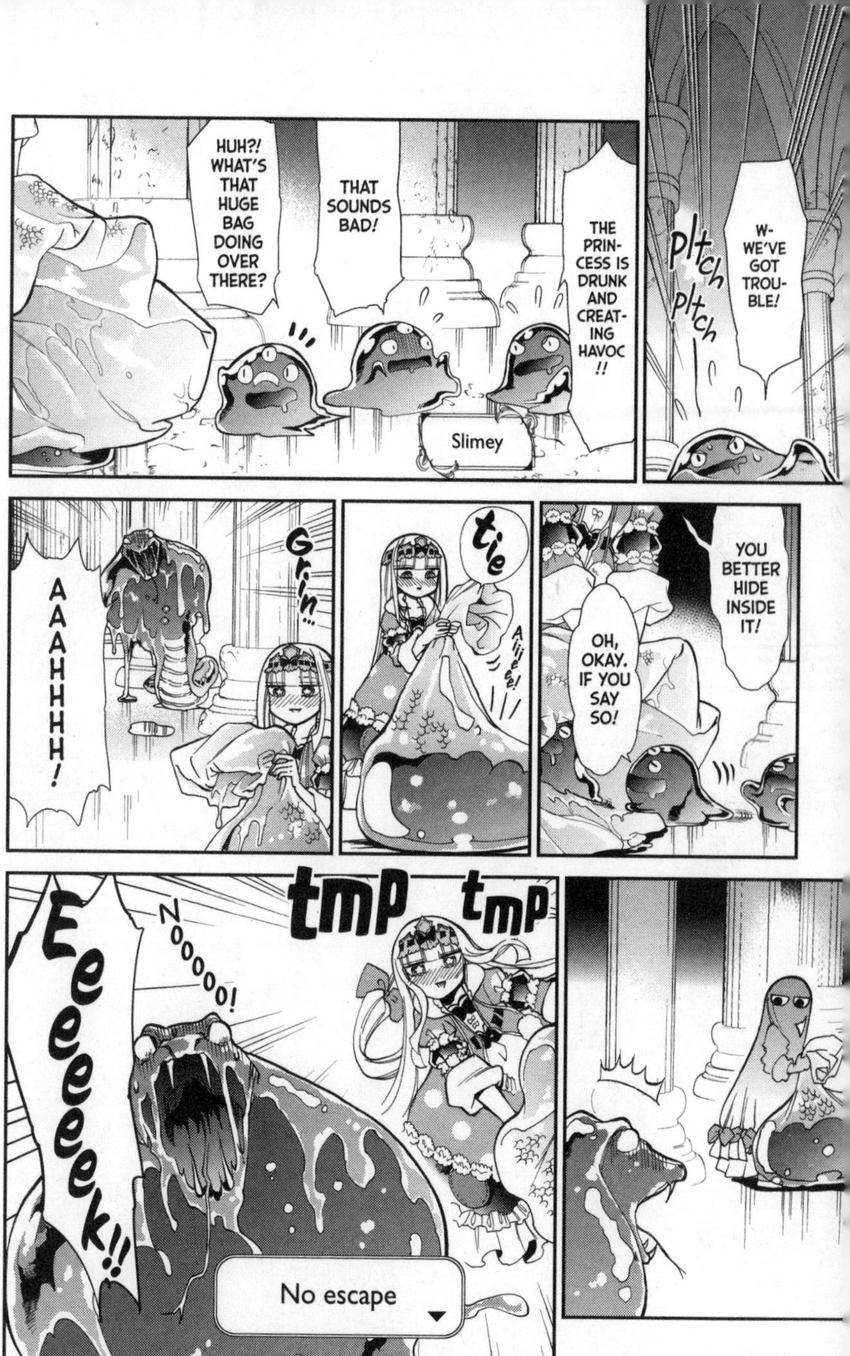
W-WE'VE GOT TROUBLE!
Pltch pltch
THE PRINCESS IS DRUNK AND CREATING HAVOC!!
THAT SOUNDS BAD!
HUH?! WHAT'S THAT HUGE BAG DOING OVER THERE?
Slimey
YOU BETTER HIDE INSIDE IT!
OH, OKAY. IF YOU SAY SO!
tie
Aiiiee!
Grin...
AAAAHHHHH!
tmp tmp
Noooooo!
Eeeeeeek!!
No escape

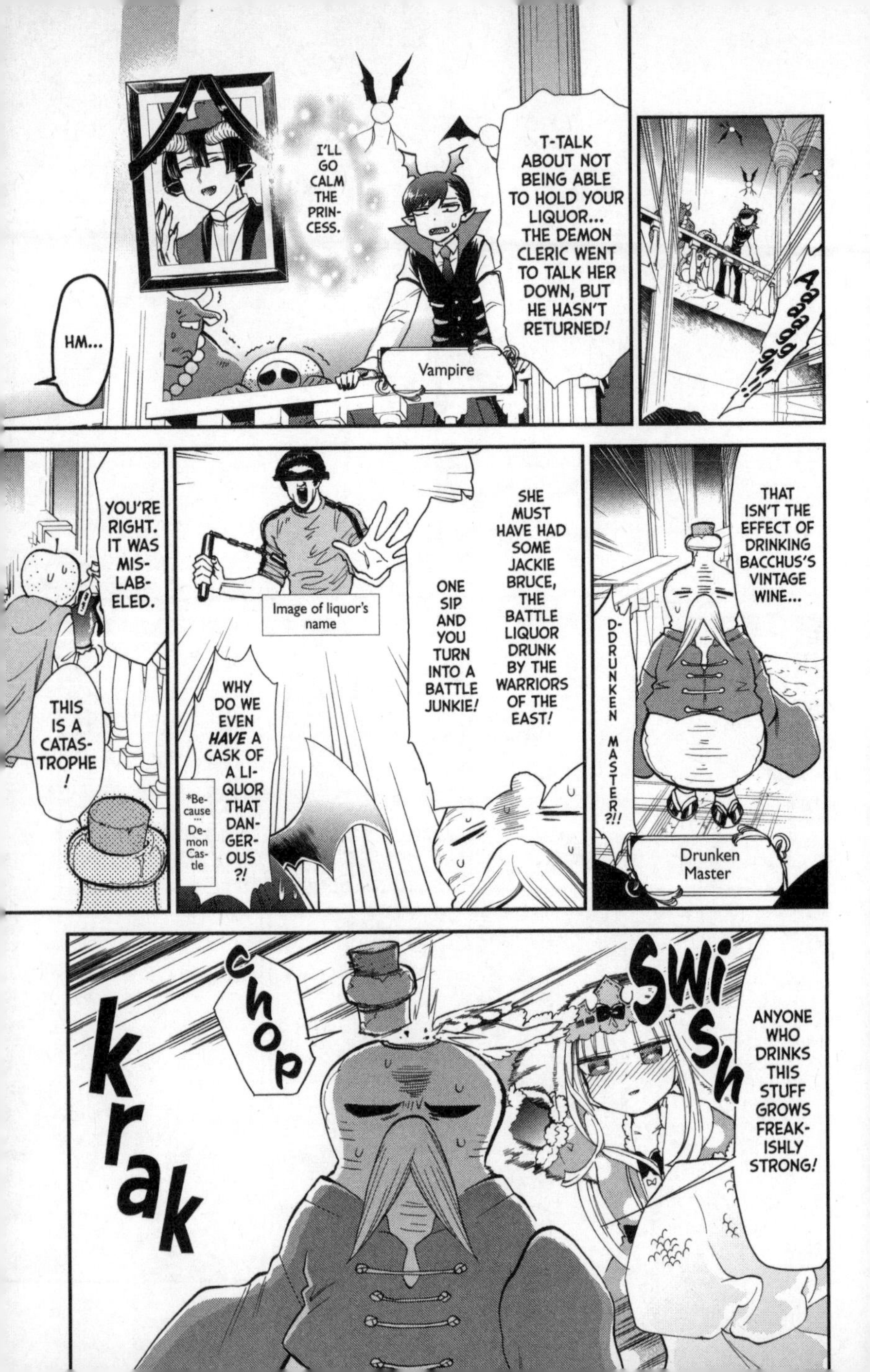
Aaaaggh!!!
T-TALK ABOUT NOT BEING ABLE TO HOLD YOUR LIQUOR... THE DEMON CLERIC WENT TO TALK HER DOWN, BUT HE HASN'T RETURNED!
I'LL GO CALM THE PRINCESS.
Vampire
HM...
THAT ISN'T THE EFFECT OF DRINKING BACCHUS'S VINTAGE WINE...
D-DRUNKEN MASTER?!!
Drunken Master
SHE MUST HAVE HAD SOME JACKIE BRUCE, THE BATTLE LIQUOR DRUNK BY THE WARRIORS OF THE EAST!
ONE SIP AND YOU TURN INTO A BATTLE JUNKIE!
Image of liquor's name
WHY DO WE EVEN *HAVE* A CASK OF A LIQUOR THAT DANGEROUS?!
*Because... Demon Castle
YOU'RE RIGHT. IT WAS MISLABELED.
THIS IS A CATASTROPHE!
ANYONE WHO DRINKS THIS STUFF GROWS FREAKISHLY STRONG!
Swish
chop
krak

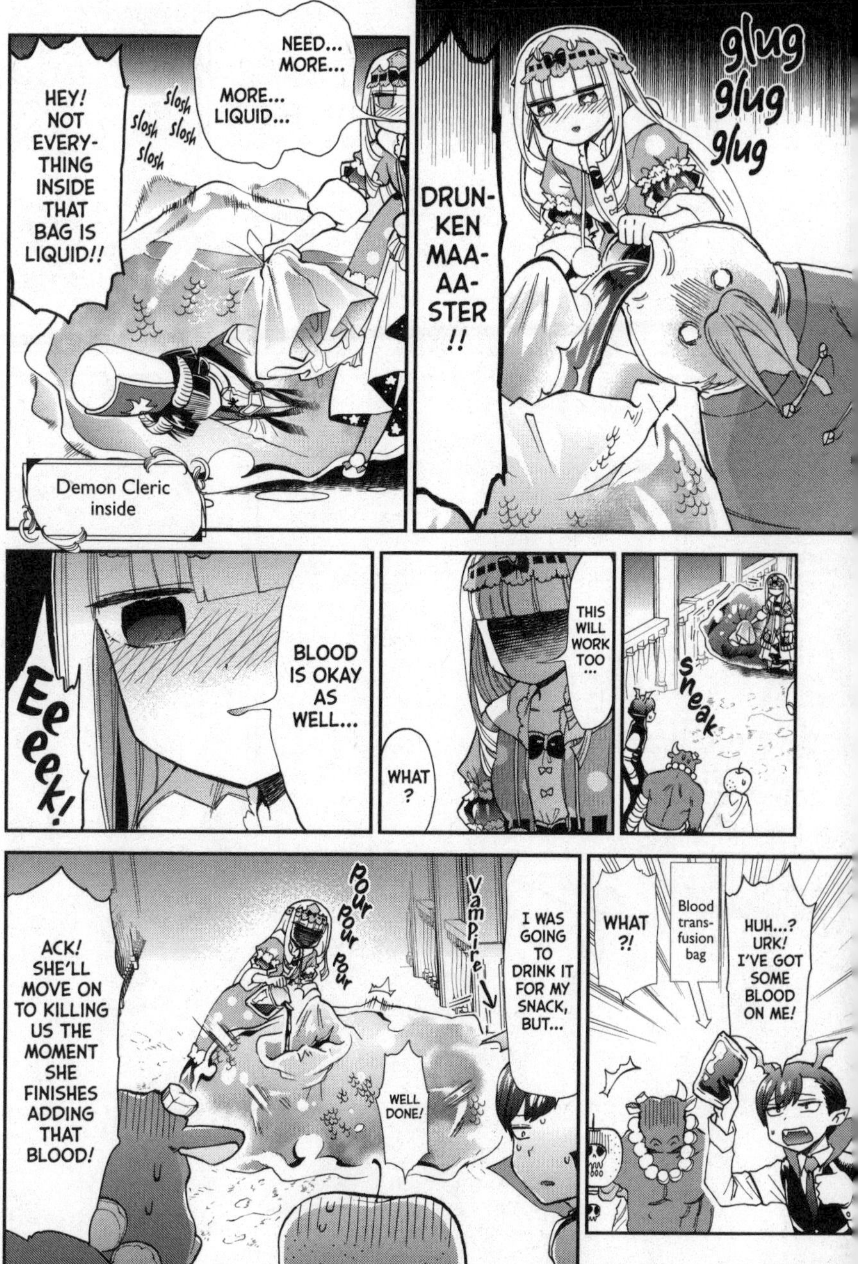
glug glug glug
DRUNKEN MAAAASTER!!
NEED... MORE...
MORE... LIQUID...
slosh slosh slosh slosh
HEY! NOT EVERYTHING INSIDE THAT BAG IS LIQUID!!
Demon Cleric inside
sneak
THIS WILL WORK TOO...
WHAT?
BLOOD IS OKAY AS WELL...
Eeeeek!
HUH...? URK! I'VE GOT SOME BLOOD ON ME!
Blood transfusion bag
WHAT?!
I WAS GOING TO DRINK IT FOR MY SNACK, BUT...
Vampire
Pour pour pour pour
ACK! SHE'LL MOVE ON TO KILLING US THE MOMENT SHE FINISHES ADDING THAT BLOOD!
WELL DONE!

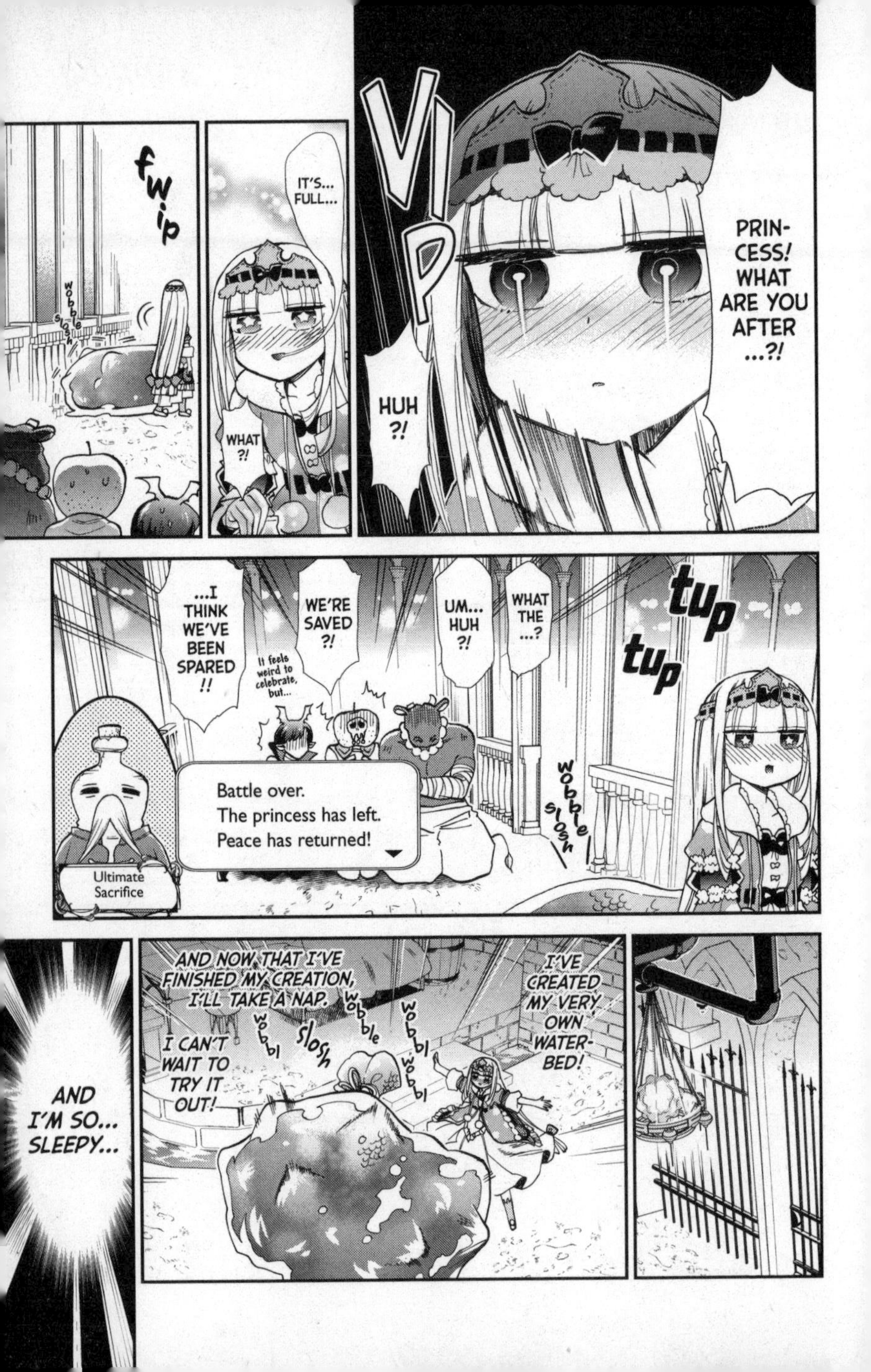
PRIN-CESS! WHAT ARE YOU AFTER ...?!
VIP
HUH ?!
IT'S... FULL...
WHAT ?!
fwip
wobble
slosh
tup
tup
WHAT THE ...?
UM... HUH ?!
WE'RE SAVED ?!
It feels weird to celebrate, but...
...I THINK WE'VE BEEN SPARED !!
wobble
slosh
Battle over.
The princess has left.
Peace has returned!
Ultimate Sacrifice
I'VE CREATED MY VERY OWN WATER-BED!
AND NOW THAT I'VE FINISHED MY CREATION, I'LL TAKE A NAP.
I CAN'T WAIT TO TRY IT OUT!
wobble
slosh
wobbl
wobbl
wobbl
wobbl
AND I'M SO... SLEEPY...

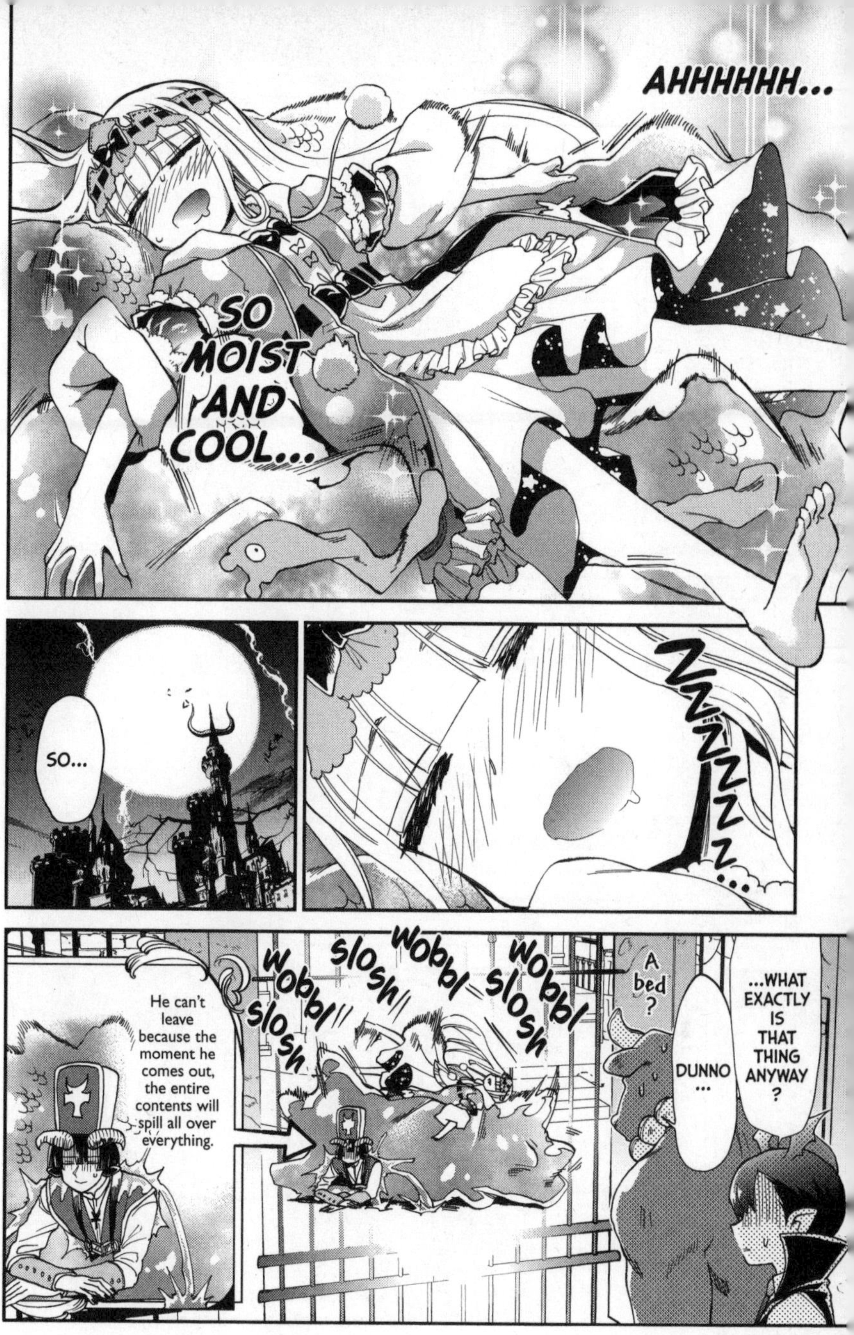
AHHHHHH...
SO MOIST AND COOL...
ZZZZZZZ...
SO...
...WHAT EXACTLY IS THAT THING ANYWAY?
DUNNO...
A bed?
wobbl slosh
wobbl slosh
wobbl slosh
He can't leave because the moment he comes out, the entire contents will spill all over everything.

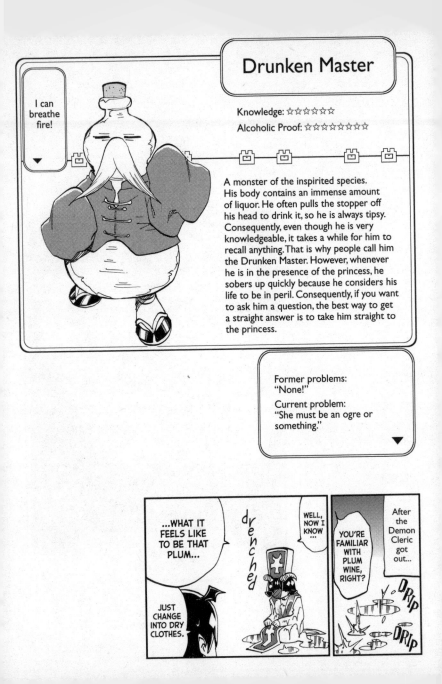

Drunken Master

I can breathe fire!

Knowledge: ☆☆☆☆☆☆
Alcoholic Proof: ☆☆☆☆☆☆☆☆☆

A monster of the inspirited species. His body contains an immense amount of liquor. He often pulls the stopper off his head to drink it, so he is always tipsy. Consequently, even though he is very knowledgeable, it takes a while for him to recall anything. That is why people call him the Drunken Master. However, whenever he is in the presence of the princess, he sobers up quickly because he considers his life to be in peril. Consequently, if you want to ask him a question, the best way to get a straight answer is to take him straight to the princess.

Former problems:
"None!"

Current problem:
"She must be an ogre or something."

After the Demon Cleric got out...

YOU'RE FAMILIAR WITH PLUM WINE, RIGHT?

WELL, NOW I KNOW...

drenched

...WHAT IT FEELS LIKE TO BE THAT PLUM...

JUST CHANGE INTO DRY CLOTHES.

DRIP DRIP

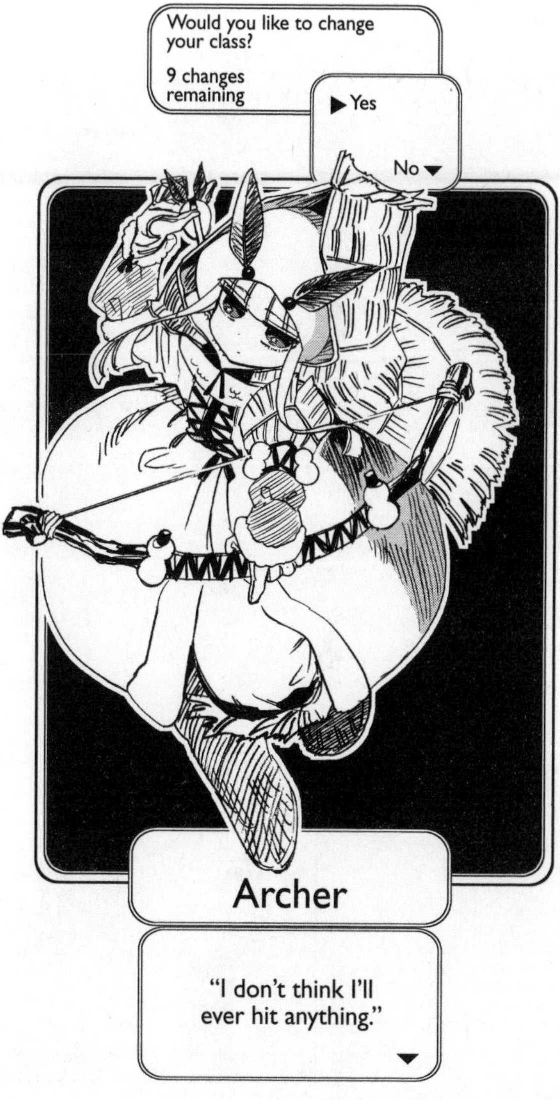
Would you like to change your class?
9 changes remaining
▶Yes
No
Archer
"I don't think I'll ever hit anything."

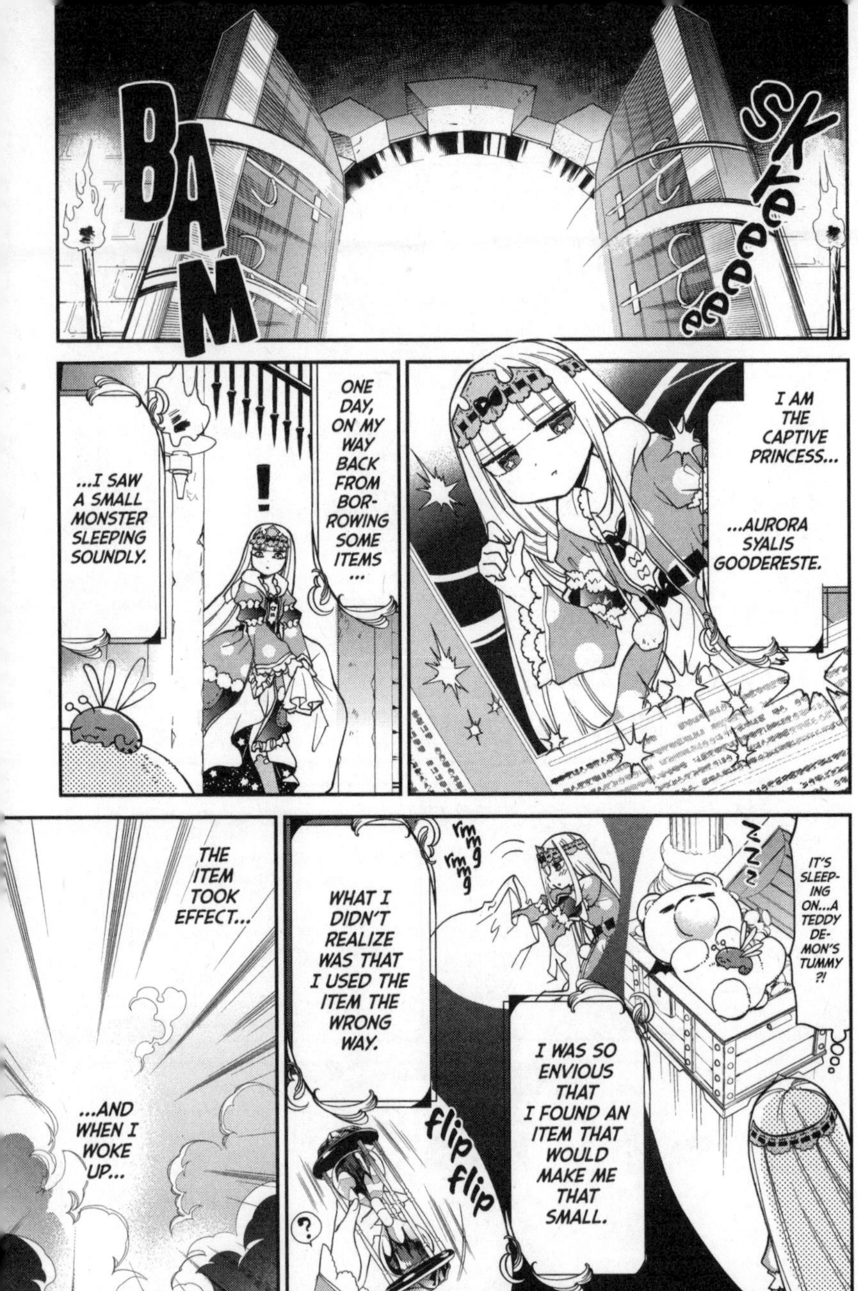
SKREEEEEE
BAM
I AM THE CAPTIVE PRINCESS...
...AURORA SYALIS GOODERESTE.
ONE DAY, ON MY WAY BACK FROM BOR-ROWING SOME ITEMS...
!
...I SAW A SMALL MONSTER SLEEPING SOUNDLY.
IT'S SLEEP-ING ON...A TEDDY DE-MON'S TUMMY ?!
ZZZ
I WAS SO ENVIOUS THAT I FOUND AN ITEM THAT WOULD MAKE ME THAT SMALL.
rmmg rmmg
flip flip
?
The Hourglass of Apoté
WHAT I DIDN'T REALIZE WAS THAT I USED THE ITEM THE WRONG WAY.
THE ITEM TOOK EFFECT...
...AND WHEN I WOKE UP...

17th Night: It Looks like a Princess and Has the Brain of a Princess

17th Night: It Looks like a Princess and Has the Brain of a Princess

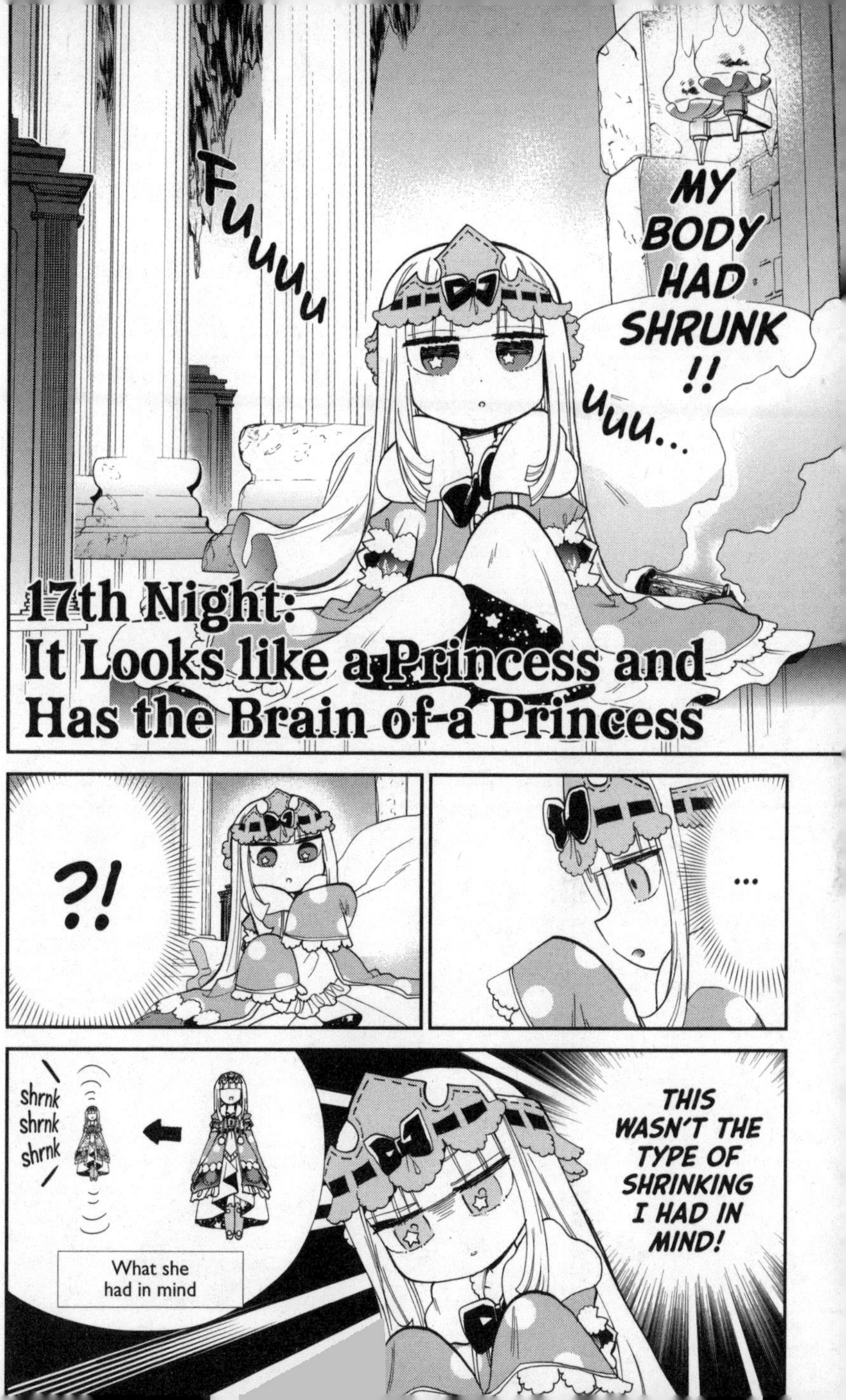
MY BODY HAD SHRUNK!!
Fuuuuu
uuu...
...
?!
THIS WASN'T THE TYPE OF SHRINKING I HAD IN MIND!
shrnk shrnk shrnk
What she had in mind

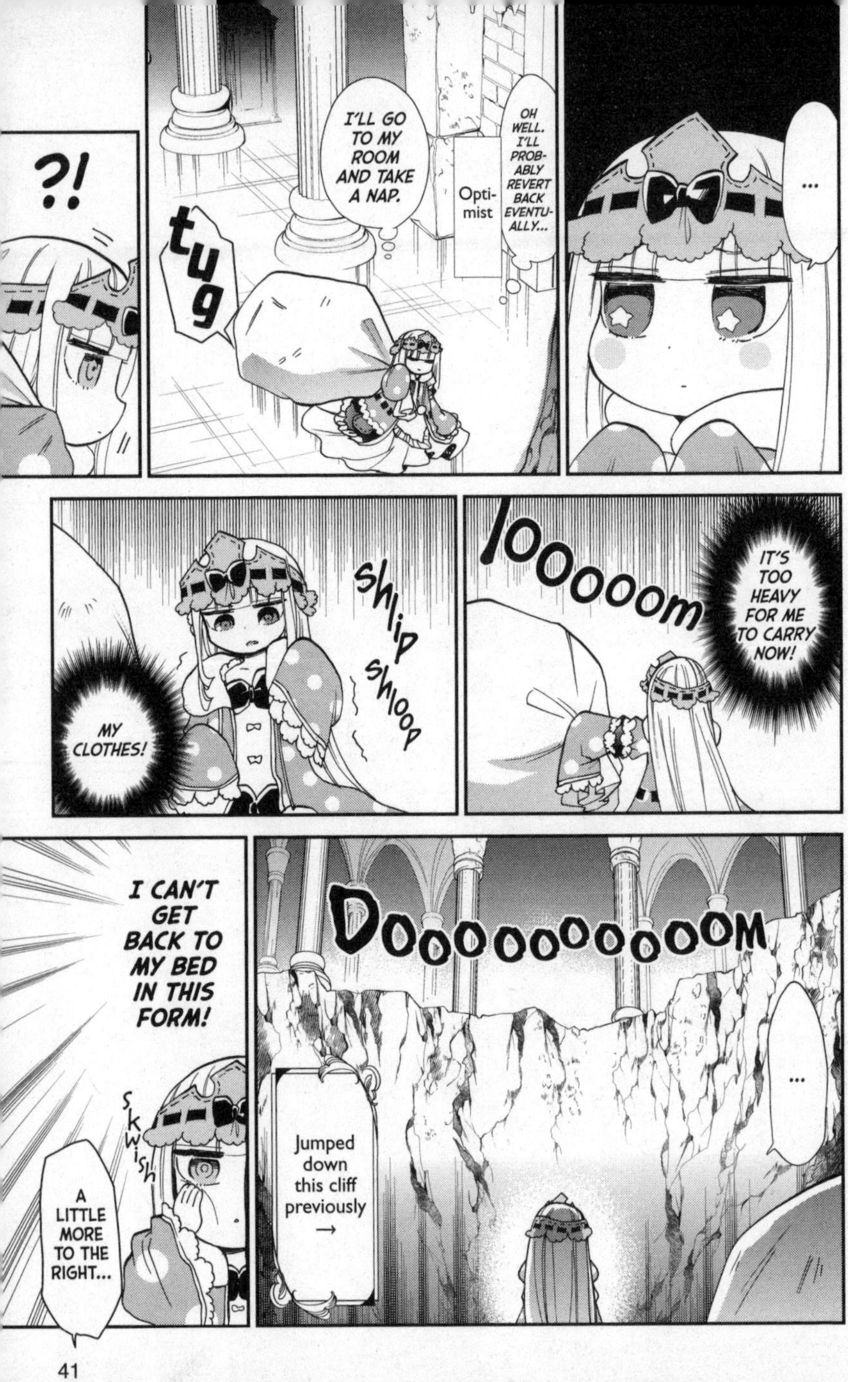
...
OH WELL. I'LL PROBABLY REVERT BACK EVENTUALLY...
Optimist
I'LL GO TO MY ROOM AND TAKE A NAP.
tug
?!
IOOOOOOM
IT'S TOO HEAVY FOR ME TO CARRY NOW!
shlip shloop
MY CLOTHES!
DOOOOOOOOOOOM
...
Jumped down this cliff previously →
I CAN'T GET BACK TO MY BED IN THIS FORM!
skwish
A LITTLE MORE TO THE RIGHT...

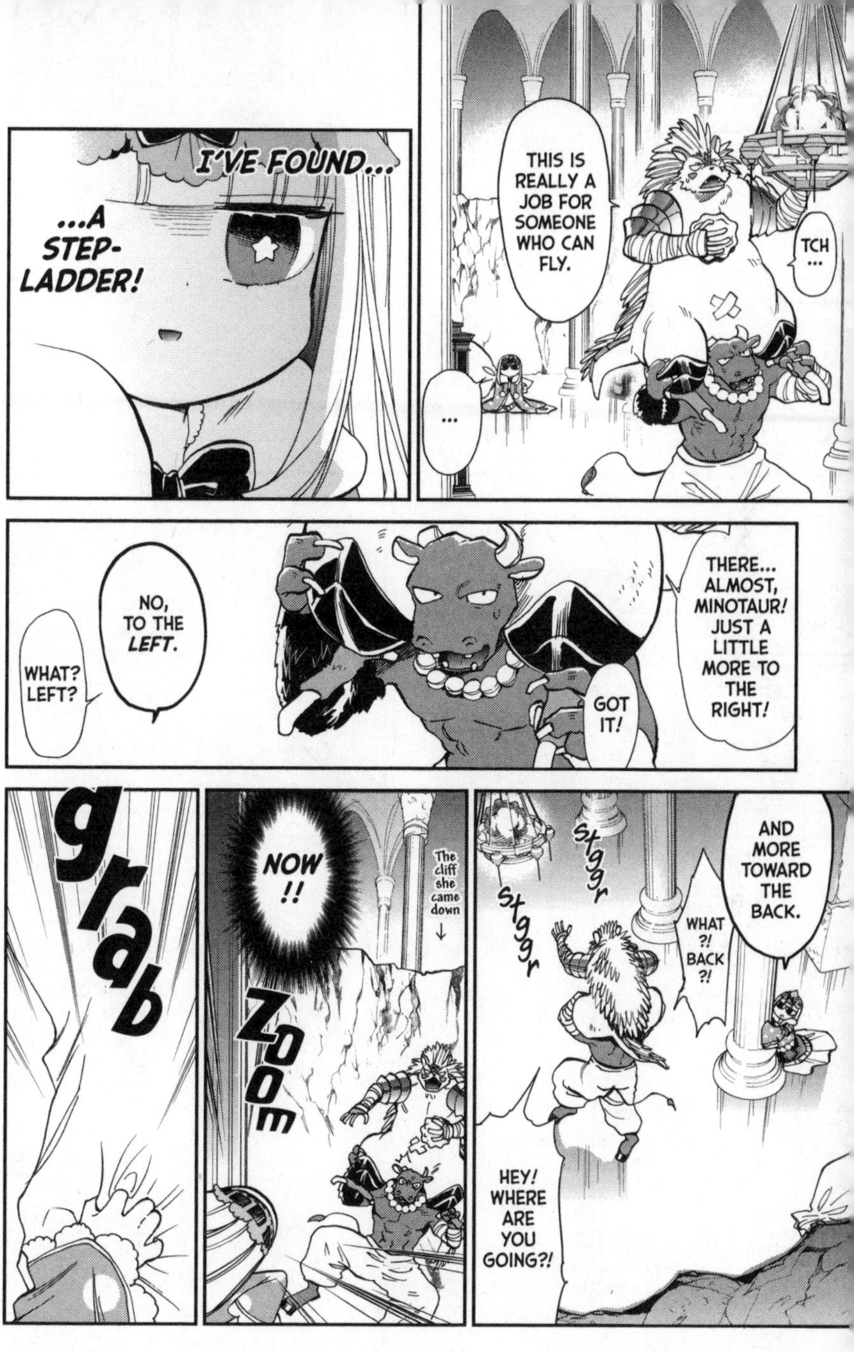
THIS IS REALLY A JOB FOR SOMEONE WHO CAN FLY.
TCH ...
...
I'VE FOUND...
...A STEP-LADDER!
THERE... ALMOST, MINOTAUR! JUST A LITTLE MORE TO THE RIGHT!
GOT IT!
NO, TO THE LEFT.
WHAT? LEFT?
AND MORE TOWARD THE BACK.
WHAT?! BACK?!
stggr
stggr
HEY! WHERE ARE YOU GOING?!
NOW!!
The cliff she came down ↓
zoom
grab

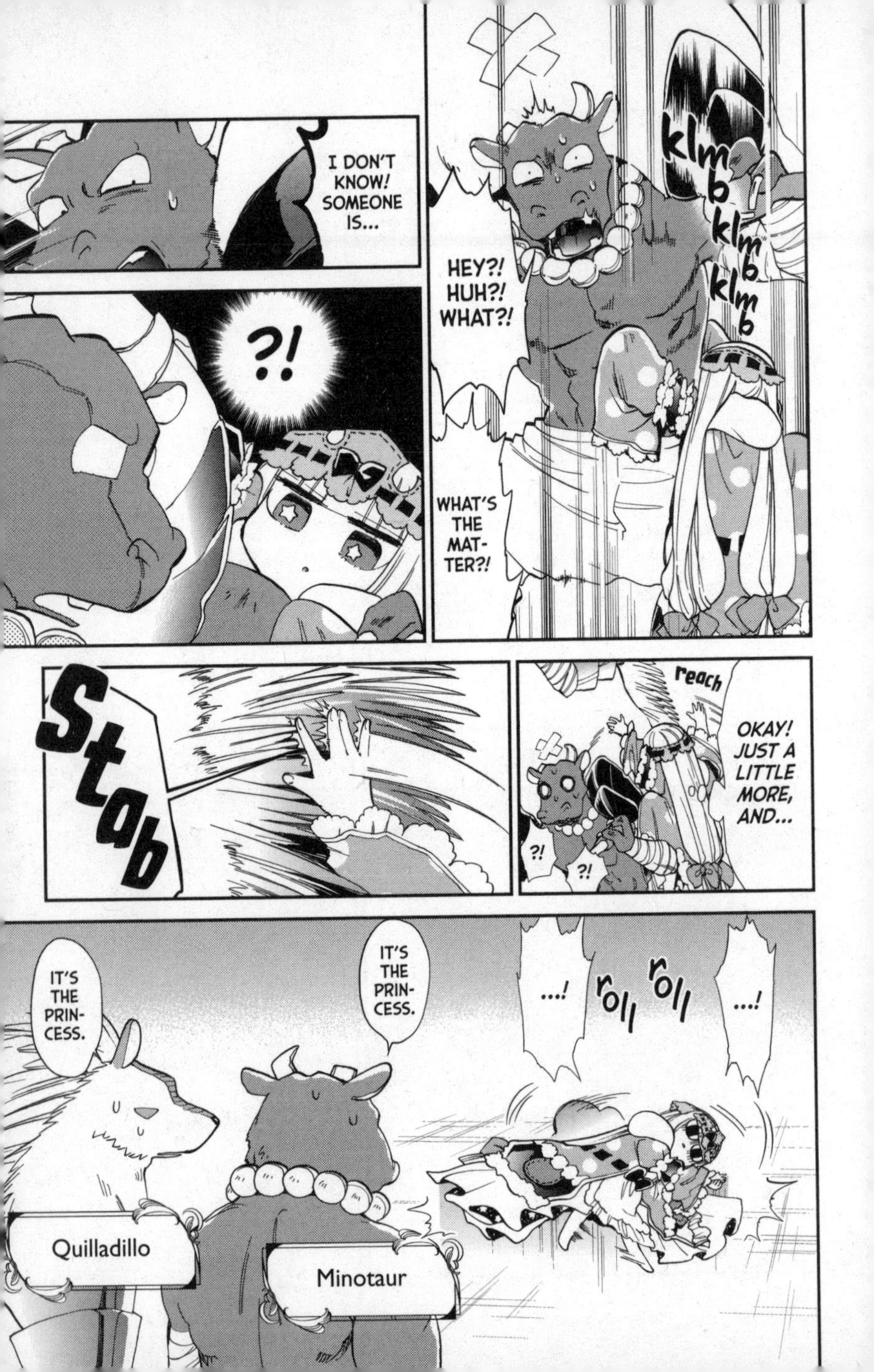
klmb
klmb
klmb
HEY?! HUH?! WHAT?!
WHAT'S THE MAT-TER?!
I DON'T KNOW! SOMEONE IS...
?!
reach
OKAY! JUST A LITTLE MORE, AND...
?!
?!
Stab
...!
roll
roll
...!
IT'S THE PRIN-CESS.
IT'S THE PRIN-CESS.
Minotaur
Quilladillo

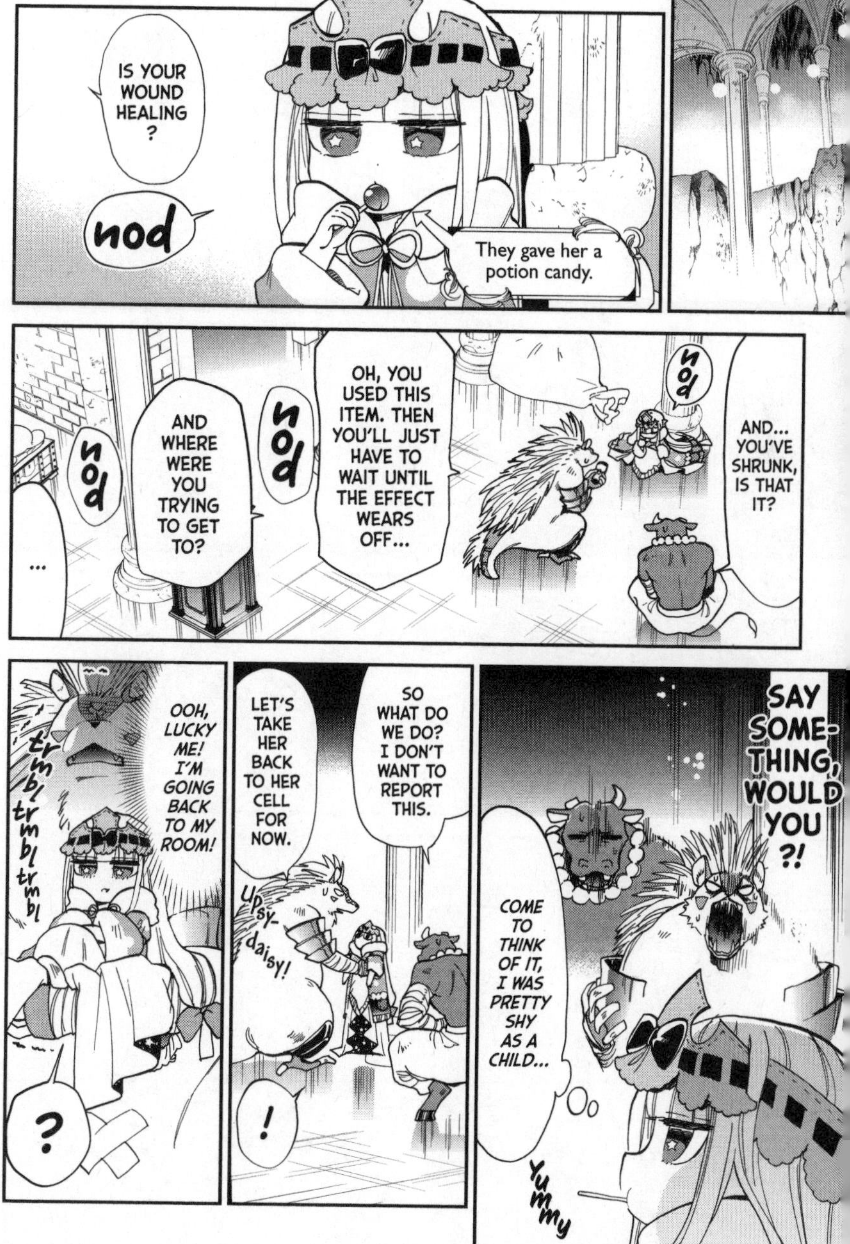
IS YOUR WOUND HEALING?
nod
They gave her a potion candy.
AND... YOU'VE SHRUNK, IS THAT IT?
nod
OH, YOU USED THIS ITEM. THEN YOU'LL JUST HAVE TO WAIT UNTIL THE EFFECT WEARS OFF...
nod
AND WHERE WERE YOU TRYING TO GET TO?
nod
...
SAY SOME-THING, WOULD YOU?!
COME TO THINK OF IT, I WAS PRETTY SHY AS A CHILD...
Yummy
SO WHAT DO WE DO? I DON'T WANT TO REPORT THIS.
LET'S TAKE HER BACK TO HER CELL FOR NOW.
Upsy-daisy!
!
OOH, LUCKY ME! I'M GOING BACK TO MY ROOM!
trmbl trmbl trmbl
?

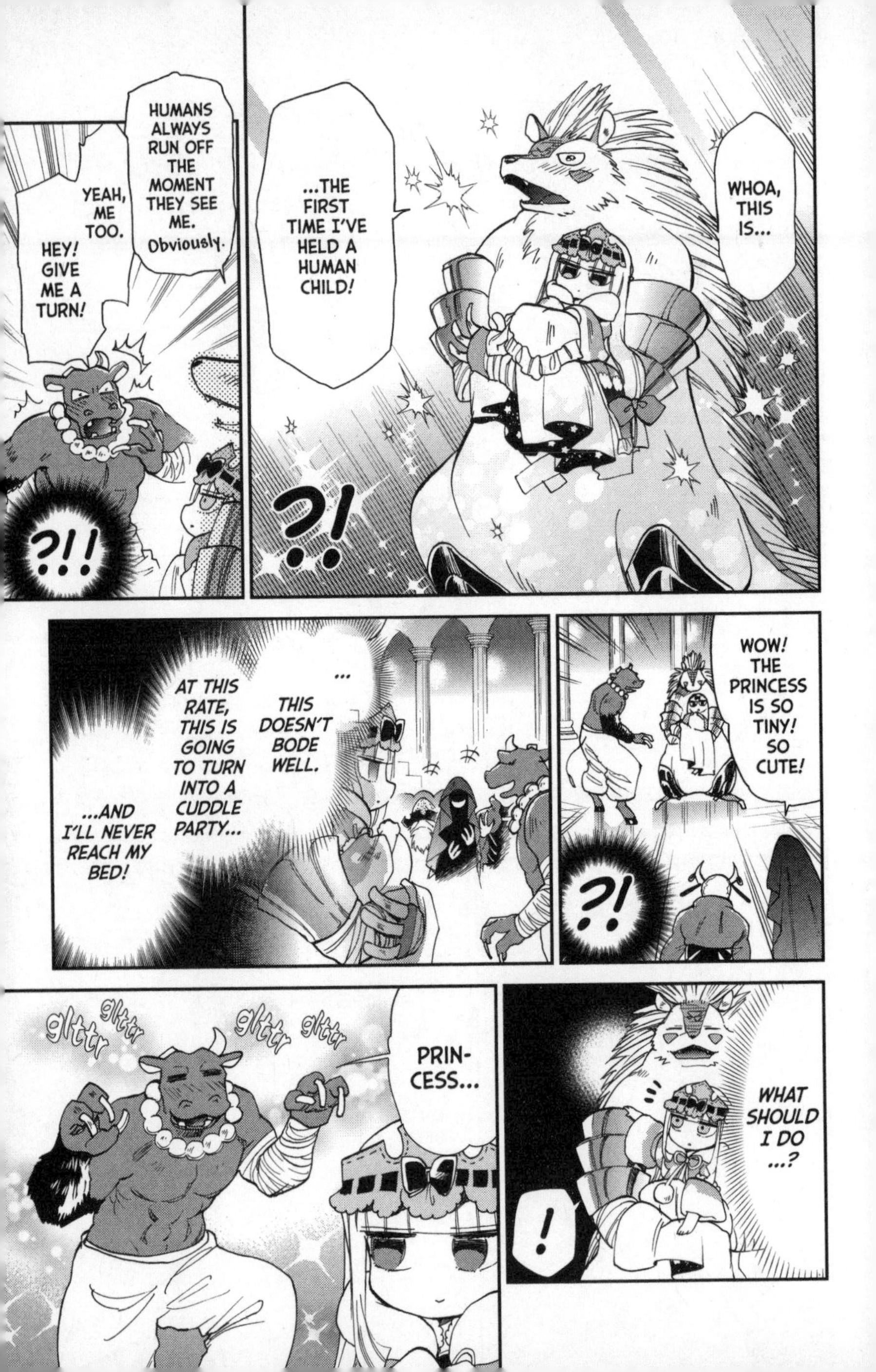
WHOA, THIS IS...
...THE FIRST TIME I'VE HELD A HUMAN CHILD!
?!
HUMANS ALWAYS RUN OFF THE MOMENT THEY SEE ME. Obviously.
YEAH, ME TOO.
HEY! GIVE ME A TURN!
?!!
WOW! THE PRINCESS IS SO TINY! SO CUTE!
?!
...
THIS DOESN'T BODE WELL.
AT THIS RATE, THIS IS GOING TO TURN INTO A CUDDLE PARTY...
...AND I'LL NEVER REACH MY BED!
WHAT SHOULD I DO ...?
!
PRIN-CESS...
glttr glttr glttr glttr

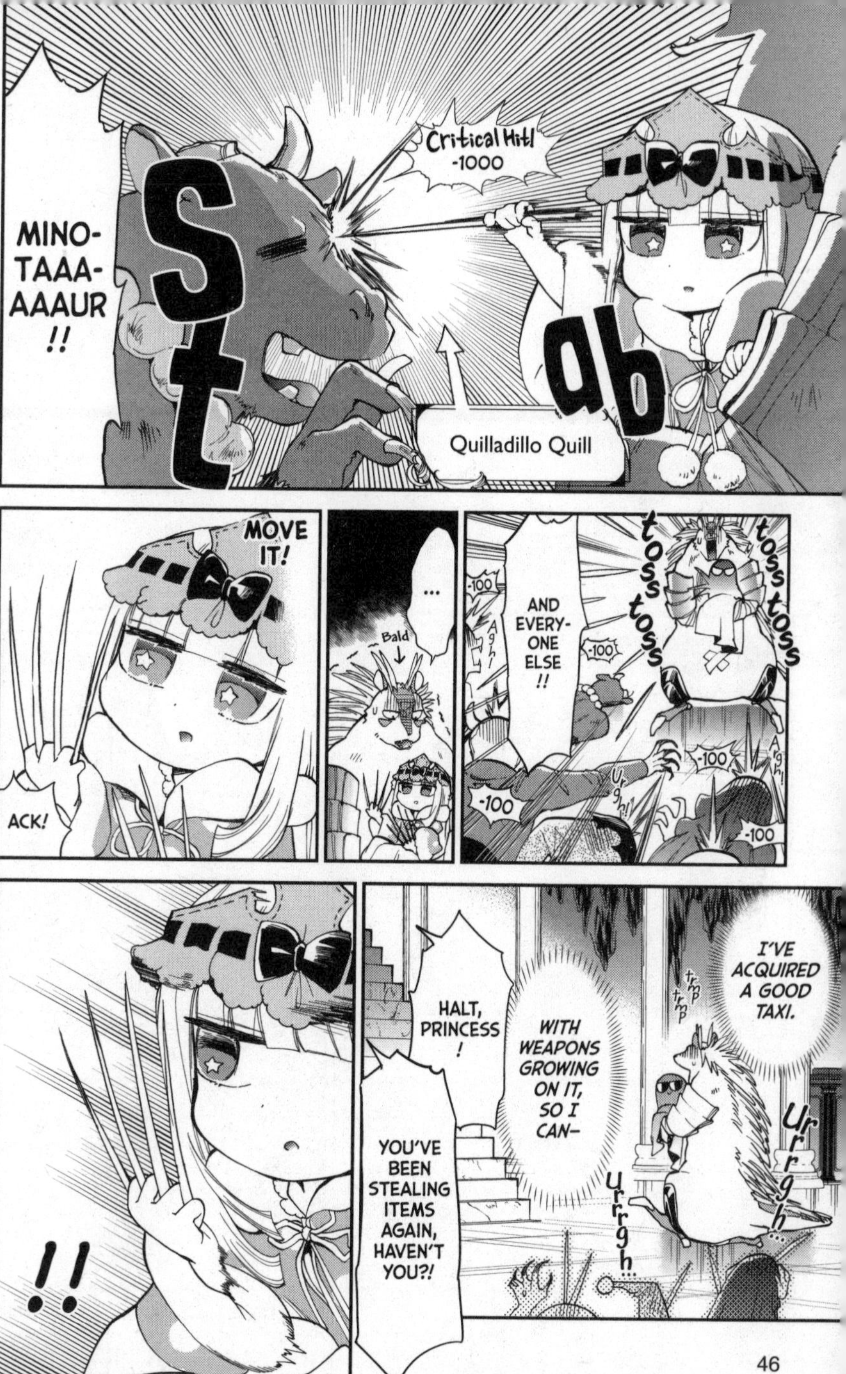
Critical Hit! -1000
Quilladillo Quill
Stab
MINO-TAAAA-AAAUR!!
toss toss
toss toss
AND EVERY-ONE ELSE!!
-100
-100
Agh!
Argh!
-100
Urgh!
-100
-100
...
Bald
MOVE IT!
ACK!
I'VE ACQUIRED A GOOD TAXI.
trmp trmp
WITH WEAPONS GROWING ON IT, SO I CAN–
HALT, PRINCESS!
YOU'VE BEEN STEALING ITEMS AGAIN, HAVEN'T YOU?!
Urrrgh...
Urrrgh...
!!

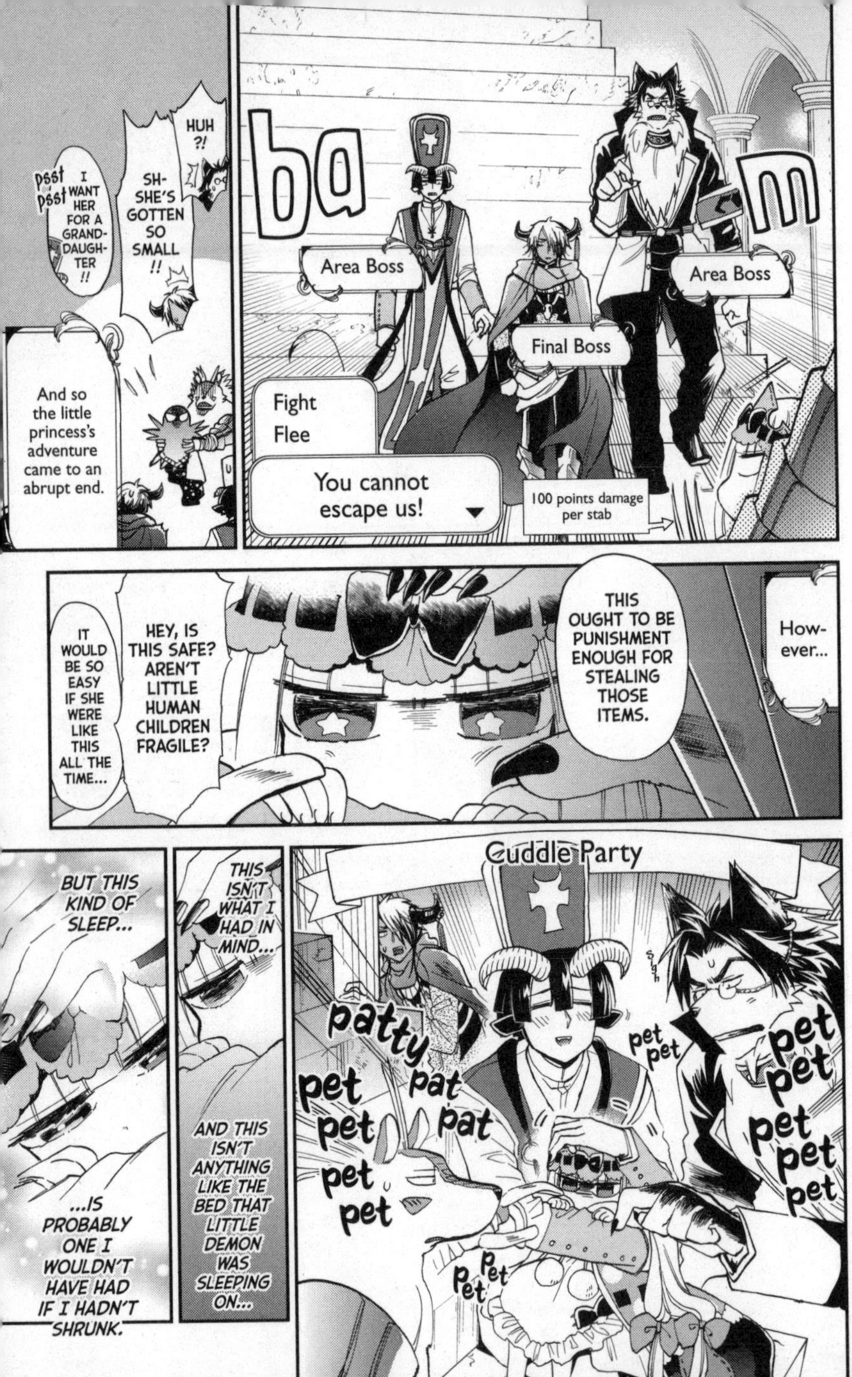
bam
Area Boss
Final Boss
Area Boss
Fight
Flee
You cannot escape us!
100 points damage per stab
HUH ?!
SH- SHE'S GOTTEN SO SMALL !!
pssst pssst
I WANT HER FOR A GRAND-DAUGHTER !!
And so the little princess's adventure came to an abrupt end.
How-ever...
THIS OUGHT TO BE PUNISHMENT ENOUGH FOR STEALING THOSE ITEMS.
HEY, IS THIS SAFE? AREN'T LITTLE HUMAN CHILDREN FRAGILE?
IT WOULD BE SO EASY IF SHE WERE LIKE THIS ALL THE TIME...
Cuddle Party
Sigh
pet pet
pet pet pet pet pet pet
patty pat pat
pet pet pet pet
Pet Pet
THIS ISN'T WHAT I HAD IN MIND...
AND THIS ISN'T ANYTHING LIKE THE BED THAT LITTLE DEMON WAS SLEEPING ON...
BUT THIS KIND OF SLEEP...
...IS PROBABLY ONE I WOULDN'T HAVE HAD IF I HADN'T SHRUNK.

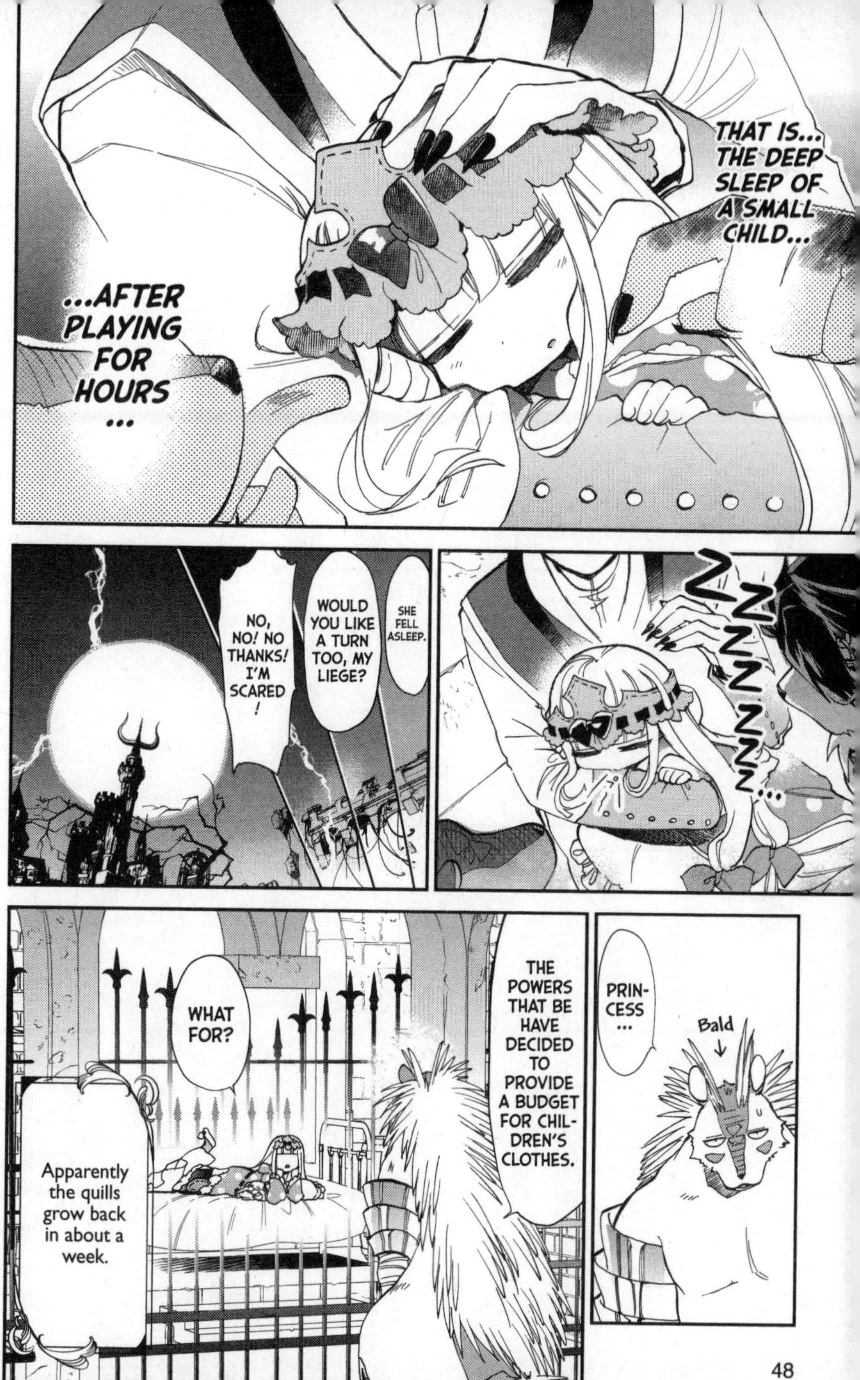
THAT IS... THE DEEP SLEEP OF A SMALL CHILD...
...AFTER PLAYING FOR HOURS...
ZZZZZZZ...
SHE FELL ASLEEP.
WOULD YOU LIKE A TURN TOO, MY LIEGE?
NO, NO! NO THANKS! I'M SCARED!
PRINCESS...
Bald
THE POWERS THAT BE HAVE DECIDED TO PROVIDE A BUDGET FOR CHILDREN'S CLOTHES.
WHAT FOR?
Apparently the quills grow back in about a week.

Minotaur

He prefers soy milk to cow's milk.

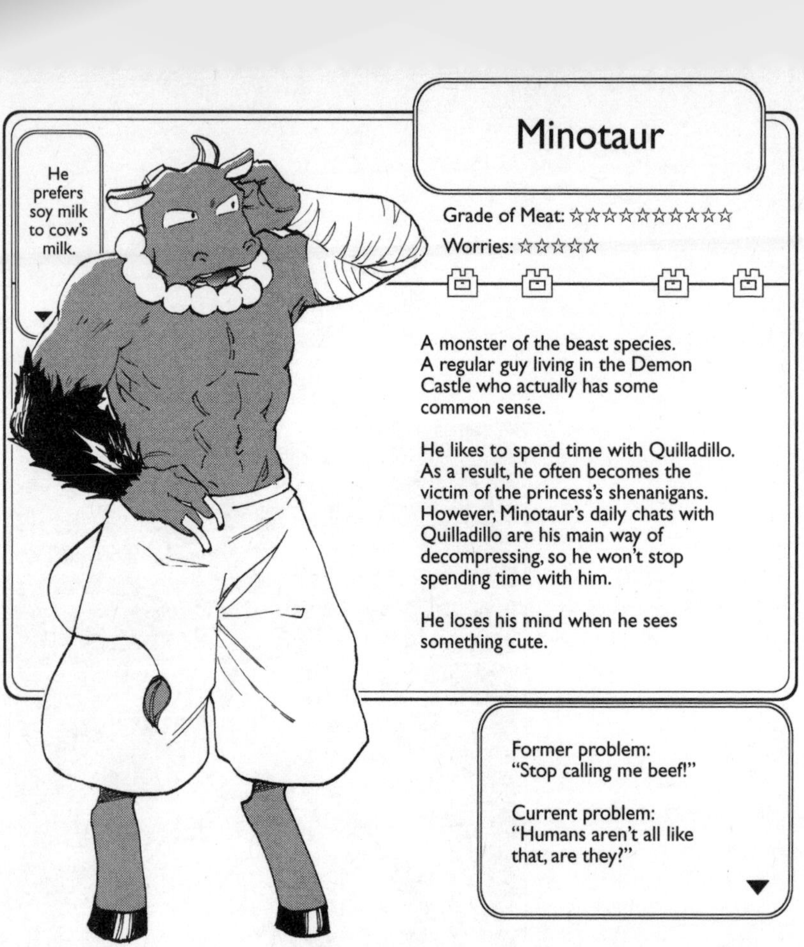

Grade of Meat: ☆☆☆☆☆☆☆☆☆☆☆

Worries: ☆☆☆☆☆

A monster of the beast species. A regular guy living in the Demon Castle who actually has some common sense.

He likes to spend time with Quilladillo. As a result, he often becomes the victim of the princess's shenanigans. However, Minotaur's daily chats with Quilladillo are his main way of decompressing, so he won't stop spending time with him.

He loses his mind when he sees something cute.

Former problem:
"Stop calling me beef!"

Current problem:
"Humans aren't all like that, are they?"

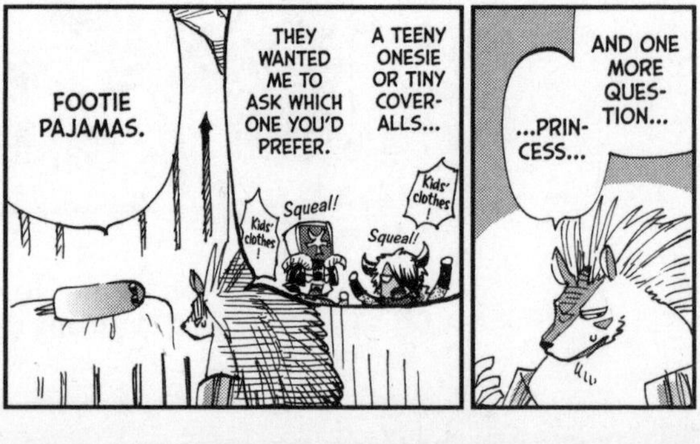
AND ONE MORE QUES-TION...
...PRIN-CESS...
A TEENY ONESIE OR TINY COVER-ALLS...
THEY WANTED ME TO ASK WHICH ONE YOU'D PREFER.
Kids' clothes!
Squeal!
Squeal!
Kids' clothes!
FOOTIE PAJAMAS.

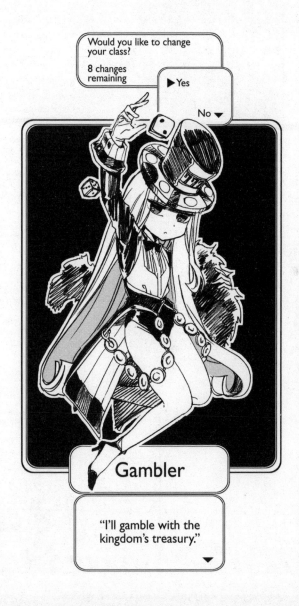

Would you like to change your class?

8 changes remaining

▶Yes

No ▼

Gambler

"I'll gamble with the kingdom's treasury."

▼

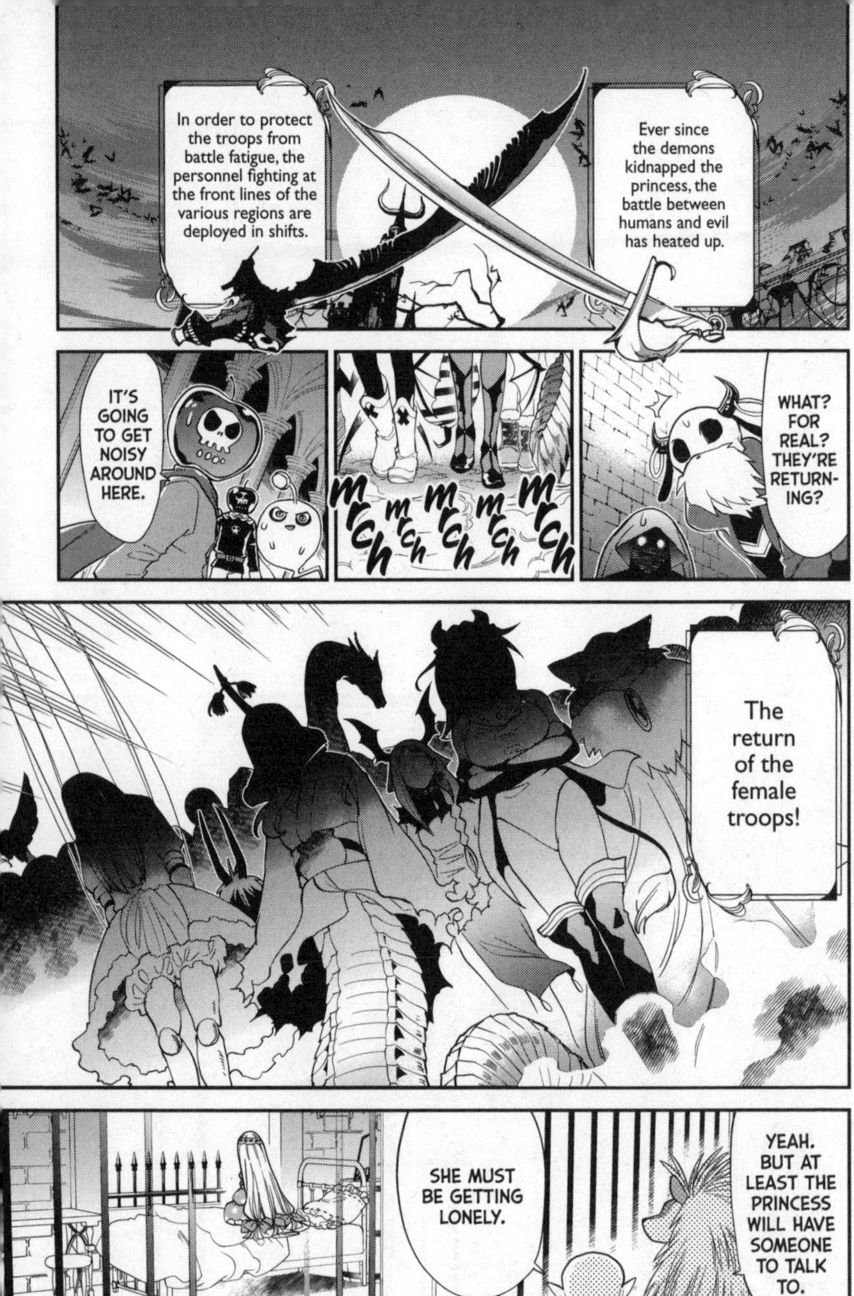
Ever since the demons kidnapped the princess, the battle between humans and evil has heated up.
In order to protect the troops from battle fatigue, the personnel fighting at the front lines of the various regions are deployed in shifts.
WHAT? FOR REAL? THEY'RE RETURNING?
mrch mrch mrch mrch mrch
IT'S GOING TO GET NOISY AROUND HERE.
The return of the female troops!
YEAH. BUT AT LEAST THE PRINCESS WILL HAVE SOMEONE TO TALK TO.
SHE MUST BE GETTING LONELY.

18th Night: Comforter = Friend

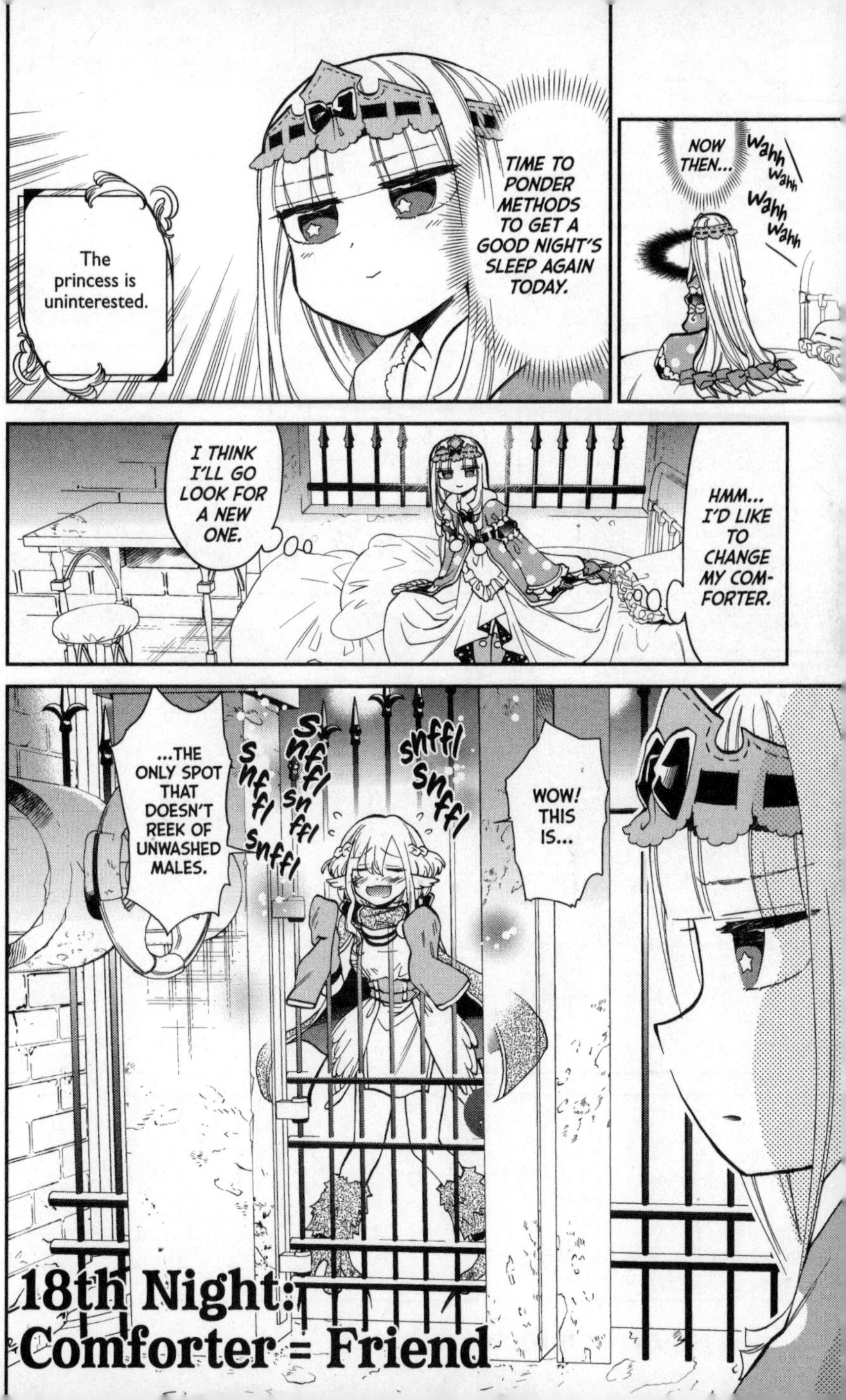
NOW THEN...
wahh wahh
wahh wahh
TIME TO PONDER METHODS TO GET A GOOD NIGHT'S SLEEP AGAIN TODAY.
The princess is uninterested.
HMM... I'D LIKE TO CHANGE MY COM-FORTER.
I THINK I'LL GO LOOK FOR A NEW ONE.
WOW! THIS IS...
snffl snffl
snffl snffl snffl
snffl snffl
...THE ONLY SPOT THAT DOESN'T REEK OF UNWASHED MALES.

18th Night: Comforter = Friend

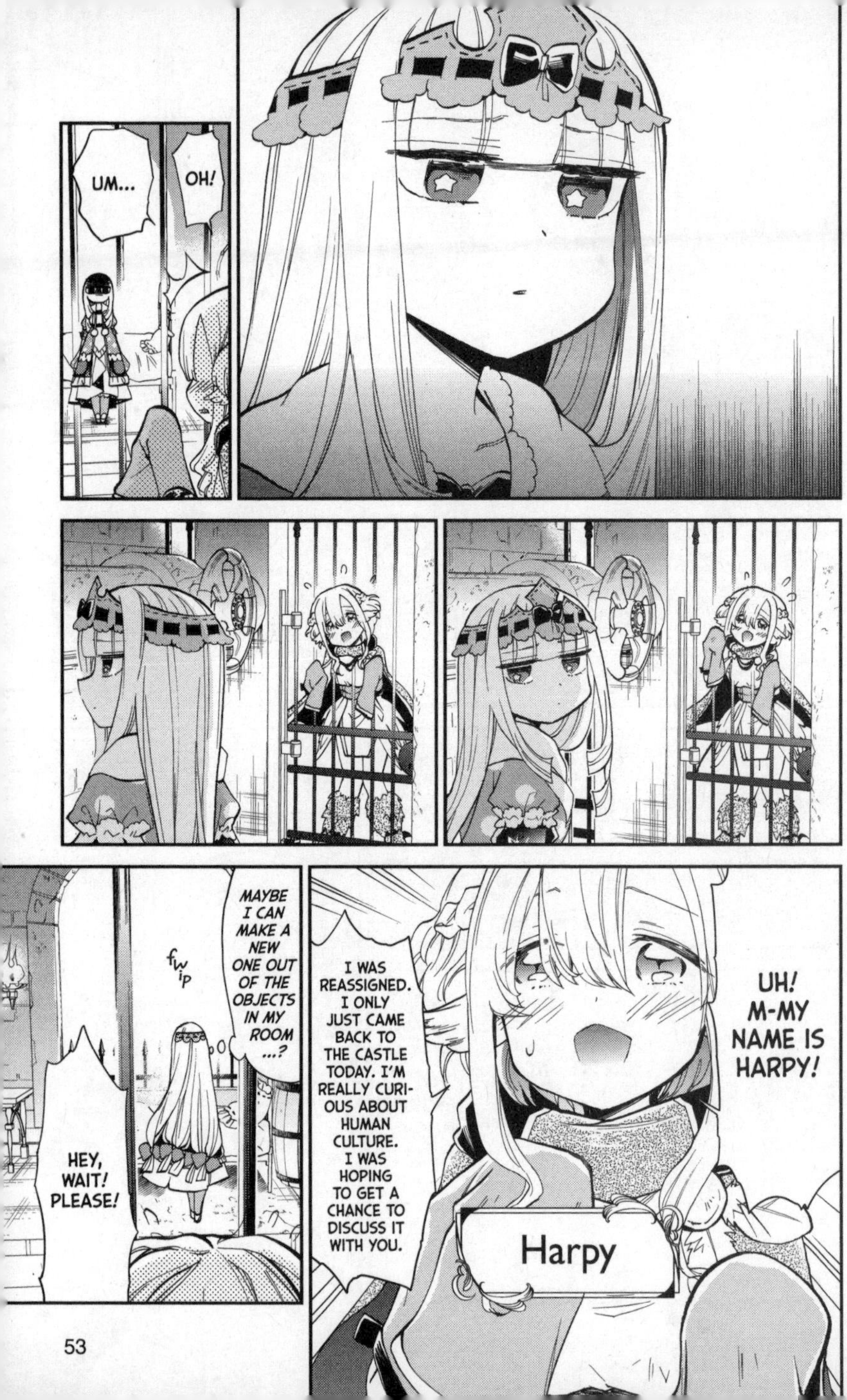
OH!
UM...
UH! M-MY NAME IS HARPY!
Harpy
I WAS REASSIGNED. I ONLY JUST CAME BACK TO THE CASTLE TODAY. I'M REALLY CURIOUS ABOUT HUMAN CULTURE. I WAS HOPING TO GET A CHANCE TO DISCUSS IT WITH YOU.
MAYBE I CAN MAKE A NEW ONE OUT OF THE OBJECTS IN MY ROOM ...?
fwip
HEY, WAIT! PLEASE!

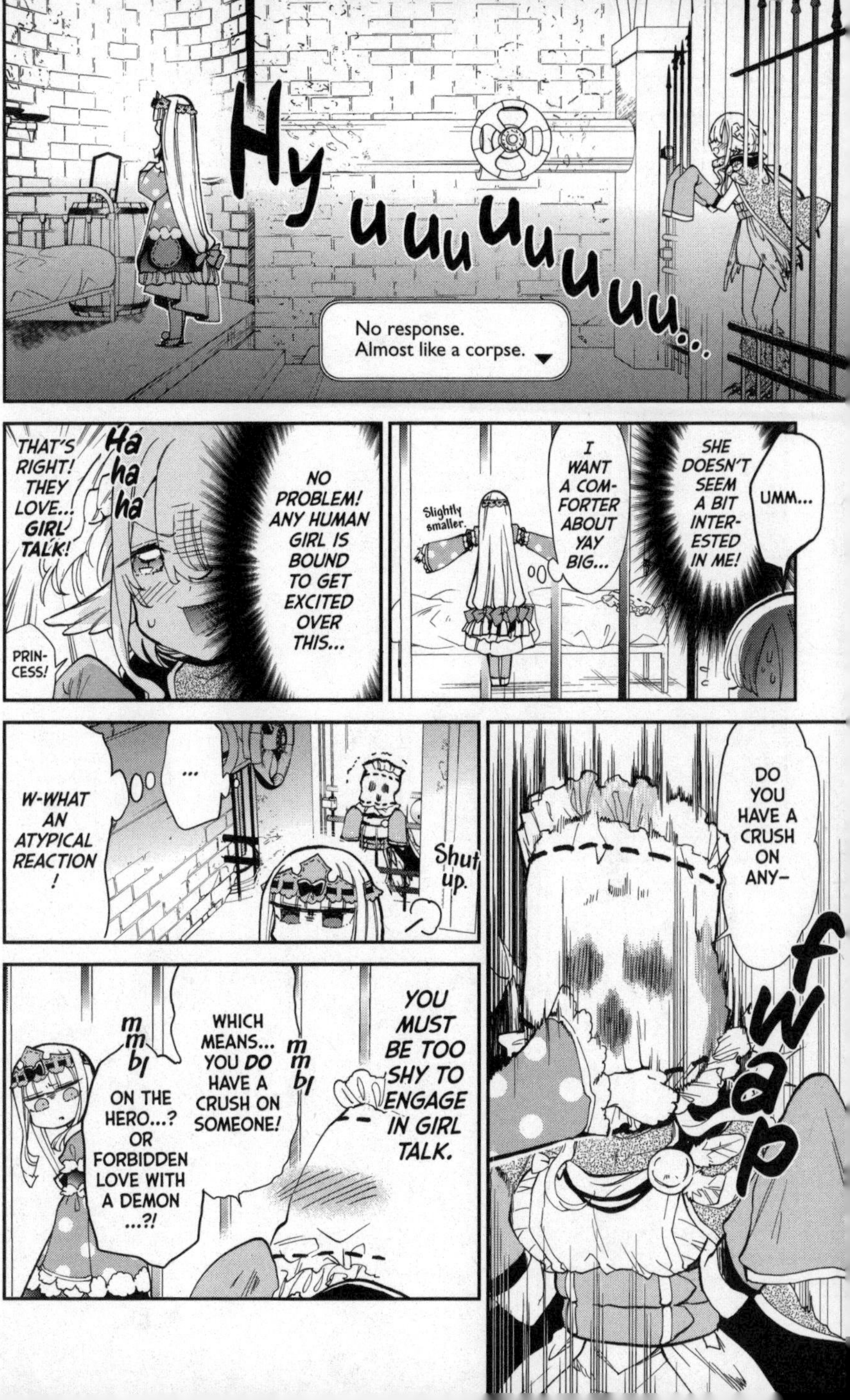
Hyuuuuuuuuuu...
No response. Almost like a corpse.
UMM...
SHE DOESN'T SEEM A BIT INTER-ESTED IN ME!
I WANT A COM-FORTER ABOUT YAY BIG...
Slightly smaller.
NO PROBLEM! ANY HUMAN GIRL IS BOUND TO GET EXCITED OVER THIS...
PRIN-CESS!
Hahaha
THAT'S RIGHT! THEY LOVE... GIRL TALK!
DO YOU HAVE A CRUSH ON ANY—
fwap
...
Shut up.
W-WHAT AN ATYPICAL REACTION!
YOU MUST BE TOO SHY TO ENGAGE IN GIRL TALK.
mmbl
WHICH MEANS... YOU DO HAVE A CRUSH ON SOMEONE!
mmbl
ON THE HERO...? OR FORBIDDEN LOVE WITH A DEMON...?!

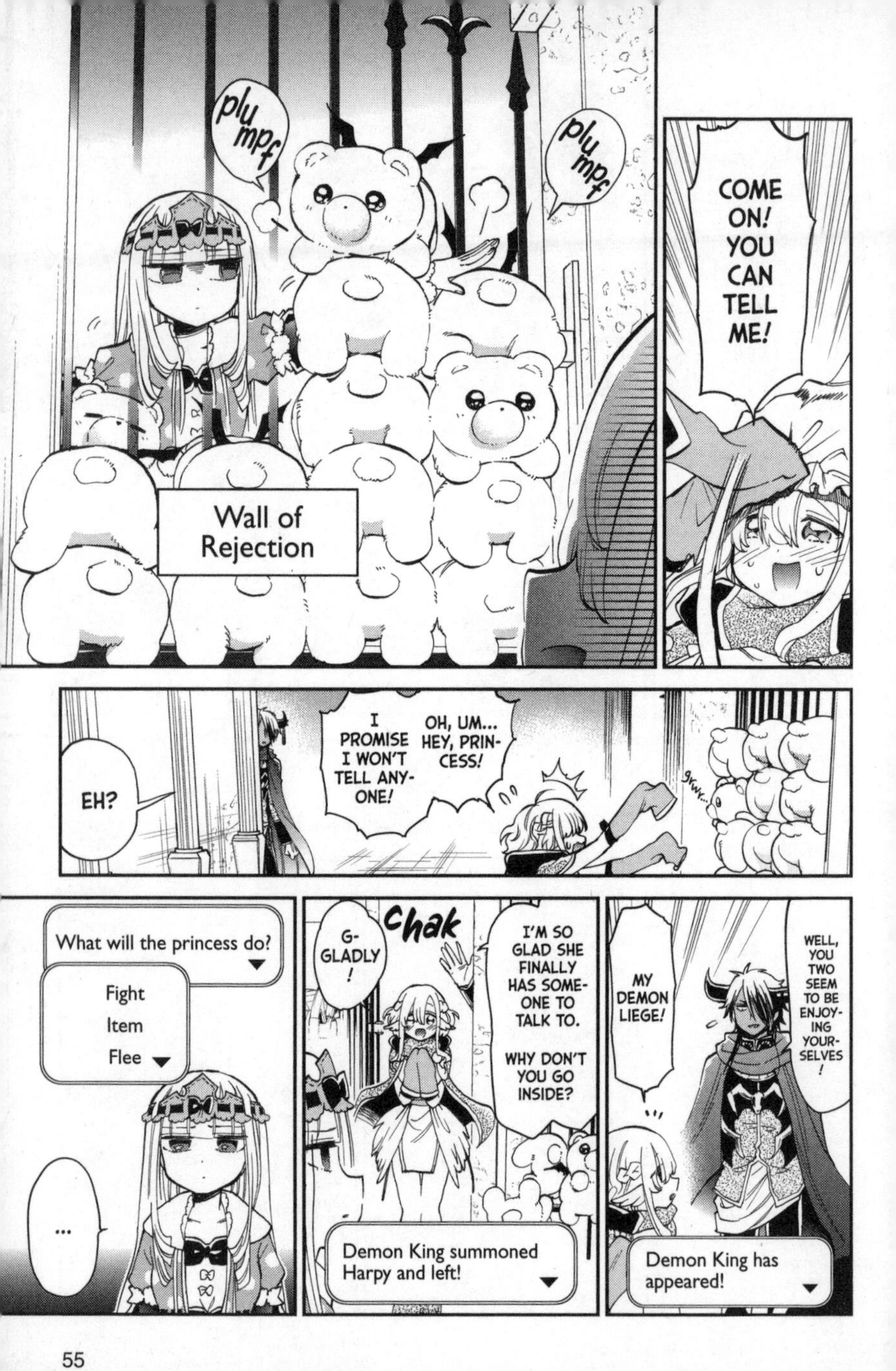
COME ON! YOU CAN TELL ME!
plumpf
plumpf
Wall of Rejection
grwr...
OH, UM... HEY, PRINCESS!
I PROMISE I WON'T TELL ANYONE!
EH?
WELL, YOU TWO SEEM TO BE ENJOYING YOURSELVES!
MY DEMON LIEGE!
Demon King has appeared!
I'M SO GLAD SHE FINALLY HAS SOMEONE TO TALK TO.
WHY DON'T YOU GO INSIDE?
Chak
G-GLADLY!
Demon King summoned Harpy and left!
What will the princess do?
Fight
Item
Flee
...

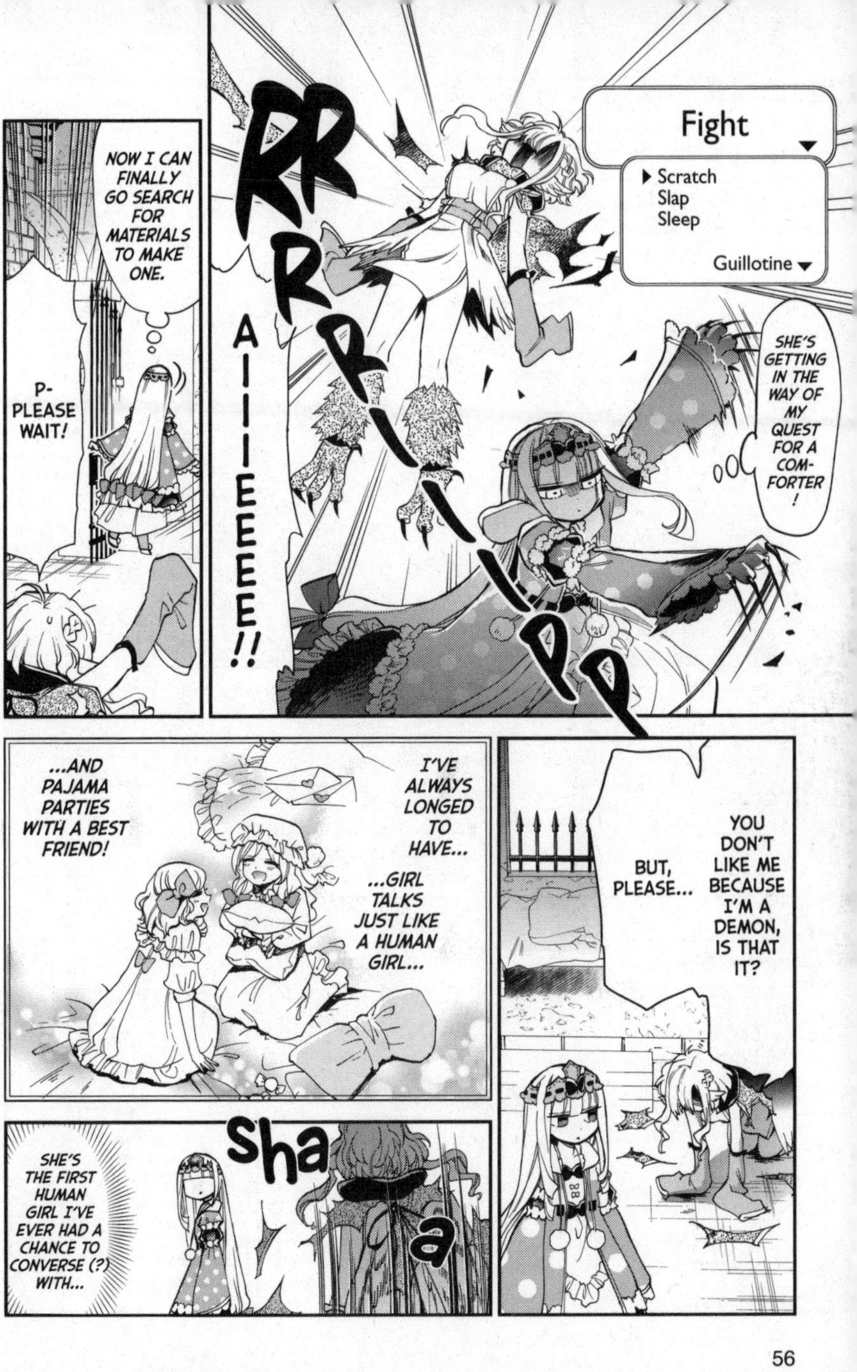
Fight
▸ Scratch
Slap
Sleep
Guillotine
SHE'S GETTING IN THE WAY OF MY QUEST FOR A COM-FORTER!
RRRRIIIPP
AIIIIEEEEE!!
NOW I CAN FINALLY GO SEARCH FOR MATERIALS TO MAKE ONE.
P-PLEASE WAIT!
YOU DON'T LIKE ME BECAUSE I'M A DEMON, IS THAT IT?
BUT, PLEASE...
I'VE ALWAYS LONGED TO HAVE...
...GIRL TALKS JUST LIKE A HUMAN GIRL...
...AND PAJAMA PARTIES WITH A BEST FRIEND!
Sha
a
SHE'S THE FIRST HUMAN GIRL I'VE EVER HAD A CHANCE TO CONVERSE (?) WITH...

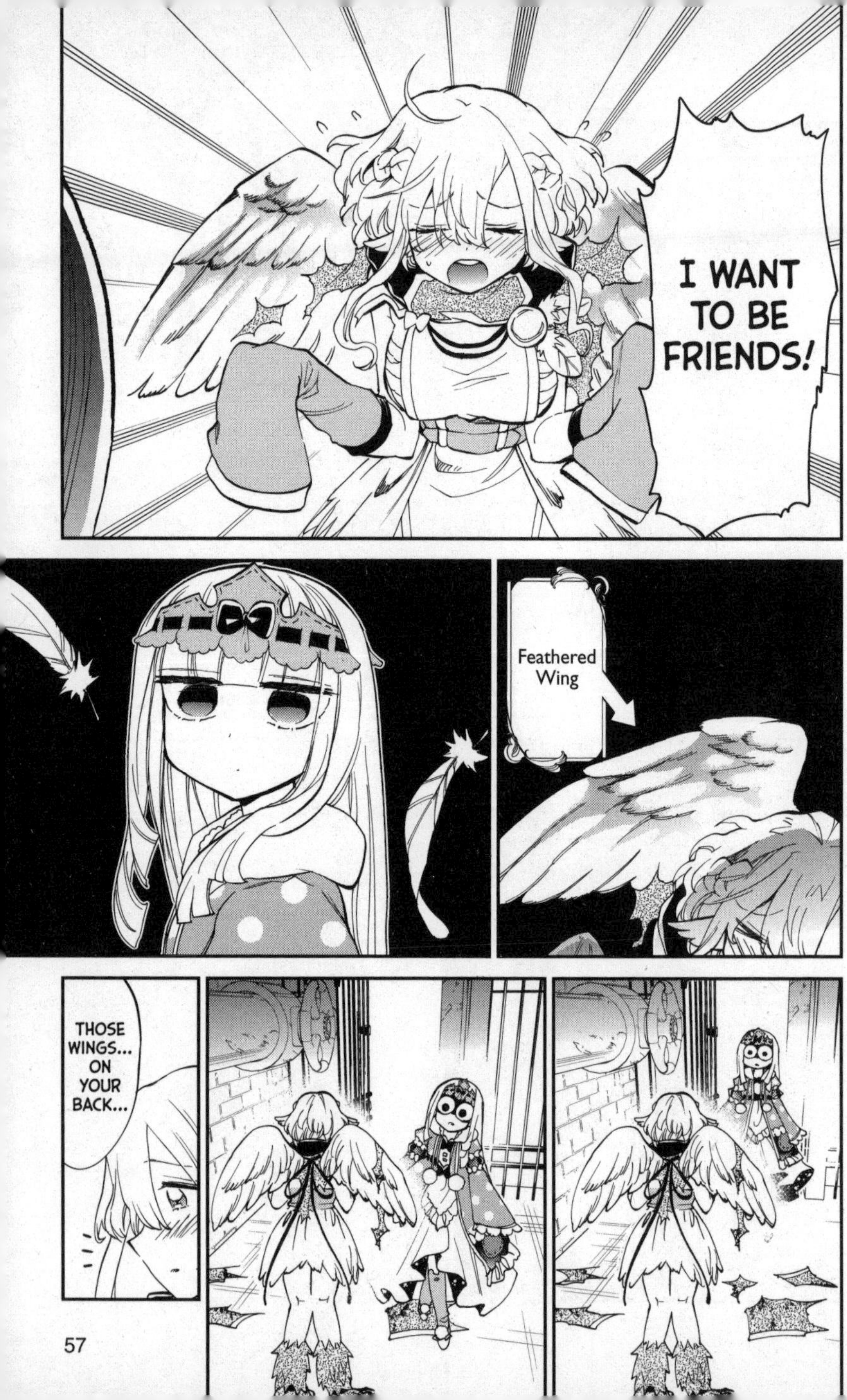
I WANT TO BE FRIENDS!
Feathered Wing
THOSE WINGS... ON YOUR BACK...

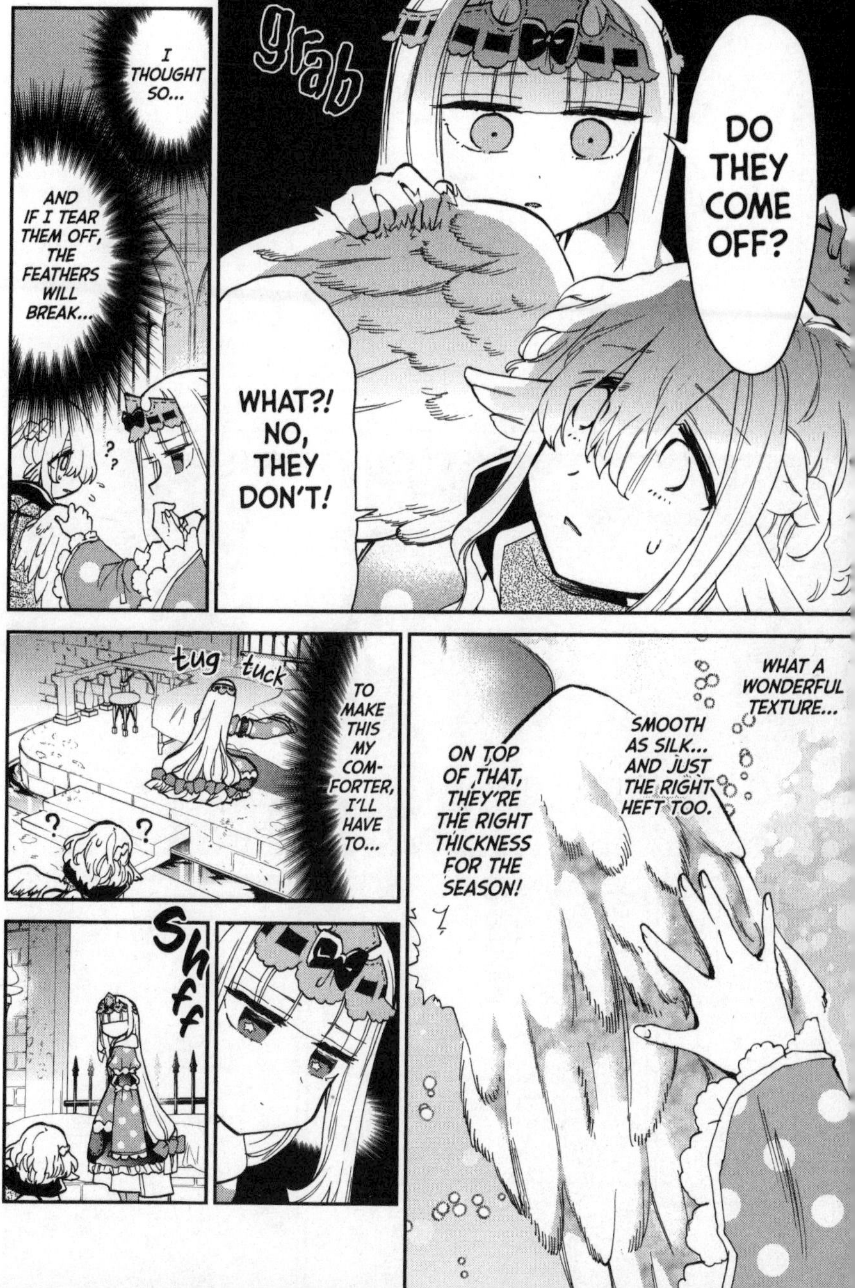
grab
DO THEY COME OFF?
WHAT?! NO, THEY DON'T!
I THOUGHT SO...
AND IF I TEAR THEM OFF, THE FEATHERS WILL BREAK...
??
WHAT A WONDERFUL TEXTURE...
SMOOTH AS SILK... AND JUST THE RIGHT HEFT TOO.
ON TOP OF THAT, THEY'RE THE RIGHT THICKNESS FOR THE SEASON!
tug
tuck
TO MAKE THIS MY COM-FORTER, I'LL HAVE TO...
? ?
Snff

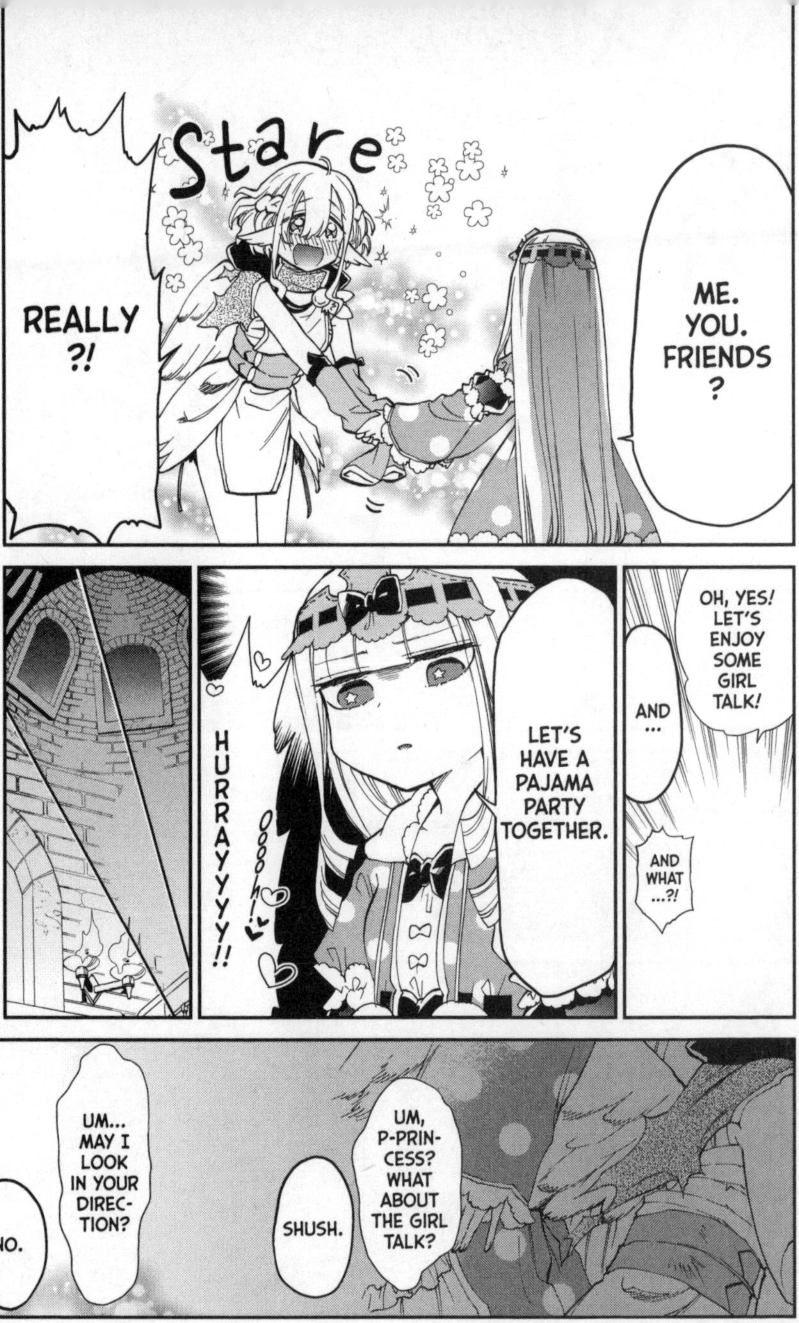
ME. YOU. FRIENDS?
Stare
REALLY?!
OH, YES! LET'S ENJOY SOME GIRL TALK!
AND...
AND WHAT...?!
LET'S HAVE A PAJAMA PARTY TOGETHER.
HURRAYYYY!!
Oooh!
UM, P-PRINCESS? WHAT ABOUT THE GIRL TALK?
SHUSH.
UM... MAY I LOOK IN YOUR DIRECTION?
NO.

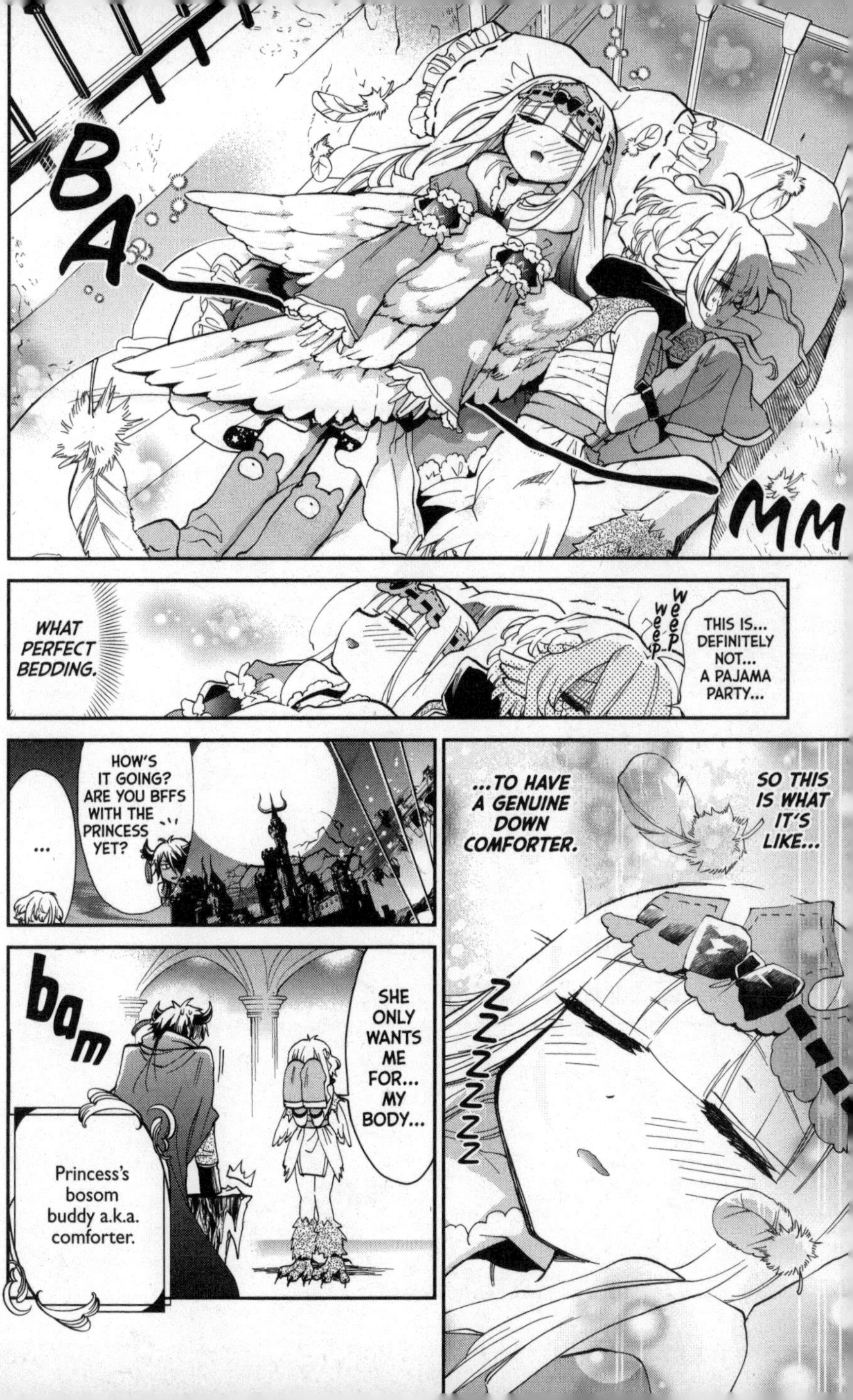
BA
MM
weep weep weep
THIS IS... DEFINITELY NOT... A PAJAMA PARTY...
WHAT PERFECT BEDDING.
SO THIS IS WHAT IT'S LIKE...
...TO HAVE A GENUINE DOWN COMFORTER.
ZZZZZZZ
HOW'S IT GOING? ARE YOU BFFS WITH THE PRINCESS YET?
...
SHE ONLY WANTS ME FOR... MY BODY...
bam
Princess's bosom buddy a.k.a. comforter.

Harpy

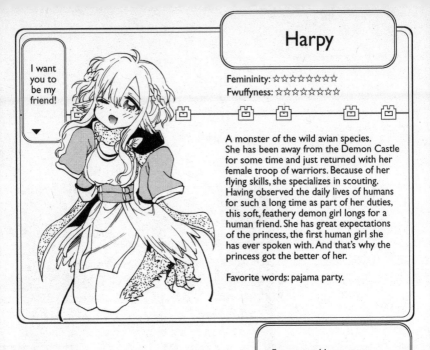

I want you to be my friend!

Femininity: ☆☆☆☆☆☆☆☆
Fwuffyness: ☆☆☆☆☆☆☆☆

A monster of the wild avian species. She has been away from the Demon Castle for some time and just returned with her female troop of warriors. Because of her flying skills, she specializes in scouting. Having observed the daily lives of humans for such a long time as part of her duties, this soft, feathery demon girl longs for a human friend. She has great expectations of the princess, the first human girl she has ever spoken with. And that's why the princess got the better of her.

Favorite words: pajama party.

Former problem:
"My hands aren't delicate."

Current problem:
"I wish I could get close to the princess..."

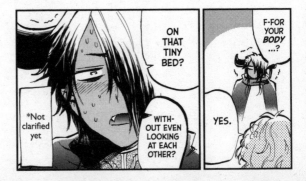

F-FOR YOUR *BODY* ...?
YES.
ON THAT TINY BED?
WITH-OUT EVEN LOOKING AT EACH OTHER?
*Not clarified yet

Would you like to change
your class?

7 changes
remaining

▶Yes

No ▼

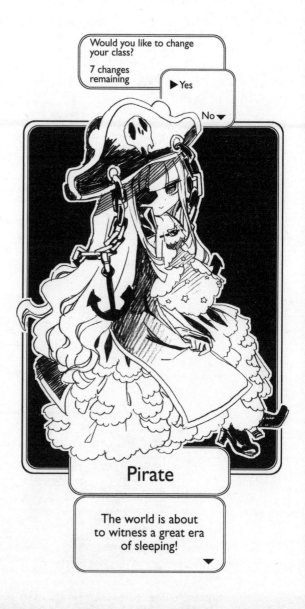

Pirate

The world is about
to witness a great era
of sleeping!

▼

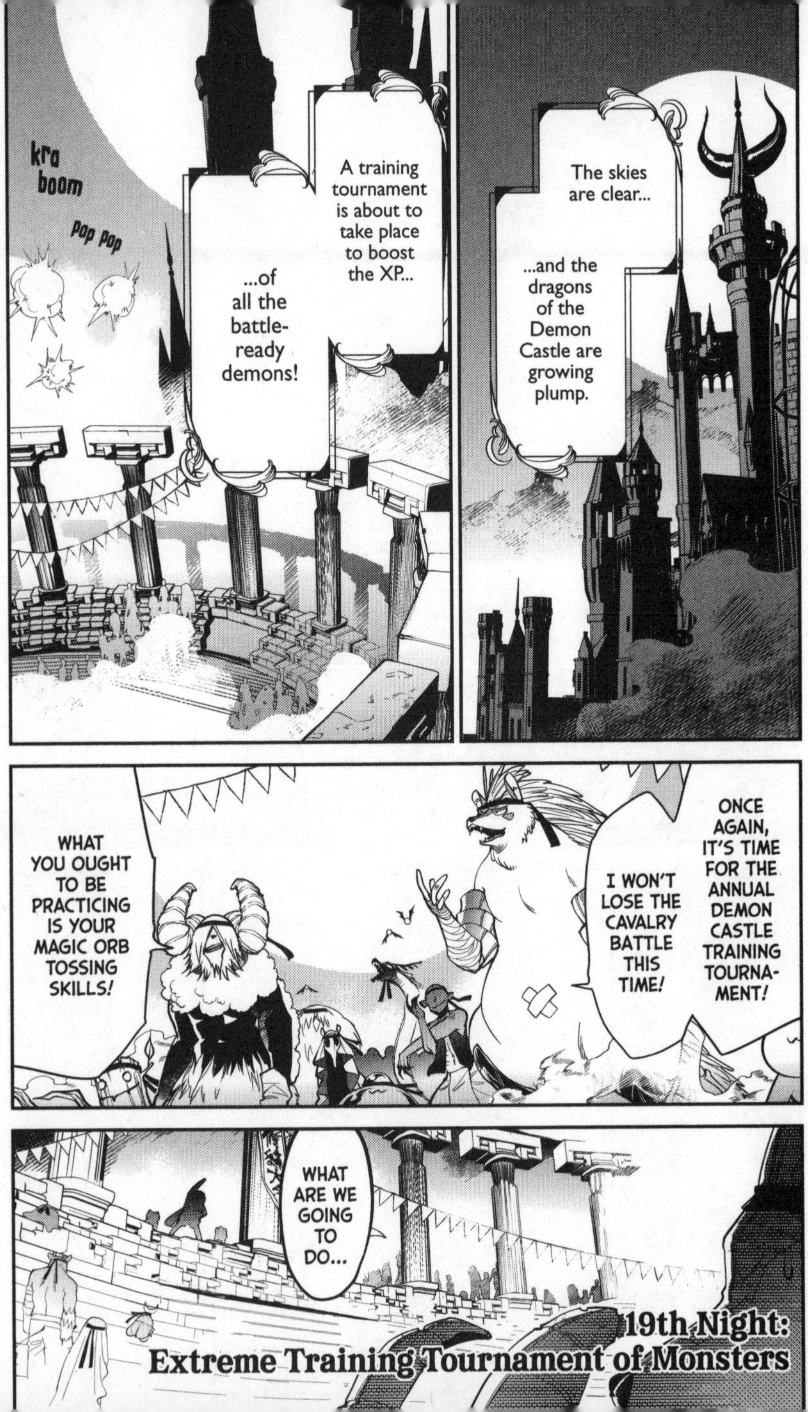
The skies are clear...
...and the dragons of the Demon Castle are growing plump.
A training tournament is about to take place to boost the XP...
...of all the battle-ready demons!
kra boom
pop pop
ONCE AGAIN, IT'S TIME FOR THE ANNUAL DEMON CASTLE TRAINING TOURNAMENT!
I WON'T LOSE THE CAVALRY BATTLE THIS TIME!
WHAT YOU OUGHT TO BE PRACTICING IS YOUR MAGIC ORB TOSSING SKILLS!
WHAT ARE WE GOING TO DO...
19th Night: Extreme Training Tournament of Monsters

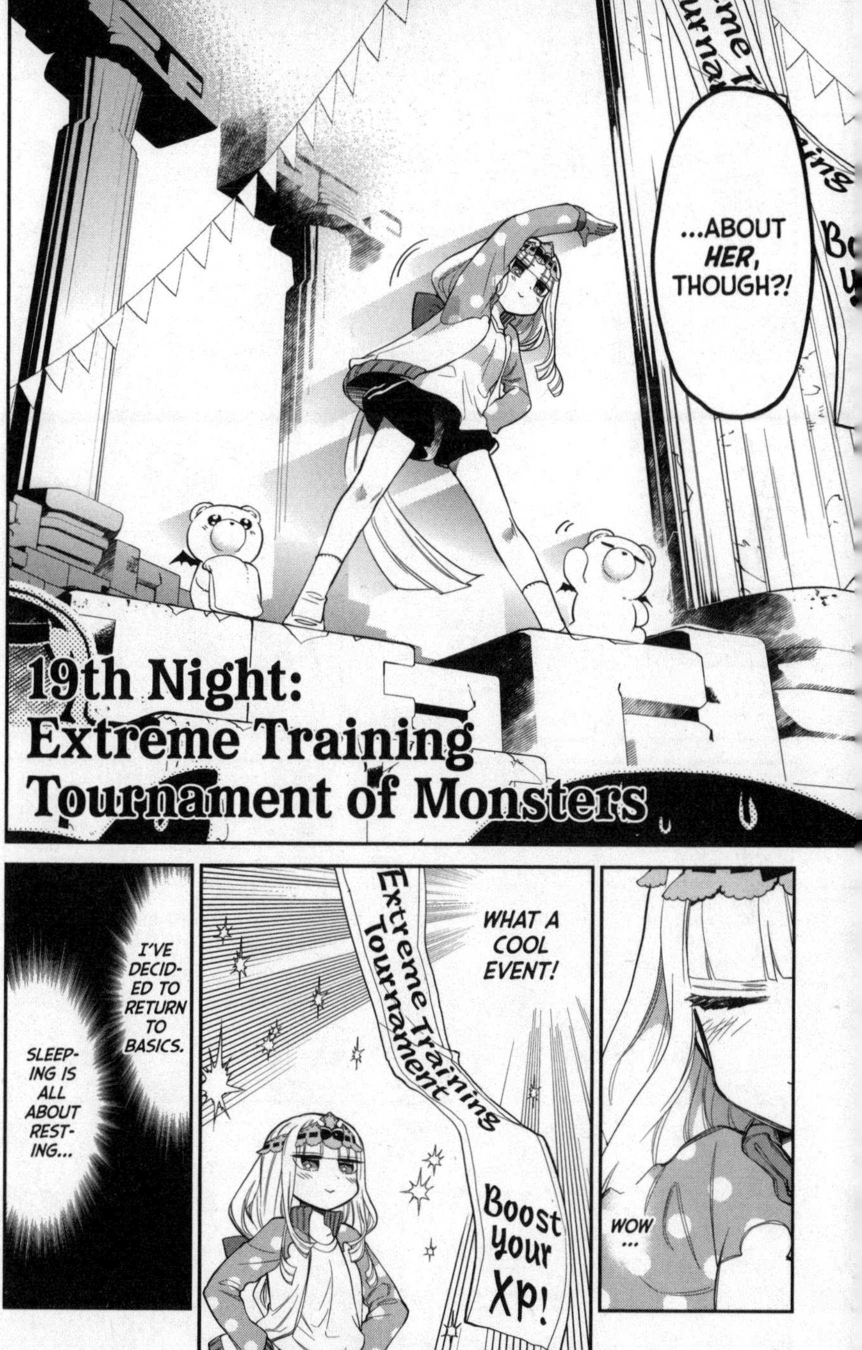
...ABOUT *HER*, THOUGH?!
19th Night: Extreme Training Tournament of Monsters
WOW...
WHAT A COOL EVENT!
Extreme Training Tournament
Boost Your XP!
I'VE DECIDED TO RETURN TO BASICS.
SLEEPING IS ALL ABOUT RESTING...

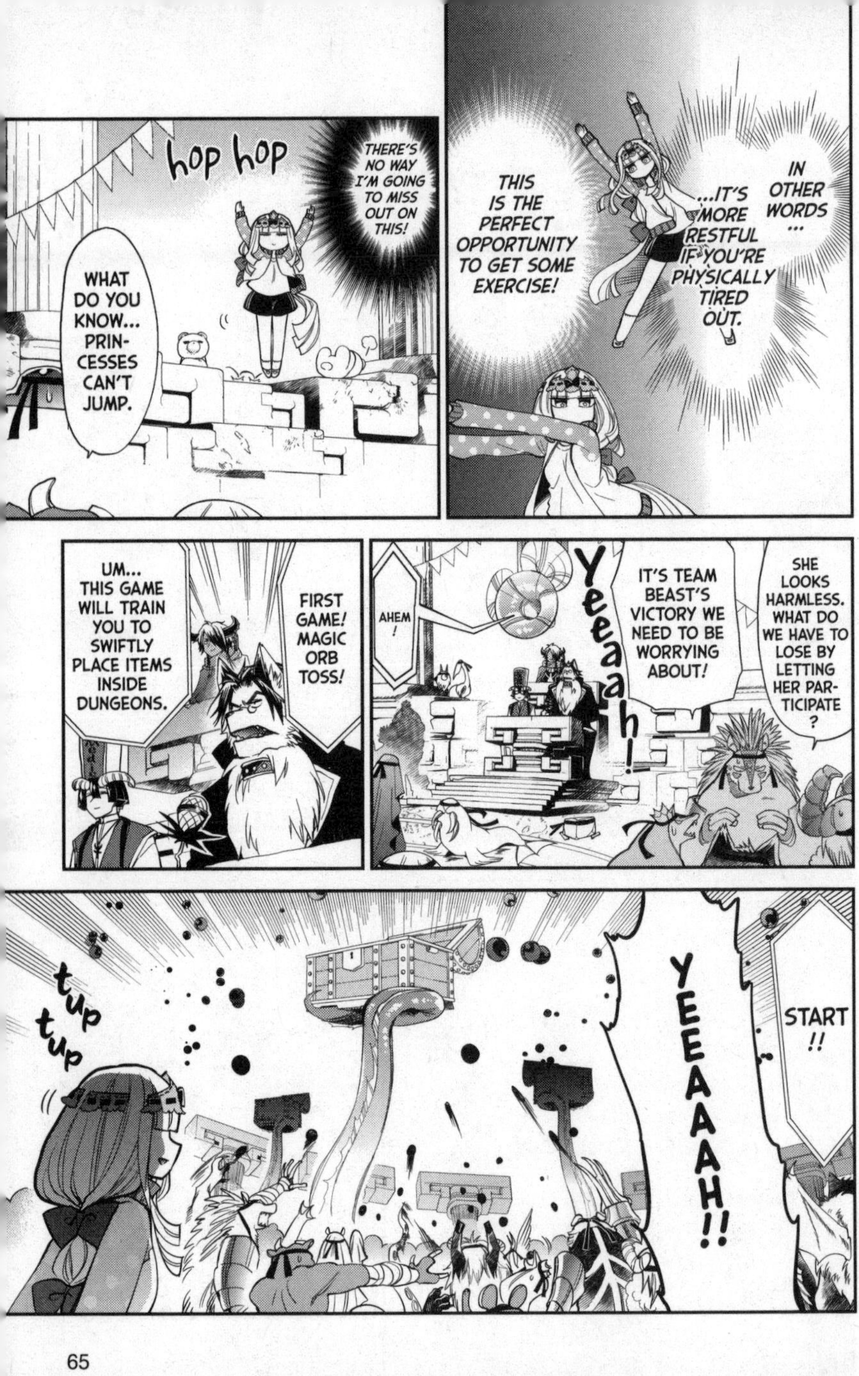
IN OTHER WORDS...
...IT'S MORE RESTFUL IF YOU'RE PHYSICALLY TIRED OUT.
THIS IS THE PERFECT OPPORTUNITY TO GET SOME EXERCISE!
THERE'S NO WAY I'M GOING TO MISS OUT ON THIS!
hop hop
WHAT DO YOU KNOW... PRINCESSES CAN'T JUMP.
SHE LOOKS HARMLESS. WHAT DO WE HAVE TO LOSE BY LETTING HER PARTICIPATE?
IT'S TEAM BEAST'S VICTORY WE NEED TO BE WORRYING ABOUT!
Yeeaah!
AHEM!
FIRST GAME! MAGIC ORB TOSS!
UM... THIS GAME WILL TRAIN YOU TO SWIFTLY PLACE ITEMS INSIDE DUNGEONS.
START!!
YEEAAAH!!
tup tup

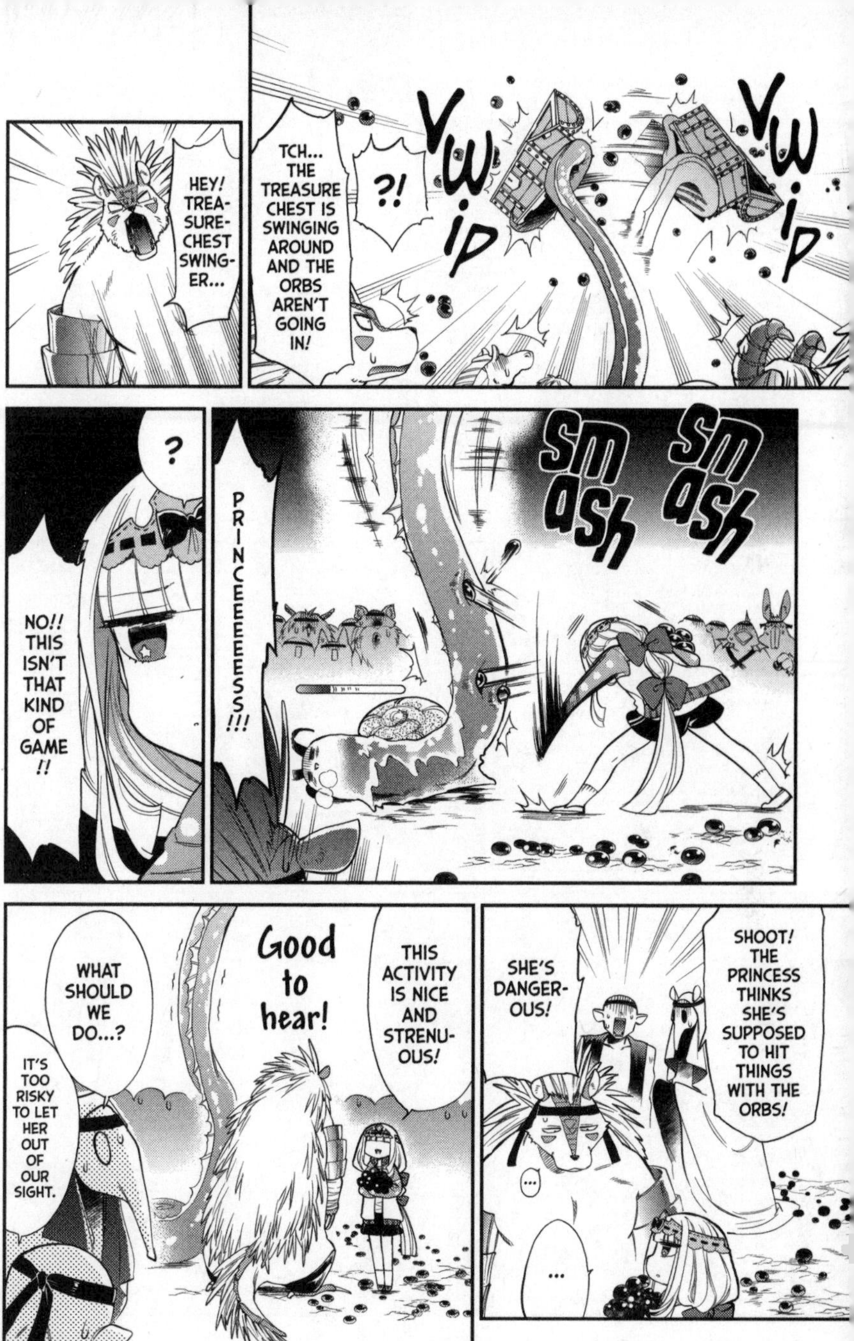
VWIP
VWIP
?!
TCH... THE TREASURE CHEST IS SWINGING AROUND AND THE ORBS AREN'T GOING IN!
HEY! TREASURE-CHEST SWINGER...
SMASH
SMASH
PRINCEEEEEESS!!!
?
NO!! THIS ISN'T THAT KIND OF GAME!!
SHOOT! THE PRINCESS THINKS SHE'S SUPPOSED TO HIT THINGS WITH THE ORBS!
SHE'S DANGEROUS!
...
...
THIS ACTIVITY IS NICE AND STRENUOUS!
Good to hear!
WHAT SHOULD WE DO...?
IT'S TOO RISKY TO LET HER OUT OF OUR SIGHT.

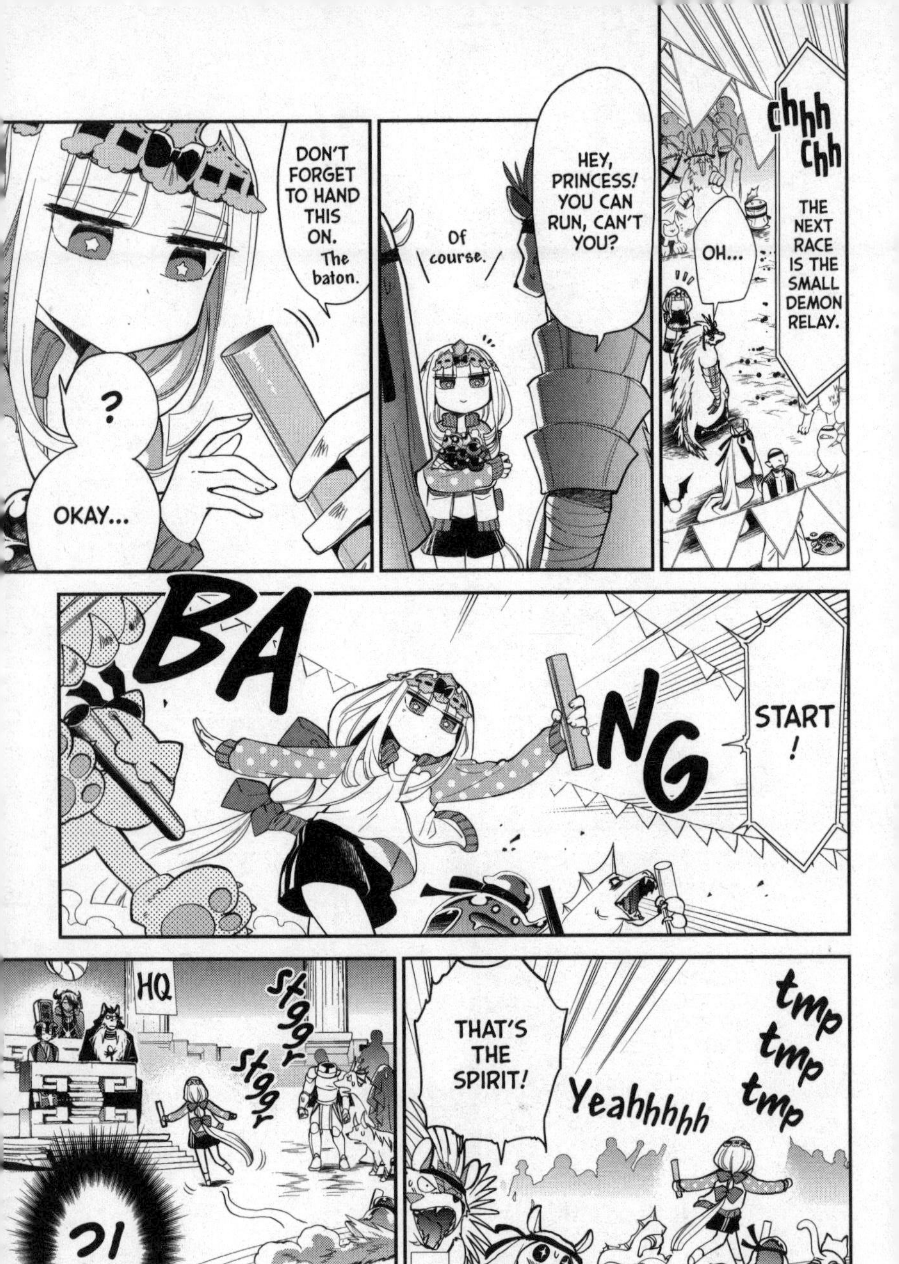
chhh chhh
THE NEXT RACE IS THE SMALL DEMON RELAY.
OH...
HEY, PRINCESS! YOU CAN RUN, CAN'T YOU?
Of course.
DON'T FORGET TO HAND THIS ON. The baton.
?
OKAY...
START!
BANG
tmp tmp tmp
THAT'S THE SPIRIT!
Yeahhhhh
Fam-ily
HQ
stggr stggr
?!

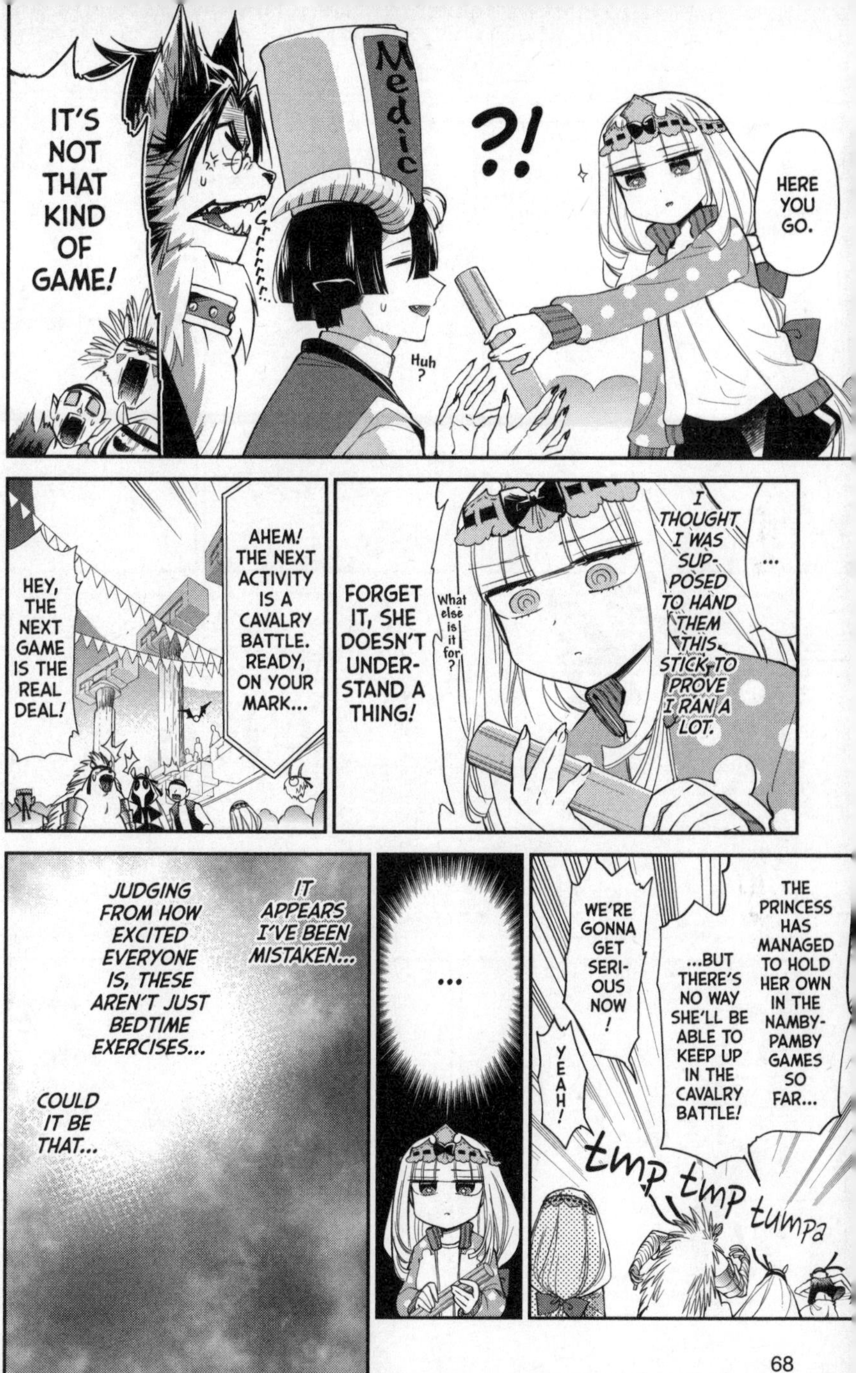
HERE YOU GO.
?!
Medic
Grrrrrr...
IT'S NOT THAT KIND OF GAME!
Huh?
I THOUGHT I WAS SUP-POSED TO HAND THEM THIS STICK TO PROVE I RAN A LOT.
...
What else is it for?
FORGET IT, SHE DOESN'T UNDER-STAND A THING!
AHEM! THE NEXT ACTIVITY IS A CAVALRY BATTLE. READY, ON YOUR MARK...
HEY, THE NEXT GAME IS THE REAL DEAL!
THE PRINCESS HAS MANAGED TO HOLD HER OWN IN THE NAMBY-PAMBY GAMES SO FAR...
...BUT THERE'S NO WAY SHE'LL BE ABLE TO KEEP UP IN THE CAVALRY BATTLE!
WE'RE GONNA GET SERI-OUS NOW!
YEAH!
tmp tmp tumpa
...
IT APPEARS I'VE BEEN MISTAKEN...
JUDGING FROM HOW EXCITED EVERYONE IS, THESE AREN'T JUST BEDTIME EXERCISES...
COULD IT BE THAT...

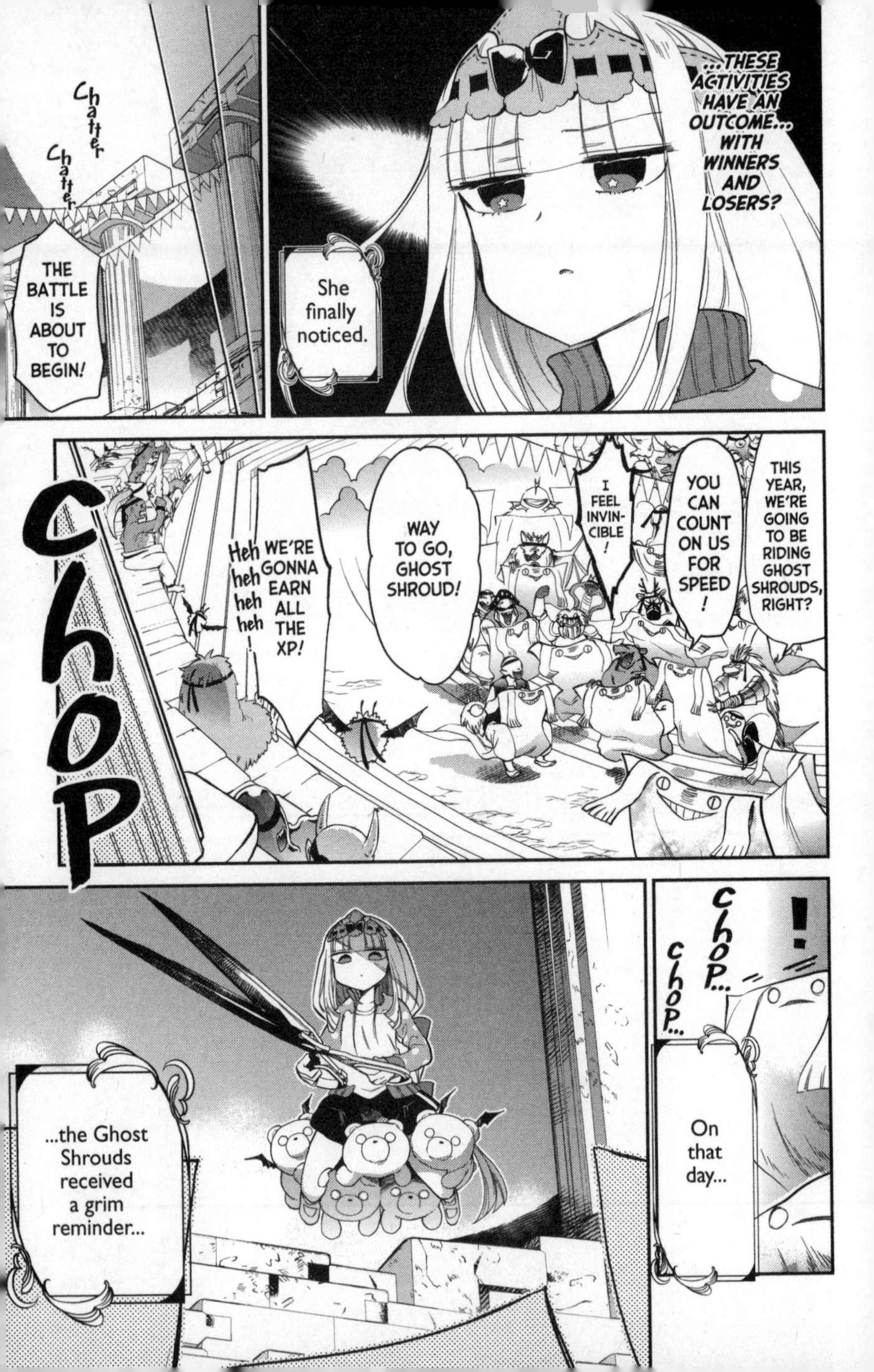
...THESE ACTIVITIES HAVE AN OUTCOME... WITH WINNERS AND LOSERS?
She finally noticed.
Chatter Chatter
THE BATTLE IS ABOUT TO BEGIN!
THIS YEAR, WE'RE GOING TO BE RIDING GHOST SHROUDS, RIGHT?
YOU CAN COUNT ON US FOR SPEED!
I FEEL INVINCIBLE!
WAY TO GO, GHOST SHROUD!
WE'RE GONNA EARN ALL THE XP!
Heh heh heh heh!
CHOP
chop... chop...
!
On that day...
...the Ghost Shrouds received a grim reminder...

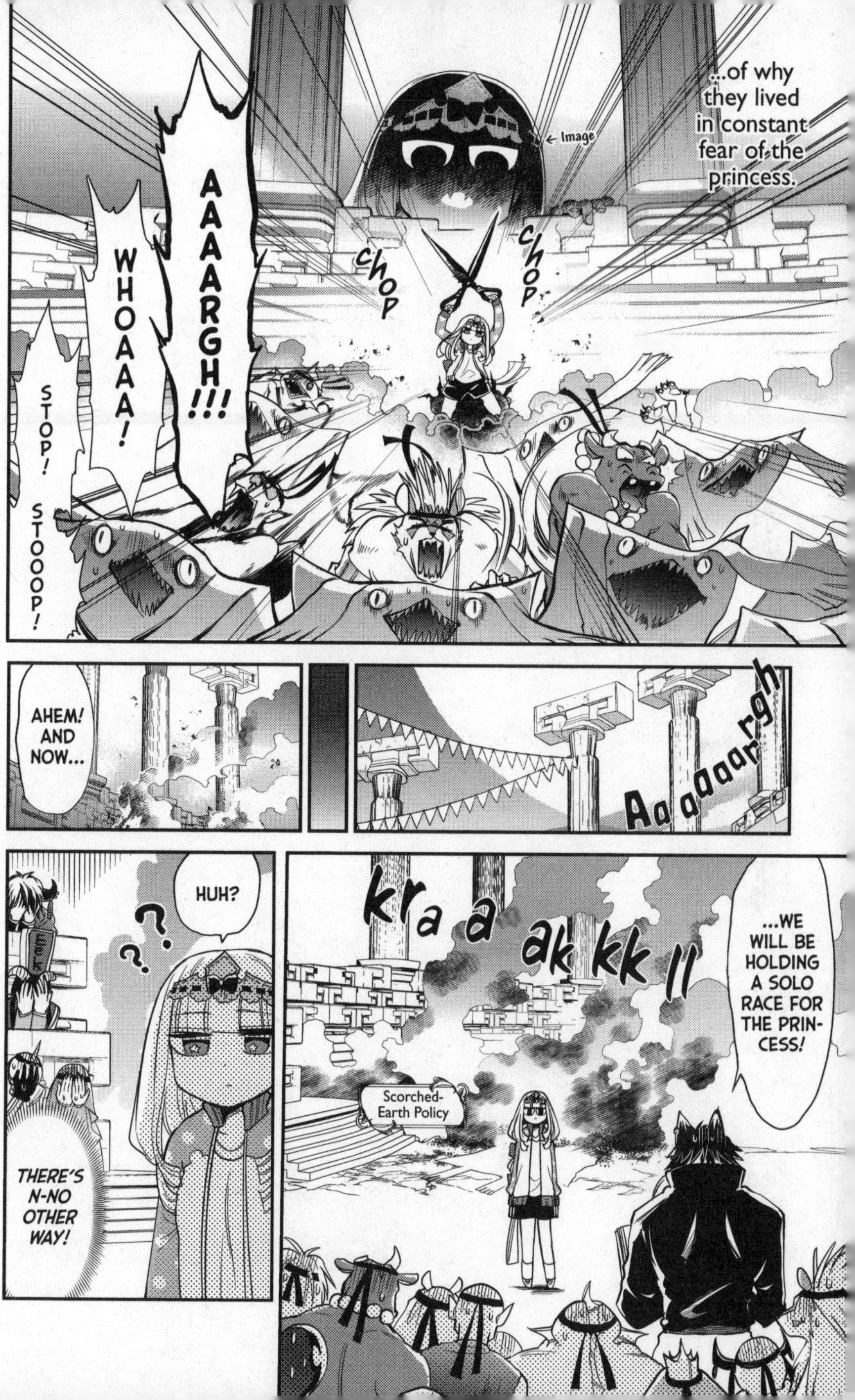
...of why they lived in constant fear of the princess.
← Image
CHOP
CHOP
AAAARGH!!!
WHOAAAA!
STOP! STOOOP!
Aaaaaargh
AHEM! AND NOW...
...WE WILL BE HOLDING A SOLO RACE FOR THE PRIN-CESS!
kraaakkll
Scorched-Earth Policy
HUH?
THERE'S N-NO OTHER WAY!

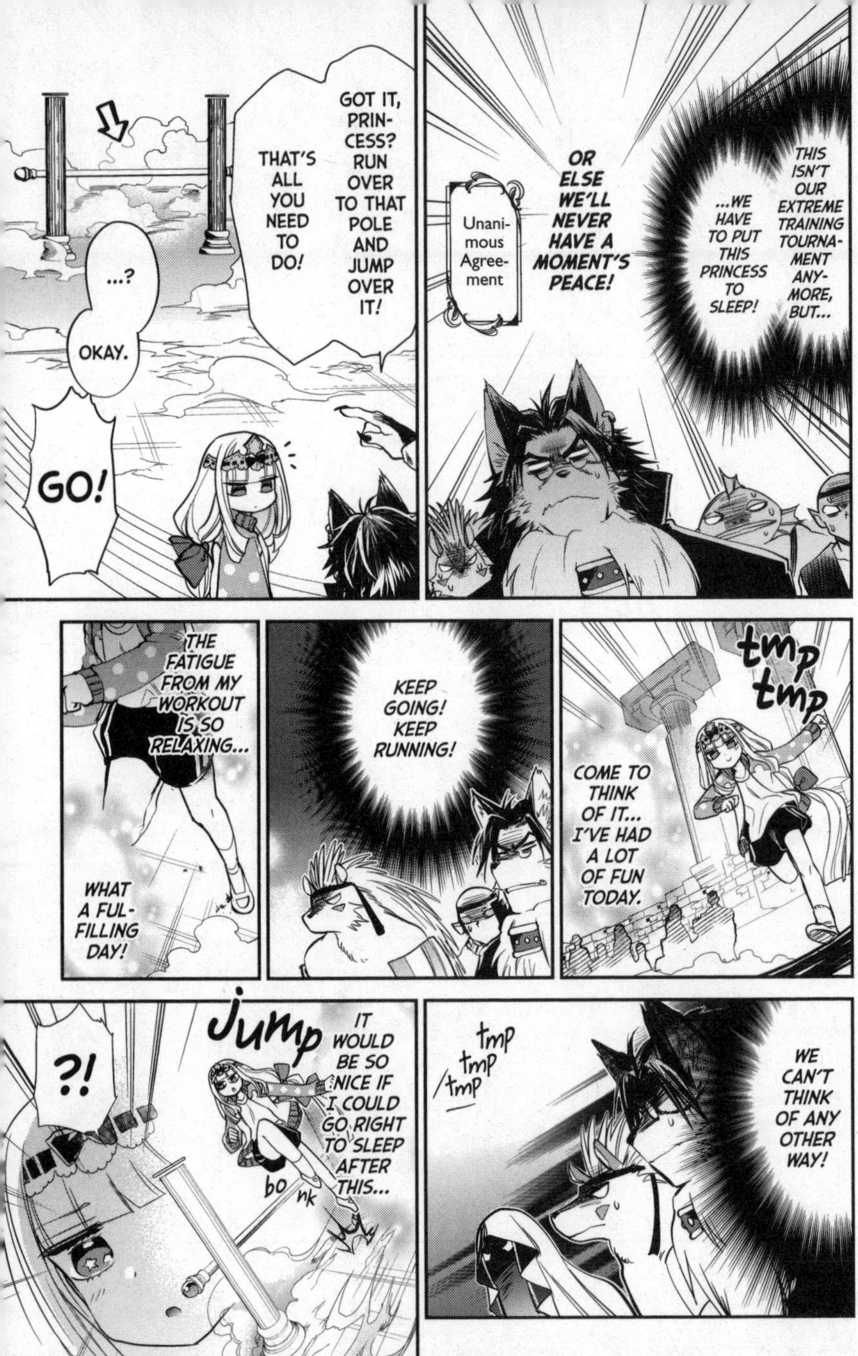
THIS ISN'T OUR EXTREME TRAINING TOURNAMENT ANYMORE, BUT...
...WE HAVE TO PUT THIS PRINCESS TO SLEEP!
OR ELSE WE'LL NEVER HAVE A MOMENT'S PEACE!
Unanimous Agreement
GOT IT, PRINCESS? RUN OVER TO THAT POLE AND JUMP OVER IT!
THAT'S ALL YOU NEED TO DO!
...?
OKAY.
GO!
tmp tmp
COME TO THINK OF IT... I'VE HAD A LOT OF FUN TODAY.
KEEP GOING! KEEP RUNNING!
THE FATIGUE FROM MY WORKOUT IS SO RELAXING...
WHAT A FULFILLING DAY!
tmp tmp tmp
WE CAN'T THINK OF ANY OTHER WAY!
IT WOULD BE SO NICE IF I COULD GO RIGHT TO SLEEP AFTER THIS...
jump
bonk
?!

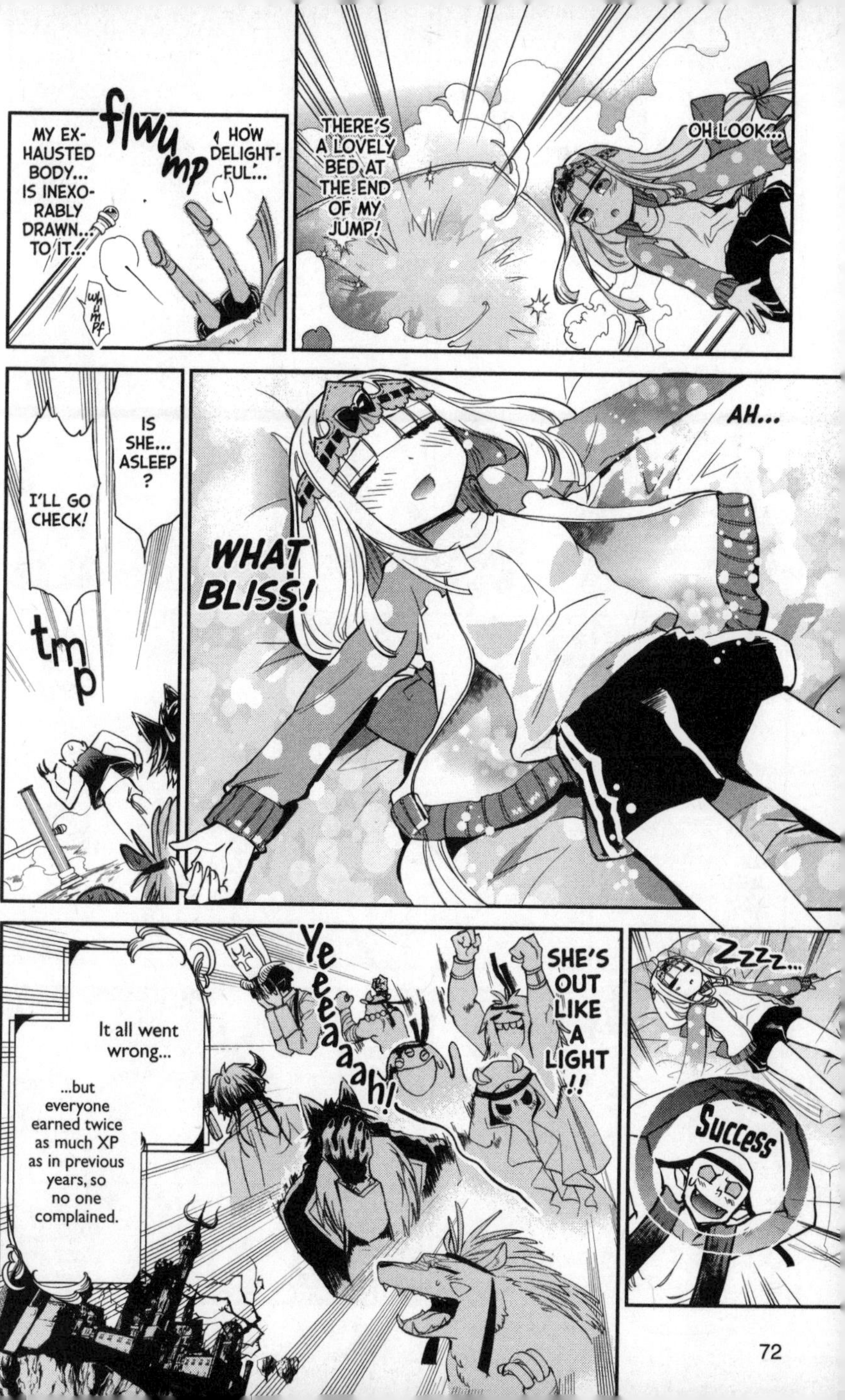
OH LOOK...
THERE'S A LOVELY BED AT THE END OF MY JUMP!
HOW DELIGHTFUL...
flwump
MY EXHAUSTED BODY... IS INEXORABLY DRAWN... TO IT...
whmpf
AH...
WHAT BLISS!
IS SHE... ASLEEP?
I'LL GO CHECK!
tmp
Zzzz...
Success
SHE'S OUT LIKE A LIGHT!!
Yeeeaaaah!
It all went wrong...
...but everyone earned twice as much XP as in previous years, so no one complained.

Dr. Anteater

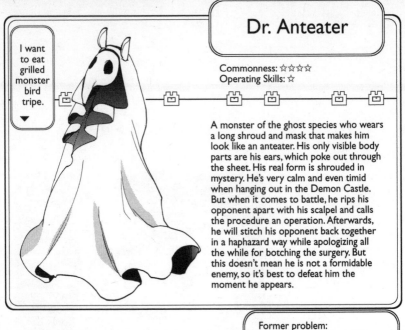

I want to eat grilled monster bird tripe.

▼

Commonness: ☆☆☆☆
Operating Skills: ☆

A monster of the ghost species who wears a long shroud and mask that makes him look like an anteater. His only visible body parts are his ears, which poke out through the sheet. His real form is shrouded in mystery. He's very calm and even timid when hanging out in the Demon Castle. But when it comes to battle, he rips his opponent apart with his scalpel and calls the procedure an operation. Afterwards, he will stitch his opponent back together in a haphazard way while apologizing all the while for botching the surgery. But this doesn't mean he is not a formidable enemy, so it's best to defeat him the moment he appears.

Former problem:
"My operating theater skills never improve."

Current problem:
"She's our hostage, yet I feel the urge to pet her every now and then."

▼

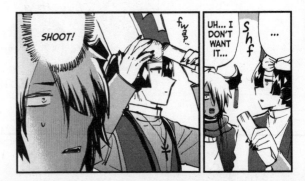

SHOOT!

fw..

UH... I DON'T WANT IT...

shf

...

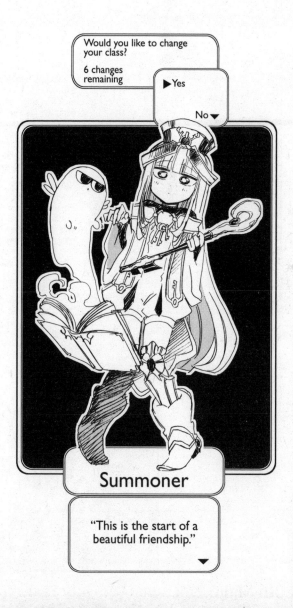

Would you like to change your class?

6 changes remaining

▶Yes

No ▼

Summoner

"This is the start of a beautiful friendship."

▼

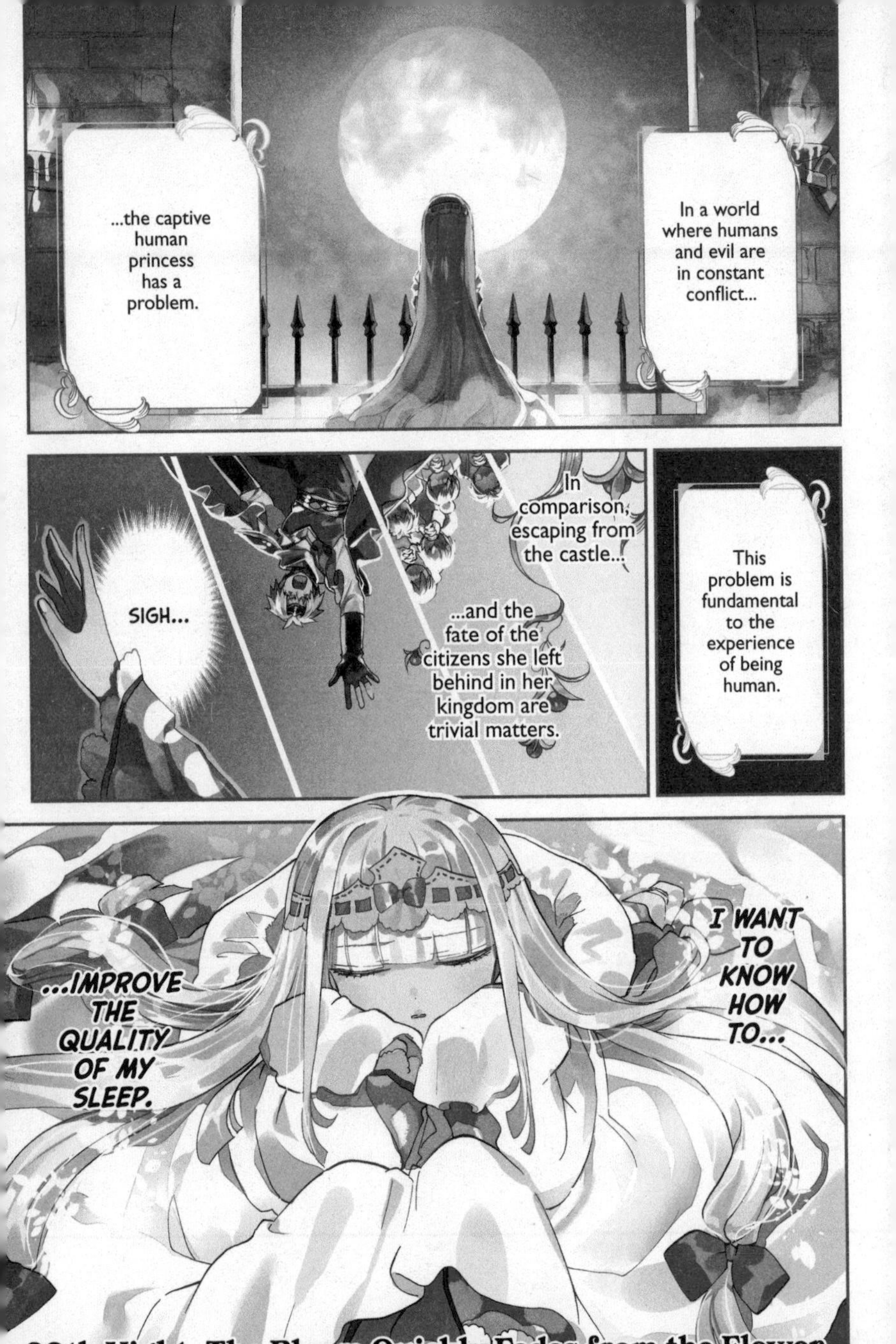
In a world where humans and evil are in constant conflict...
...the captive human princess has a problem.
This problem is fundamental to the experience of being human.
In comparison, escaping from the castle...
...and the fate of the citizens she left behind in her kingdom are trivial matters.
SIGH...
I WANT TO KNOW HOW TO...
...IMPROVE THE QUALITY OF MY SLEEP.

20th Night: The Bloom Quickly Fades from the Flower

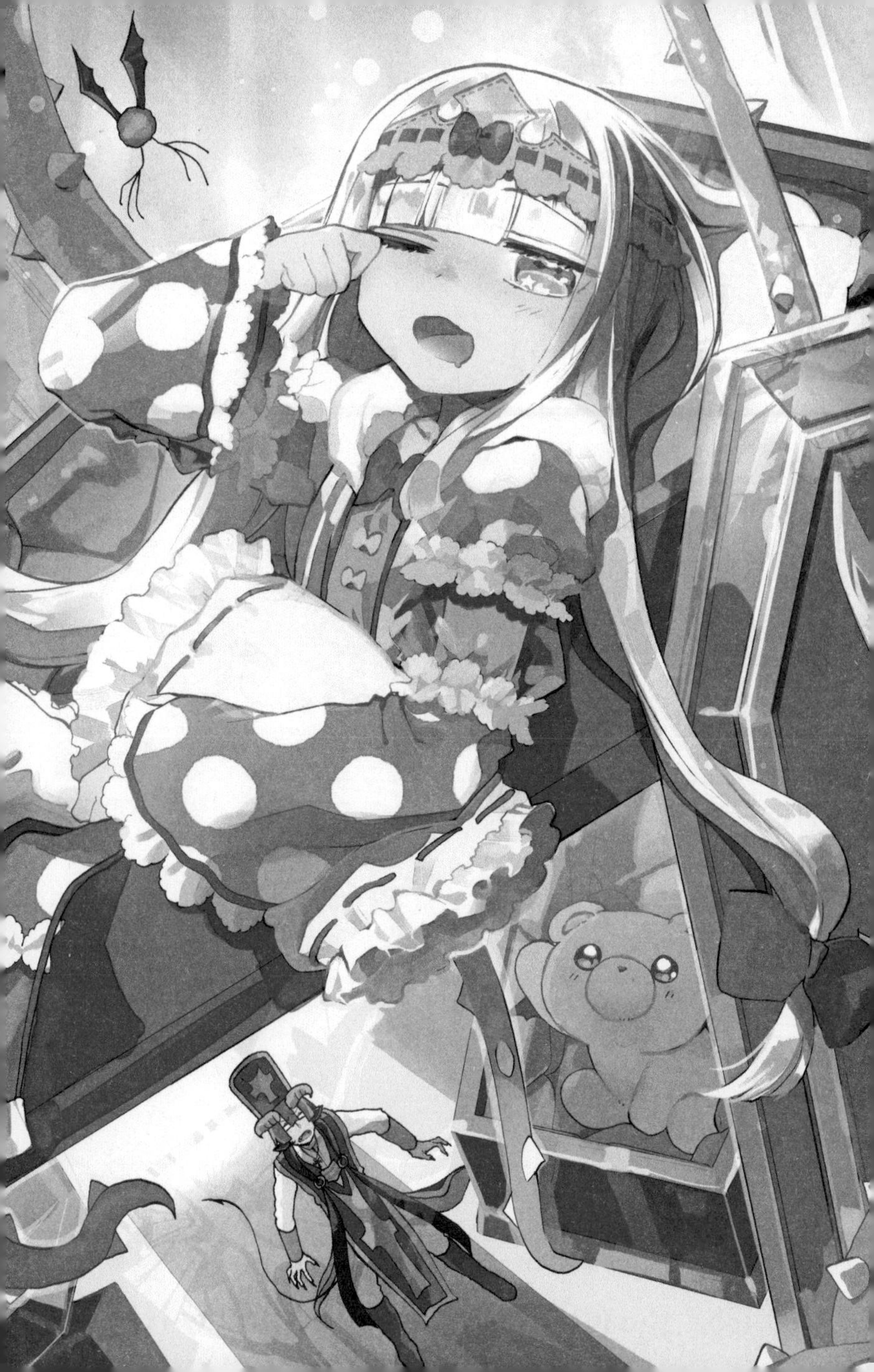

20th Night: The Bloom Quickly Fades from the Flower

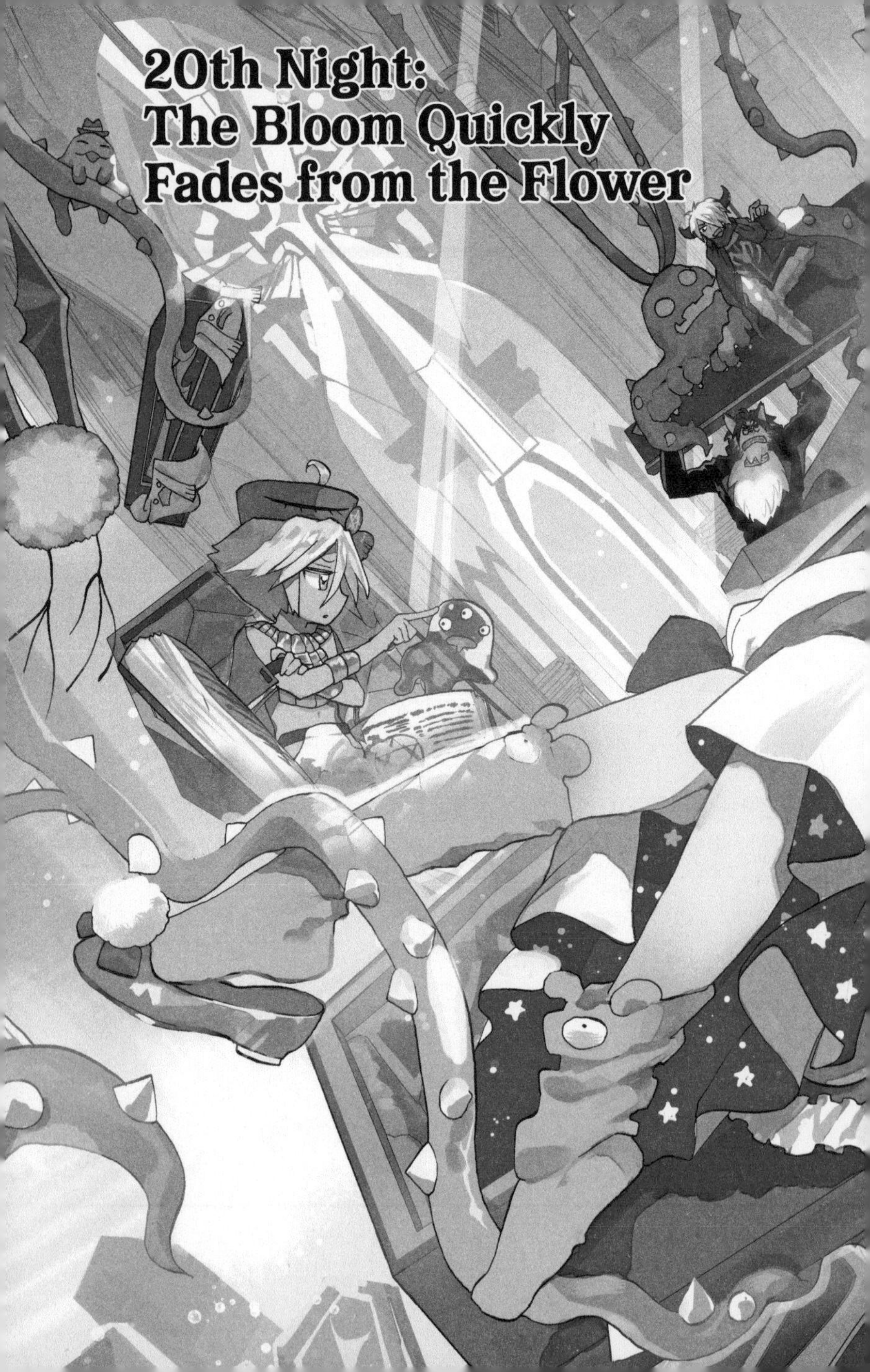

SLEEPY PRINCESS
IN THE DEMON CASTLE

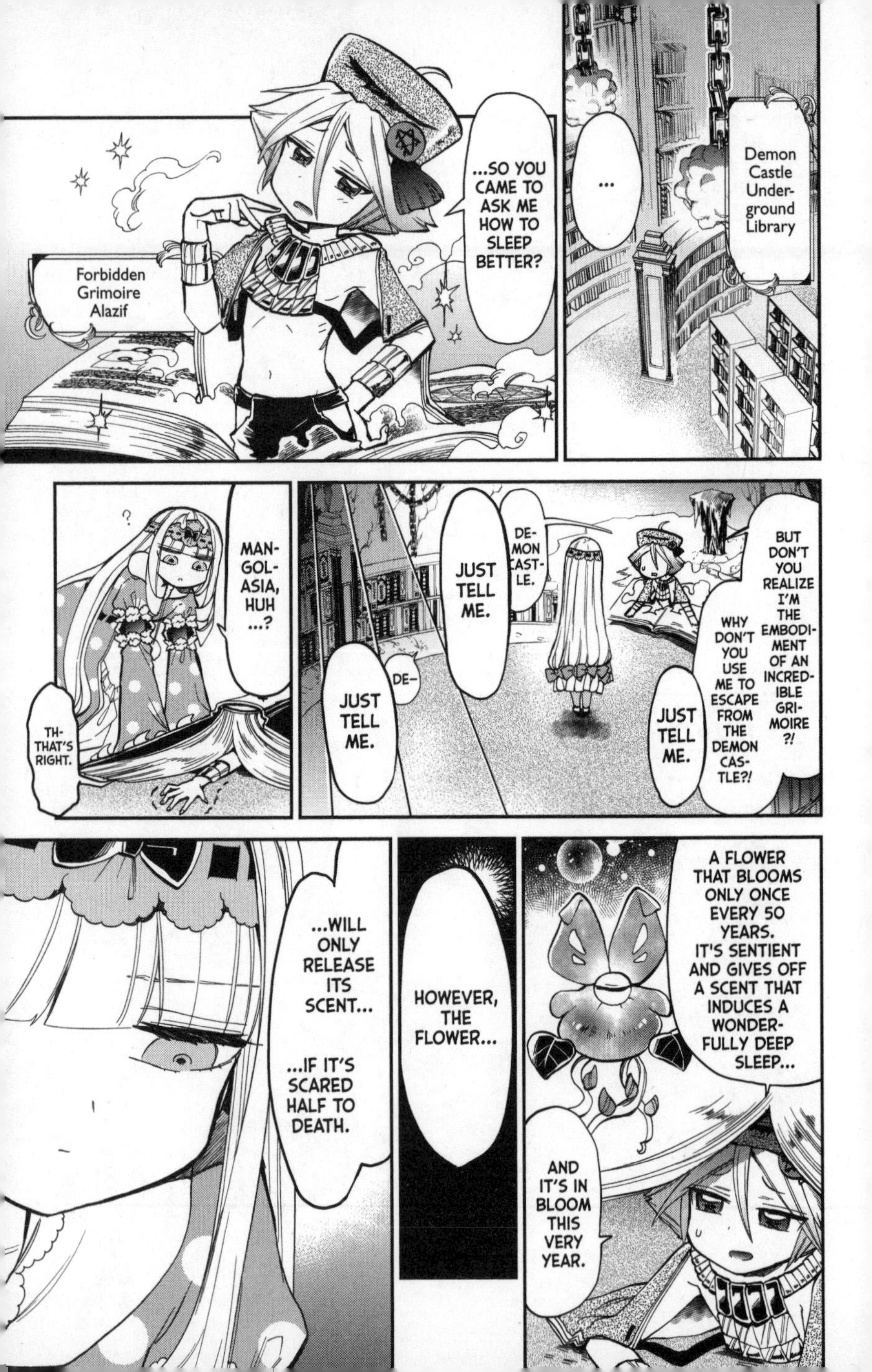
Demon Castle Under-ground Library
...
...SO YOU CAME TO ASK ME HOW TO SLEEP BETTER?
Forbidden Grimoire Alazif
BUT DON'T YOU REALIZE I'M THE EMBODI-MENT OF AN INCRED-IBLE GRI-MOIRE?!
WHY DON'T YOU USE ME TO ESCAPE FROM THE DEMON CAS-TLE?!
JUST TELL ME.
DE-MON CAST-LE.
JUST TELL ME.
DE-
JUST TELL ME.
MAN-GOL-ASIA, HUH ...?
TH-THAT'S RIGHT.
A FLOWER THAT BLOOMS ONLY ONCE EVERY 50 YEARS. IT'S SENTIENT AND GIVES OFF A SCENT THAT INDUCES A WONDER-FULLY DEEP SLEEP...
AND IT'S IN BLOOM THIS VERY YEAR.
HOWEVER, THE FLOWER...
...WILL ONLY RELEASE ITS SCENT...
...IF IT'S SCARED HALF TO DEATH.

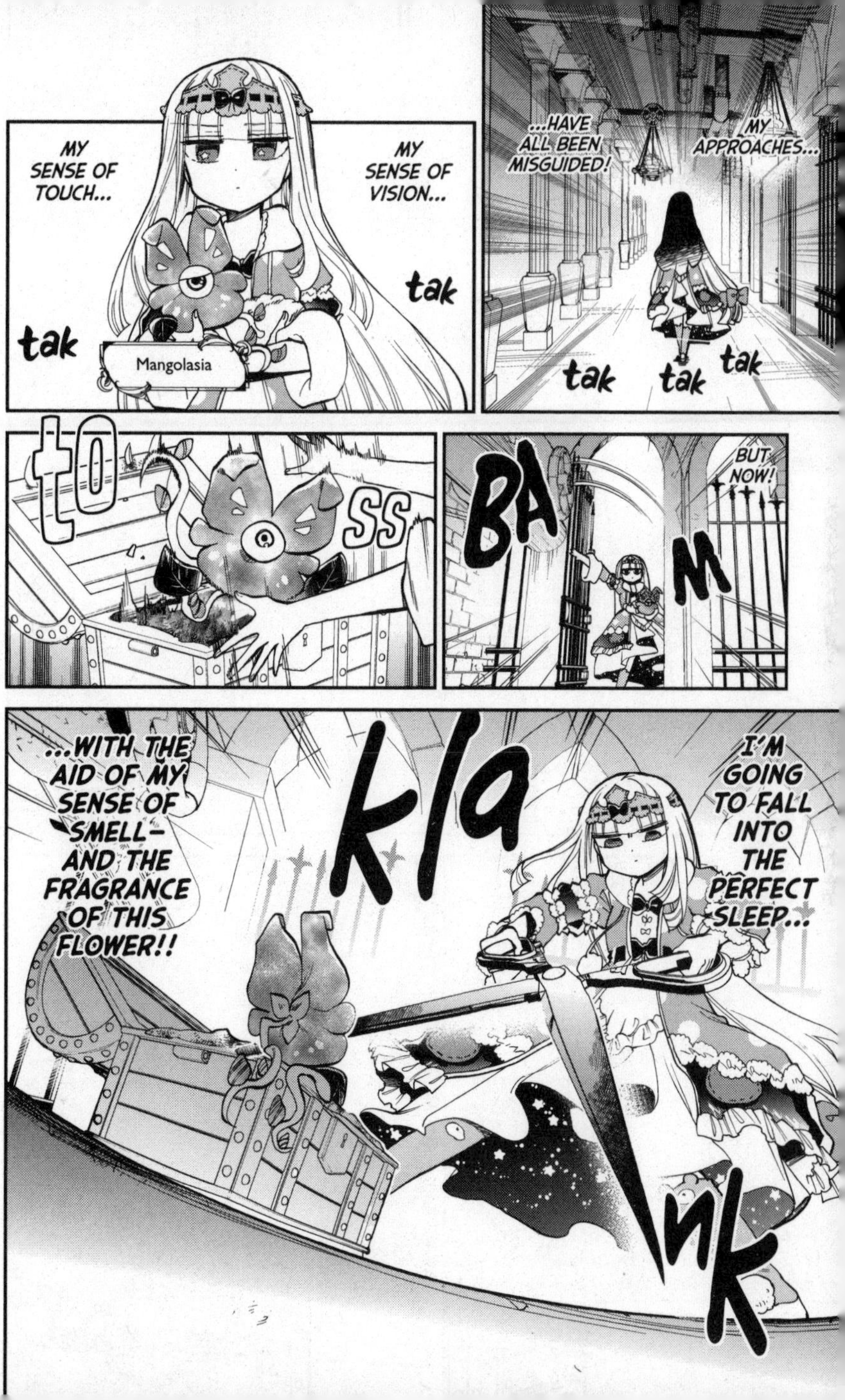
MY APPROACHES...
...HAVE ALL BEEN MISGUIDED!
tak
tak
tak
MY SENSE OF VISION...
MY SENSE OF TOUCH...
tak
tak
Mangolasia
BUT NOW!
BAM
TOSS
I'M GOING TO FALL INTO THE PERFECT SLEEP...
...WITH THE AID OF MY SENSE OF SMELL—AND THE FRAGRANCE OF THIS FLOWER!!
klank

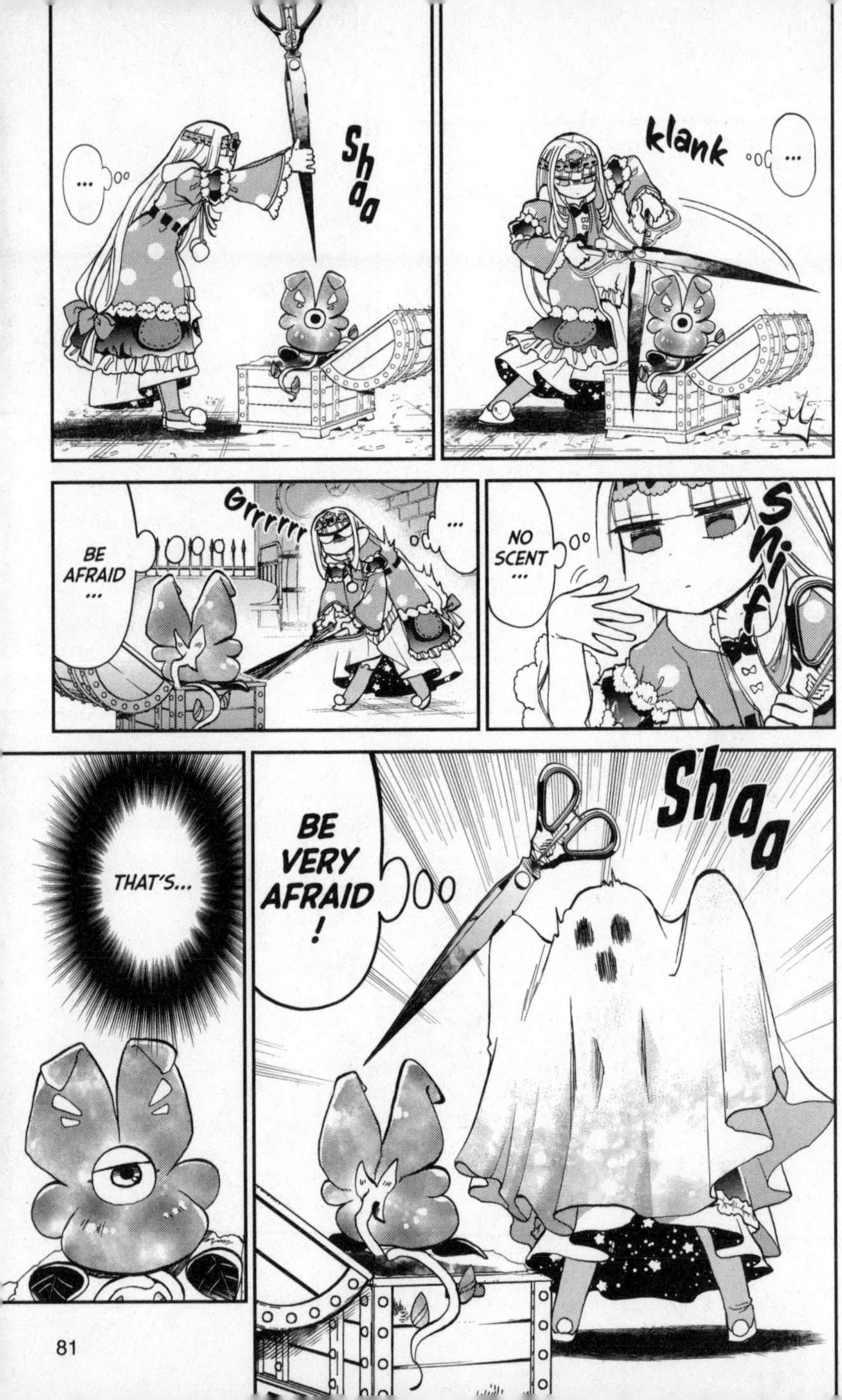
klank
...
Shaa
...
Snif
NO SCENT ...
...
Grrrrrr
BE AFRAID ...
Shaa
BE VERY AFRAID !
THAT'S...

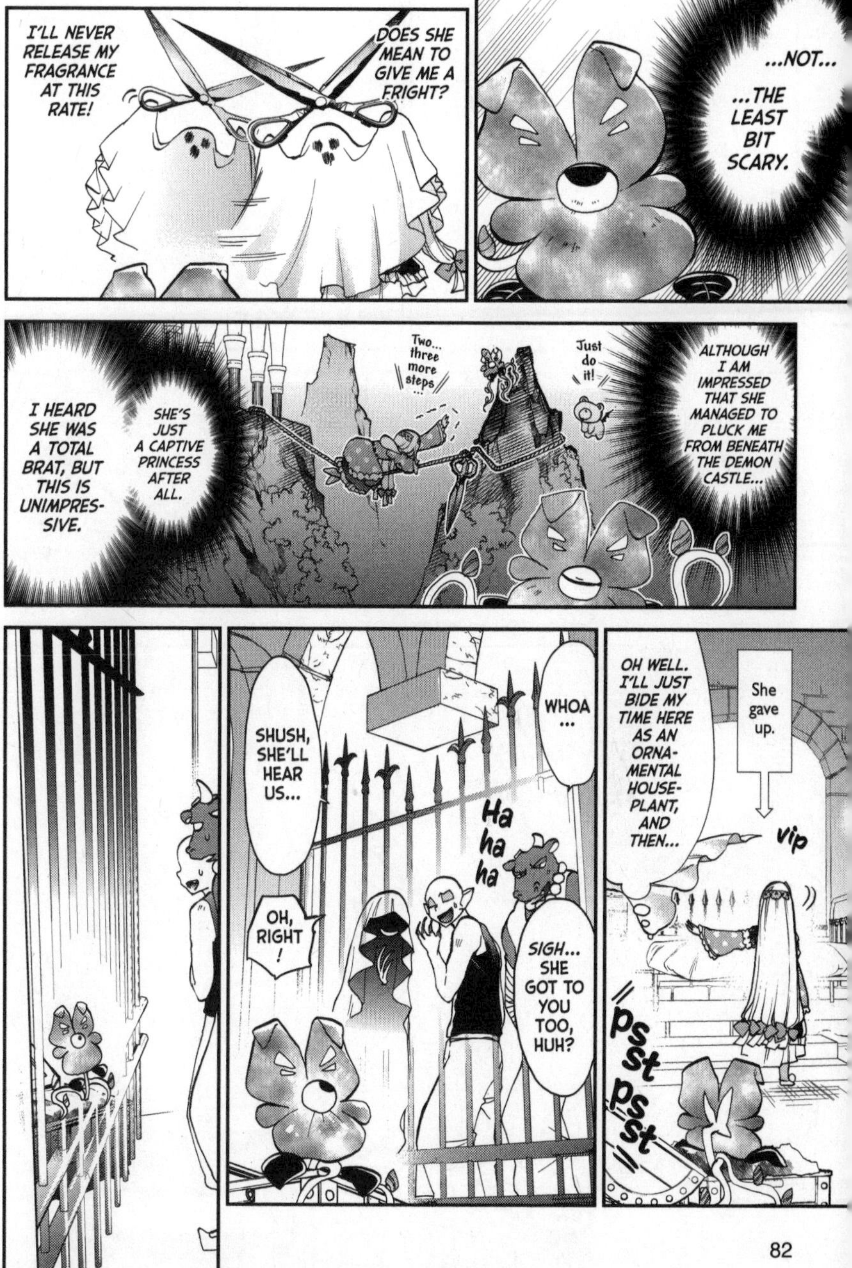
...NOT...
...THE LEAST BIT SCARY.
DOES SHE MEAN TO GIVE ME A FRIGHT?
I'LL NEVER RELEASE MY FRAGRANCE AT THIS RATE!
ALTHOUGH I AM IMPRESSED THAT SHE MANAGED TO PLUCK ME FROM BENEATH THE DEMON CASTLE...
Just do it!
Two... three more steps...
SHE'S JUST A CAPTIVE PRINCESS AFTER ALL.
I HEARD SHE WAS A TOTAL BRAT, BUT THIS IS UNIMPRES-SIVE.
She gave up.
OH WELL. I'LL JUST BIDE MY TIME HERE AS AN ORNA-MENTAL HOUSE-PLANT, AND THEN...
vip
pst pst pst pst
WHOA...
SHUSH, SHE'LL HEAR US...
Ha ha ha
OH, RIGHT!
SIGH... SHE GOT TO YOU TOO, HUH?

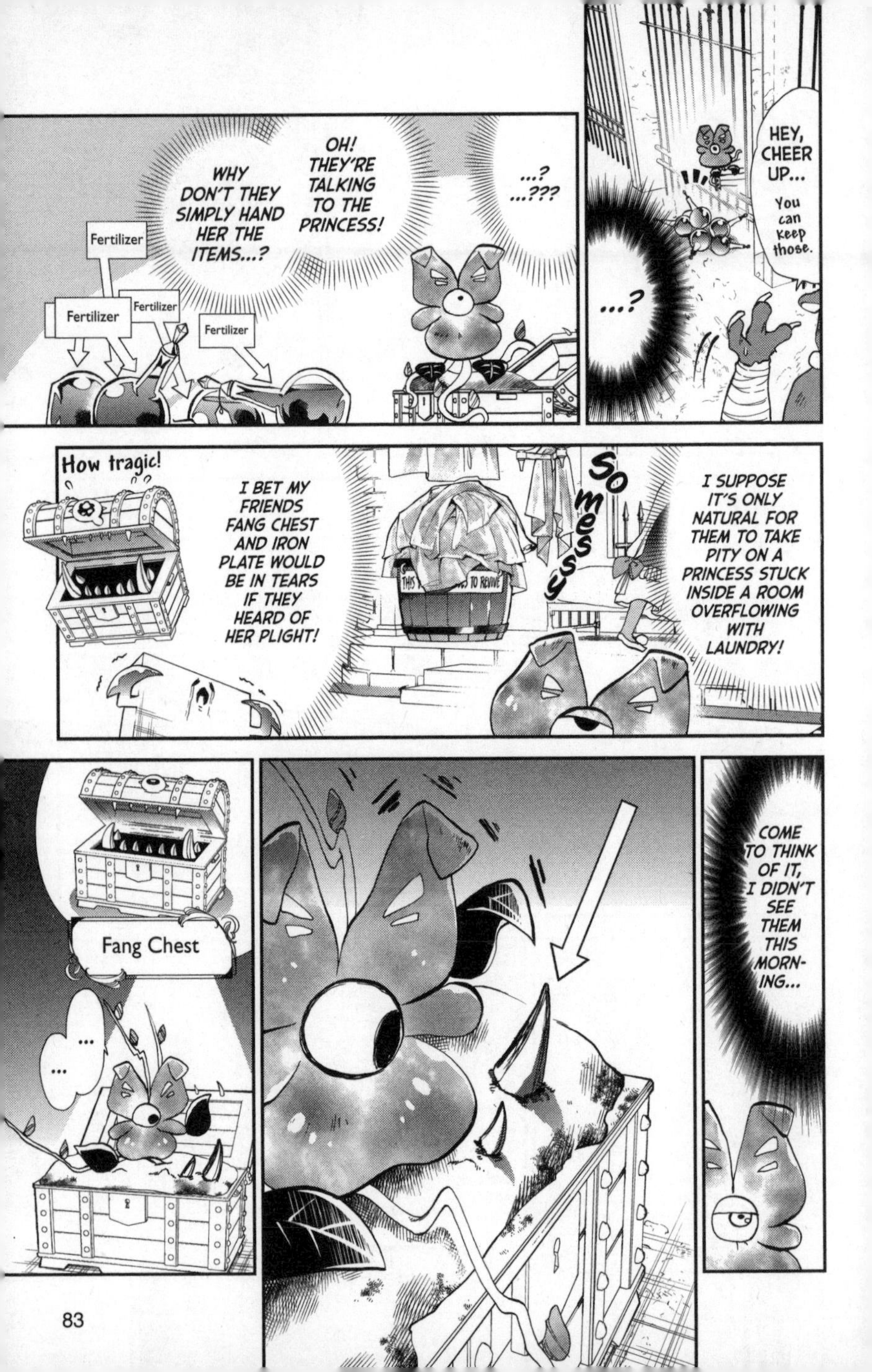
HEY, CHEER UP...
You can keep those.
...?
...?
...???
OH! THEY'RE TALKING TO THE PRINCESS!
WHY DON'T THEY SIMPLY HAND HER THE ITEMS...?
Fertilizer
Fertilizer
Fertilizer
Fertilizer
I SUPPOSE IT'S ONLY NATURAL FOR THEM TO TAKE PITY ON A PRINCESS STUCK INSIDE A ROOM OVERFLOWING WITH LAUNDRY!
So messy
I BET MY FRIENDS FANG CHEST AND IRON PLATE WOULD BE IN TEARS IF THEY HEARD OF HER PLIGHT!
How tragic!
COME TO THINK OF IT, I DIDN'T SEE THEM THIS MORN-ING...
Fang Chest
...
...

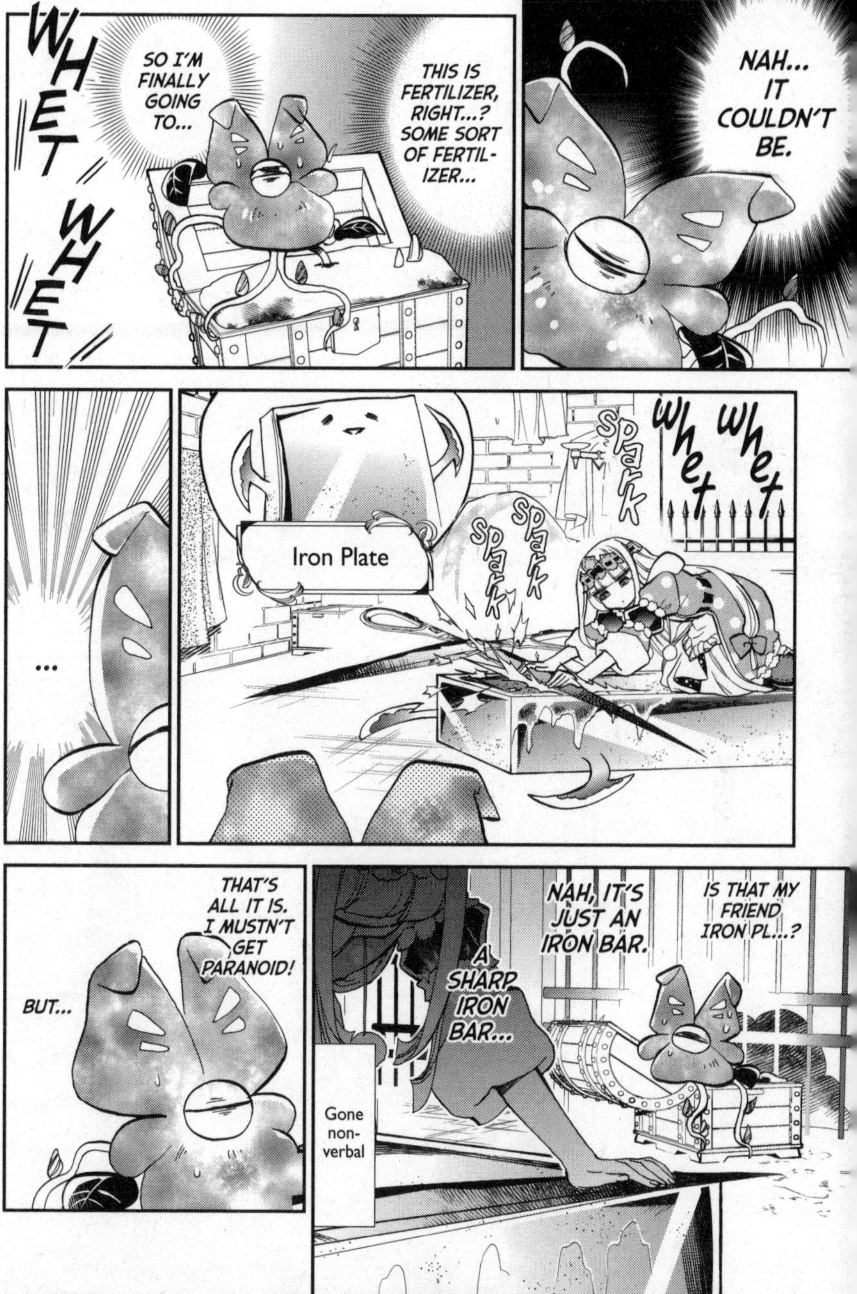
NAH... IT COULDN'T BE.
THIS IS FERTILIZER, RIGHT...? SOME SORT OF FERTIL-IZER...
SO I'M FINALLY GOING TO...
WHET WHET WHET
whet whet
spark
spark
spark
Iron Plate
...
IS THAT MY FRIEND IRON PL...?
NAH, IT'S JUST AN IRON BAR.
A SHARP IRON BAR...
Gone non-verbal
THAT'S ALL IT IS. I MUSTN'T GET PARANOID!
BUT...

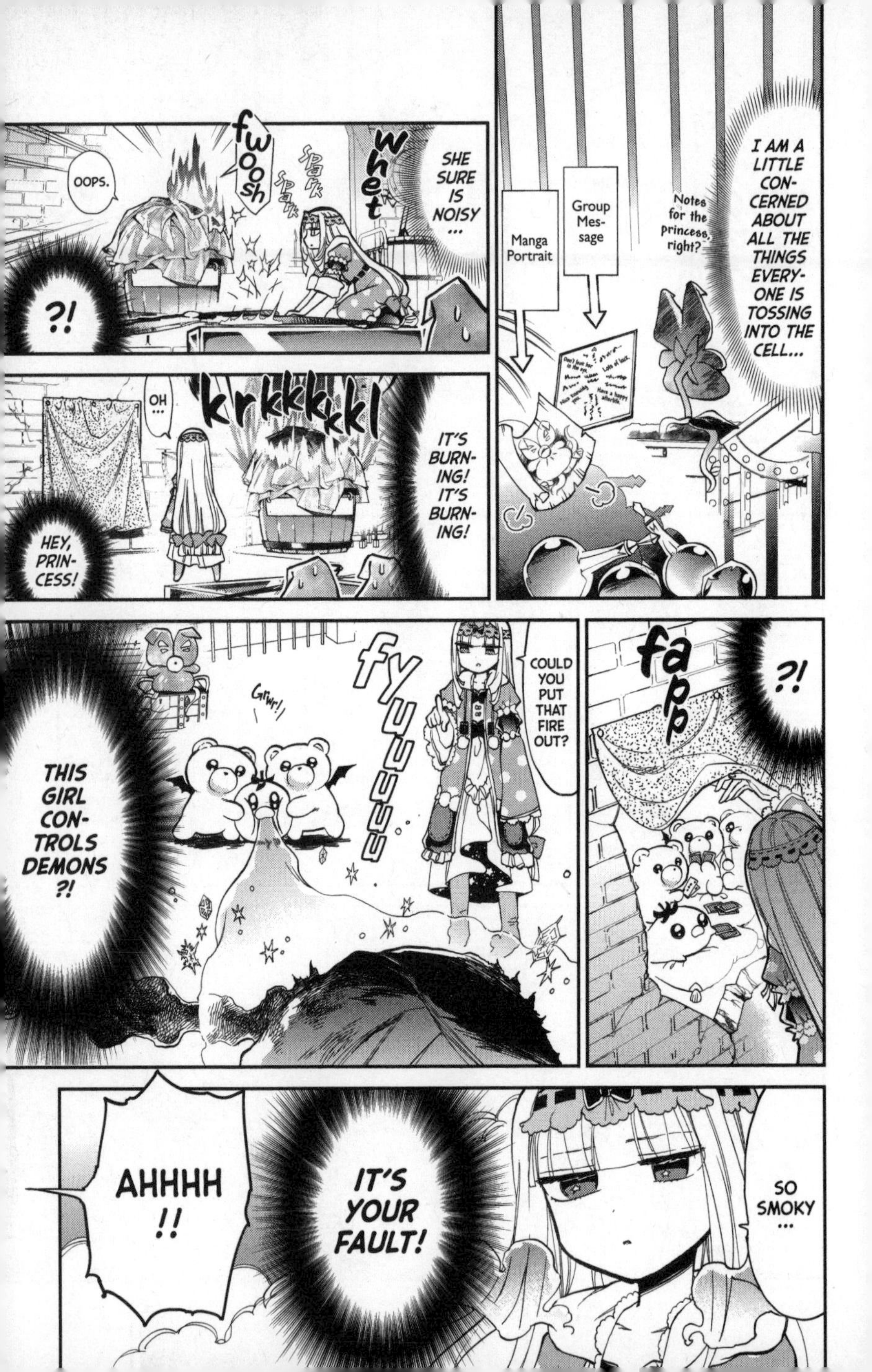
I AM A LITTLE CONCERNED ABOUT ALL THE THINGS EVERYONE IS TOSSING INTO THE CELL...
Notes for the princess, right?
Group Message
Manga Portrait
SHE SURE IS NOISY...
whet
spark spark
fwoosh
OOPS.
?!
IT'S BURNING! IT'S BURNING!
krkkkkkl
OH...
HEY, PRINCESS!
fapp
?!
COULD YOU PUT THAT FIRE OUT?
fyuuuuu
Grwr!
THIS GIRL CONTROLS DEMONS?!
SO SMOKY...
IT'S YOUR FAULT!
AHHHH!!

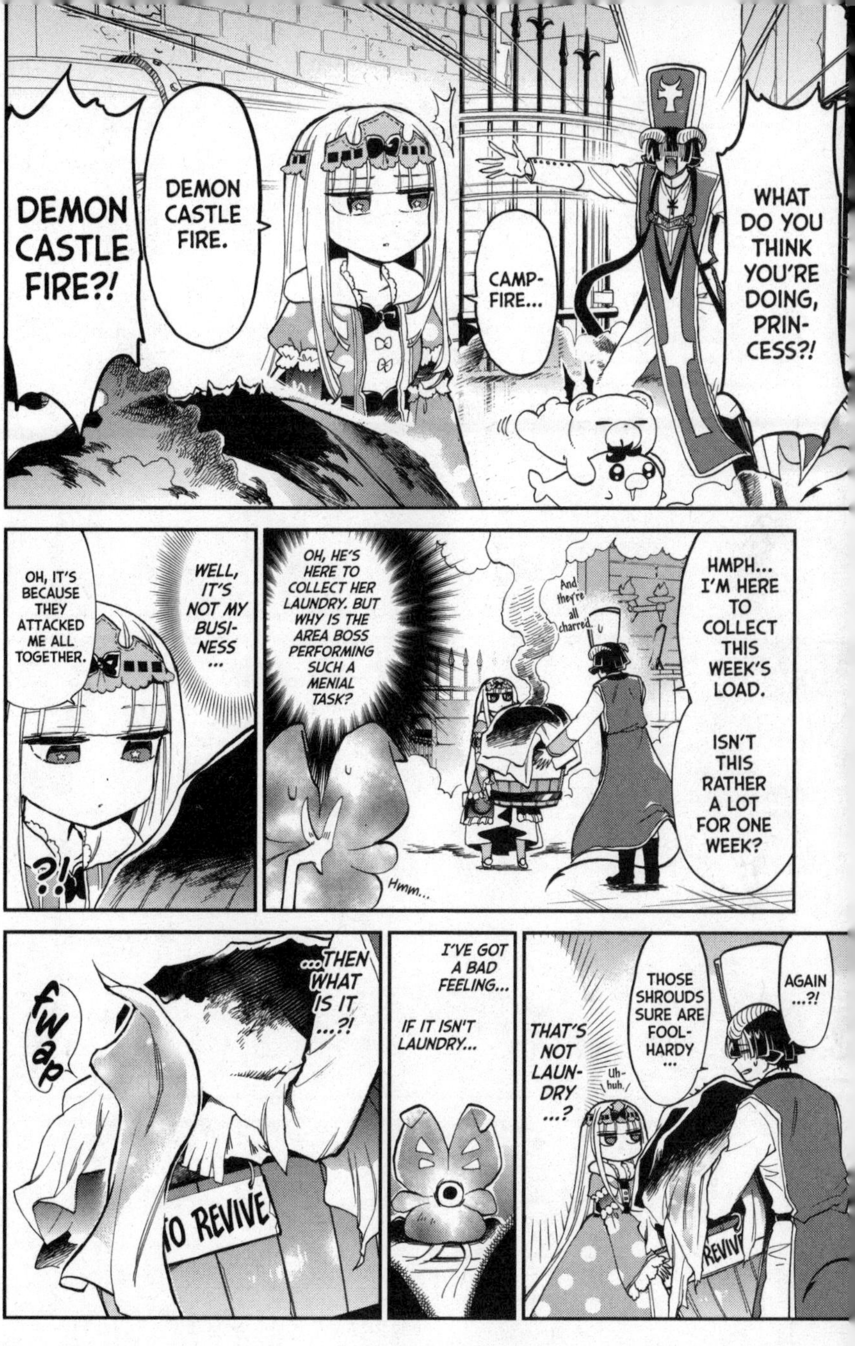
WHAT DO YOU THINK YOU'RE DOING, PRINCESS?!
CAMP-FIRE...
DEMON CASTLE FIRE.
DEMON CASTLE FIRE?!
HMPH... I'M HERE TO COLLECT THIS WEEK'S LOAD.
ISN'T THIS RATHER A LOT FOR ONE WEEK?
And they're all charred.
OH, HE'S HERE TO COLLECT HER LAUNDRY. BUT WHY IS THE AREA BOSS PERFORMING SUCH A MENIAL TASK?
Hmm...
WELL, IT'S NOT MY BUSINESS...
OH, IT'S BECAUSE THEY ATTACKED ME ALL TOGETHER.
?!
AGAIN...?!
THOSE SHROUDS SURE ARE FOOL-HARDY...
Uh-huh.
THAT'S NOT LAUN-DRY...?
REVIVE
I'VE GOT A BAD FEELING...
IF IT ISN'T LAUNDRY...
...THEN WHAT IS IT...?!
fwap
TO REVIVE

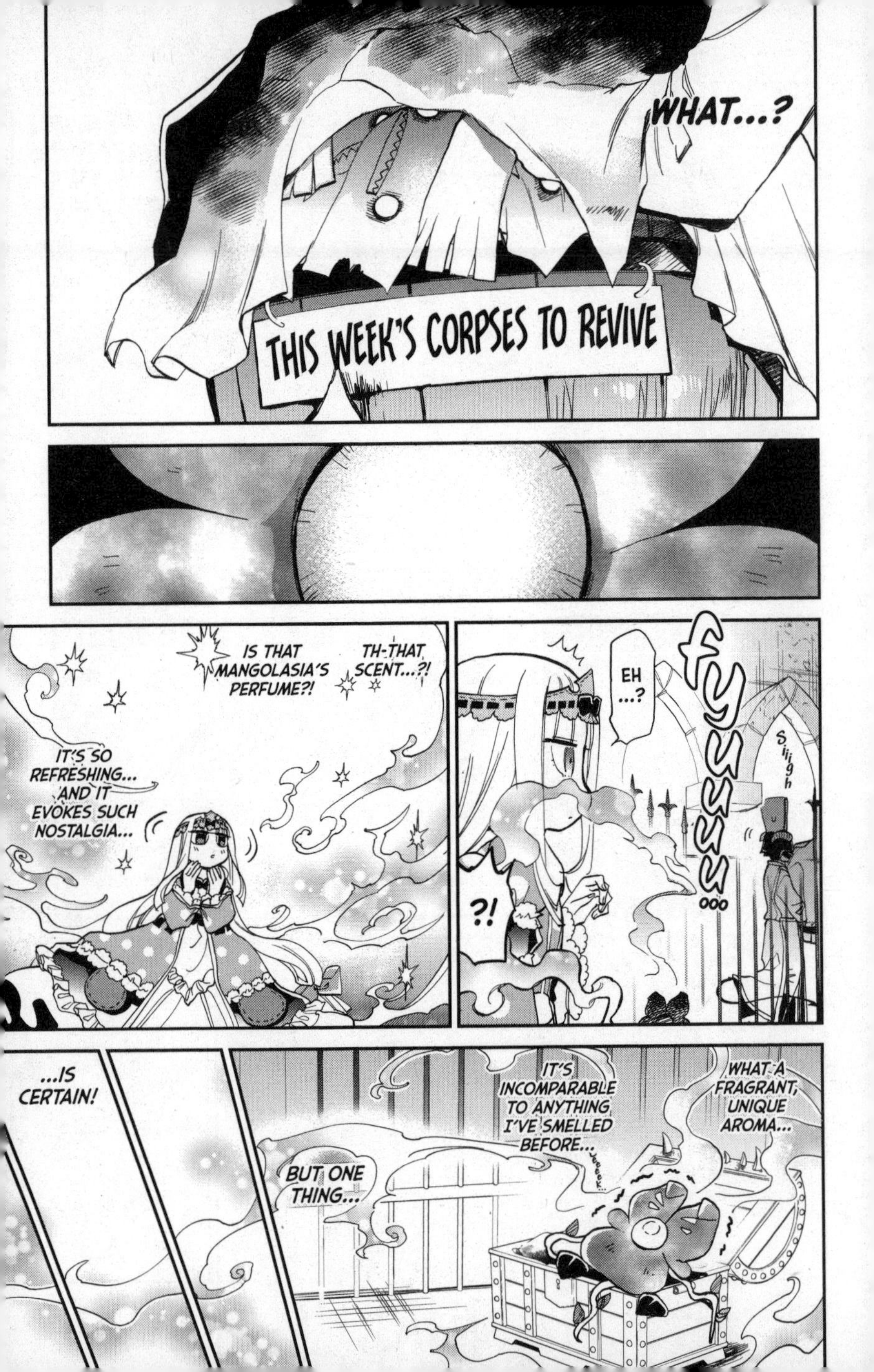
WHAT...?
THIS WEEK'S CORPSES TO REVIVE
EH ...?
fyuuuuu...
Siiigh
?!
TH-THAT SCENT...?!
IS THAT MANGOLASIA'S PERFUME?!
IT'S SO REFRESHING... AND IT EVOKES SUCH NOSTALGIA...
WHAT A FRAGRANT, UNIQUE AROMA...
IT'S INCOMPARABLE TO ANYTHING I'VE SMELLED BEFORE...
BUT ONE THING...
...IS CERTAIN!

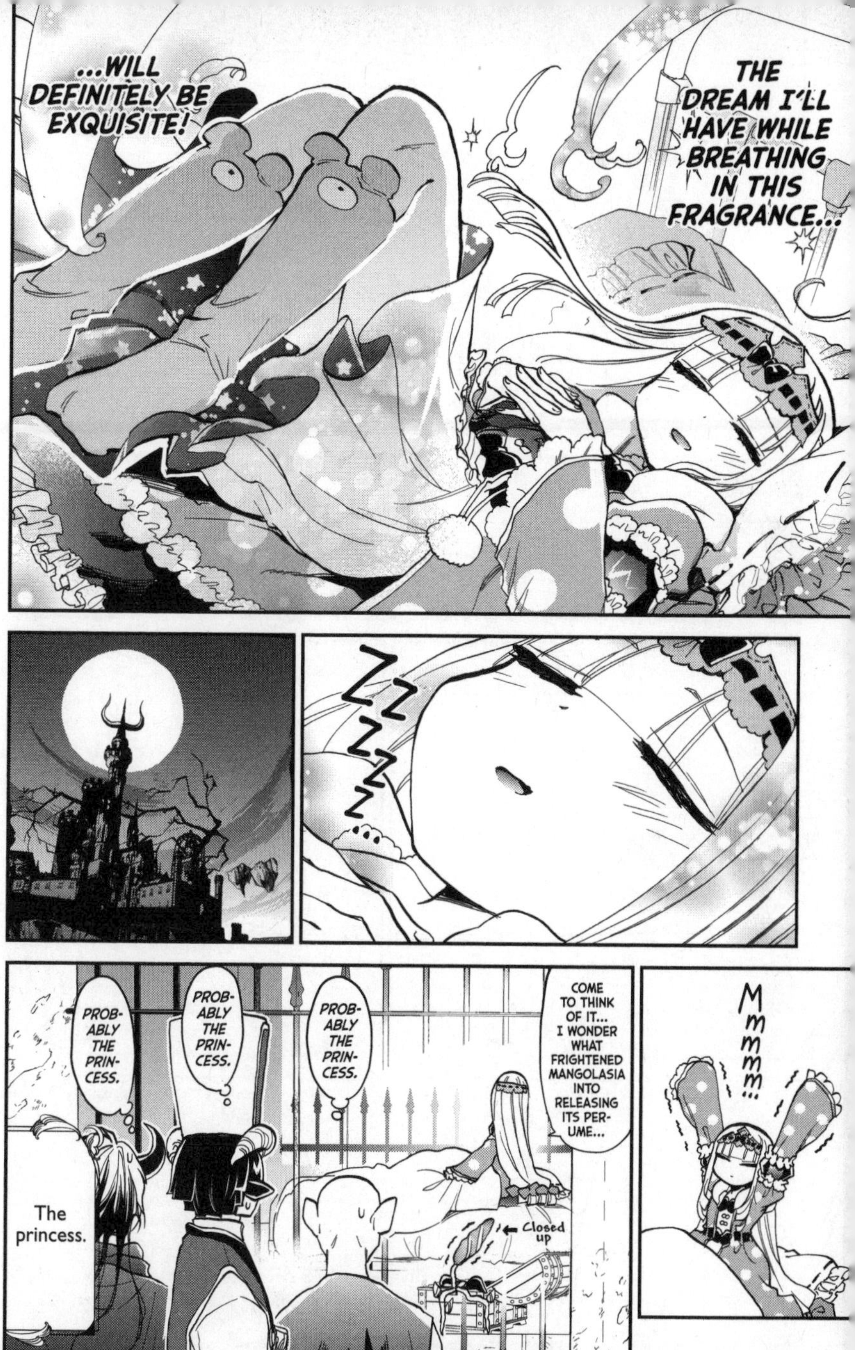
THE DREAM I'LL HAVE WHILE BREATHING IN THIS FRAGRANCE...
...WILL DEFINITELY BE EXQUISITE!
ZZZZZ...
Mmmmm..
COME TO THINK OF IT... I WONDER WHAT FRIGHTENED MANGOLASIA INTO RELEASING ITS PERFUME...
Closed up
PROBABLY THE PRINCESS.
PROBABLY THE PRINCESS.
PROBABLY THE PRINCESS.
The princess.

Mangolasia

Rarity: ☆☆☆☆☆☆☆☆☆☆
Fragrance: ☆☆☆☆☆☆☆☆☆☆

I'll never show fear!

A monster of the botanical species who blooms every 50 years and gives off a wonderful scent that puts everyone to sleep. However, it only releases its fragrance when frightened half to death.

It remains conscious even with its petals closed and can converse with certain demons via telepathy. It's a rather argumentative demon but is fond of its friends. It likes to chat with Fang Chest and Iron Plate daily as well as play tabletop games with them.

Their current hot conversation topic is "How to crush super-annoying power players in tabletop role-playing games using the game master's authority." But no one other than Fang Chest and Iron Plate is interested in this, let alone understands what they are even talking about. Mangolasia uses its vines as whips and releases spores in battle that cause status ailments.

Former problem:
"Once every 50 years is a bit too infrequent, isn't it?"

Current problem:
"The princess messed up my 50-year cycle."

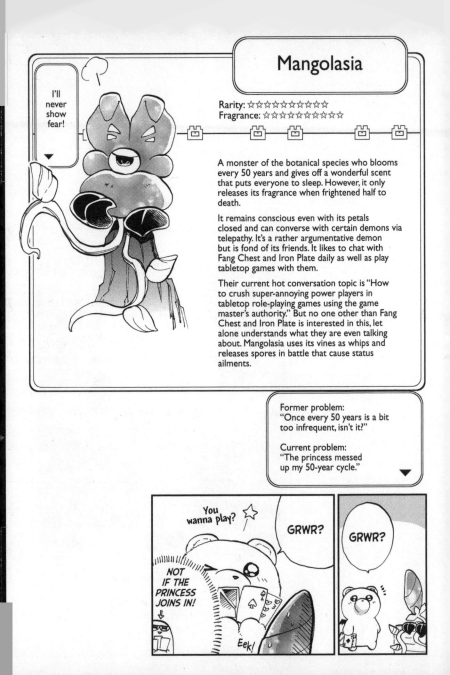

You wanna play?

GRWR?

GRWR?

NOT IF THE PRINCESS JOINS IN!

Eek!

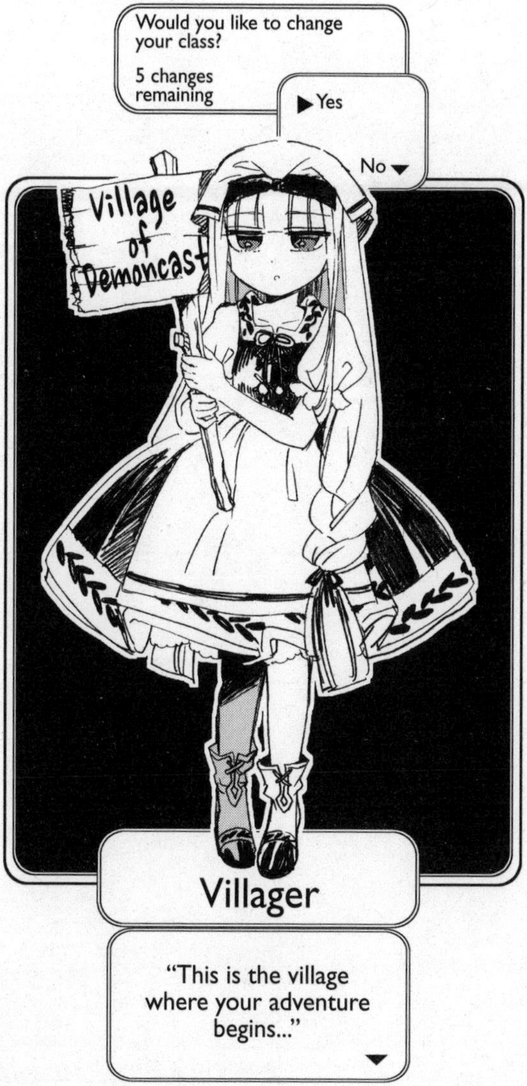
Would you like to change your class?
5 changes remaining
▶Yes
No
Village of Demoncast
Villager
"This is the village where your adventure begins..."

21st Night: Squeezing Honey out of Nothing?

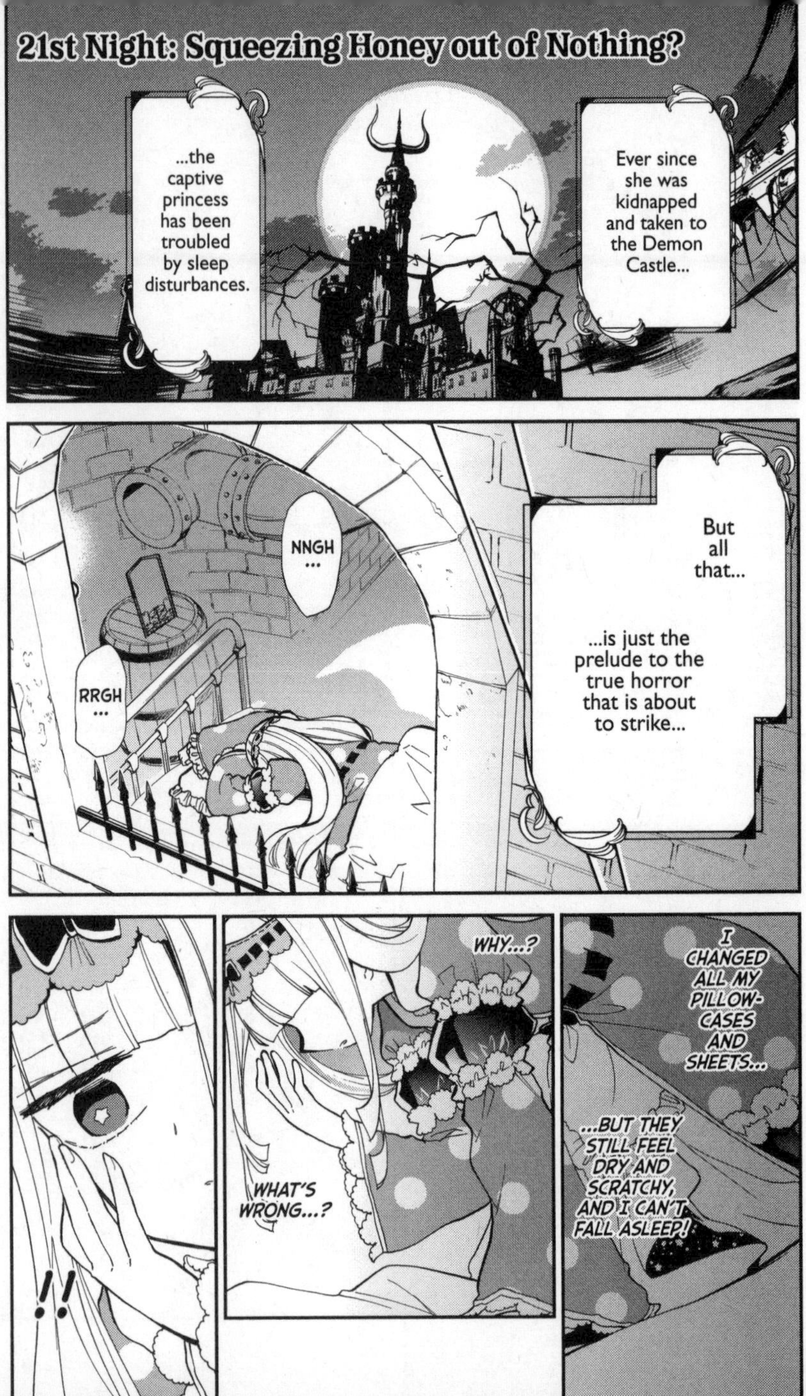
Ever since she was kidnapped and taken to the Demon Castle...
...the captive princess has been troubled by sleep disturbances.
But all that...
...is just the prelude to the true horror that is about to strike...
NNGH...
RRGH...
I CHANGED ALL MY PILLOWCASES AND SHEETS...
...BUT THEY STILL FEEL DRY AND SCRATCHY, AND I CAN'T FALL ASLEEP!
WHY...?
WHAT'S WRONG...?
!!

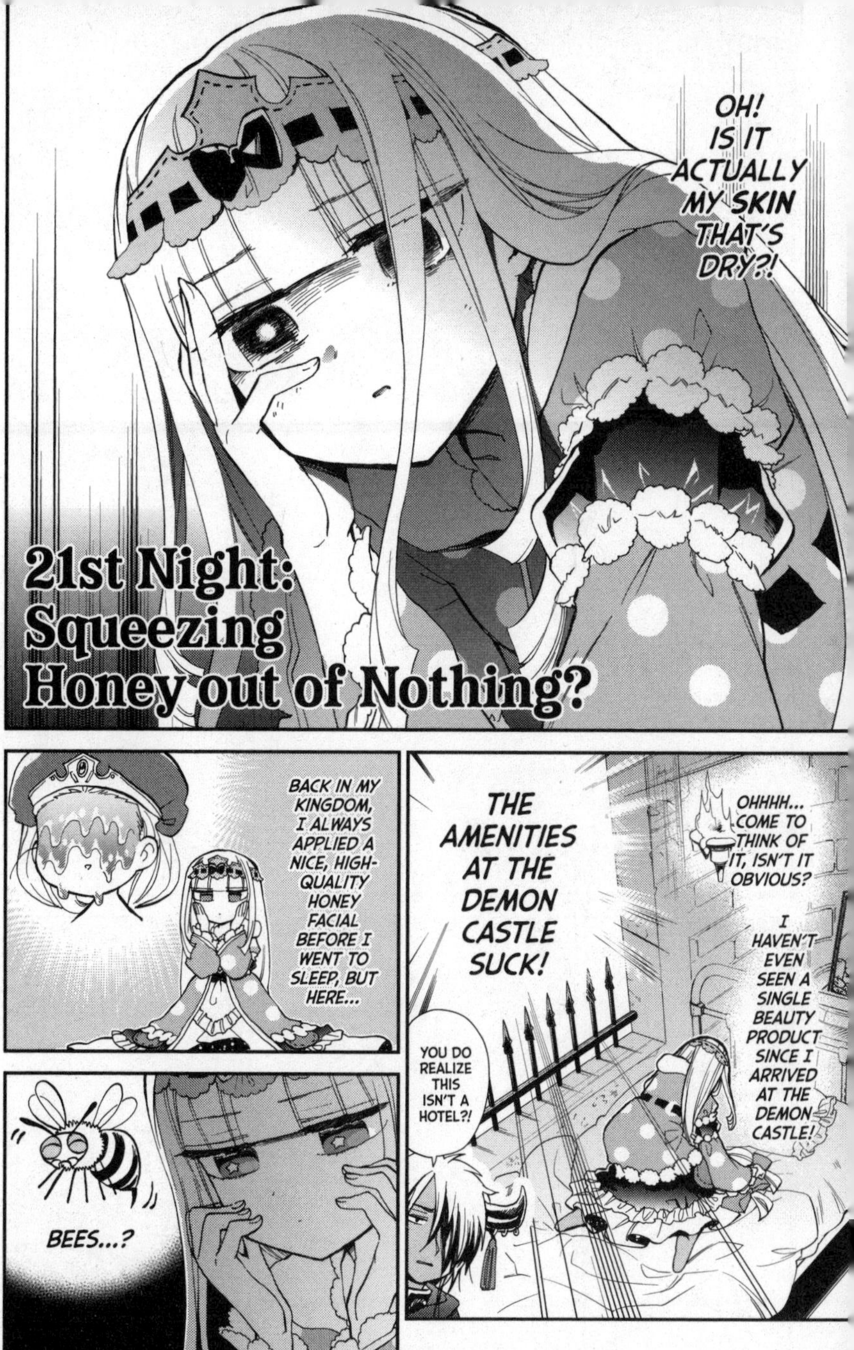
OH! IS IT ACTUALLY MY SKIN THAT'S DRY?!
21st Night: Squeezing Honey out of Nothing?
OHHHH... COME TO THINK OF IT, ISN'T IT OBVIOUS?
THE AMENITIES AT THE DEMON CASTLE SUCK!
I HAVEN'T EVEN SEEN A SINGLE BEAUTY PRODUCT SINCE I ARRIVED AT THE DEMON CASTLE!
YOU DO REALIZE THIS ISN'T A HOTEL?!
BACK IN MY KINGDOM, I ALWAYS APPLIED A NICE, HIGH-QUALITY HONEY FACIAL BEFORE I WENT TO SLEEP, BUT HERE...
BEES...?

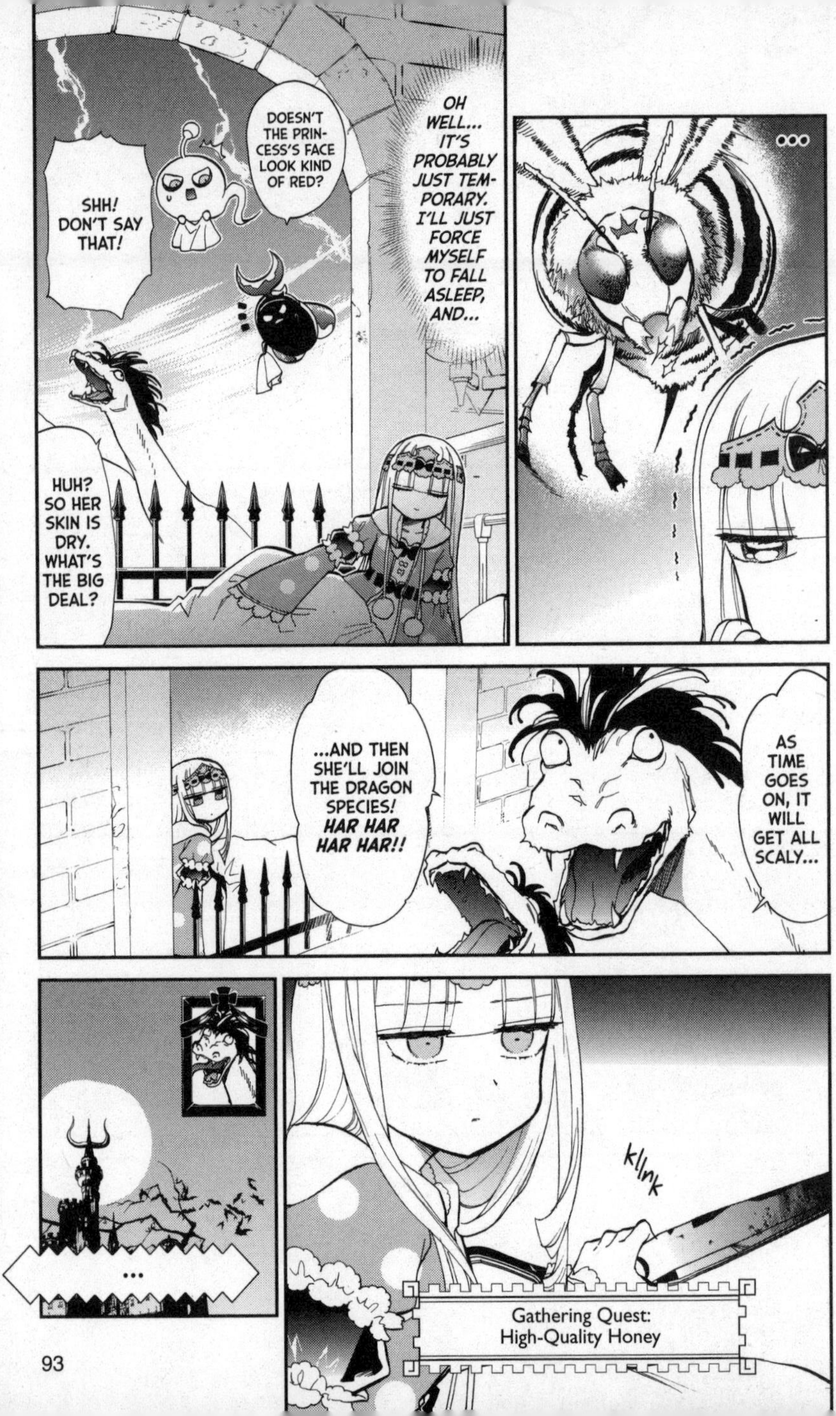

OH WELL... IT'S PROBABLY JUST TEMPORARY. I'LL JUST FORCE MYSELF TO FALL ASLEEP, AND...
DOESN'T THE PRINCESS'S FACE LOOK KIND OF RED?
SHH! DON'T SAY THAT!
HUH? SO HER SKIN IS DRY. WHAT'S THE BIG DEAL?
AS TIME GOES ON, IT WILL GET ALL SCALY...
...AND THEN SHE'LL JOIN THE DRAGON SPECIES! *HAR HAR HAR HAR!!*
kllnk
Gathering Quest: High-Quality Honey
...

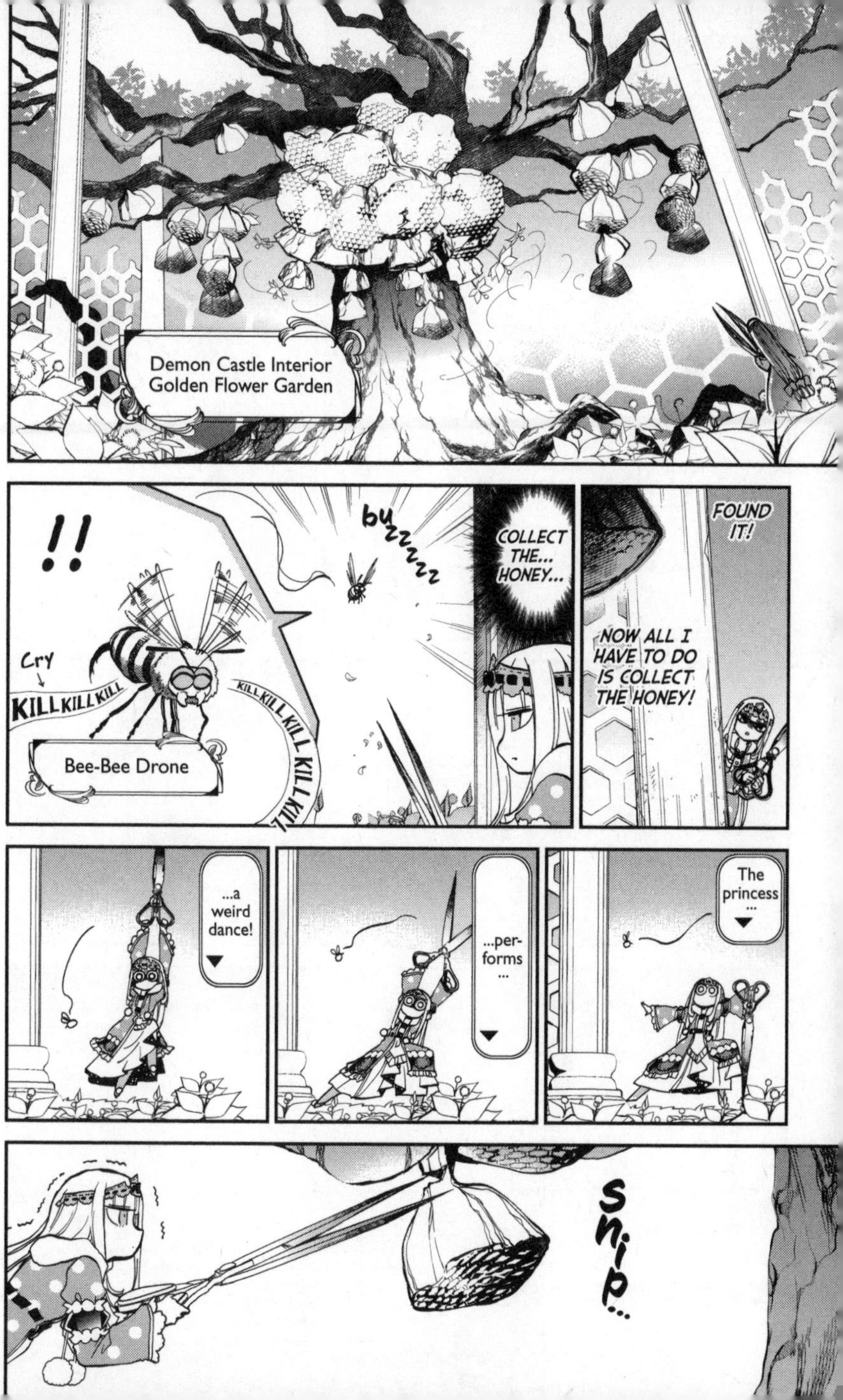
Demon Castle Interior
Golden Flower Garden
FOUND IT!
NOW ALL I HAVE TO DO IS COLLECT THE HONEY!
COLLECT THE... HONEY...
buzzzzzz
!!
Cry
KILLKILLKILL
KILLKILLKILLKILLKILL
Bee-Bee Drone
The princess ...
...per-forms ...
...a weird dance!
snip...

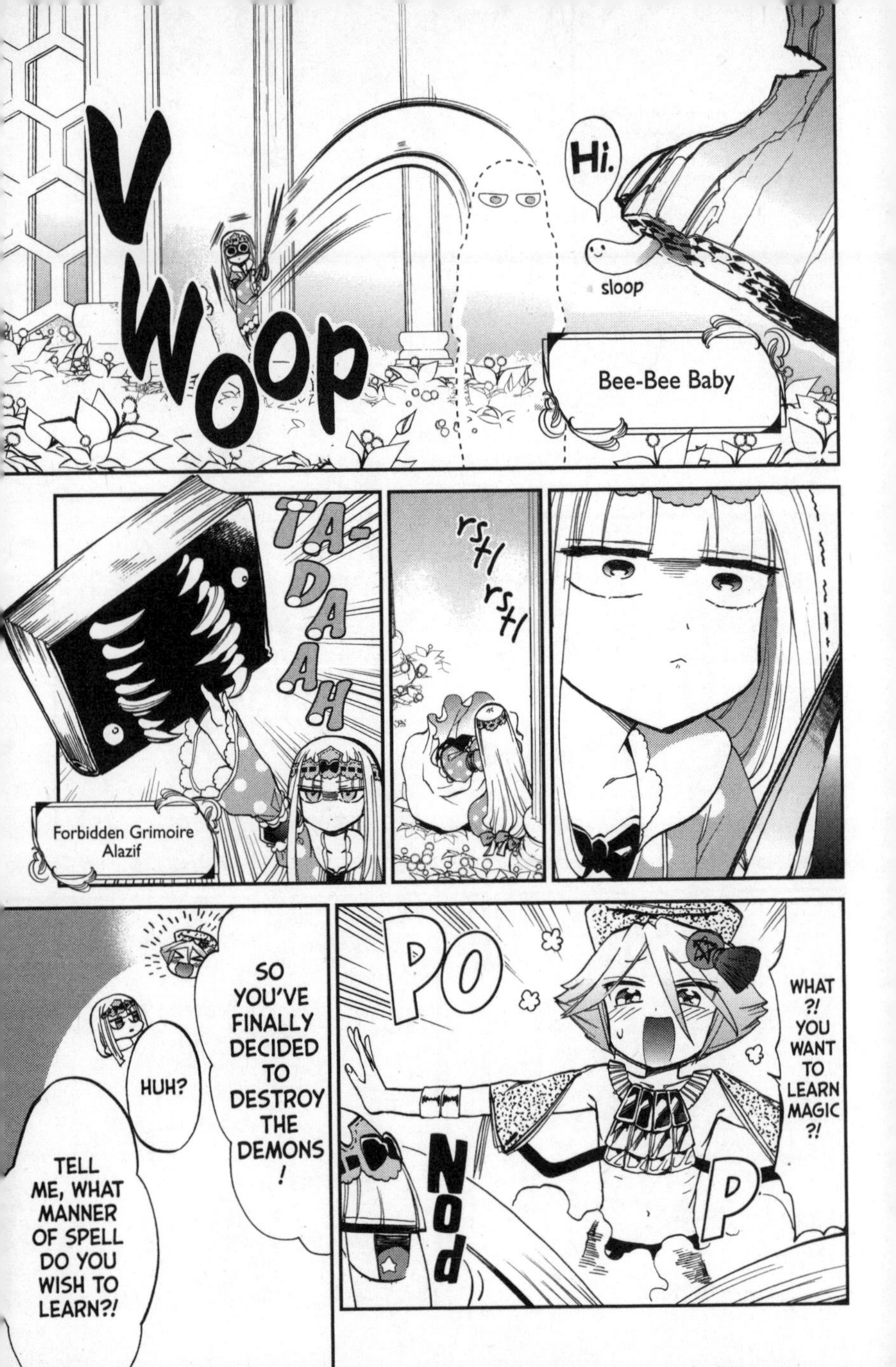
Hi.
sloop
Bee-Bee Baby
VWOOP
rstl rstl
TA-DAAAH
Forbidden Grimoire Alazif
WHAT?! YOU WANT TO LEARN MAGIC?!
POP
Nod
SO YOU'VE FINALLY DECIDED TO DESTROY THE DEMONS!
HUH?
TELL ME, WHAT MANNER OF SPELL DO YOU WISH TO LEARN?!

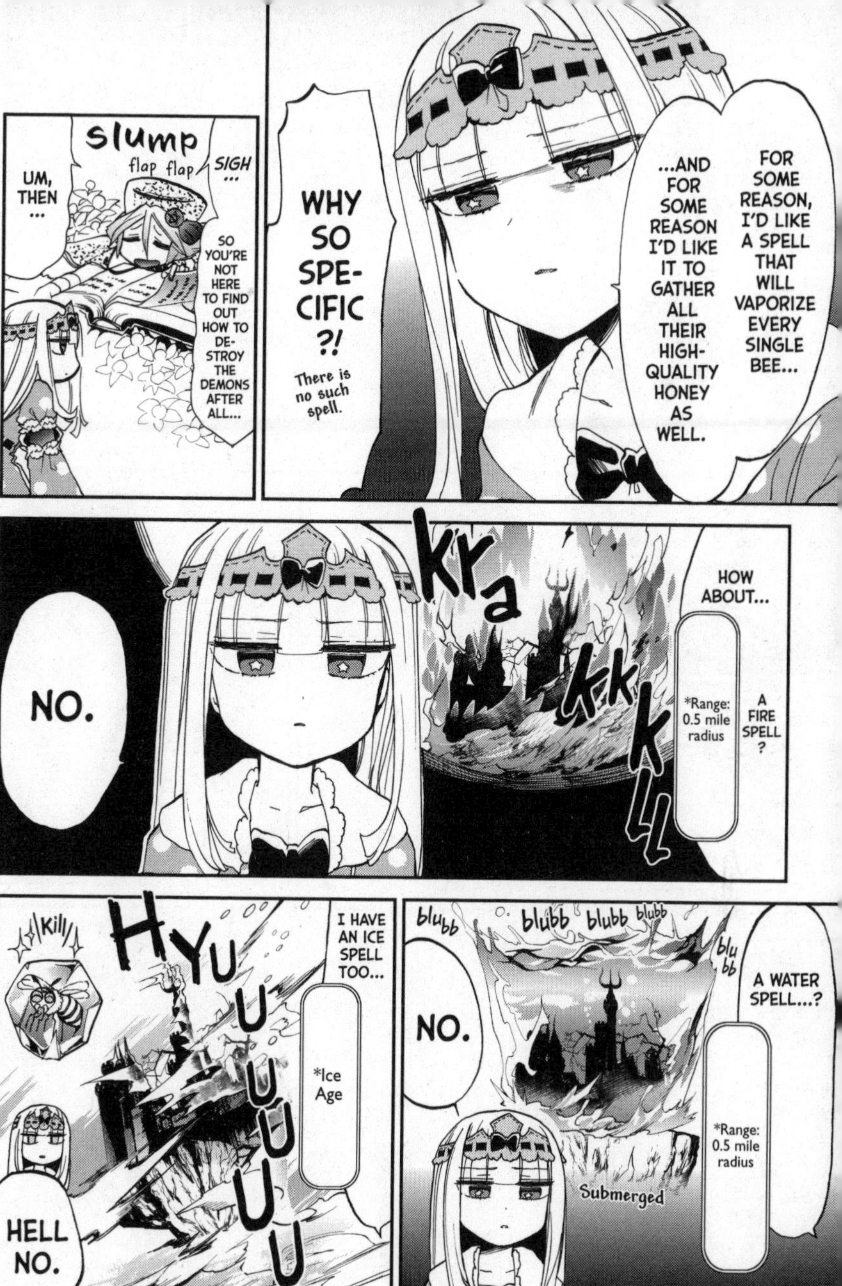
FOR SOME REASON, I'D LIKE A SPELL THAT WILL VAPORIZE EVERY SINGLE BEE...
...AND FOR SOME REASON I'D LIKE IT TO GATHER ALL THEIR HIGH-QUALITY HONEY AS WELL.
WHY SO SPE-CIFIC?!
There is no such spell.
SIGH...
slump
flap flap
UM, THEN...
SO YOU'RE NOT HERE TO FIND OUT HOW TO DE-STROY THE DEMONS AFTER ALL...
HOW ABOUT...
A FIRE SPELL?
*Range: 0.5 mile radius
KRAKKKLL
NO.
A WATER SPELL...?
blubb blubb blubb blubb blubb
*Range: 0.5 mile radius
Submerged
NO.
I HAVE AN ICE SPELL TOO...
*Ice Age
HYUUUUUUUU
Kill
HELL NO.

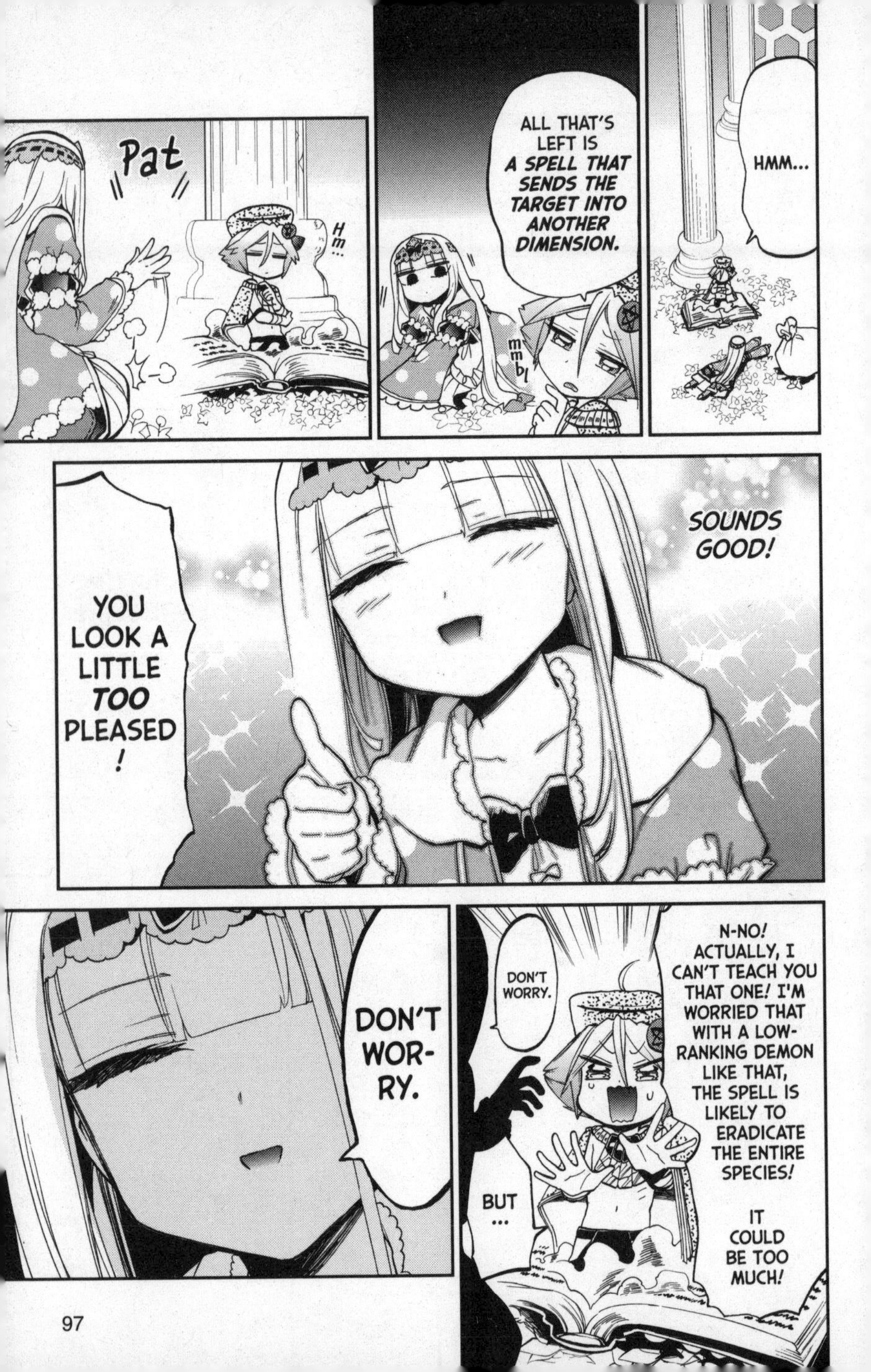
HMM...
ALL THAT'S LEFT IS A SPELL THAT SENDS THE TARGET INTO ANOTHER DIMENSION.
mmbl
Pat
Hm...
SOUNDS GOOD!
YOU LOOK A LITTLE TOO PLEASED!
N-NO! ACTUALLY, I CAN'T TEACH YOU THAT ONE! I'M WORRIED THAT WITH A LOW-RANKING DEMON LIKE THAT, THE SPELL IS LIKELY TO ERADICATE THE ENTIRE SPECIES!
DON'T WORRY.
BUT...
IT COULD BE TOO MUCH!
DON'T WORRY.

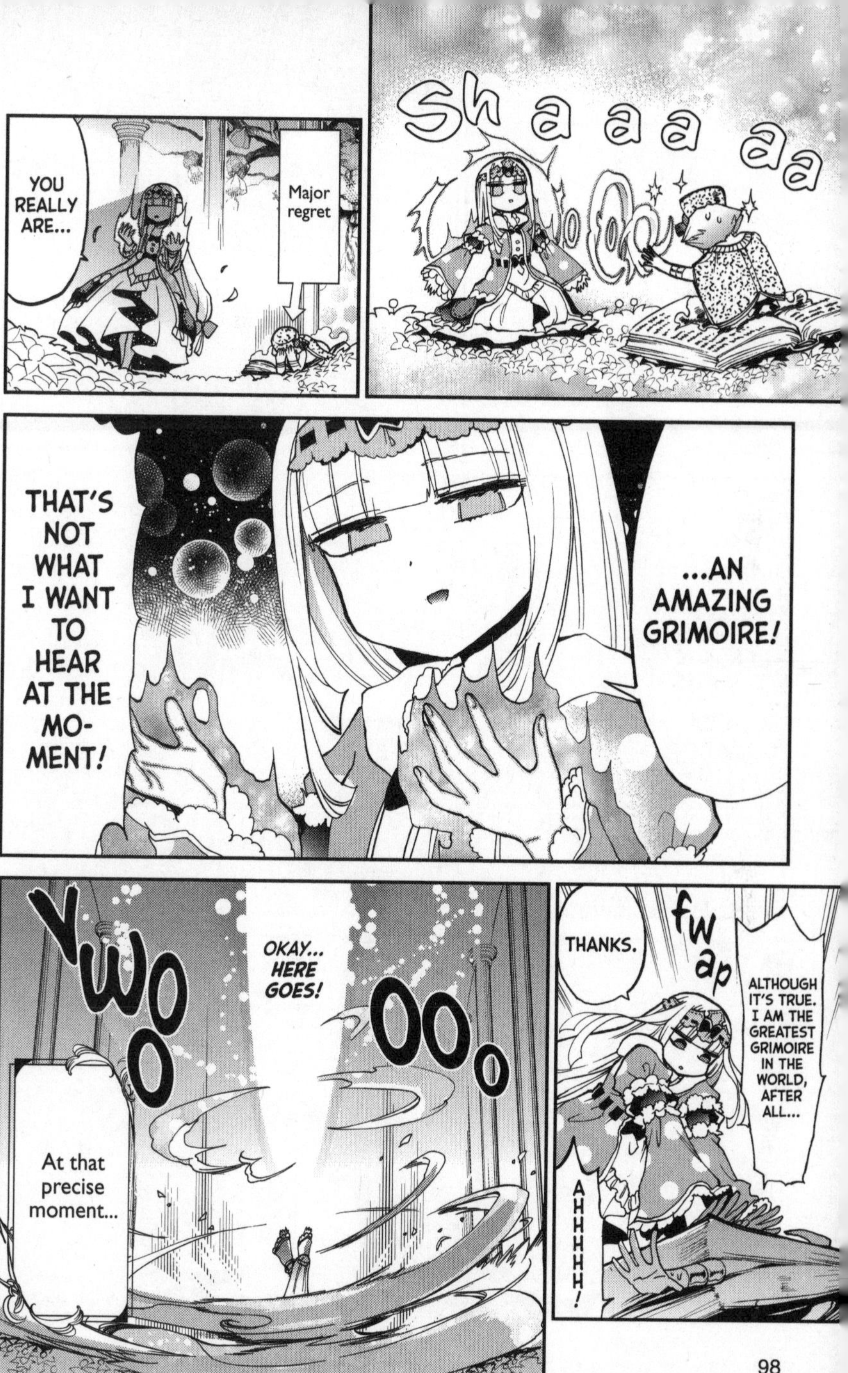
Sh a a a aa
YOU REALLY ARE...
Major regret
...AN AMAZING GRIMOIRE!
THAT'S NOT WHAT I WANT TO HEAR AT THE MO- MENT!
ALTHOUGH IT'S TRUE. I AM THE GREATEST GRIMOIRE IN THE WORLD, AFTER ALL...
fwap
THANKS.
AHHHHH!
YWOOOOo
OKAY... HERE GOES!
At that precise moment...

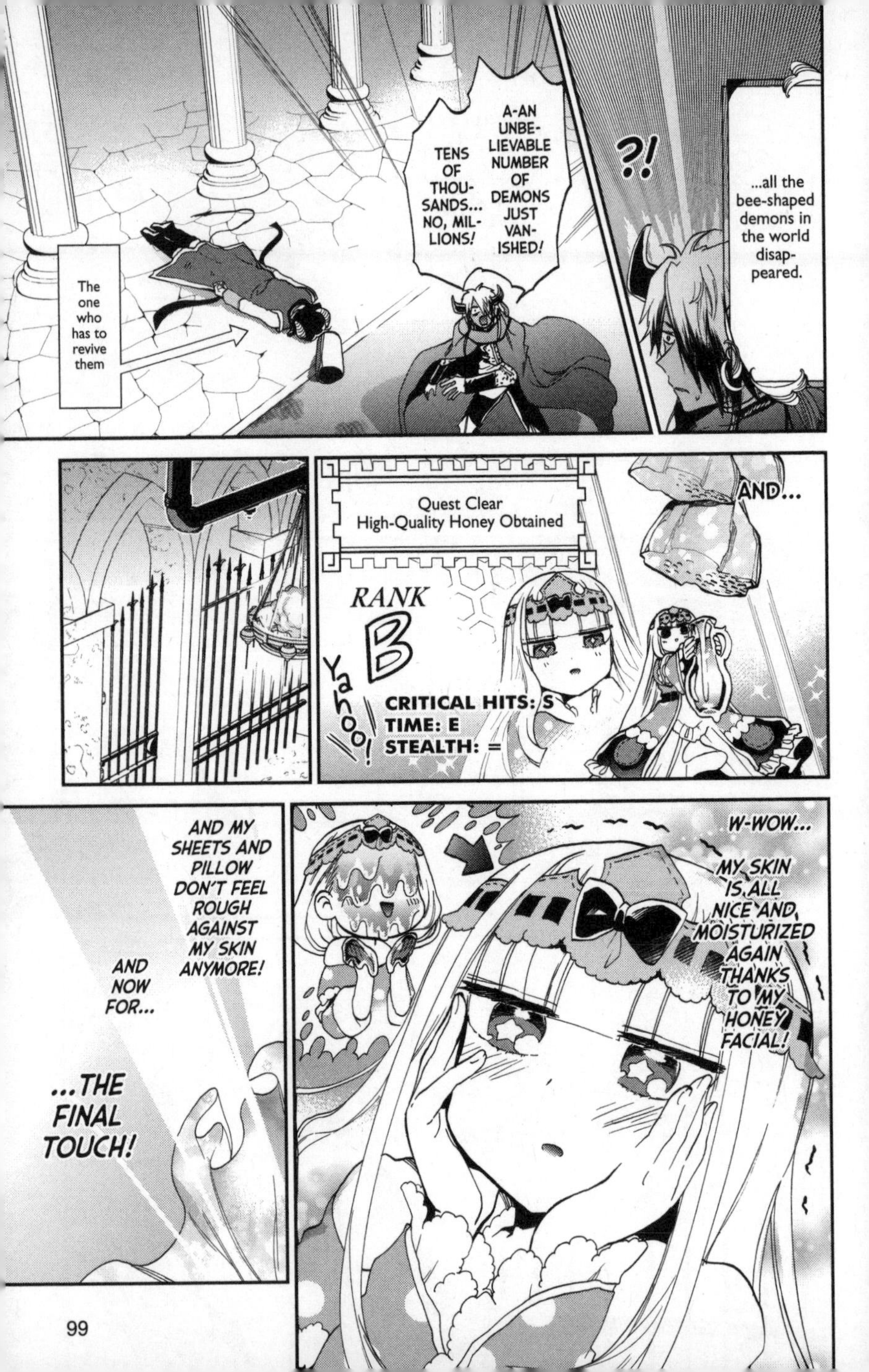
?!
...all the bee-shaped demons in the world disappeared.
A-AN UNBE-LIEVABLE NUMBER OF DEMONS JUST VAN-ISHED!
TENS OF THOU-SANDS... NO, MIL-LIONS!
The one who has to revive them
Quest Clear
High-Quality Honey Obtained
RANK B
CRITICAL HITS: S
TIME: E
STEALTH: =
Yahoo!
AND...
W-WOW...
MY SKIN IS ALL NICE AND MOISTURIZED AGAIN THANKS TO MY HONEY FACIAL!
AND MY SHEETS AND PILLOW DON'T FEEL ROUGH AGAINST MY SKIN ANYMORE!
AND NOW FOR...
...THE FINAL TOUCH!

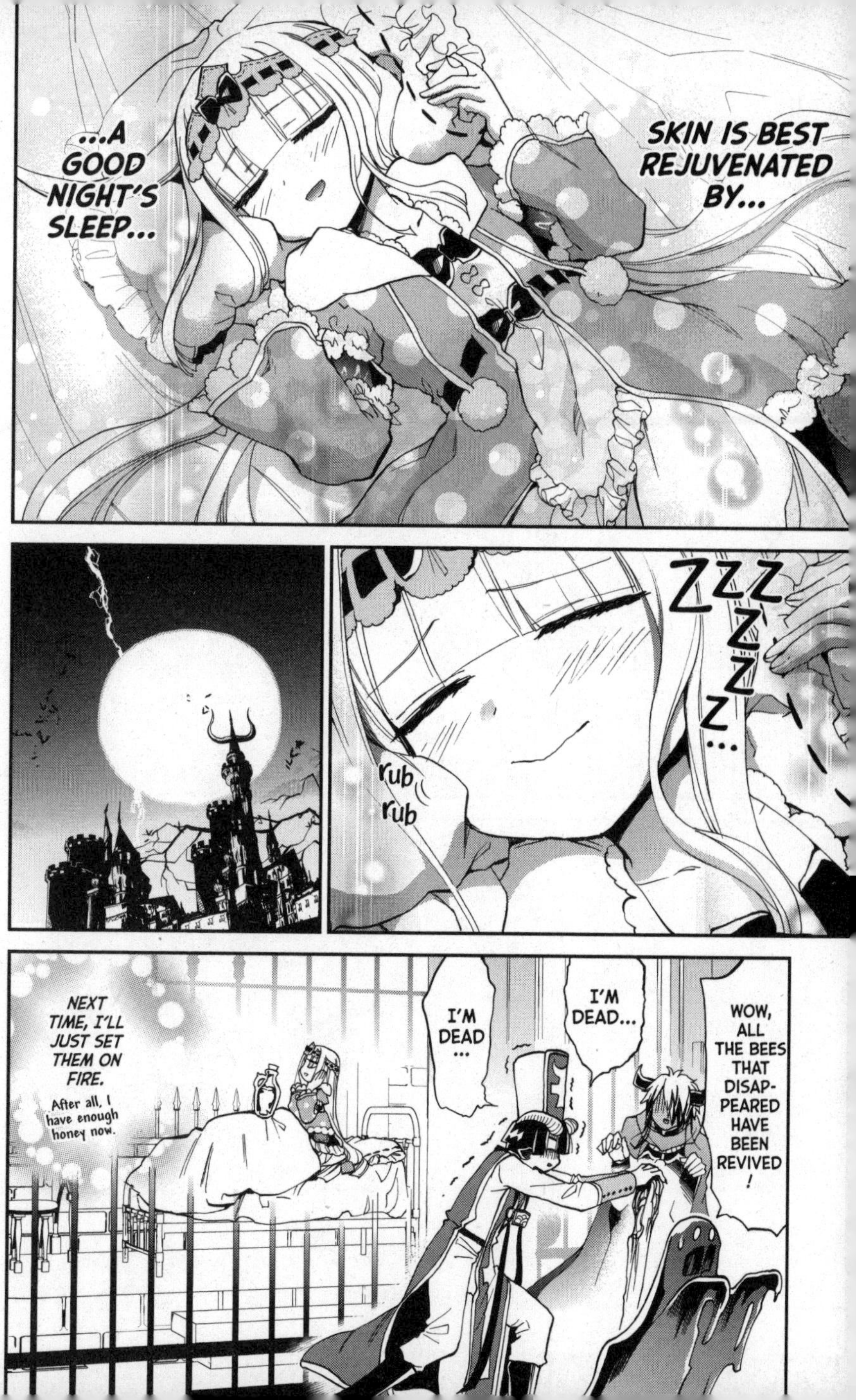
SKIN IS BEST REJUVENATED BY...
...A GOOD NIGHT'S SLEEP...
ZZZ ZZZ...
rub rub
WOW, ALL THE BEES THAT DISAP-PEARED HAVE BEEN REVIVED!
I'M DEAD...
I'M DEAD ...
NEXT TIME, I'LL JUST SET THEM ON FIRE.
After all, I have enough honey now.

Bee-Bee Drone

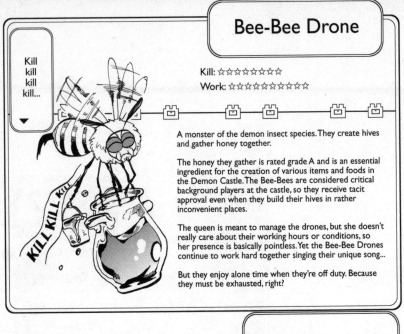

Kill
kill
kill
kill...

KILL KILL KILL KILL

Kill: ☆☆☆☆☆☆☆☆☆

Work: ☆☆☆☆☆☆☆☆☆☆☆

A monster of the demon insect species. They create hives and gather honey together.

The honey they gather is rated grade A and is an essential ingredient for the creation of various items and foods in the Demon Castle. The Bee-Bees are considered critical background players at the castle, so they receive tacit approval even when they build their hives in rather inconvenient places.

The queen is meant to manage the drones, but she doesn't really care about their working hours or conditions, so her presence is basically pointless. Yet the Bee-Bee Drones continue to work hard together singing their unique song...

But they enjoy alone time when they're off duty. Because they must be exhausted, right?

Former problem:
"Kill kill kill kill."

Current problem:
"Kill kill kill kill kill kill."

HONEY AND BEARS GO TOGETHER.
WOULD IT HAVE BEEN EASIER TO JUST ASK THE TEDDY DEMONS FOR SOME HONEY?
....
Facial expression: "No, because I don't like to get sticky."

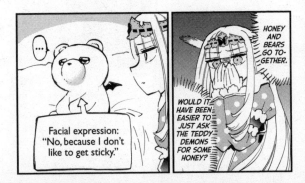

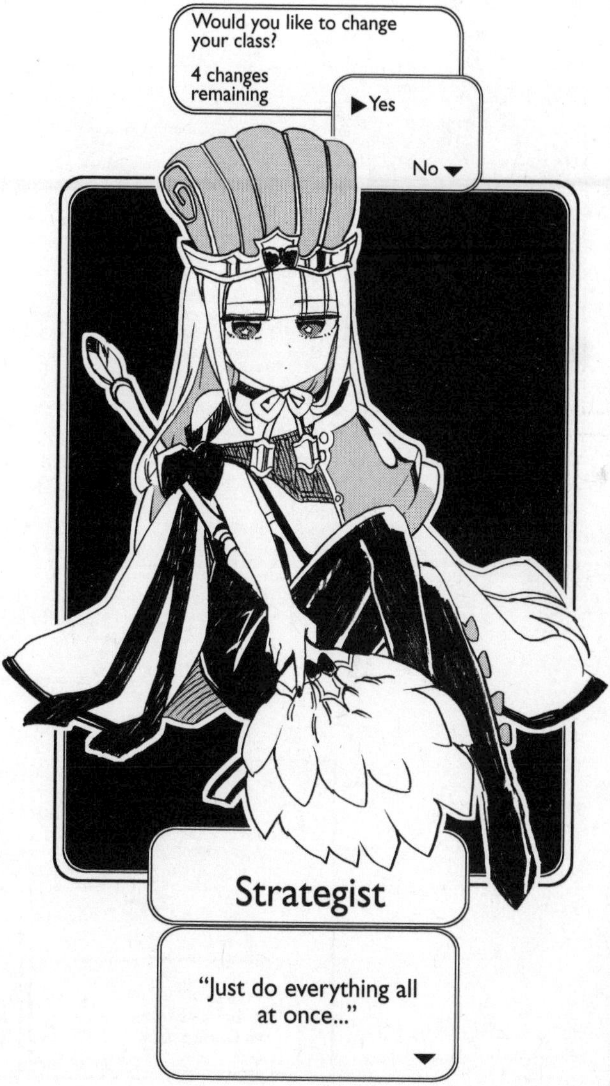
Would you like to change your class?
4 changes remaining
▶Yes
No
Strategist
"Just do everything all at once..."

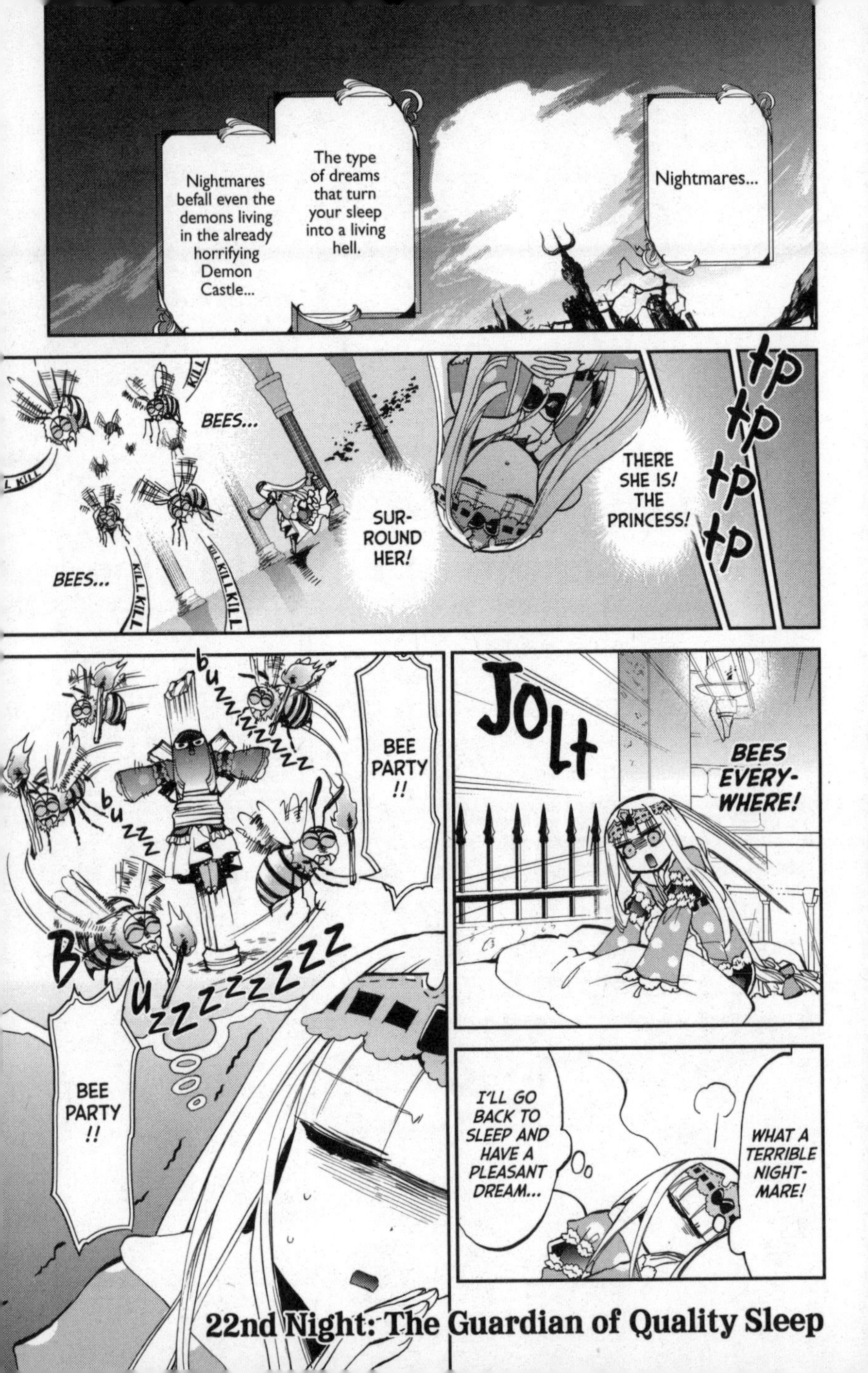
Nightmares...
The type of dreams that turn your sleep into a living hell.
Nightmares befall even the demons living in the already horrifying Demon Castle...
tp tp tp tp
THERE SHE IS! THE PRINCESS!
SUR-ROUND HER!
BEES...
BEES...
KILL KILL
KILL KILL
JOLT
BEES EVERY-WHERE!
WHAT A TERRIBLE NIGHT-MARE!
I'LL GO BACK TO SLEEP AND HAVE A PLEASANT DREAM...
BEE PARTY !!
buzzzzzzzz
buzzz
BEE PARTY !!
BUZZZZZZZZZ

22nd Night: The Guardian of Quality Sleep

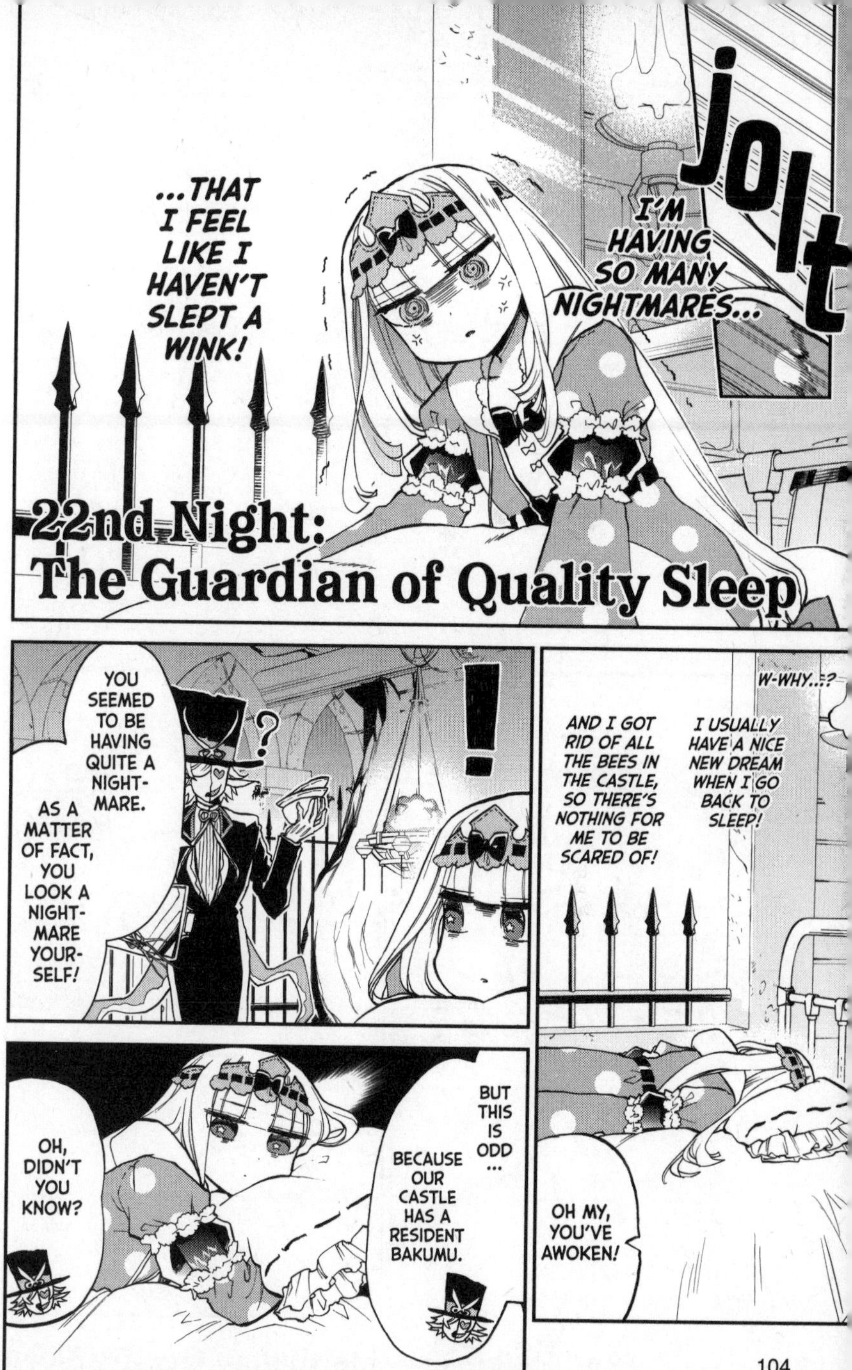
JOLT
I'M HAVING SO MANY NIGHTMARES...
...THAT I FEEL LIKE I HAVEN'T SLEPT A WINK!
22nd Night: The Guardian of Quality Sleep
W-WHY...?
I USUALLY HAVE A NICE NEW DREAM WHEN I GO BACK TO SLEEP!
AND I GOT RID OF ALL THE BEES IN THE CASTLE, SO THERE'S NOTHING FOR ME TO BE SCARED OF!
OH MY, YOU'VE AWOKEN!
!
?
YOU SEEMED TO BE HAVING QUITE A NIGHT-MARE.
AS A MATTER OF FACT, YOU LOOK A NIGHT-MARE YOUR-SELF!
BUT THIS IS ODD...
BECAUSE OUR CASTLE HAS A RESIDENT BAKUMU.
OH, DIDN'T YOU KNOW?

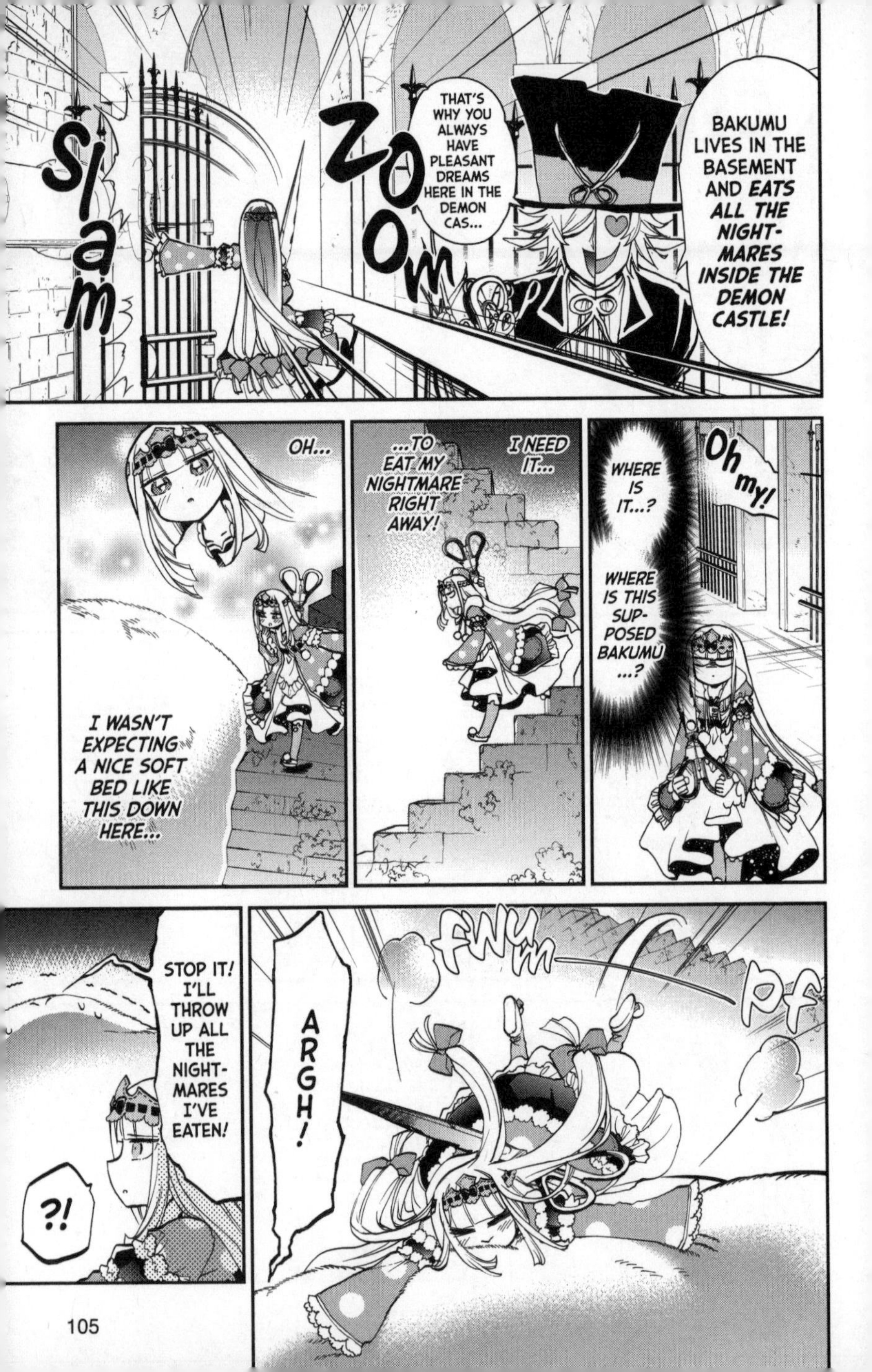
BAKUMU LIVES IN THE BASEMENT AND *EATS ALL THE NIGHTMARES INSIDE THE DEMON CASTLE!*
THAT'S WHY YOU ALWAYS HAVE PLEASANT DREAMS HERE IN THE DEMON CAS...
ZOOM
Slam
Oh my!
WHERE IS IT...?
WHERE IS THIS SUPPOSED BAKUMU ...?
I NEED IT...
...TO EAT MY NIGHTMARE RIGHT AWAY!
OH...
I WASN'T EXPECTING A NICE SOFT BED LIKE THIS DOWN HERE...
FWUMPF
ARGH!
STOP IT! I'LL THROW UP ALL THE NIGHTMARES I'VE EATEN!
?!

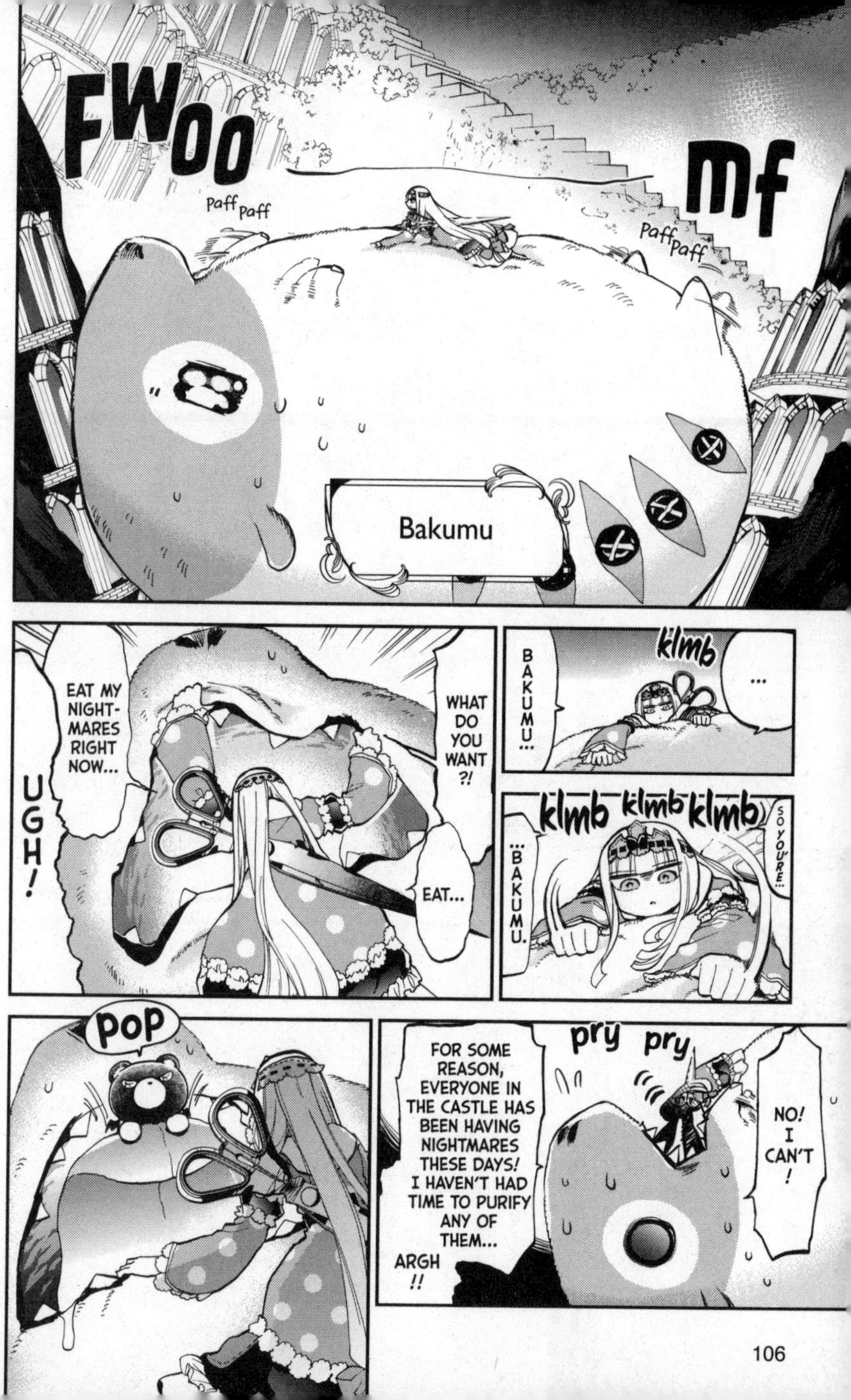
FWOOMF
Paff paff
Paff paff
Bakumu
...
klmb
BAKUMU...
SO YOU'RE...
klmb klmb klmb
...BAKUMU.
WHAT DO YOU WANT?!
EAT...
EAT MY NIGHTMARES RIGHT NOW...
UGH!
NO! I CAN'T!
pry pry
FOR SOME REASON, EVERYONE IN THE CASTLE HAS BEEN HAVING NIGHTMARES THESE DAYS! I HAVEN'T HAD TIME TO PURIFY ANY OF THEM...
ARGH!!
pop

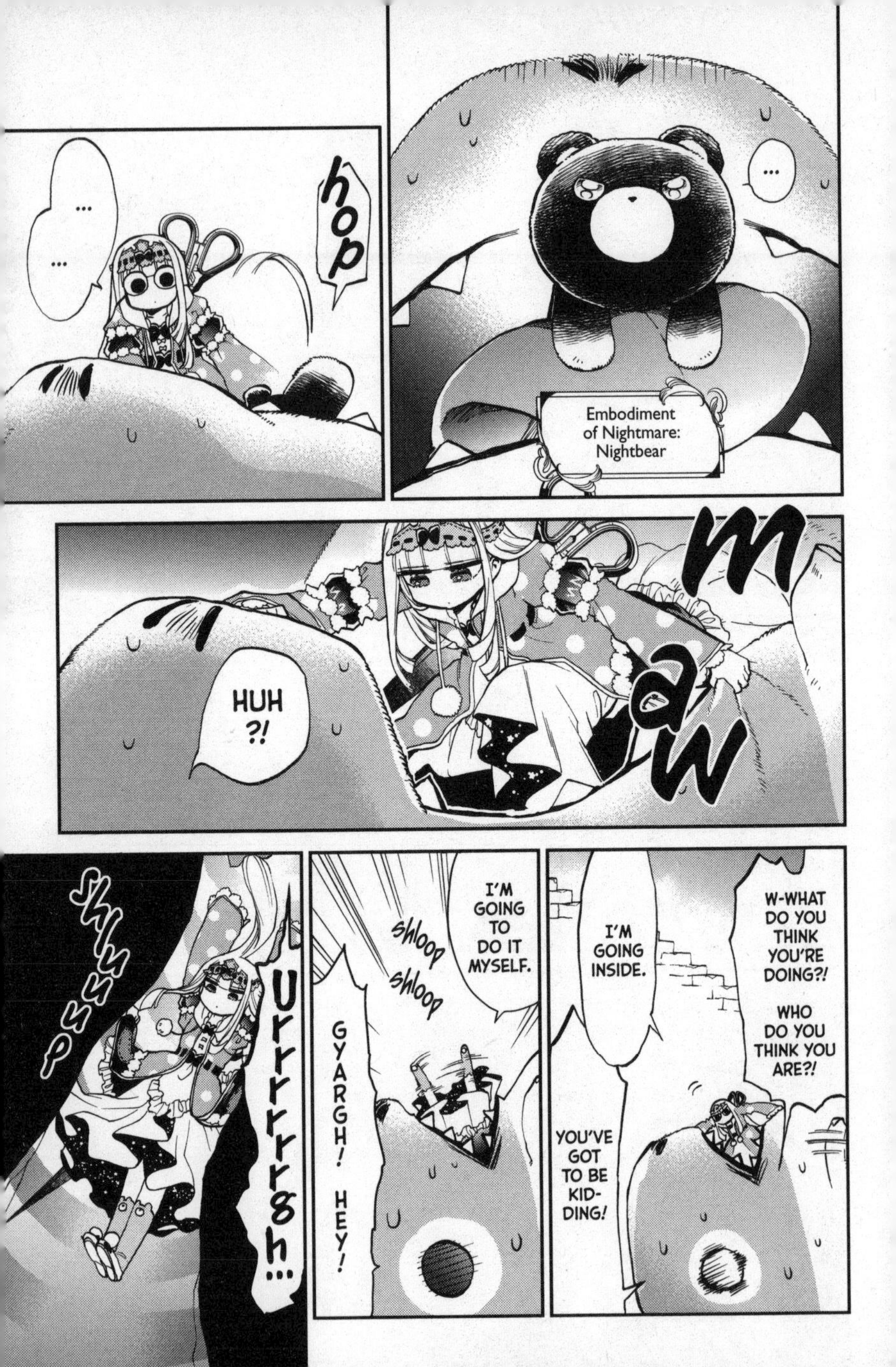
...
Embodiment of Nightmare: Nightbear
hop
... ...
maw
HUH ?!
W-WHAT DO YOU THINK YOU'RE DOING?!
WHO DO YOU THINK YOU ARE?!
I'M GOING INSIDE.
YOU'VE GOT TO BE KID-DING!
I'M GOING TO DO IT MYSELF.
shloop shloop
GYARGH! HEY!
Urrrrrrgh!!
shluuup

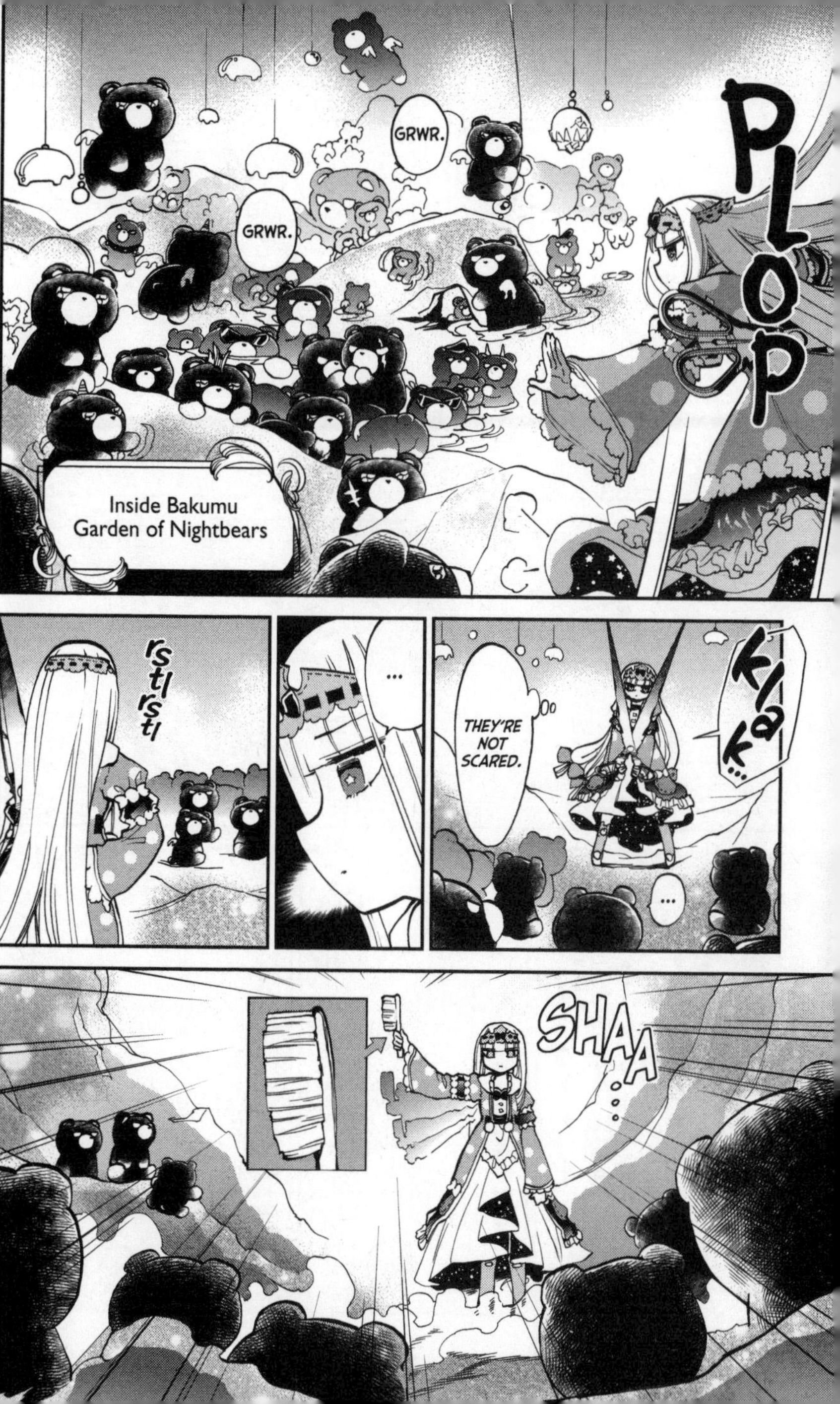
PLOP
GRWR.
GRWR.
Inside Bakumu Garden of Nightbears
klak...
THEY'RE NOT SCARED.
...
...
rstl rstl
SHAA...

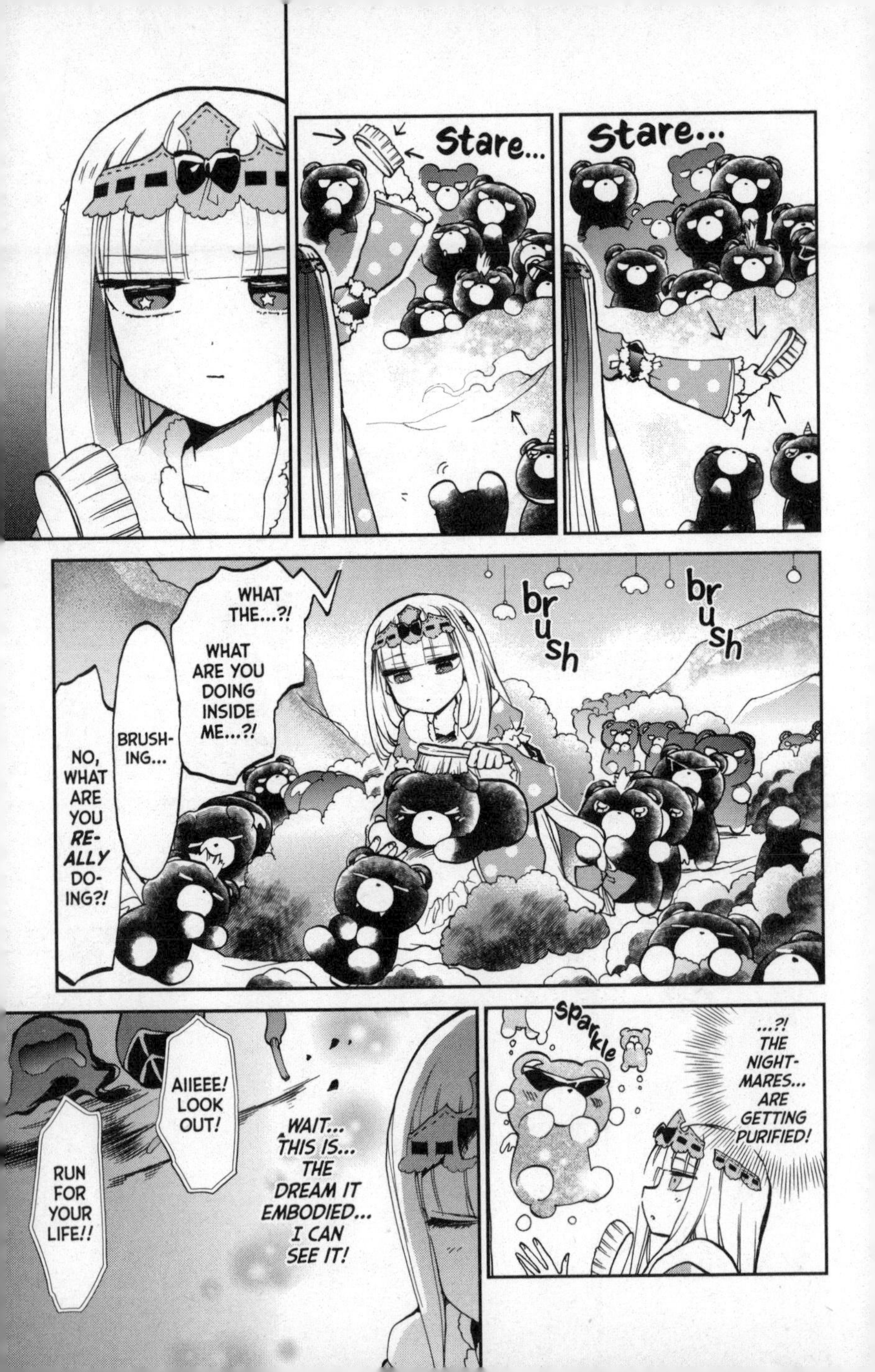
Stare...
Stare...
brush
brush
WHAT THE...?!
WHAT ARE YOU DOING INSIDE ME...?!
BRUSHING...
NO, WHAT ARE YOU *REALLY* DOING?!
sparkle
...?! THE NIGHTMARES... ARE GETTING PURIFIED!
WAIT... THIS IS... THE DREAM IT EMBODIED... I CAN SEE IT!
AIIEEE! LOOK OUT!
RUN FOR YOUR LIFE!!

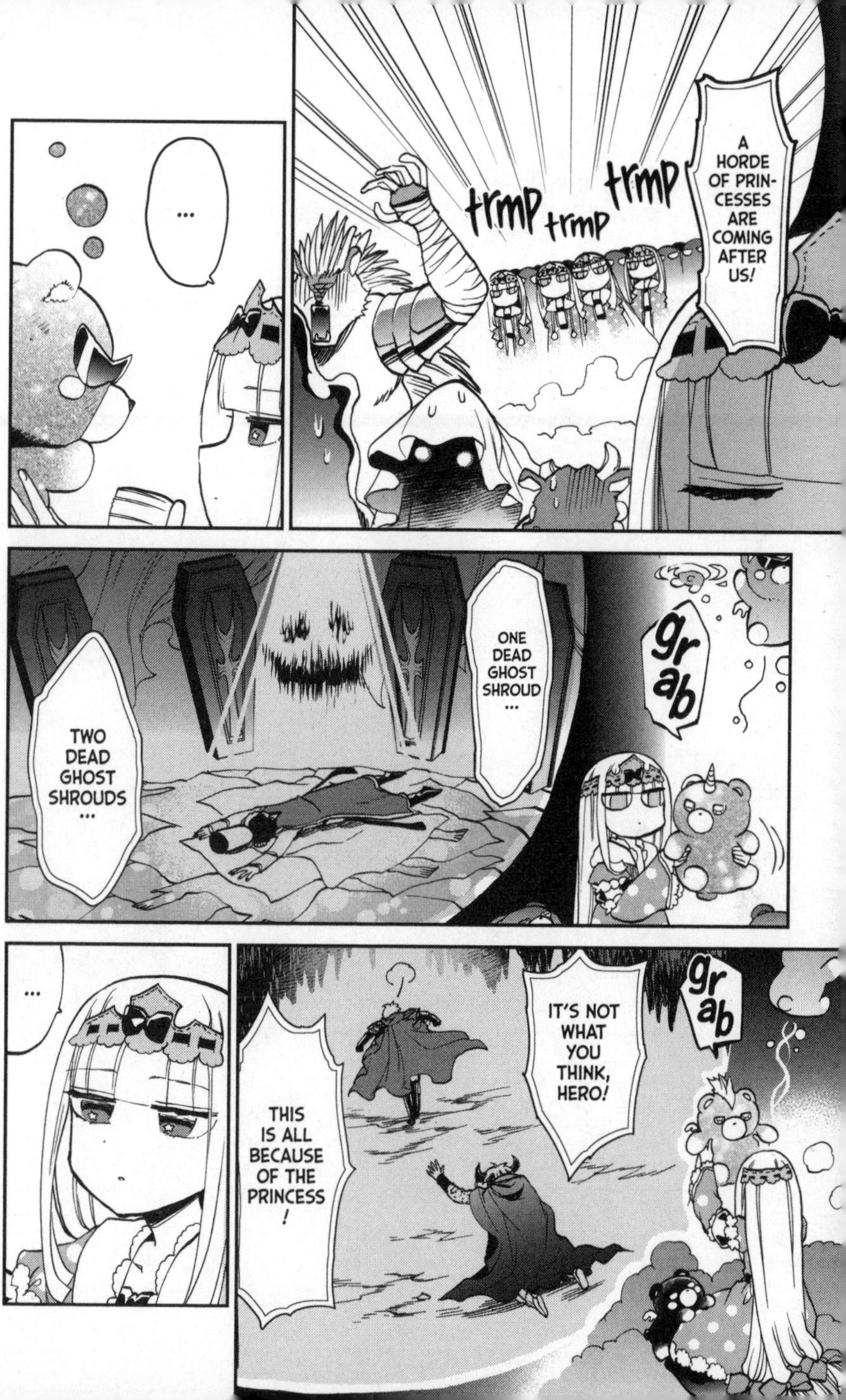
A HORDE OF PRINCESSES ARE COMING AFTER US!
trmp
trmp
trmp
...
grab
ONE DEAD GHOST SHROUD ...
TWO DEAD GHOST SHROUDS ...
grab
IT'S NOT WHAT YOU THINK, HERO!
THIS IS ALL BECAUSE OF THE PRINCESS!
...

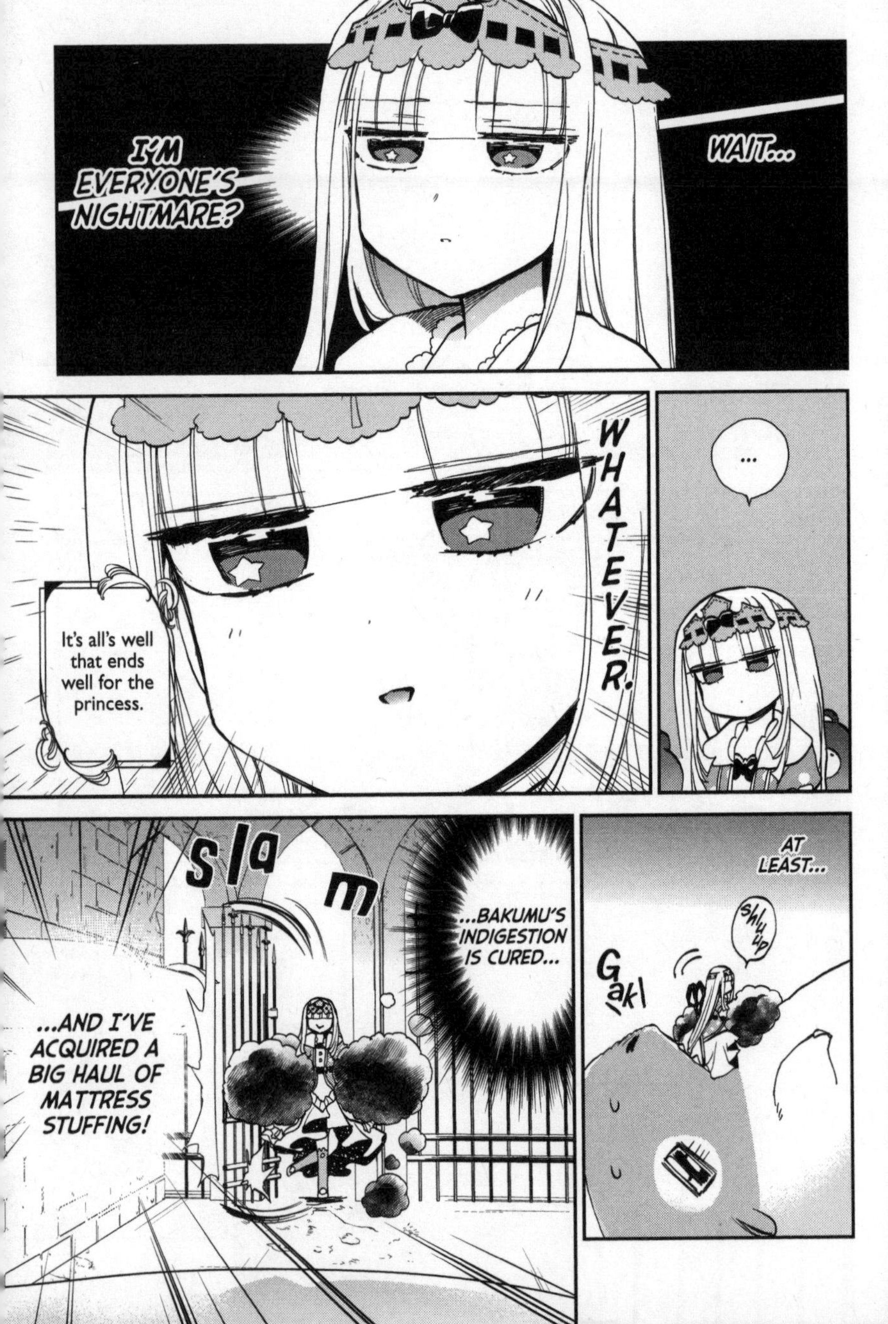
WAIT...
I'M EVERYONE'S NIGHTMARE?
...
WHATEVER.
It's all's well that ends well for the princess.
AT LEAST...
shluup
Gak!
slam
...BAKUMU'S INDIGESTION IS CURED...
...AND I'VE ACQUIRED A BIG HAUL OF MATTRESS STUFFING!

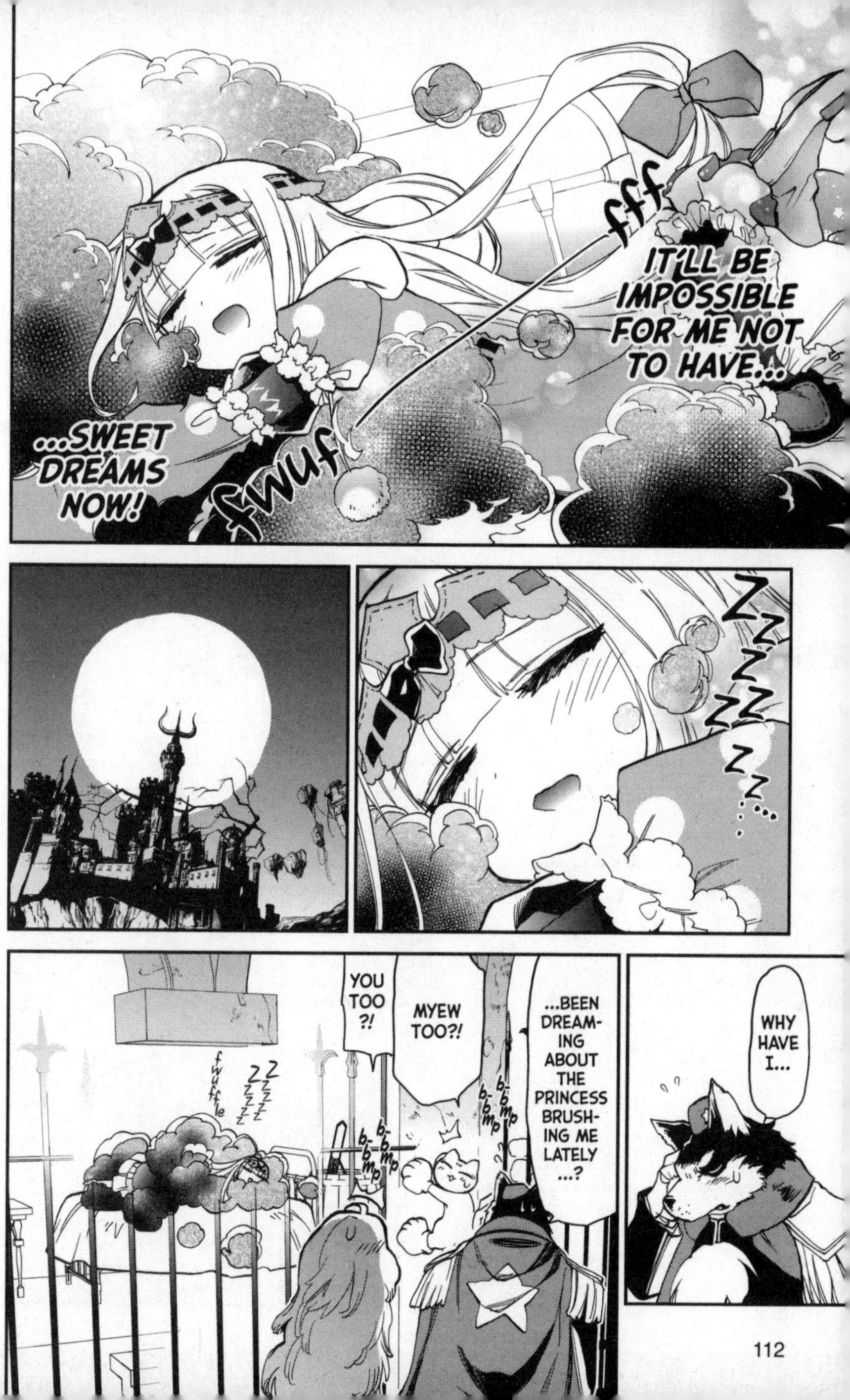
IT'LL BE IMPOSSIBLE FOR ME NOT TO HAVE...
fff
...SWEET DREAMS NOW!
fwuf
ZZZZZZZ...
WHY HAVE I...
...BEEN DREAMING ABOUT THE PRINCESS BRUSHING ME LATELY...?
MYEW TOO?!
YOU TOO?!
b-bmp b-bmp
b-bmp b-bmp
fwuffle
ZZZZZZZ

Bakumu & Nightbear

Marsh-mallow body.

Furriness: ☆☆☆☆☆☆☆☆☆☆☆
Dreaminess: ☆☆☆☆

They are both monsters of the beast species. But Nightbear and Bakumu are also unique demons in that they exist in both the real world and the dream world. Their relationship is...

Someone in the Demon Castle has a dream.
↓
No matter what kind of dream it is, it enters a Nightbear.
↓
If the dream is a nightmare, the Nightbear automatically dispenses "Nightmare Fog." (Status ailment from the fog: Silence)
↓
Nightmare Fog is Bakumu's food source, so it consumes the Nightbear and purifies it inside its stomach.
↓
The Nightbear goes out and hangs out in the dream world again.

This is their natural symbiotic cycle. Nightbears don't come out into the real world very often, but these ones have become attached to Syalis and like to visit her with a brush in hand.

Former problem of the last 100 years:
"I want quantity over quality in my nightmare meals."

Current problem:
"I was wrong about my former problem."

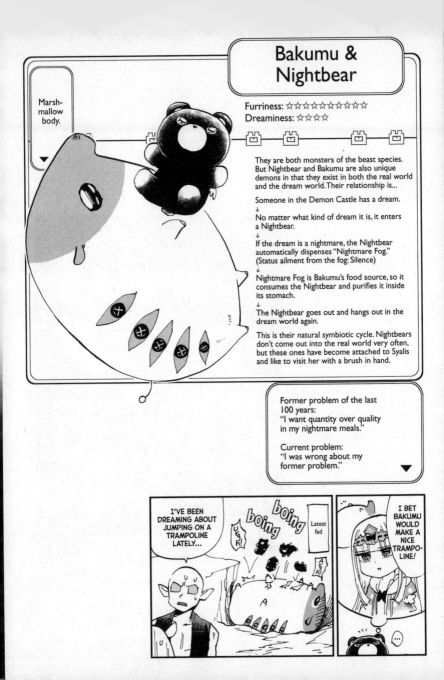

I BET BAKUMU WOULD MAKE A NICE TRAMPO-LINE!
...
Latest fad
boing
boing
Argh!
I'VE BEEN DREAMING ABOUT JUMPING ON A TRAMPOLINE LATELY...
Urgh!

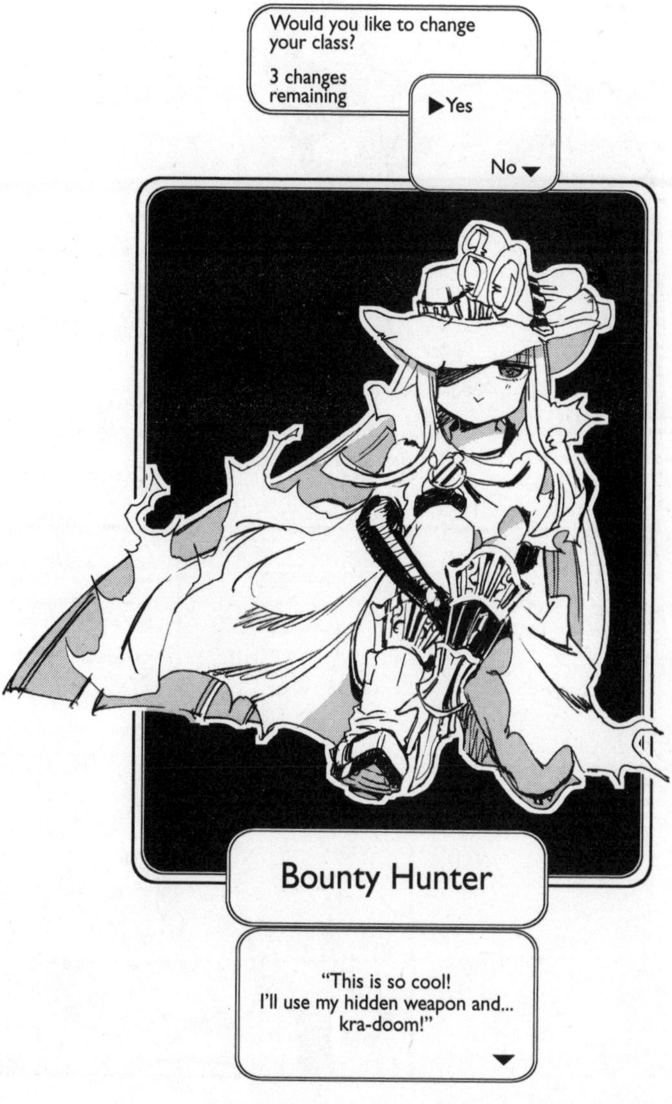
Would you like to change your class?
3 changes remaining
▶Yes
No
Bounty Hunter
"This is so cool! I'll use my hidden weapon and... kra-doom!"

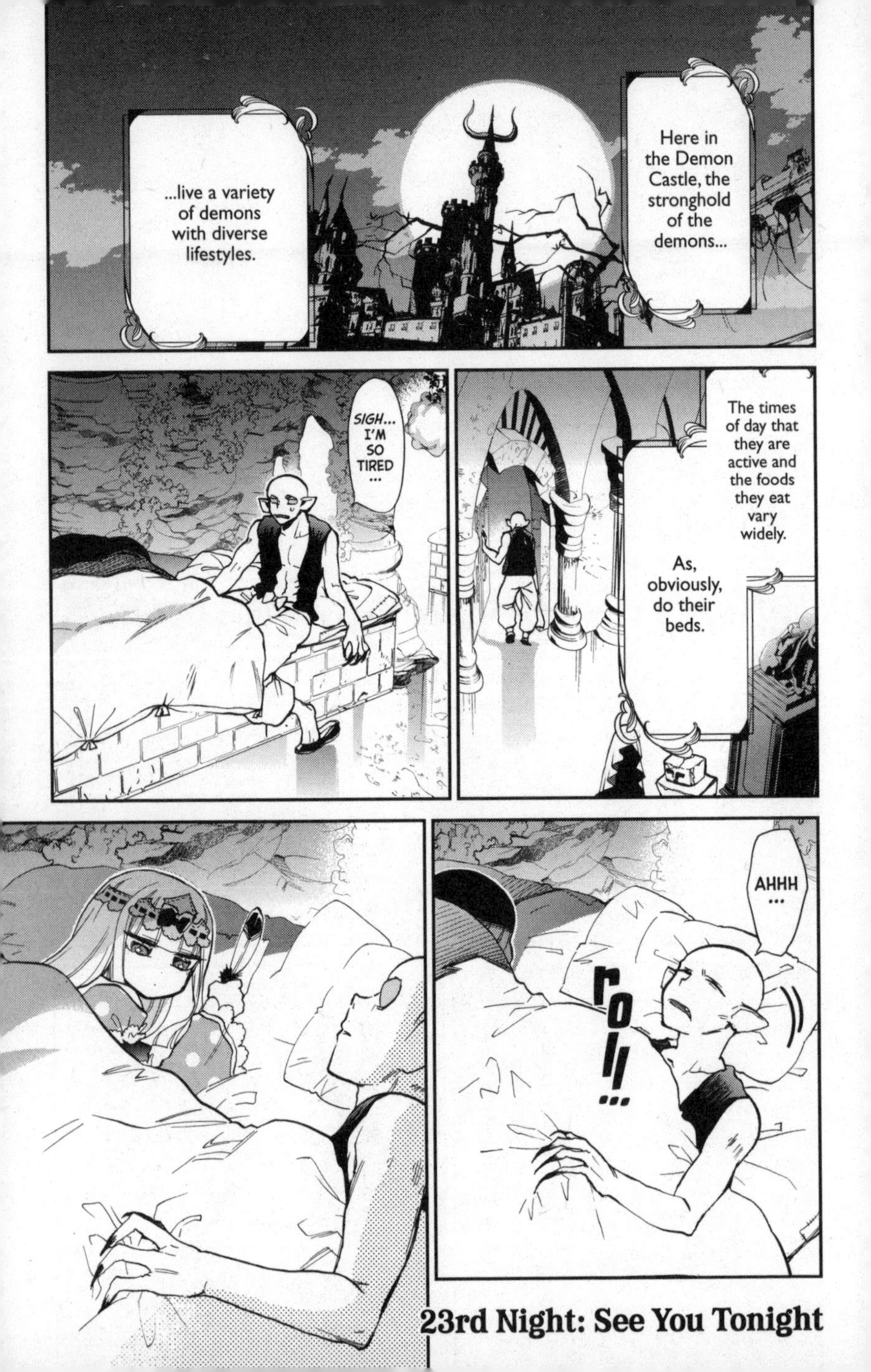
Here in the Demon Castle, the stronghold of the demons...
...live a variety of demons with diverse lifestyles.
The times of day that they are active and the foods they eat vary widely.
As, obviously, do their beds.
SIGH... I'M SO TIRED...
AHHH...
roll!..

23rd Night: See You Tonight

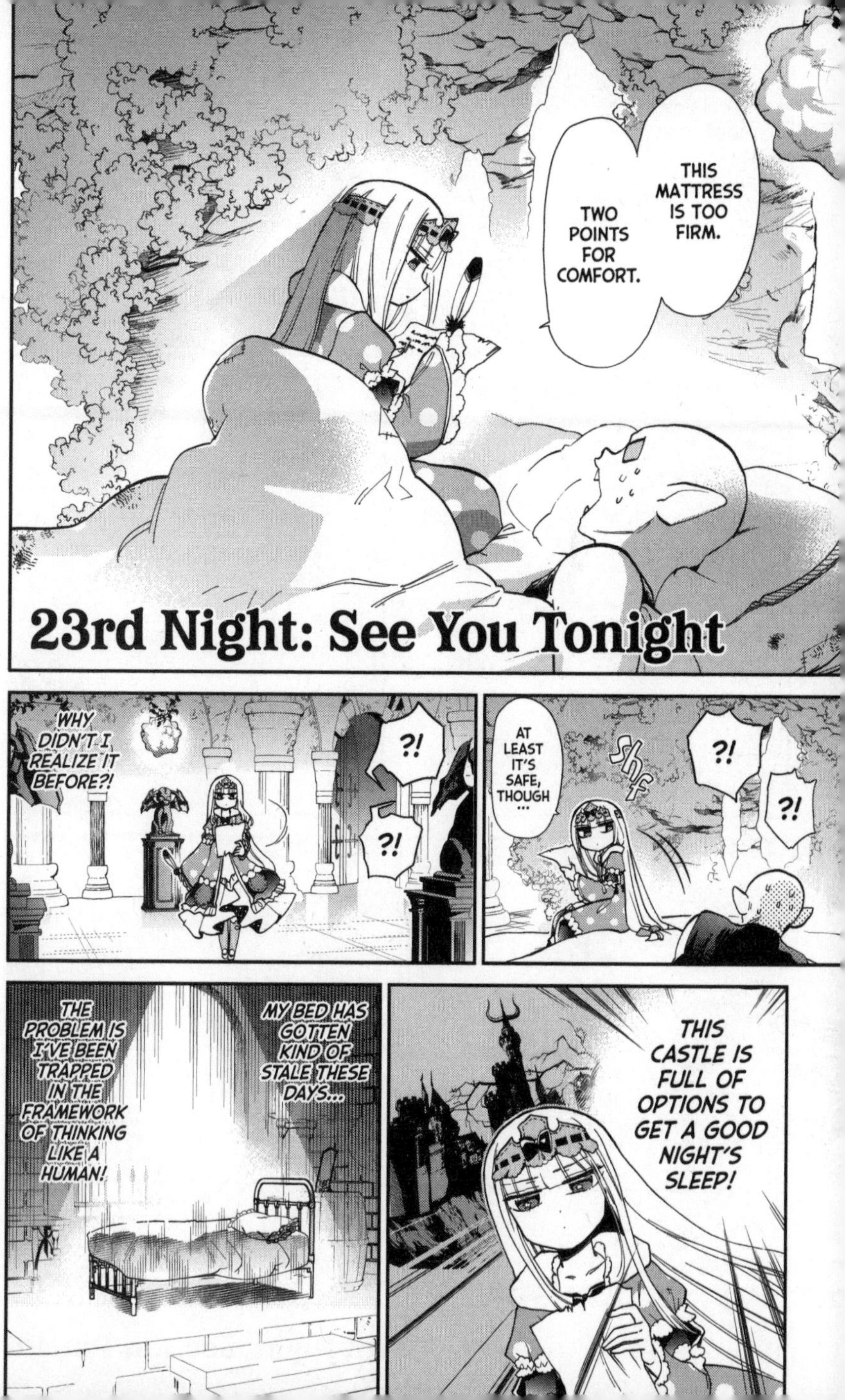
THIS MATTRESS IS TOO FIRM.
TWO POINTS FOR COMFORT.
23rd Night: See You Tonight
?!
?!
shf
AT LEAST IT'S SAFE, THOUGH...
?!
?!
WHY DIDN'T I REALIZE IT BEFORE?!
THIS CASTLE IS FULL OF OPTIONS TO GET A GOOD NIGHT'S SLEEP!
MY BED HAS GOTTEN KIND OF STALE THESE DAYS...
THE PROBLEM IS I'VE BEEN TRAPPED IN THE FRAMEWORK OF THINKING LIKE A HUMAN!

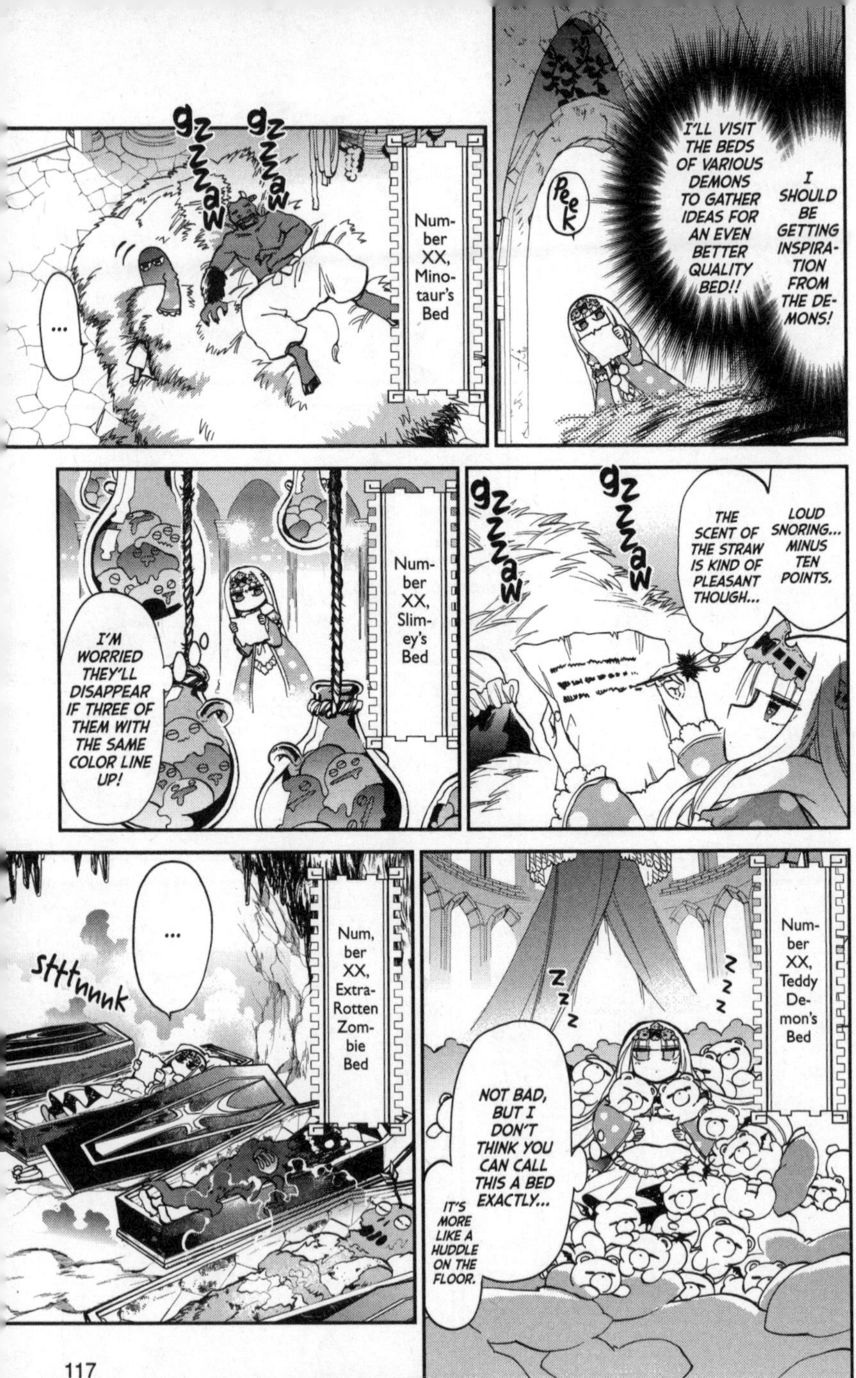

Peek
I SHOULD BE GETTING INSPIRATION FROM THE DEMONS!
I'LL VISIT THE BEDS OF VARIOUS DEMONS TO GATHER IDEAS FOR AN EVEN BETTER QUALITY BED!!
gzzzaw
gzzzaw
Number XX, Minotaur's Bed
...
gzzzaw
gzzzaw
LOUD SNORING... MINUS TEN POINTS.
THE SCENT OF THE STRAW IS KIND OF PLEASANT THOUGH...
Number XX, Slimey's Bed
I'M WORRIED THEY'LL DISAPPEAR IF THREE OF THEM WITH THE SAME COLOR LINE UP!
Number XX, Teddy Demon's Bed
zzz
zzz
NOT BAD, BUT I DON'T THINK YOU CAN CALL THIS A BED EXACTLY...
IT'S MORE LIKE A HUDDLE ON THE FLOOR.
Num, ber XX, Extra-Rotten Zombie Bed
...
stttnnnk

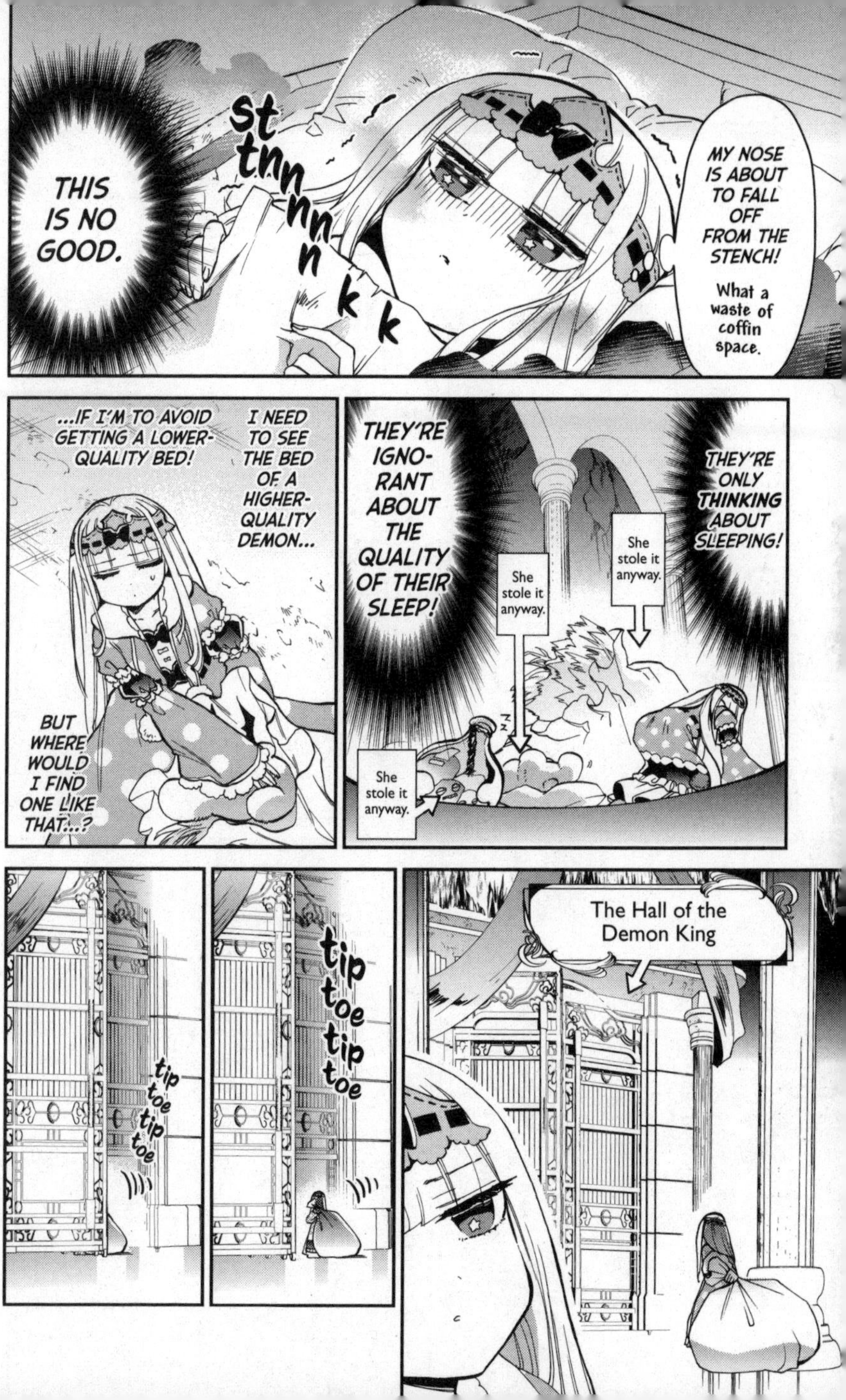
MY NOSE IS ABOUT TO FALL OFF FROM THE STENCH!
What a waste of coffin space.
st tnnnnnkk
THIS IS NO GOOD.
THEY'RE ONLY THINKING ABOUT SLEEPING!
She stole it anyway.
She stole it anyway.
She stole it anyway.
THEY'RE IGNORANT ABOUT THE QUALITY OF THEIR SLEEP!
I NEED TO SEE THE BED OF A HIGHER-QUALITY DEMON...
...IF I'M TO AVOID GETTING A LOWER-QUALITY BED!
BUT WHERE WOULD I FIND ONE LIKE THAT...?
The Hall of the Demon King
tip toe tip toe
tip toe tip toe

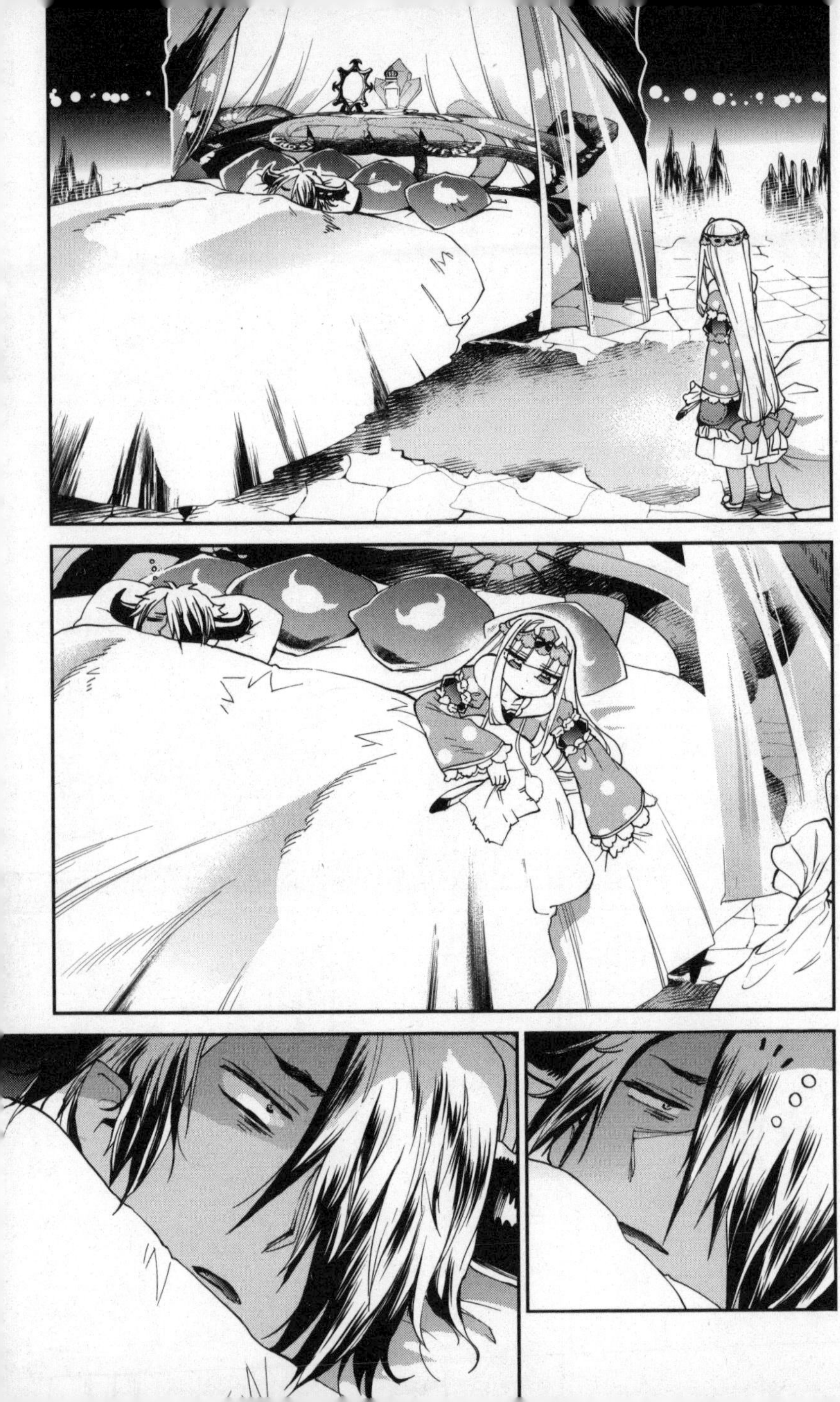

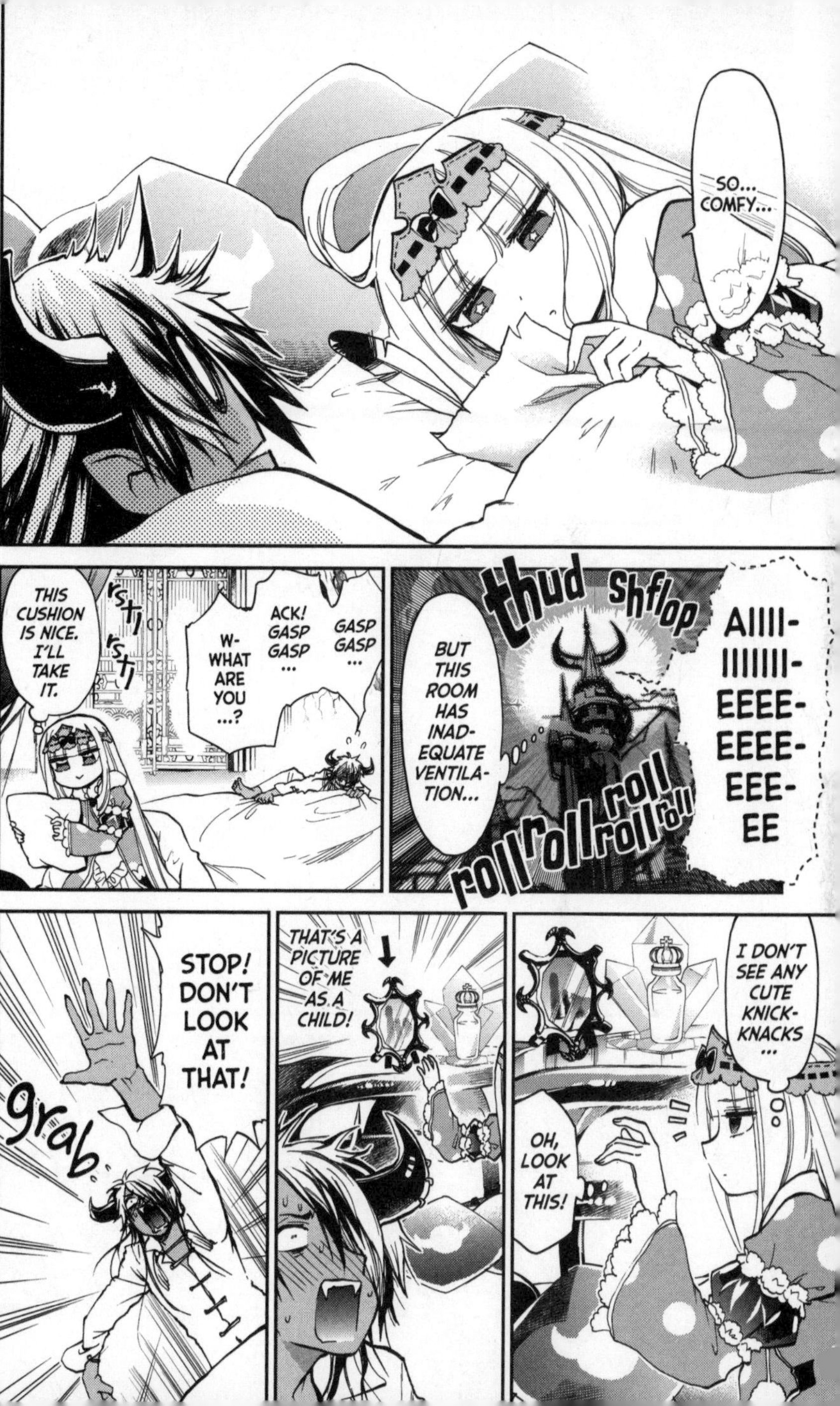
SO... COMFY...
AIIII-IIIIIII-EEEE-EEEE-EEE-EE
thud
shflop
BUT THIS ROOM HAS INADEQUATE VENTILATION...
roll roll roll roll roll
GASP GASP ...
ACK! GASP GASP ...
W-WHAT ARE YOU ...?
rstl rstl
THIS CUSHION IS NICE. I'LL TAKE IT.
I DON'T SEE ANY CUTE KNICK-KNACKS ...
OH, LOOK AT THIS!
THAT'S A PICTURE OF ME AS A CHILD!
STOP! DON'T LOOK AT THAT!
grab

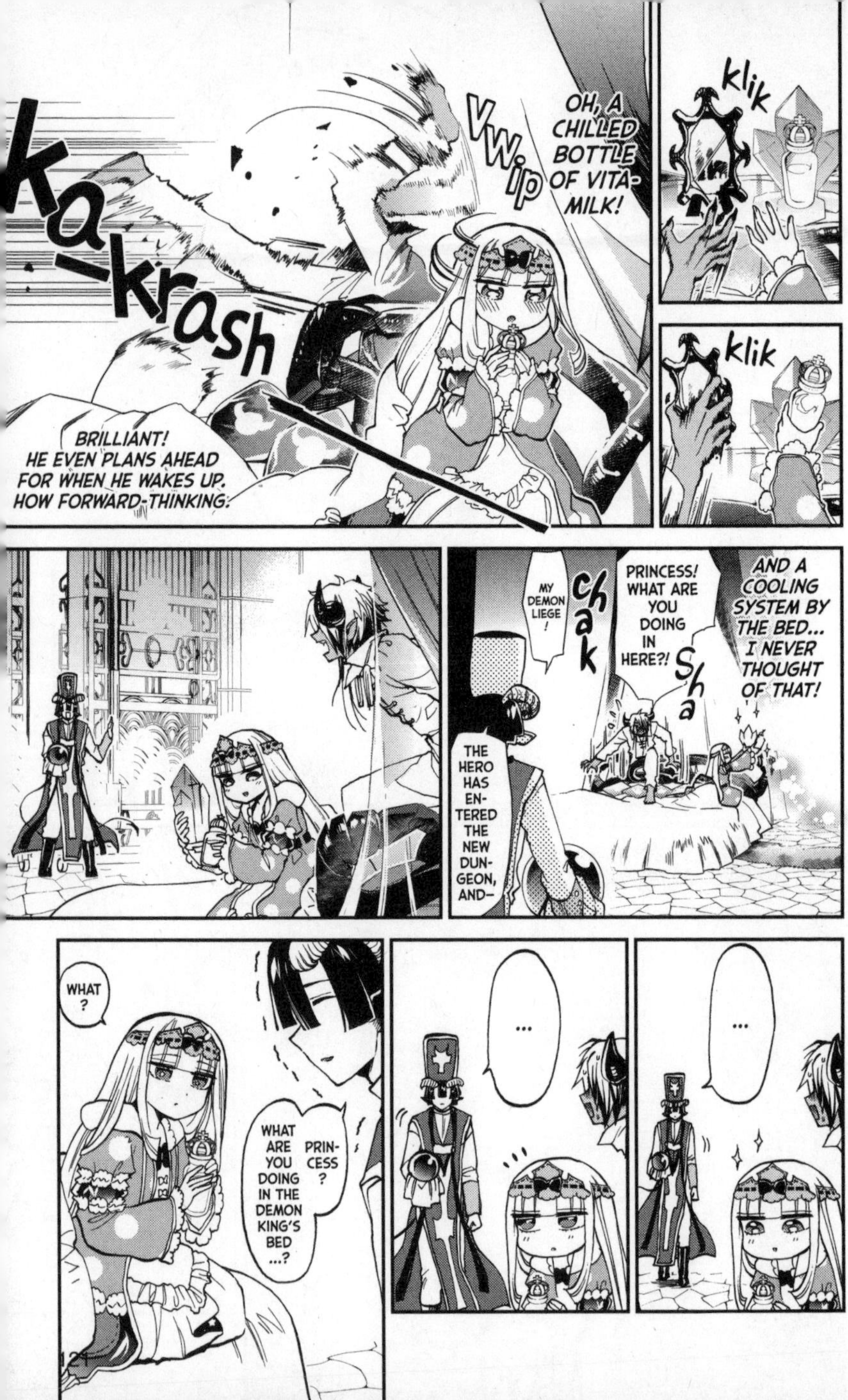
klik
klik
OH, A CHILLED BOTTLE OF VITA-MILK!
VWip
ka-krash
BRILLIANT! HE EVEN PLANS AHEAD FOR WHEN HE WAKES UP. HOW FORWARD-THINKING.
AND A COOLING SYSTEM BY THE BED... I NEVER THOUGHT OF THAT!
PRINCESS! WHAT ARE YOU DOING IN HERE?!
Sha
chak
MY DEMON LIEGE!
THE HERO HAS ENTERED THE NEW DUNGEON, AND—
...
...
WHAT?
PRINCESS?
WHAT ARE YOU DOING IN THE DEMON KING'S BED...?

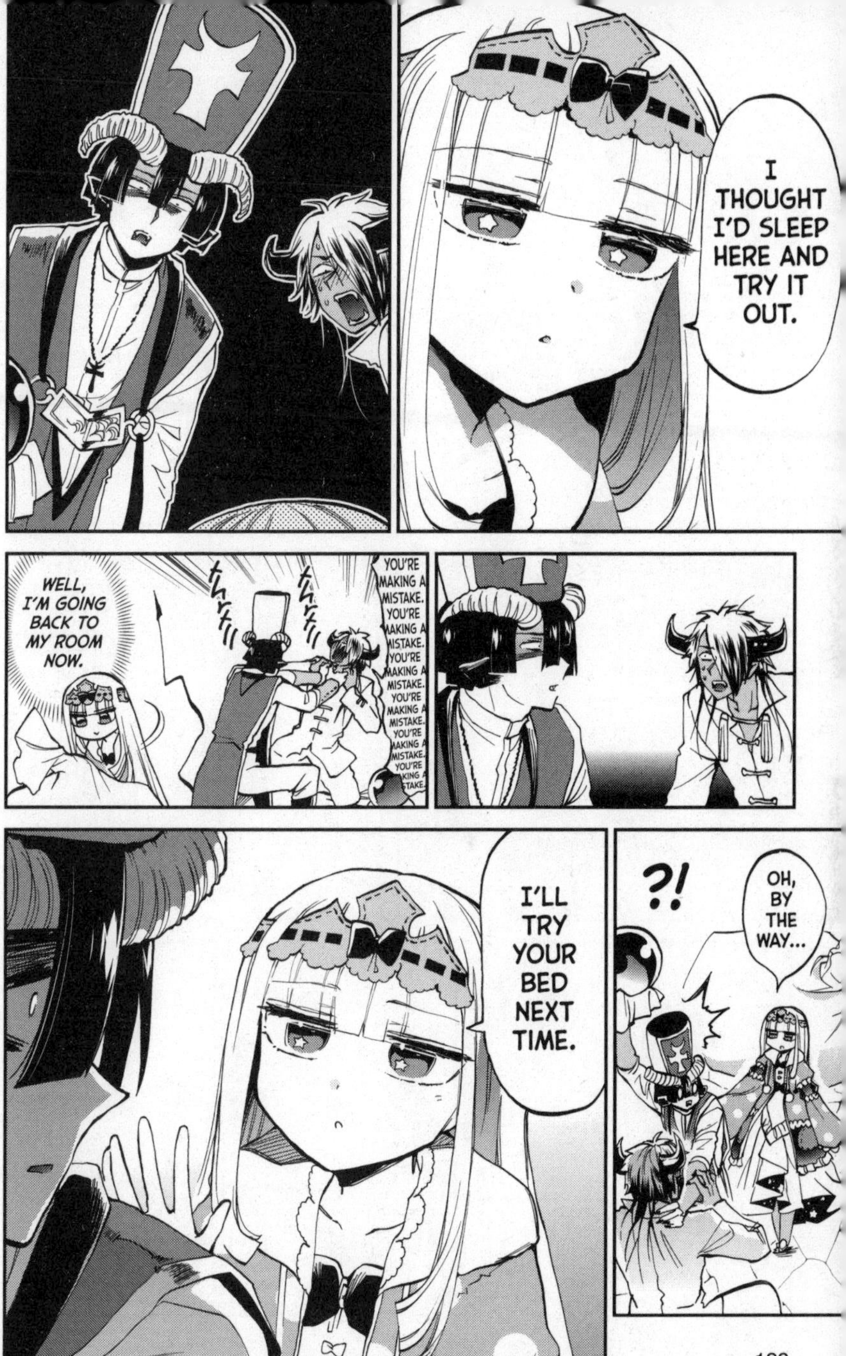
I THOUGHT I'D SLEEP HERE AND TRY IT OUT.
YOU'RE MAKING A MISTAKE. YOU'RE MAKING A MISTAKE. YOU'RE MAKING A MISTAKE. YOU'RE MAKING A MISTAKE. YOU'RE MAKING A MISTAKE. YOU'RE MAKING A MISTAKE.
WELL, I'M GOING BACK TO MY ROOM NOW.
OH, BY THE WAY...
?!
I'LL TRY YOUR BED NEXT TIME.

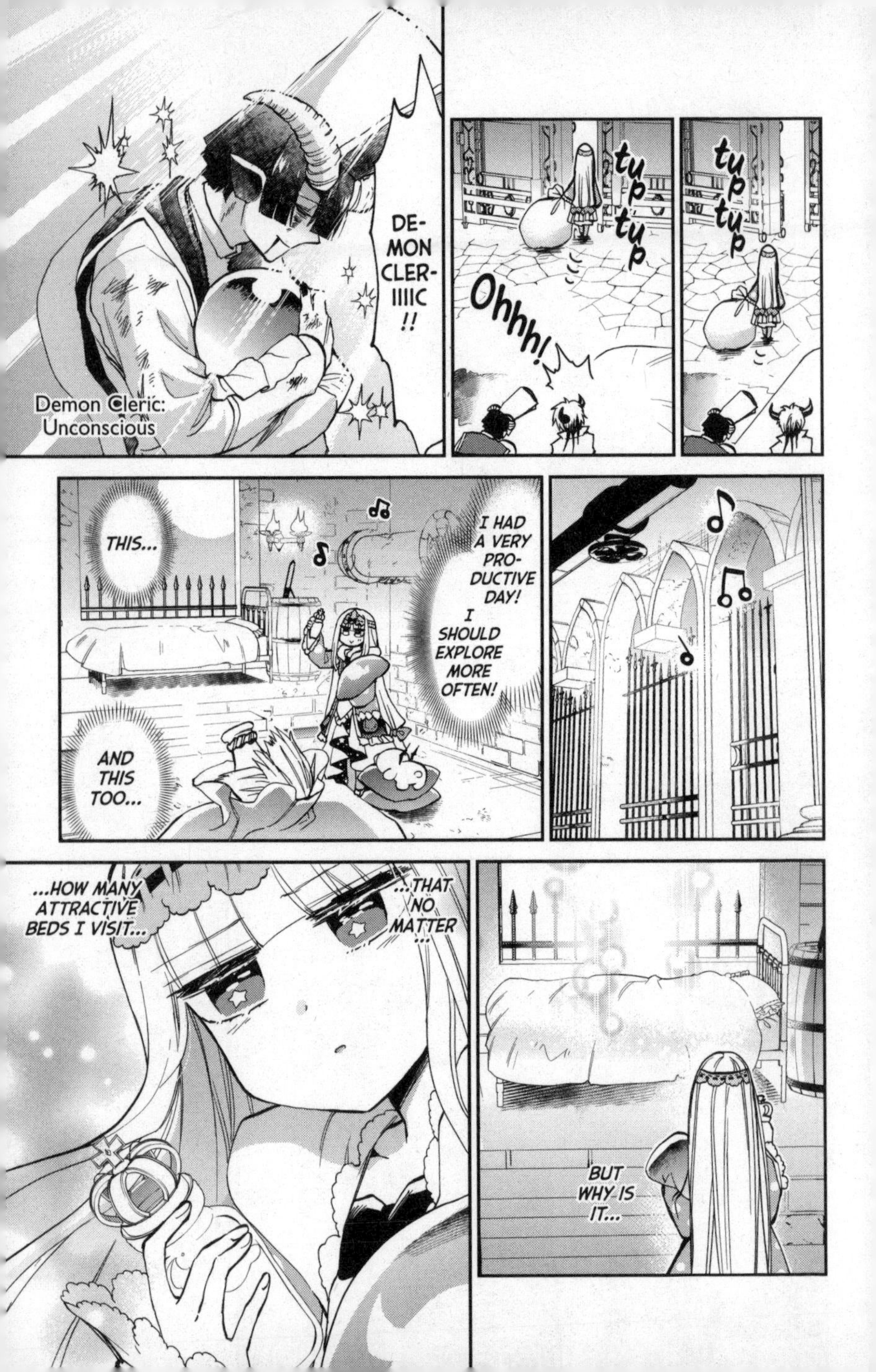
tup tup
tup tup
tup tup
Ohhh!
DE-MON CLER-IIIIC !!
Demon Cleric: Unconscious
I HAD A VERY PRO-DUCTIVE DAY!
I SHOULD EXPLORE MORE OFTEN!
THIS...
AND THIS TOO...
BUT WHY IS IT...
...THAT NO MATTER...
...HOW MANY ATTRACTIVE BEDS I VISIT...

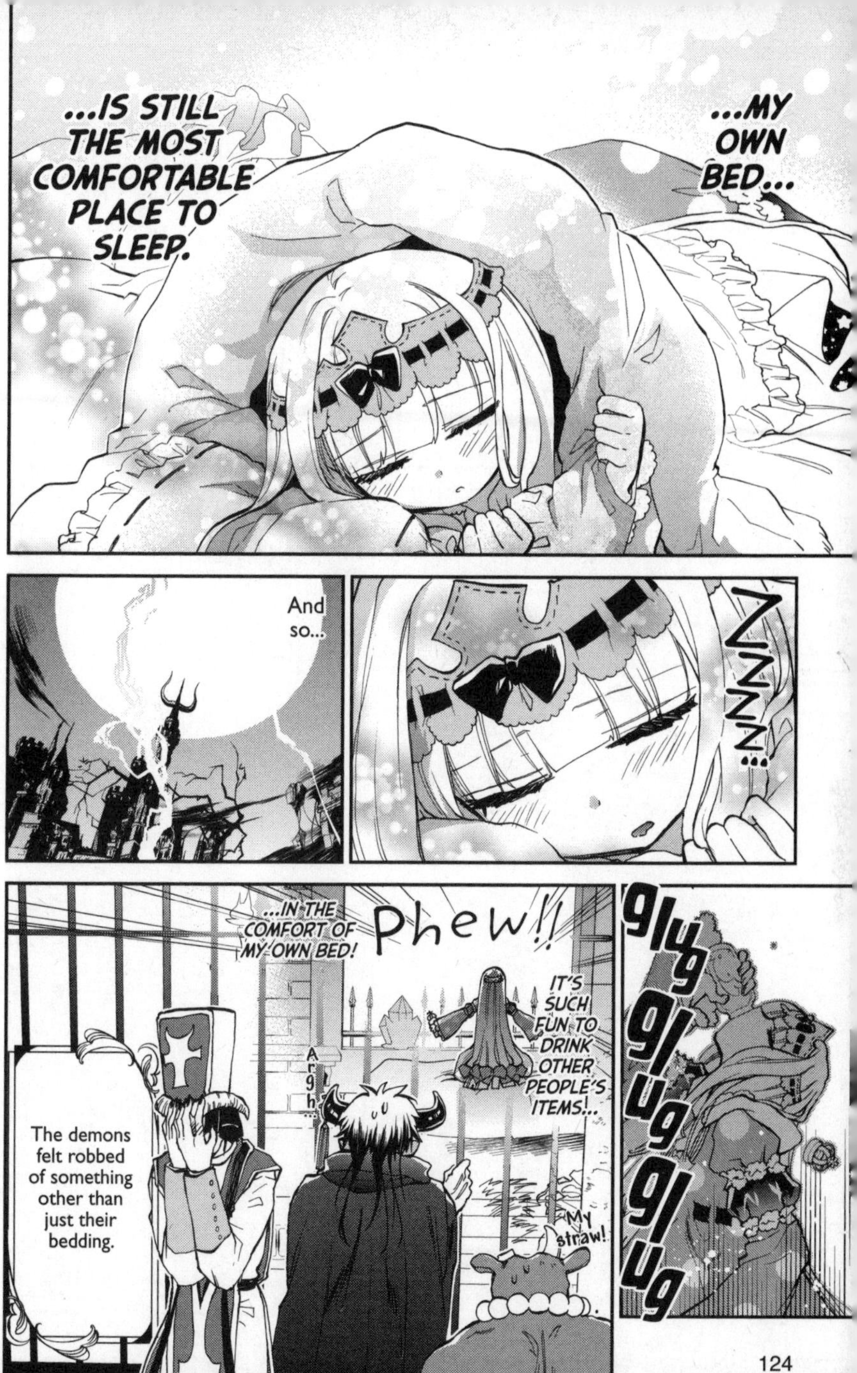
...MY OWN BED...
...IS STILL THE MOST COMFORTABLE PLACE TO SLEEP.
ZZZZ...
And so...
glug glug glug
...IN THE COMFORT OF MY OWN BED!
Phew!!
IT'S SUCH FUN TO DRINK OTHER PEOPLE'S ITEMS!...
Argh...
My straw!
The demons felt robbed of something other than just their bedding.

Castle Grunt Goblin

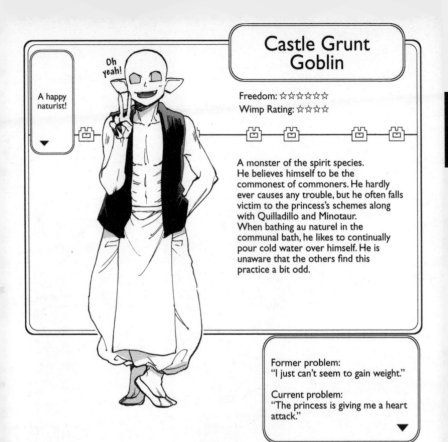

A happy naturist!

Oh yeah!

Freedom: ☆☆☆☆☆☆
Wimp Rating: ☆☆☆☆

A monster of the spirit species. He believes himself to be the commonest of commoners. He hardly ever causes any trouble, but he often falls victim to the princess's schemes along with Quilladillo and Minotaur. When bathing au naturel in the communal bath, he likes to continually pour cold water over himself. He is unaware that the others find this practice a bit odd.

Former problem:
"I just can't seem to gain weight."

Current problem:
"The princess is giving me a heart attack."

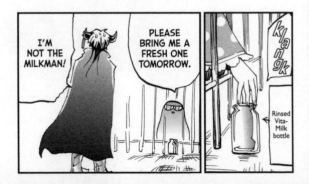

klangk
Rinsed Vita-Milk bottle
PLEASE BRING ME A FRESH ONE TOMORROW.
I'M NOT THE MILKMAN!

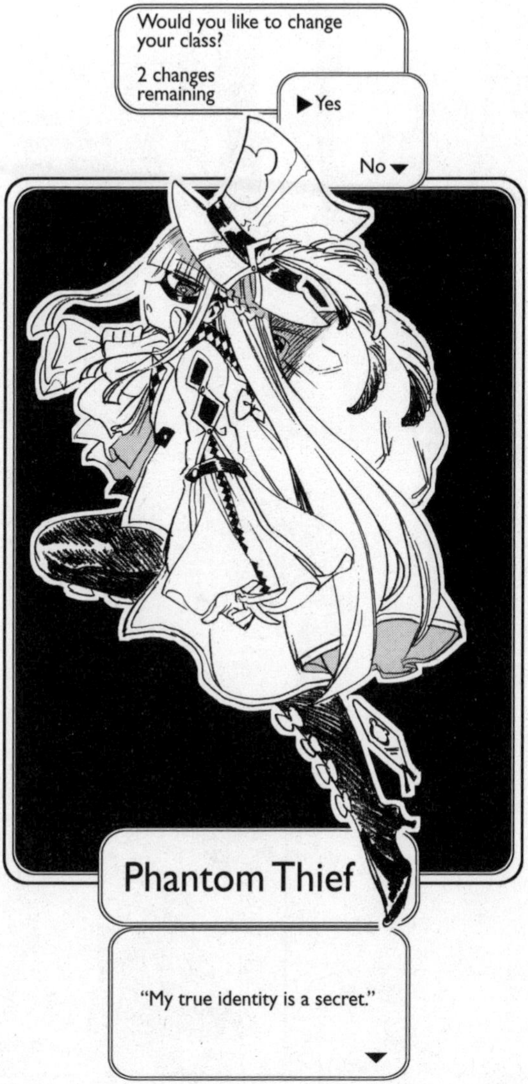
Would you like to change your class?
2 changes remaining
▶Yes
No
Phantom Thief
"My true identity is a secret."

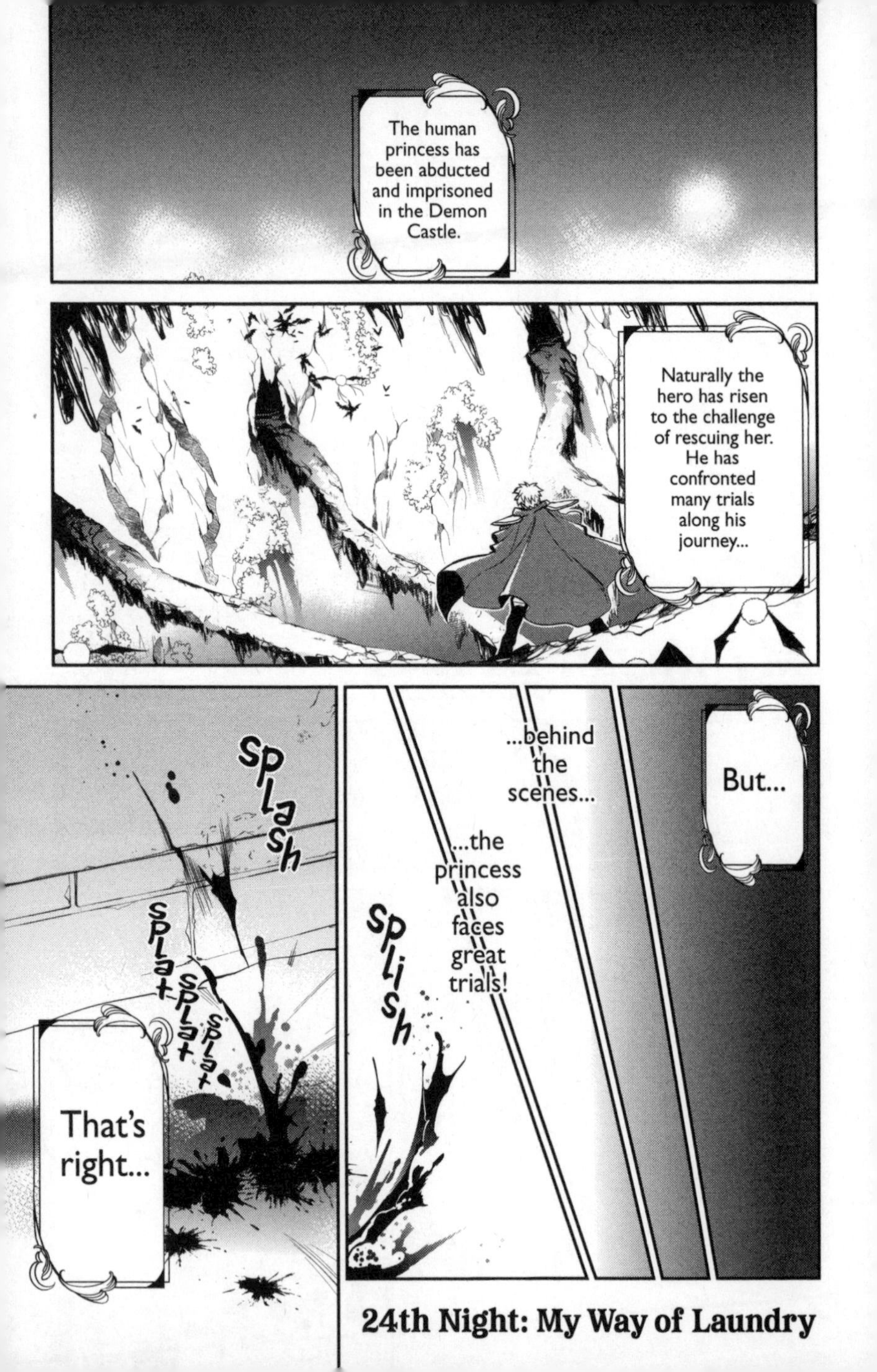
The human princess has been abducted and imprisoned in the Demon Castle.
Naturally the hero has risen to the challenge of rescuing her. He has confronted many trials along his journey...
But...
...behind the scenes...
...the princess also faces great trials!
Splish
Splash
Splat
Splat
Splat
That's right...

24th Night: My Way of Laundry

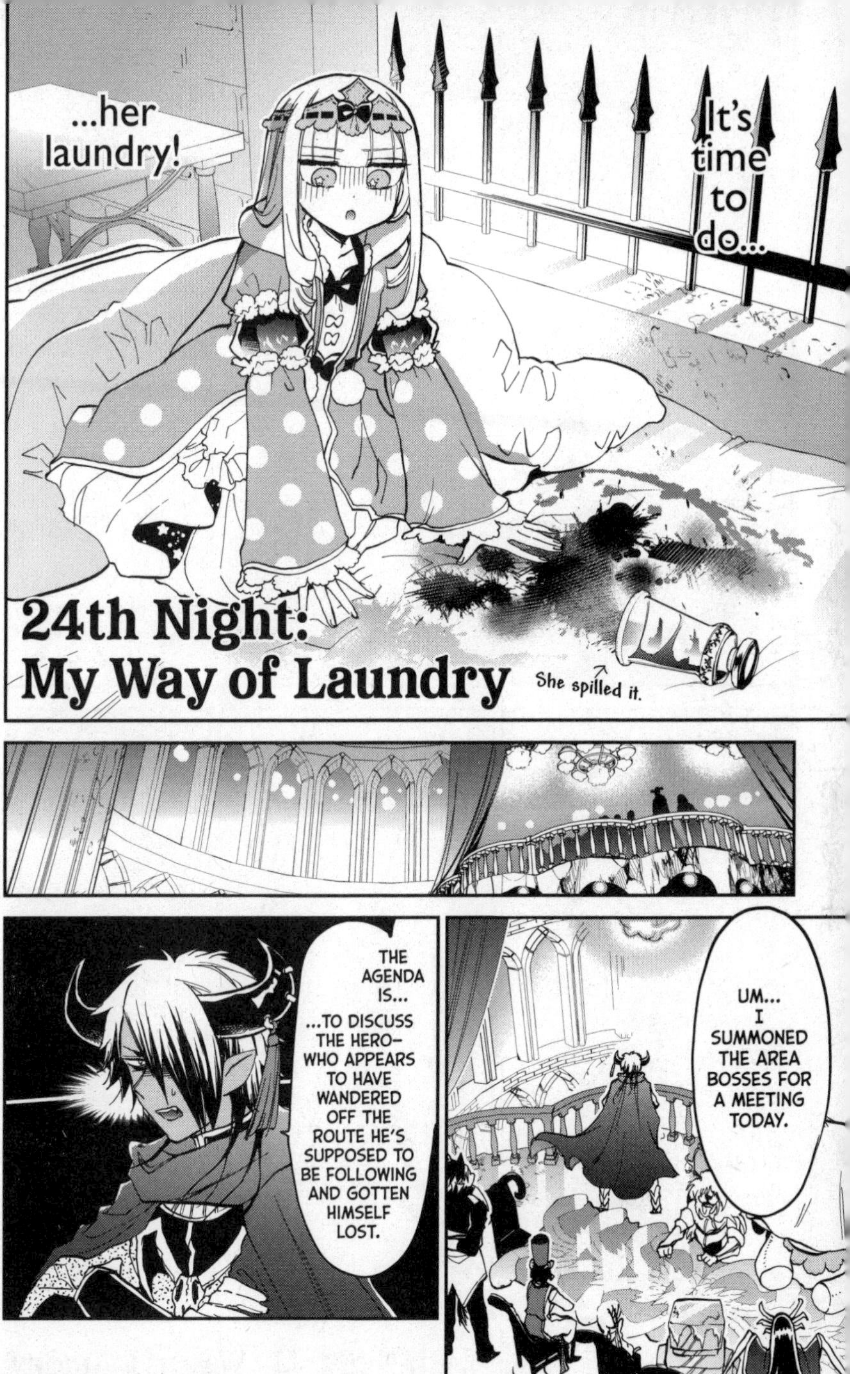
It's time to do...
...her laundry!
24th Night: My Way of Laundry
She spilled it.
UM... I SUMMONED THE AREA BOSSES FOR A MEETING TODAY.
THE AGENDA IS...
...TO DISCUSS THE HERO—WHO APPEARS TO HAVE WANDERED OFF THE ROUTE HE'S SUPPOSED TO BE FOLLOWING AND GOTTEN HIMSELF LOST.

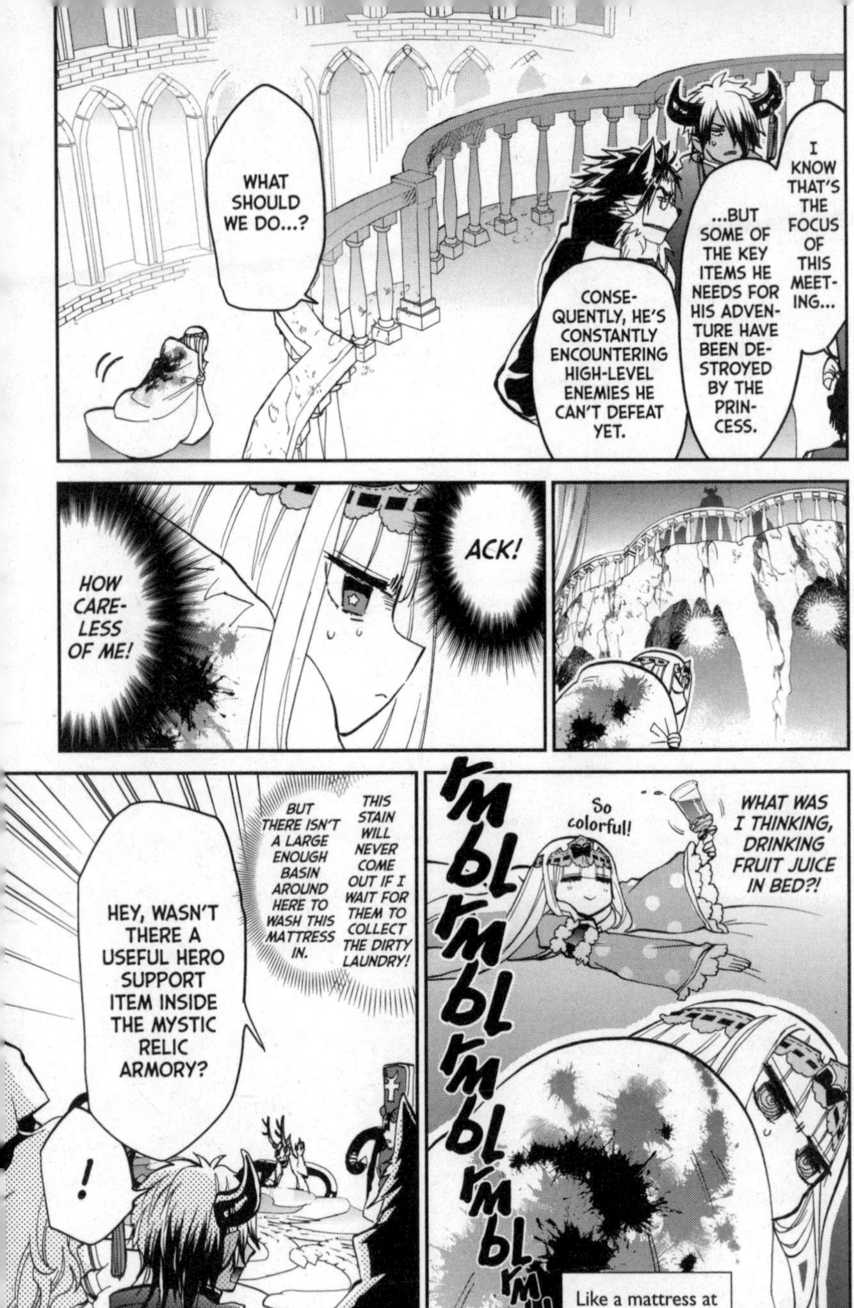
I KNOW THAT'S THE FOCUS OF THIS MEETING...
...BUT SOME OF THE KEY ITEMS HE NEEDS FOR HIS ADVENTURE HAVE BEEN DESTROYED BY THE PRINCESS.
CONSEQUENTLY, HE'S CONSTANTLY ENCOUNTERING HIGH-LEVEL ENEMIES HE CAN'T DEFEAT YET.
WHAT SHOULD WE DO...?
ACK!
HOW CARELESS OF ME!
WHAT WAS I THINKING, DRINKING FRUIT JUICE IN BED?!
So colorful!
rmbl rmbl rmbl rmbl rmbl rmbl
Like a mattress at a crime scene
THIS STAIN WILL NEVER COME OUT IF I WAIT FOR THEM TO COLLECT THE DIRTY LAUNDRY!
BUT THERE ISN'T A LARGE ENOUGH BASIN AROUND HERE TO WASH THIS MATTRESS IN.
HEY, WASN'T THERE A USEFUL HERO SUPPORT ITEM INSIDE THE MYSTIC RELIC ARMORY?
!

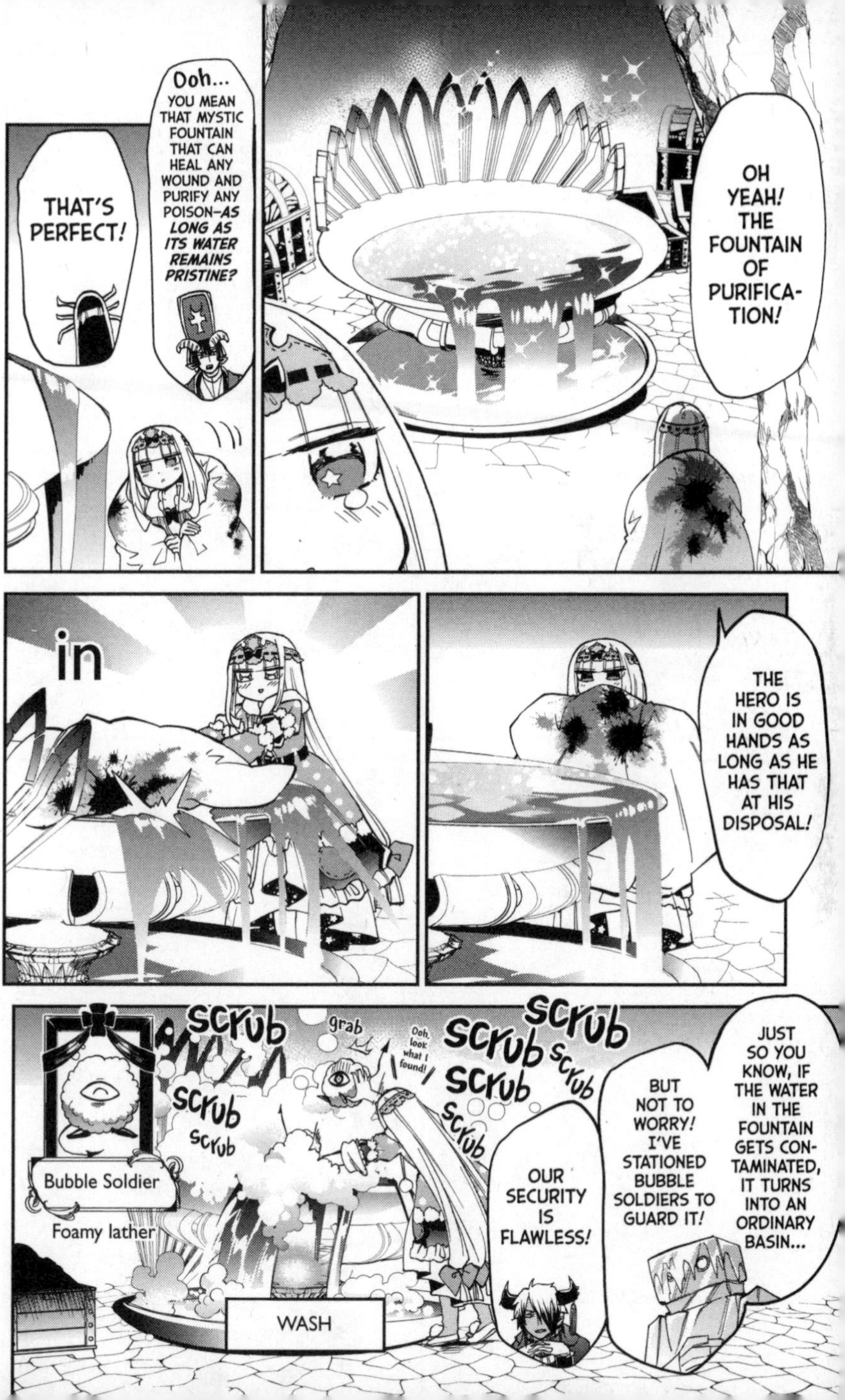
OH YEAH! THE FOUNTAIN OF PURIFICA-TION!
Ooh... YOU MEAN THAT MYSTIC FOUNTAIN THAT CAN HEAL ANY WOUND AND PURIFY ANY POISON—*AS LONG AS ITS WATER REMAINS PRISTINE?*
THAT'S PERFECT!
THE HERO IS IN GOOD HANDS AS LONG AS HE HAS THAT AT HIS DISPOSAL!
in
JUST SO YOU KNOW, IF THE WATER IN THE FOUNTAIN GETS CON-TAMINATED, IT TURNS INTO AN ORDINARY BASIN...
BUT NOT TO WORRY! I'VE STATIONED BUBBLE SOLDIERS TO GUARD IT!
OUR SECURITY IS FLAWLESS!
scrub
scrub
scrub
scrub
scrub
Ooh, look what I found!
grab
scrub
scrub
scrub
Bubble Soldier
Foamy lather
WASH

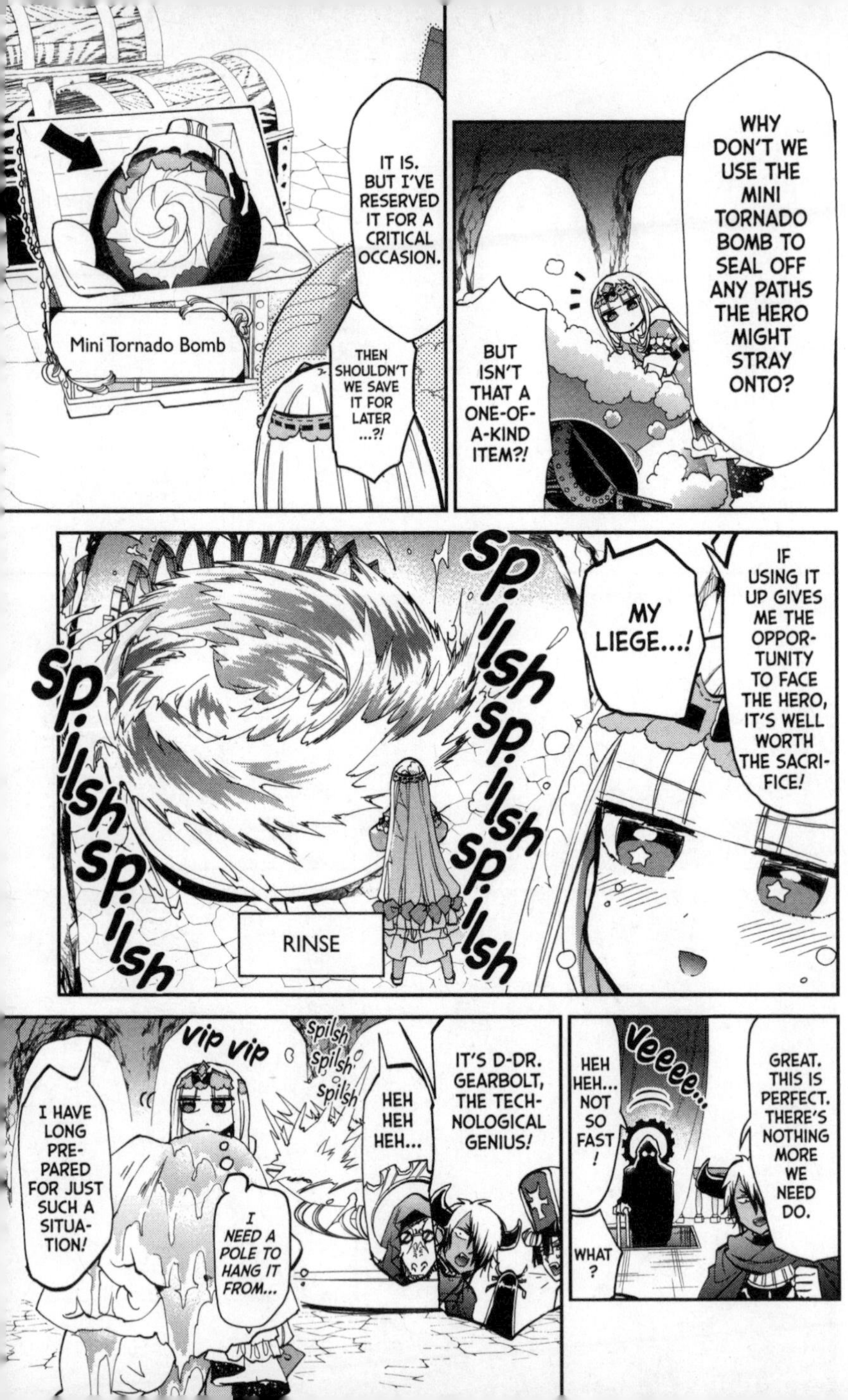
WHY DON'T WE USE THE MINI TORNADO BOMB TO SEAL OFF ANY PATHS THE HERO MIGHT STRAY ONTO?
BUT ISN'T THAT A ONE-OF-A-KIND ITEM?!
IT IS. BUT I'VE RESERVED IT FOR A CRITICAL OCCASION.
THEN SHOULDN'T WE SAVE IT FOR LATER ...?!
Mini Tornado Bomb
IF USING IT UP GIVES ME THE OPPORTUNITY TO FACE THE HERO, IT'S WELL WORTH THE SACRIFICE!
MY LIEGE...!
spilish spilish spilish spilish
RINSE
spilish spilish
GREAT. THIS IS PERFECT. THERE'S NOTHING MORE WE NEED DO.
veeee...
HEH HEH... NOT SO FAST!
WHAT?
IT'S D-DR. GEARBOLT, THE TECHNOLOGICAL GENIUS!
HEH HEH HEH...
spilsh spilsh spilsh
vip vip
I HAVE LONG PREPARED FOR JUST SUCH A SITUATION!
I NEED A POLE TO HANG IT FROM...

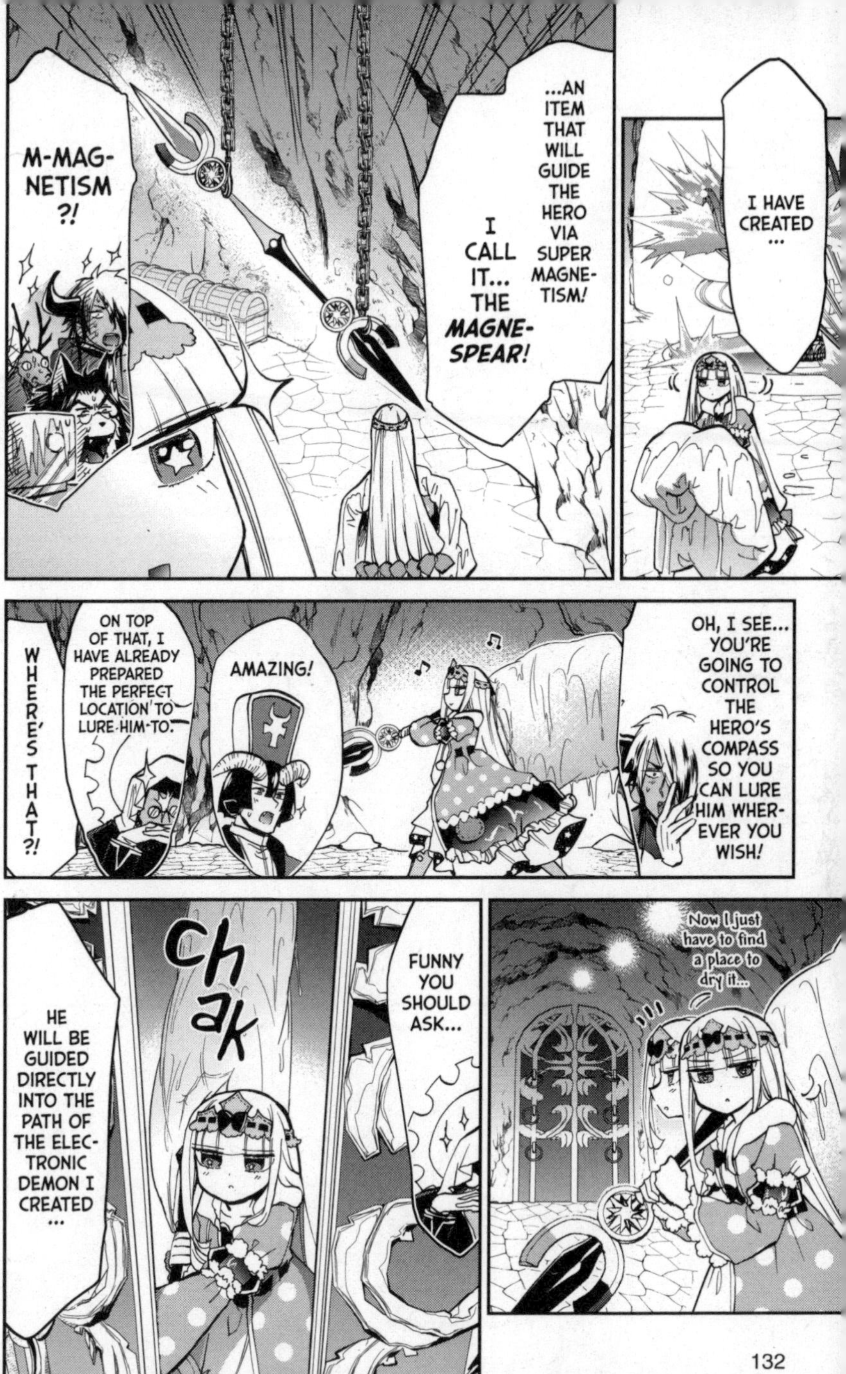
I HAVE CREATED ...
...AN ITEM THAT WILL GUIDE THE HERO VIA SUPER MAGNETISM!
I CALL IT... THE MAGNE-SPEAR!
M-MAGNETISM?!
OH, I SEE... YOU'RE GOING TO CONTROL THE HERO'S COMPASS SO YOU CAN LURE HIM WHEREVER YOU WISH!
AMAZING!
ON TOP OF THAT, I HAVE ALREADY PREPARED THE PERFECT LOCATION TO LURE HIM TO.
WHERE'S THAT?!
Now I just have to find a place to dry it...
FUNNY YOU SHOULD ASK...
chak
HE WILL BE GUIDED DIRECTLY INTO THE PATH OF THE ELECTRONIC DEMON I CREATED ...

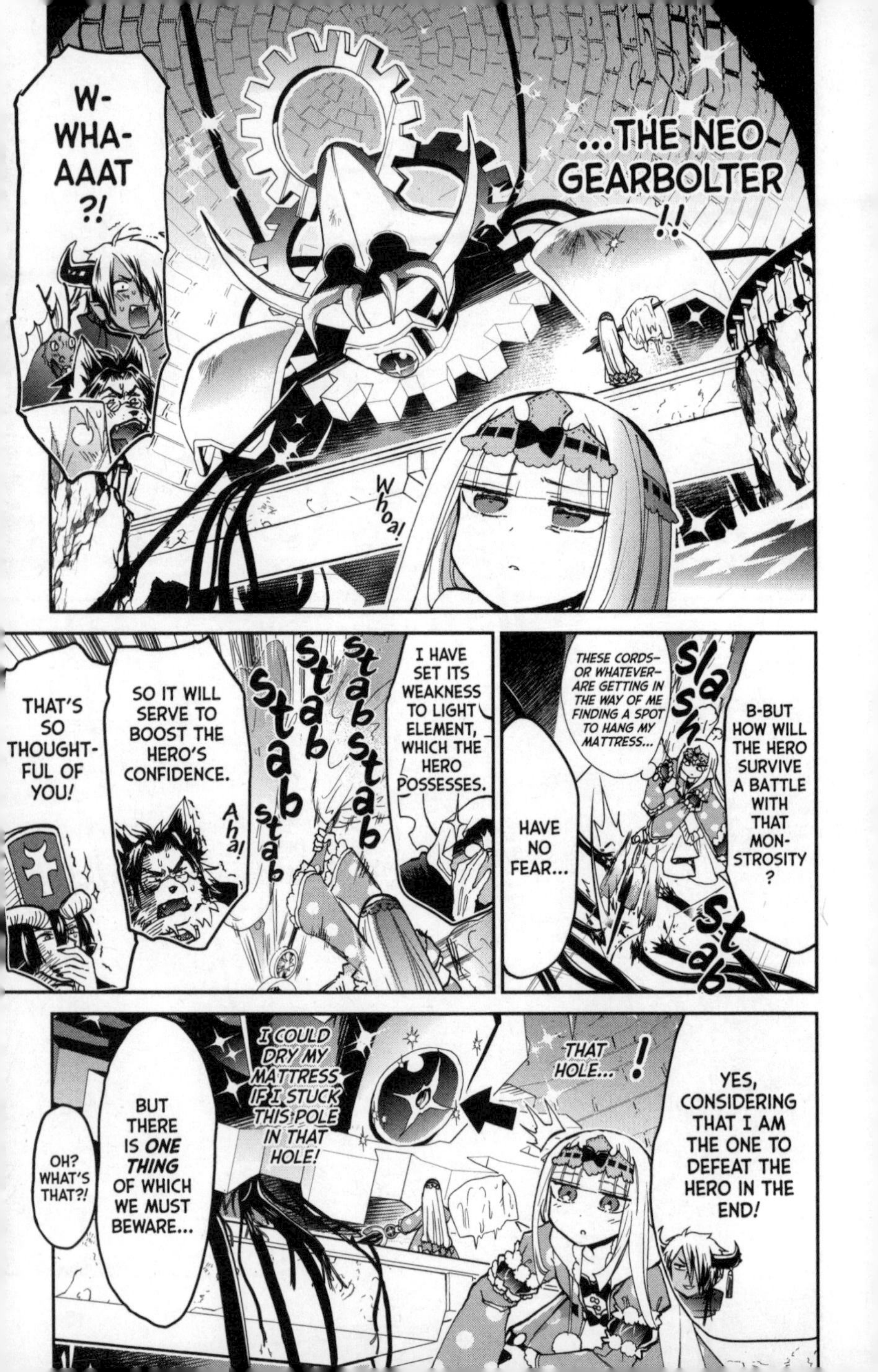
...THE NEO GEARBOLTER!!
W-WHA-AAAT?!
Whoa!
B-BUT HOW WILL THE HERO SURVIVE A BATTLE WITH THAT MONSTROSITY?
Slash
THESE CORDS—OR WHATEVER—ARE GETTING IN THE WAY OF ME FINDING A SPOT TO HANG MY MATTRESS...
HAVE NO FEAR...
Stab
I HAVE SET ITS WEAKNESS TO LIGHT ELEMENT, WHICH THE HERO POSSESSES.
stab stab stab
stab
stab
stab
SO IT WILL SERVE TO BOOST THE HERO'S CONFIDENCE.
Aha!
THAT'S SO THOUGHTFUL OF YOU!
YES, CONSIDERING THAT I AM THE ONE TO DEFEAT THE HERO IN THE END!
THAT HOLE... !
I COULD DRY MY MATTRESS IF I STUCK THIS POLE IN THAT HOLE!
BUT THERE IS *ONE THING* OF WHICH WE MUST BEWARE...
OH? WHAT'S THAT?!

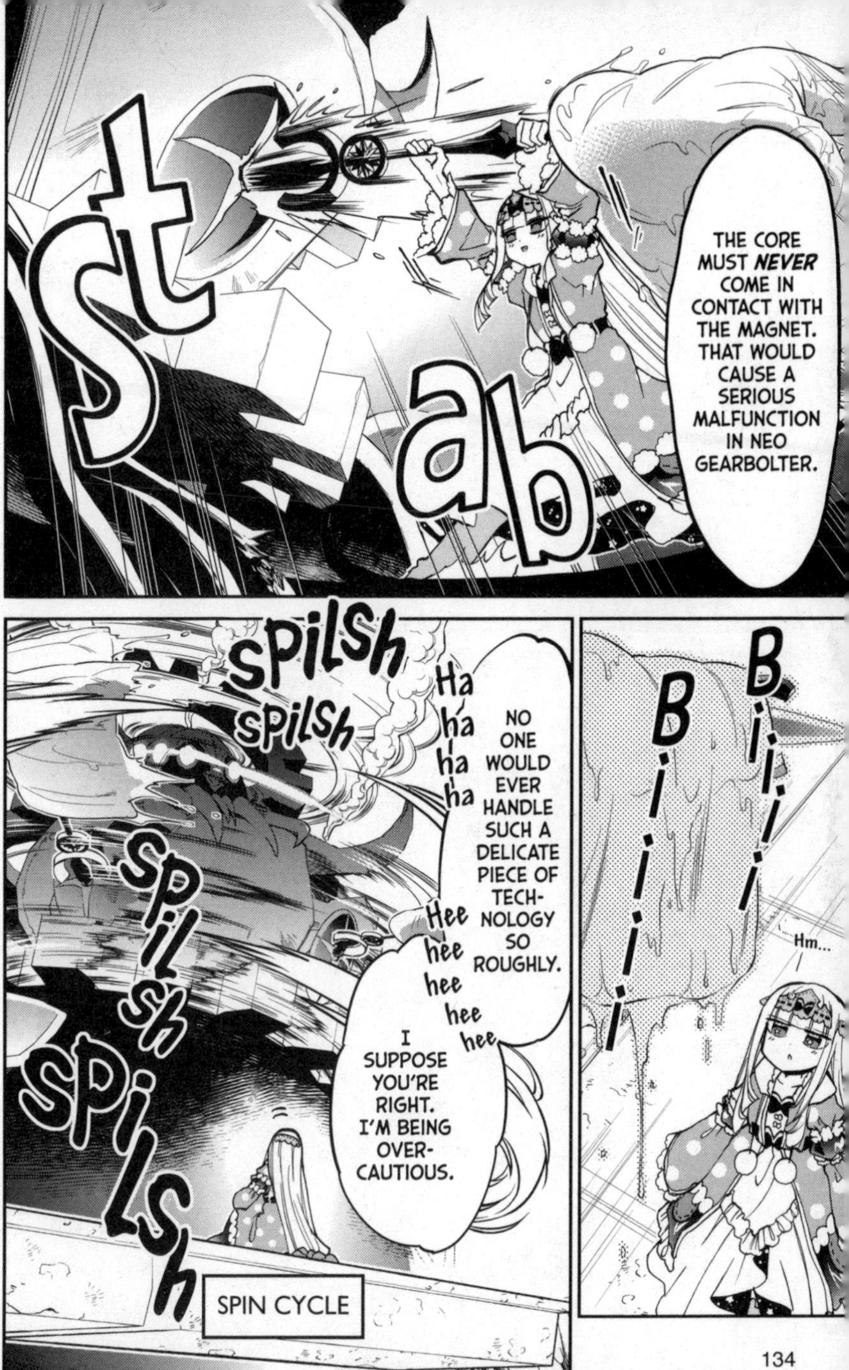
THE CORE MUST *NEVER* COME IN CONTACT WITH THE MAGNET. THAT WOULD CAUSE A SERIOUS MALFUNCTION IN NEO GEARBOLTER.
stab
B
B
Hm...
NO ONE WOULD EVER HANDLE SUCH A DELICATE PIECE OF TECH-NOLOGY SO ROUGHLY.
Ha ha ha ha
Hee hee hee hee hee
spilsh spilsh
spilsh spilsh
I SUPPOSE YOU'RE RIGHT. I'M BEING OVER-CAUTIOUS.
SPIN CYCLE

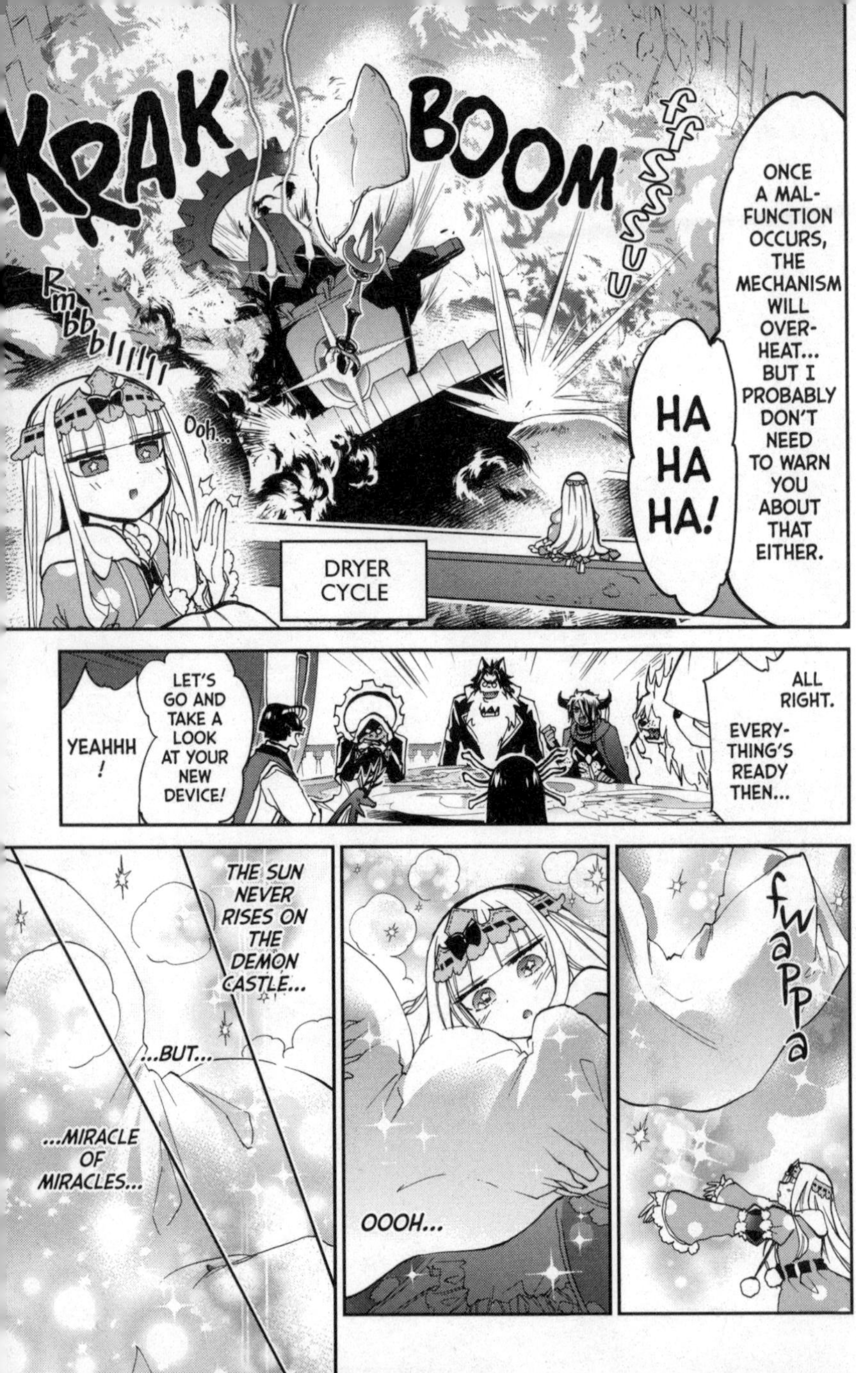
ONCE A MAL-FUNCTION OCCURS, THE MECHANISM WILL OVER-HEAT... BUT I PROBABLY DON'T NEED TO WARN YOU ABOUT THAT EITHER.
HA HA HA!
ffsssuuu
BOOM
KRAK
Rmbbblllll
Ooh...
DRYER CYCLE
ALL RIGHT.
EVERY-THING'S READY THEN...
LET'S GO AND TAKE A LOOK AT YOUR NEW DEVICE!
YEAHHH!
fwappa
OOOH...
THE SUN NEVER RISES ON THE DEMON CASTLE...
...BUT...
...MIRACLE OF MIRACLES...

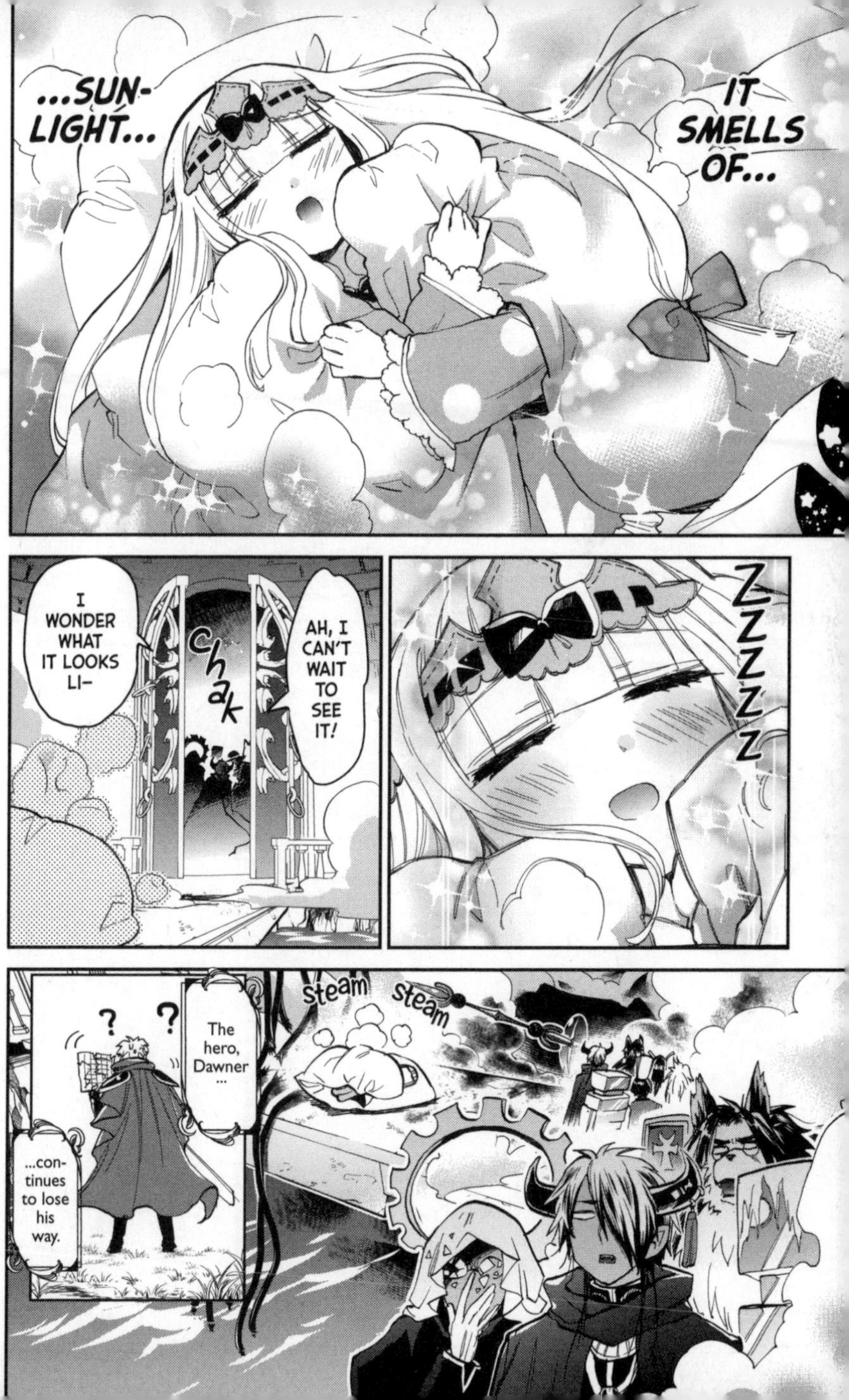
IT SMELLS OF...
...SUN-LIGHT...
ZZZZZZ
AH, I CAN'T WAIT TO SEE IT!
chak
I WONDER WHAT IT LOOKS LI–
steam
steam
? ?
The hero, Dawner ...
...con-tinues to lose his way.

Neo Gearbolter

Spilsh spilsh kraka-doom.

Emotions: —

Sturdiness: ☆☆☆☆

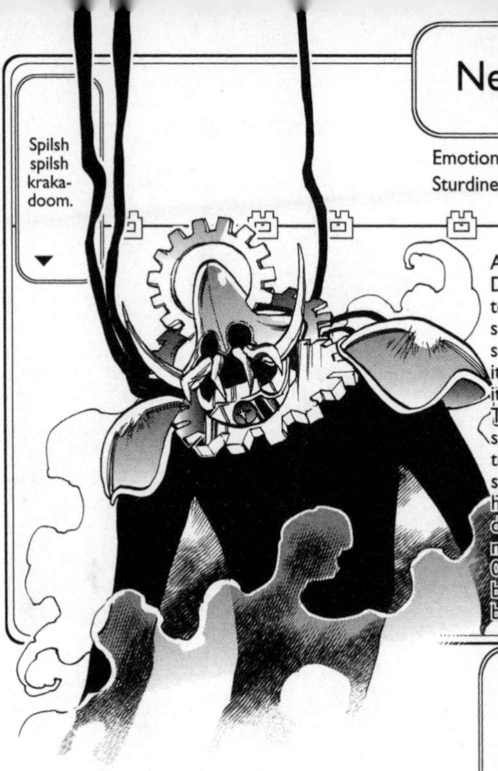

A mechanical demon created by Dr. Gearbolt. Although it is referred to as a demon, it has no emotions, so it's closer to a plant. Energy is supplied to it through the pipe on its back. Dr. Gearbolt claims that it can continue to grow forever. There is a risk of it malfunctioning, so it wears a restraint on its body to both prevent accidents and stop it from growing too large. It has basically been created to be defeated by Dawner, so they only need one, but in addition to Unit 00, which the Princess destroyed, backup Units 01 and 02 have also been secretly created.

Former problem:
"—"

Current problem:
"—"

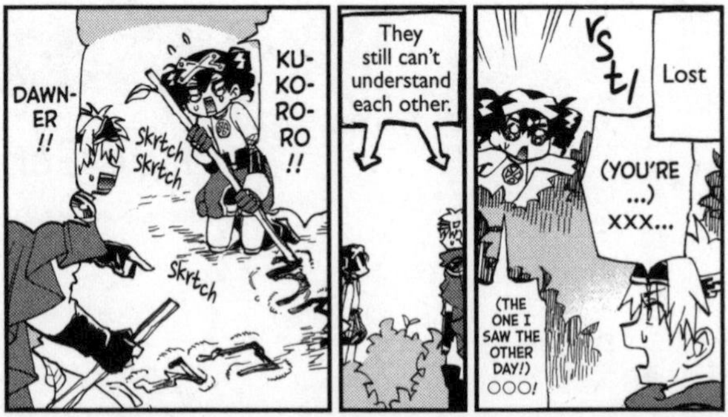
Lost
rs t/
(YOU'RE ...) XXX...
(THE ONE I SAW THE OTHER DAY!) OOO!
They still can't understand each other.
KU-KO-RO-RO!!
Skrtch Skrtch
DAWN-ER!!
Skrtch

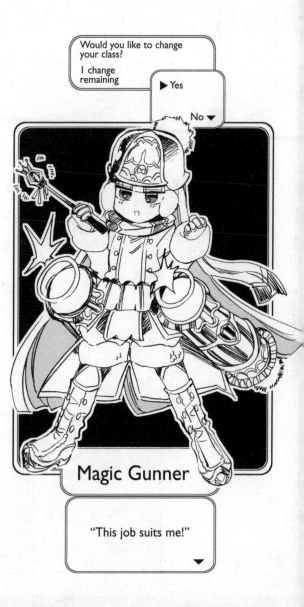

Would you like to change your class?

I change remaining

▶ Yes

No ▼

Magic Gunner

"This job suits me!"

▼

25th Night: From Cradle to Grave

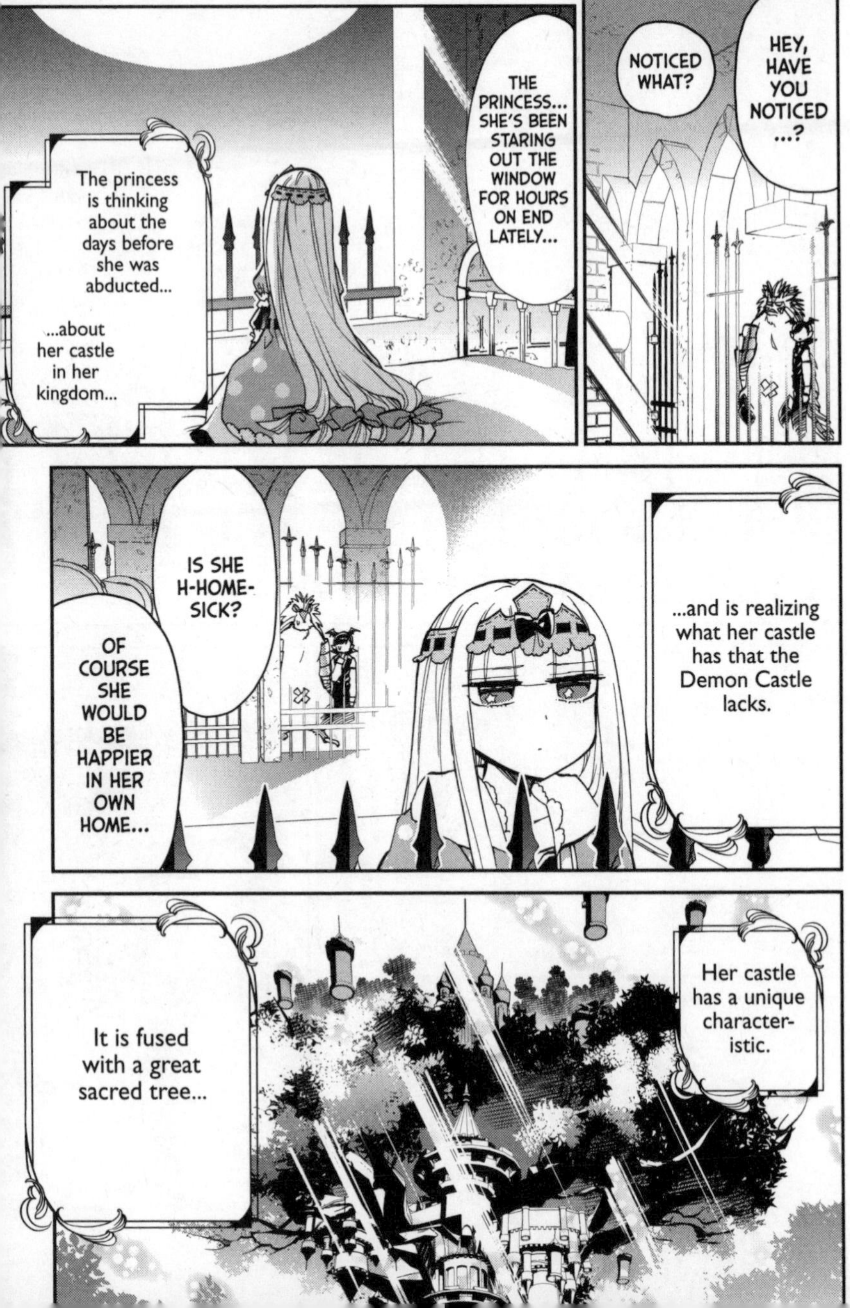
HEY, HAVE YOU NOTICED ...?
NOTICED WHAT?
THE PRINCESS... SHE'S BEEN STARING OUT THE WINDOW FOR HOURS ON END LATELY...
The princess is thinking about the days before she was abducted...
...about her castle in her kingdom...
...and is realizing what her castle has that the Demon Castle lacks.
IS SHE H-HOME-SICK?
OF COURSE SHE WOULD BE HAPPIER IN HER OWN HOME...
Her castle has a unique character-istic.
It is fused with a great sacred tree...

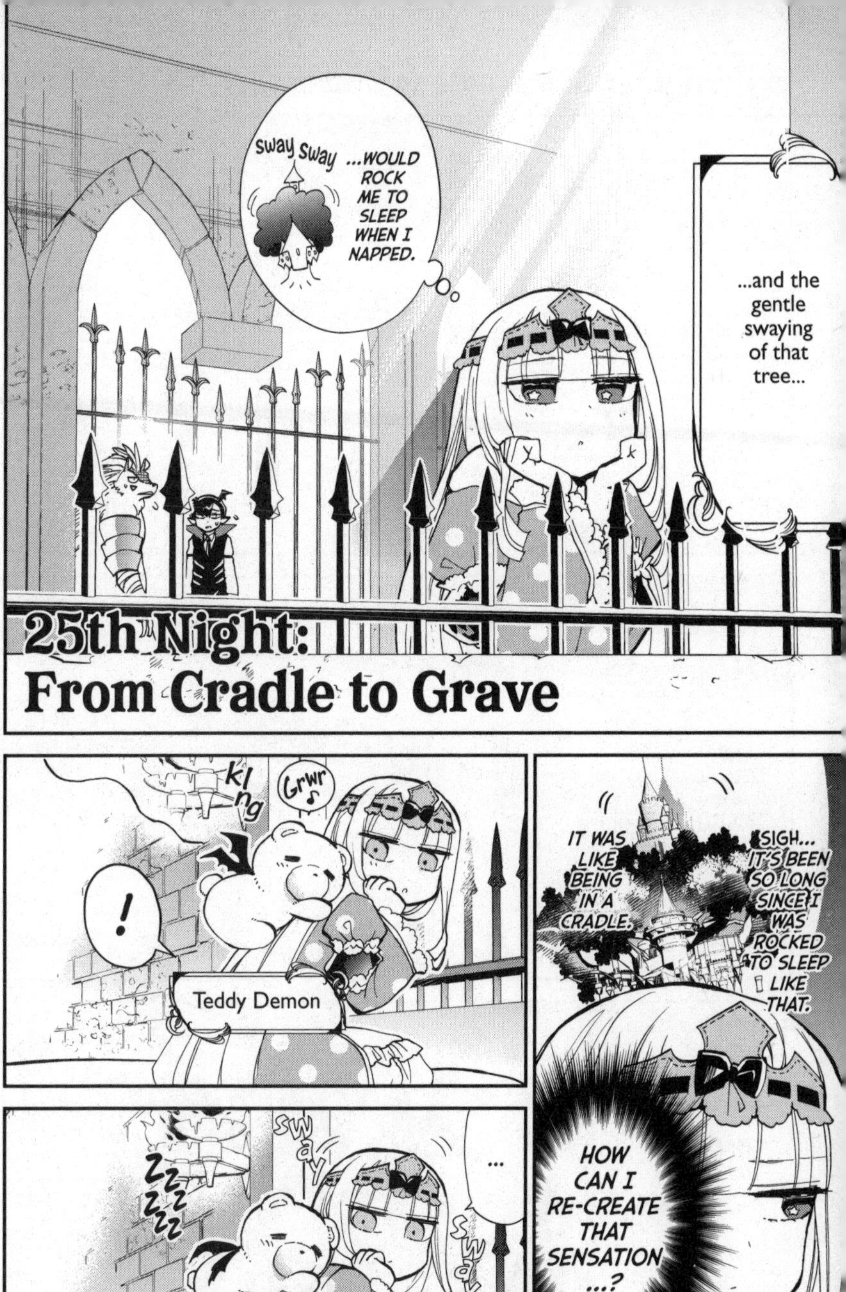
...and the gentle swaying of that tree...
sway sway
...WOULD ROCK ME TO SLEEP WHEN I NAPPED.
25th Night:
From Cradle to Grave
SIGH... IT'S BEEN SO LONG SINCE I WAS ROCKED TO SLEEP LIKE THAT.
IT WAS LIKE BEING IN A CRADLE.
HOW CAN I RE-CREATE THAT SENSATION ...?
kling
Grwr ♪
!
Teddy Demon
...
sway
sway
ZZZZZZ

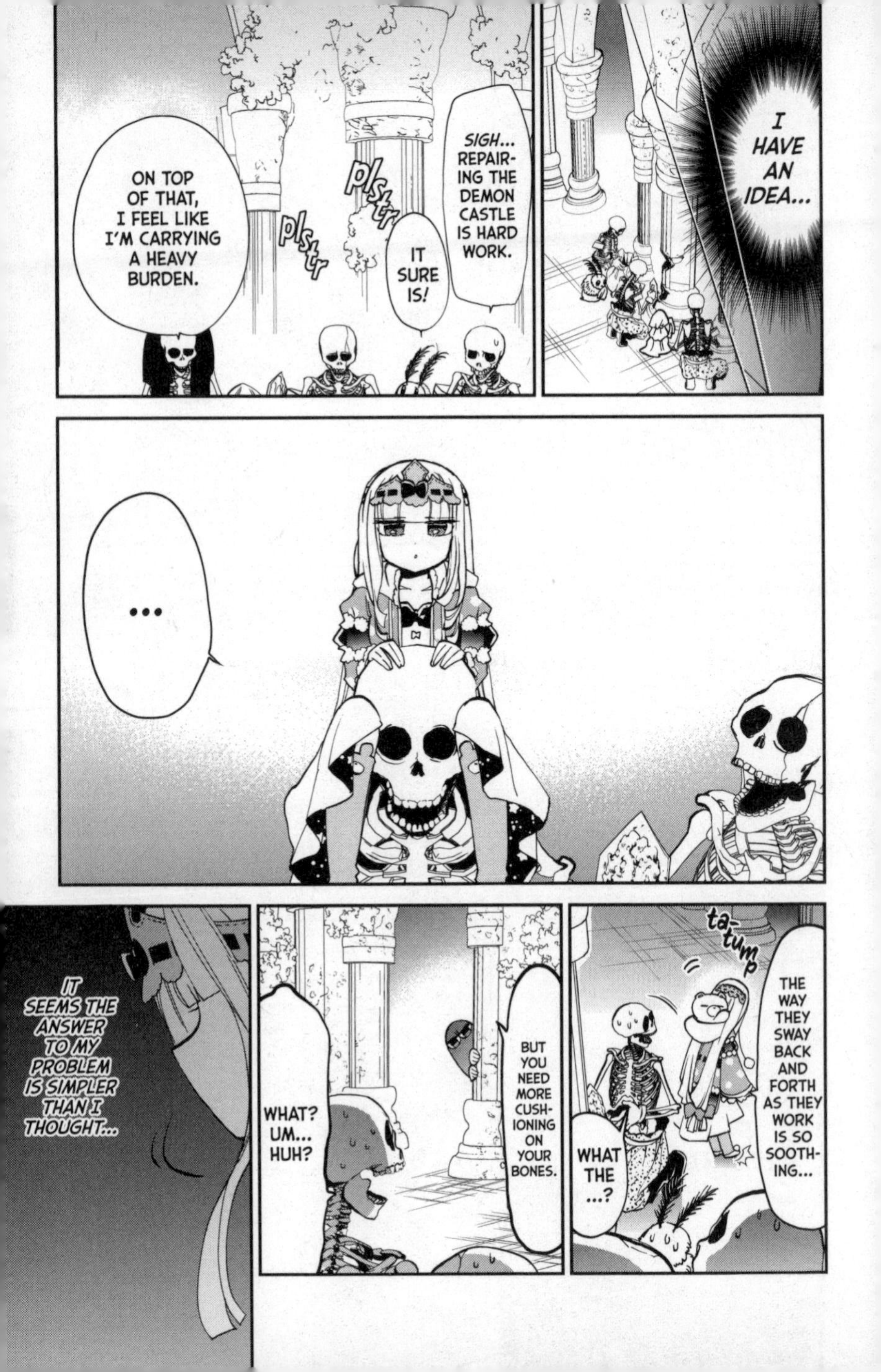
I HAVE AN IDEA...
SIGH... REPAIR-ING THE DEMON CASTLE IS HARD WORK.
IT SURE IS!
plstr
plstr
ON TOP OF THAT, I FEEL LIKE I'M CARRYING A HEAVY BURDEN.
...
ta-tump
THE WAY THEY SWAY BACK AND FORTH AS THEY WORK IS SO SOOTH-ING...
WHAT THE ...?
BUT YOU NEED MORE CUSH-IONING ON YOUR BONES.
WHAT? UM... HUH?
IT SEEMS THE ANSWER TO MY PROBLEM IS SIMPLER THAN I THOUGHT...

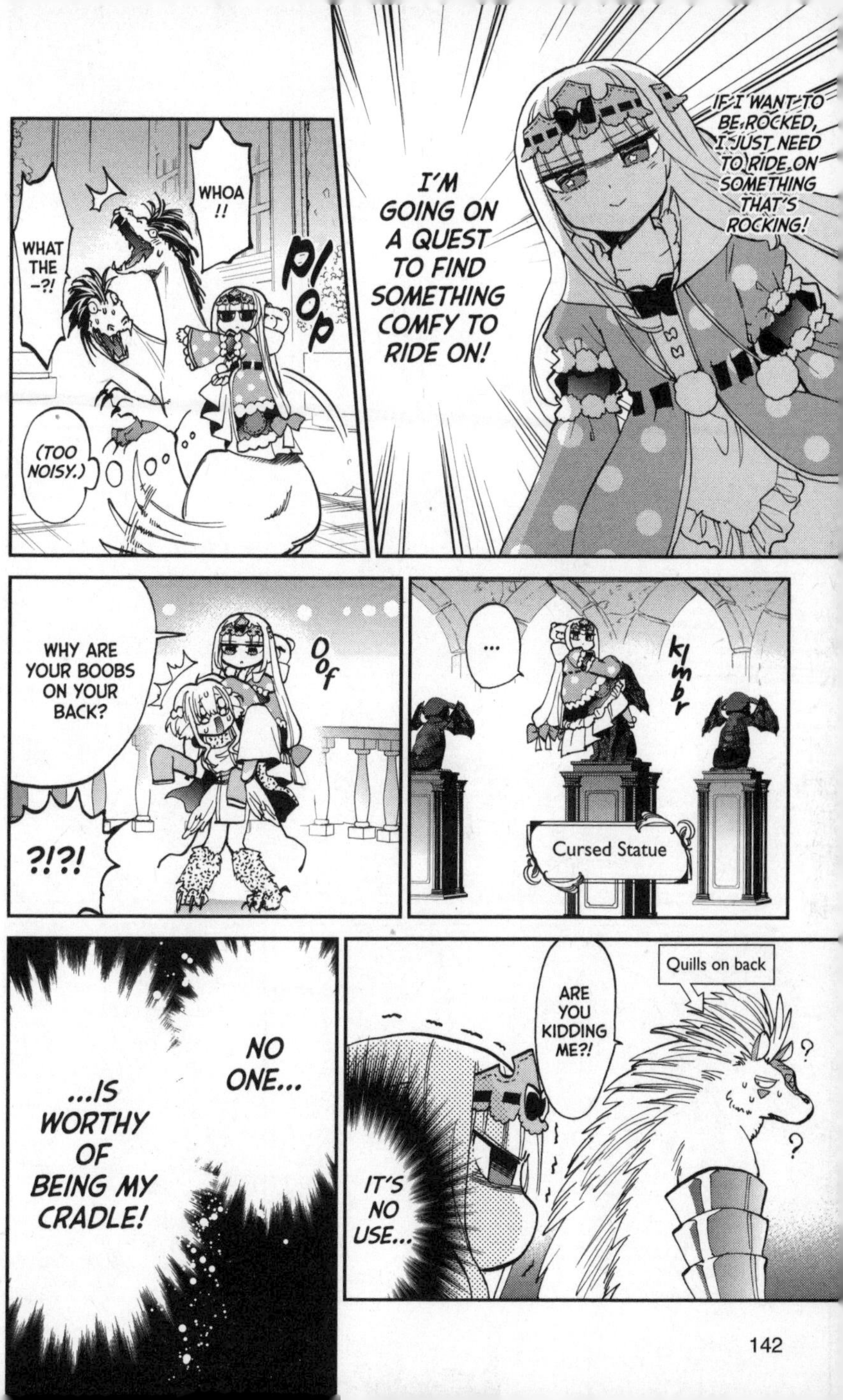
IF I WANT TO BE ROCKED, I JUST NEED TO RIDE ON SOMETHING THAT'S ROCKING!
I'M GOING ON A QUEST TO FIND SOMETHING COMFY TO RIDE ON!
WHOA!!
WHAT THE—?!
plop
(TOO NOISY.)
...
klmbr
Cursed Statue
Oof
WHY ARE YOUR BOOBS ON YOUR BACK?
?!?!
Quills on back
ARE YOU KIDDING ME?!
IT'S NO USE...
NO ONE...
...IS WORTHY OF BEING MY CRADLE!

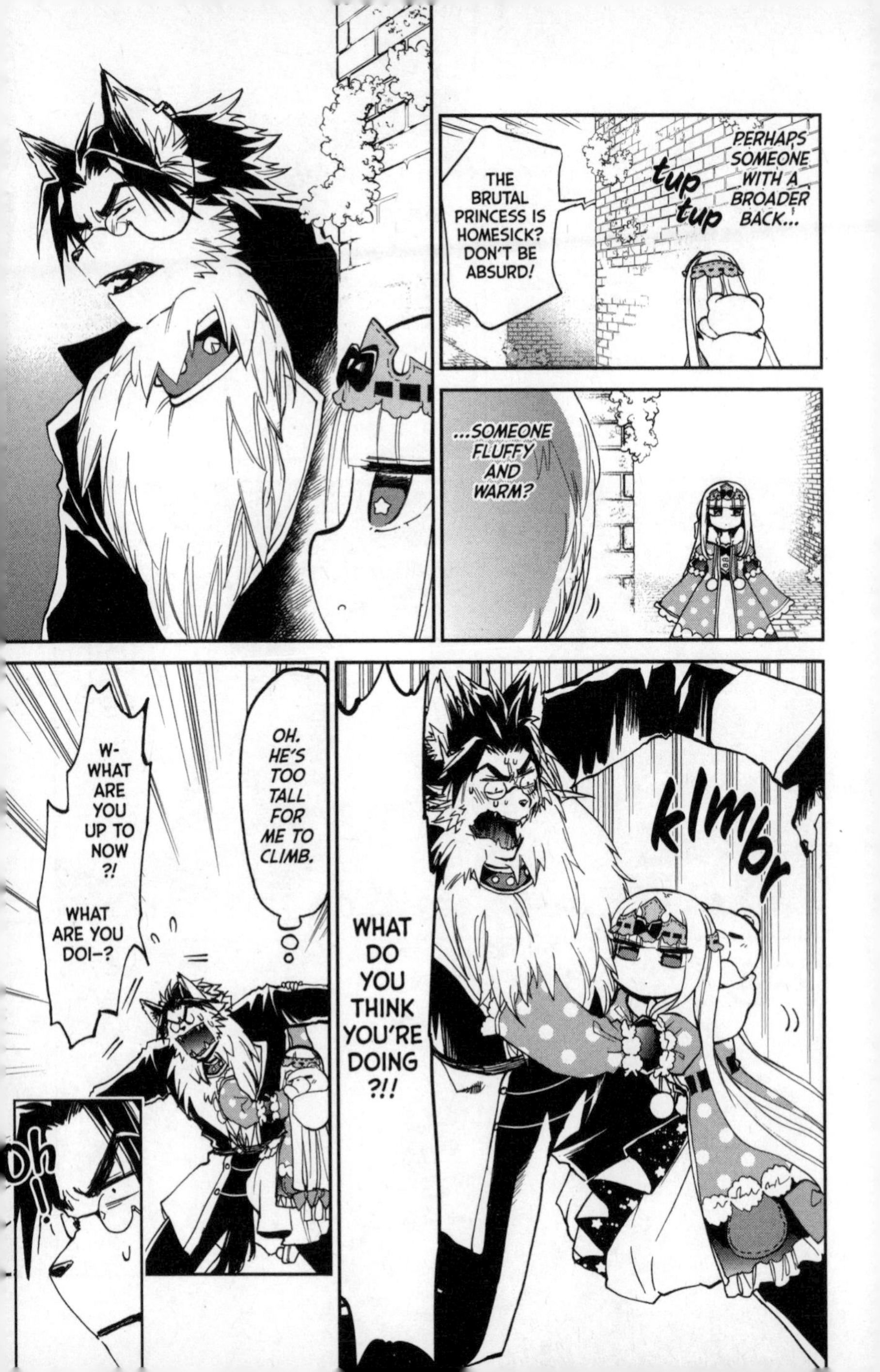
PERHAPS SOMEONE WITH A BROADER BACK...
tup tup
THE BRUTAL PRINCESS IS HOMESICK? DON'T BE ABSURD!
...SOMEONE FLUFFY AND WARM?
klmbr
WHAT DO YOU THINK YOU'RE DOING?!!
OH. HE'S TOO TALL FOR ME TO CLIMB.
W- WHAT ARE YOU UP TO NOW?!
WHAT ARE YOU DOI-?
Oh!

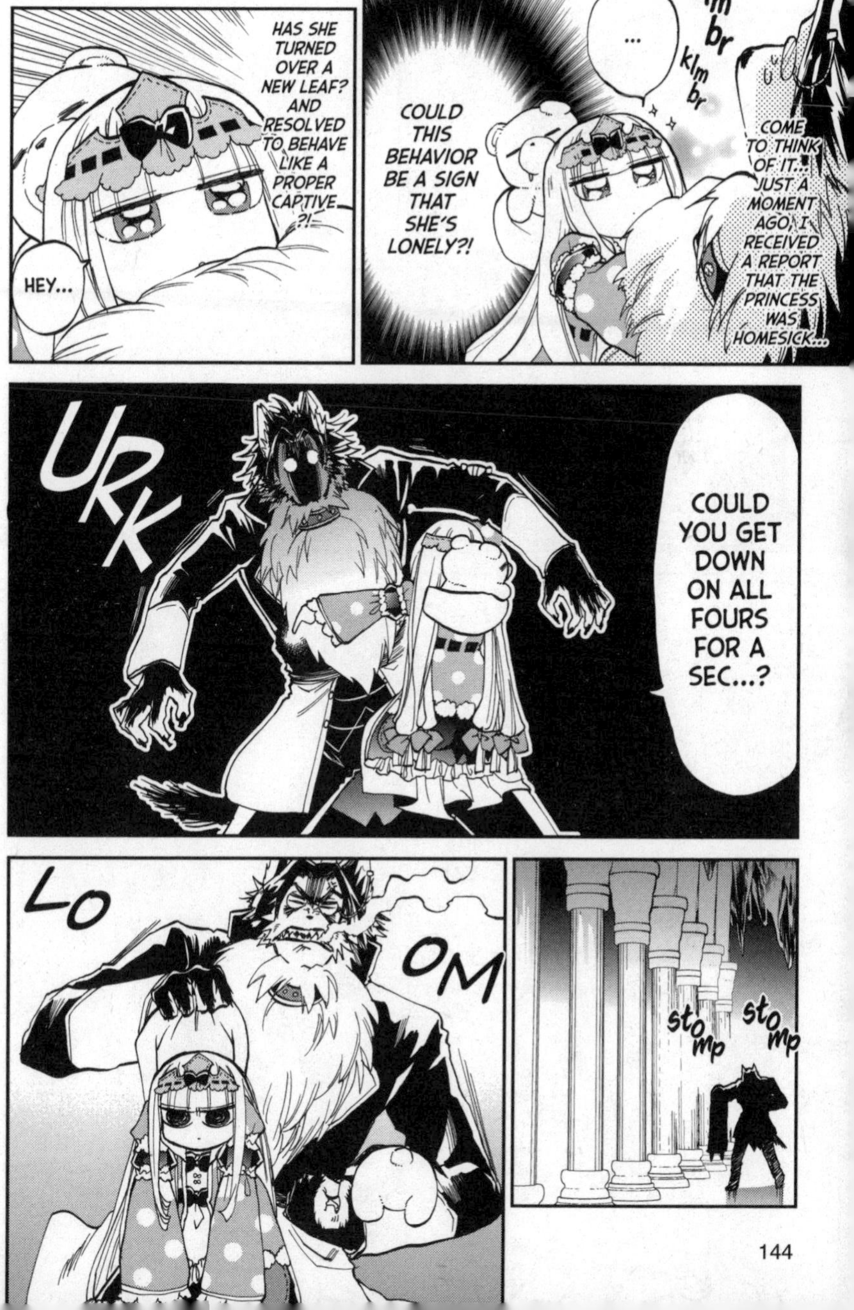
klm br klm br
...
COME TO THINK OF IT... JUST A MOMENT AGO, I RECEIVED A REPORT THAT THE PRINCESS WAS HOMESICK...
COULD THIS BEHAVIOR BE A SIGN THAT SHE'S LONELY?!
HAS SHE TURNED OVER A NEW LEAF? AND RESOLVED TO BEHAVE LIKE A PROPER CAPTIVE?!
HEY...
COULD YOU GET DOWN ON ALL FOURS FOR A SEC...?
URK
stomp stomp
LOOM

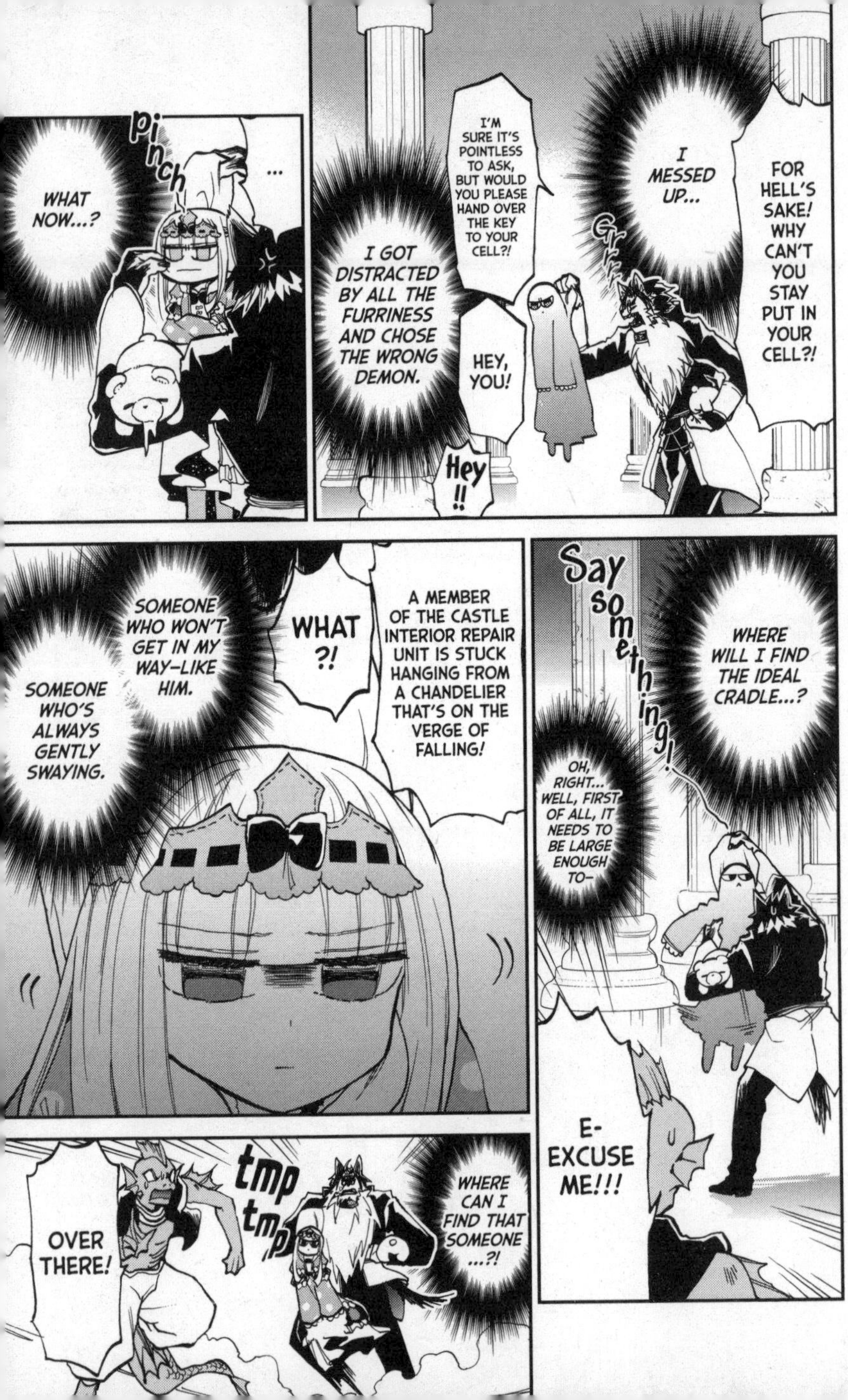
FOR HELL'S SAKE! WHY CAN'T YOU STAY PUT IN YOUR CELL?!
I MESSED UP...
Grrr
I'M SURE IT'S POINTLESS TO ASK, BUT WOULD YOU PLEASE HAND OVER THE KEY TO YOUR CELL?!
I GOT DISTRACTED BY ALL THE FURRINESS AND CHOSE THE WRONG DEMON.
HEY, YOU!
Hey!!
pinch
...
WHAT NOW...?
Say something!
WHERE WILL I FIND THE IDEAL CRADLE...?
OH, RIGHT... WELL, FIRST OF ALL, IT NEEDS TO BE LARGE ENOUGH TO–
E-EXCUSE ME!!!
A MEMBER OF THE CASTLE INTERIOR REPAIR UNIT IS STUCK HANGING FROM A CHANDELIER THAT'S ON THE VERGE OF FALLING!
WHAT?!
SOMEONE WHO WON'T GET IN MY WAY–LIKE HIM.
SOMEONE WHO'S ALWAYS GENTLY SWAYING.
WHERE CAN I FIND THAT SOMEONE...?!
tmp tmp
OVER THERE!

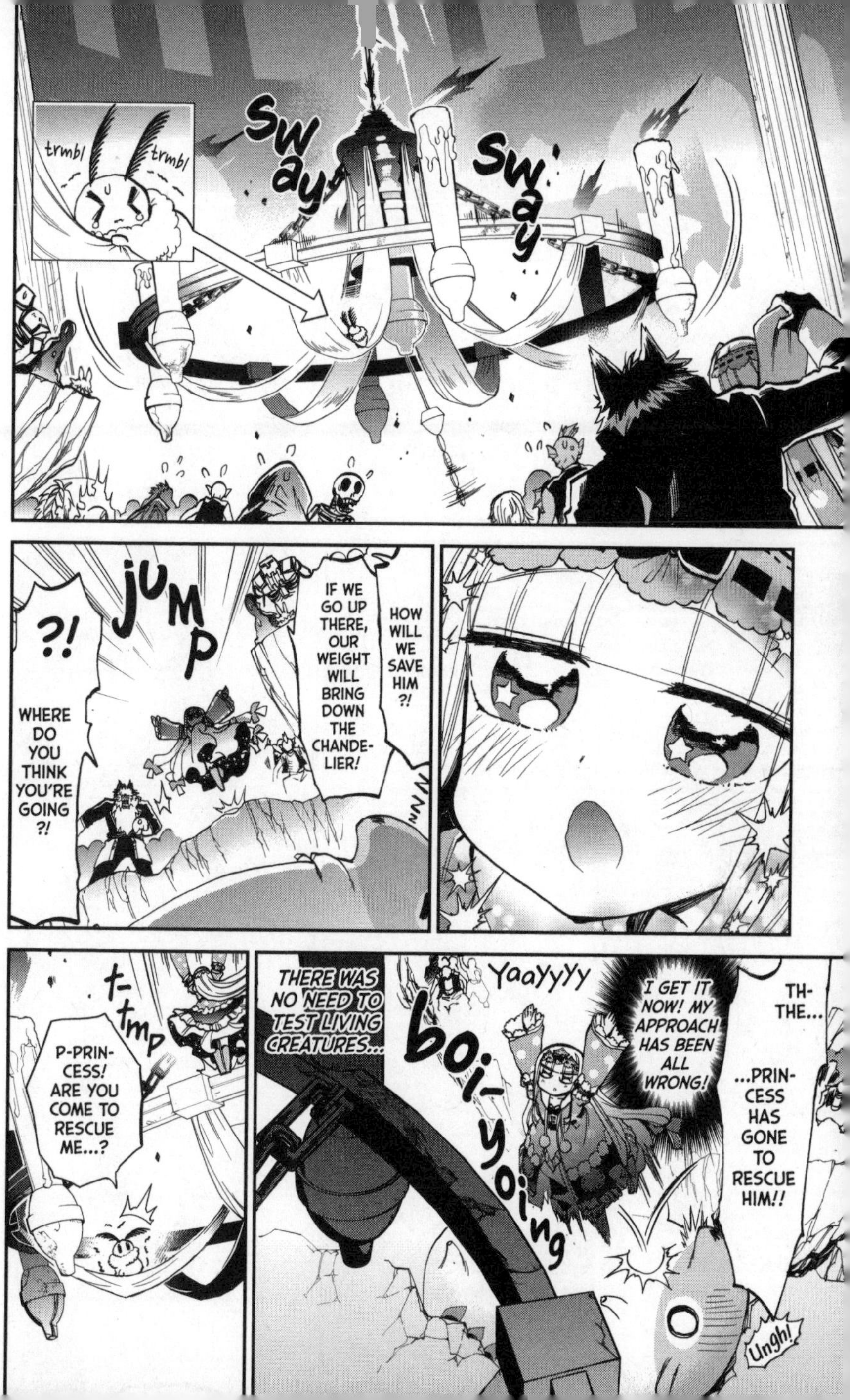
Sway
Sway
trmbl
trmbl
HOW WILL WE SAVE HIM?!
IF WE GO UP THERE, OUR WEIGHT WILL BRING DOWN THE CHANDELIER!
JUMP
?!
WHERE DO YOU THINK YOU'RE GOING?!
NNN
TH-THE...
...PRINCESS HAS GONE TO RESCUE HIM!!
I GET IT NOW! MY APPROACH HAS BEEN ALL WRONG!
Yaayyyy
THERE WAS NO NEED TO TEST LIVING CREATURES...
boi-yoing
Ungh!
t-tmp
P-PRINCESS! ARE YOU COME TO RESCUE ME...?

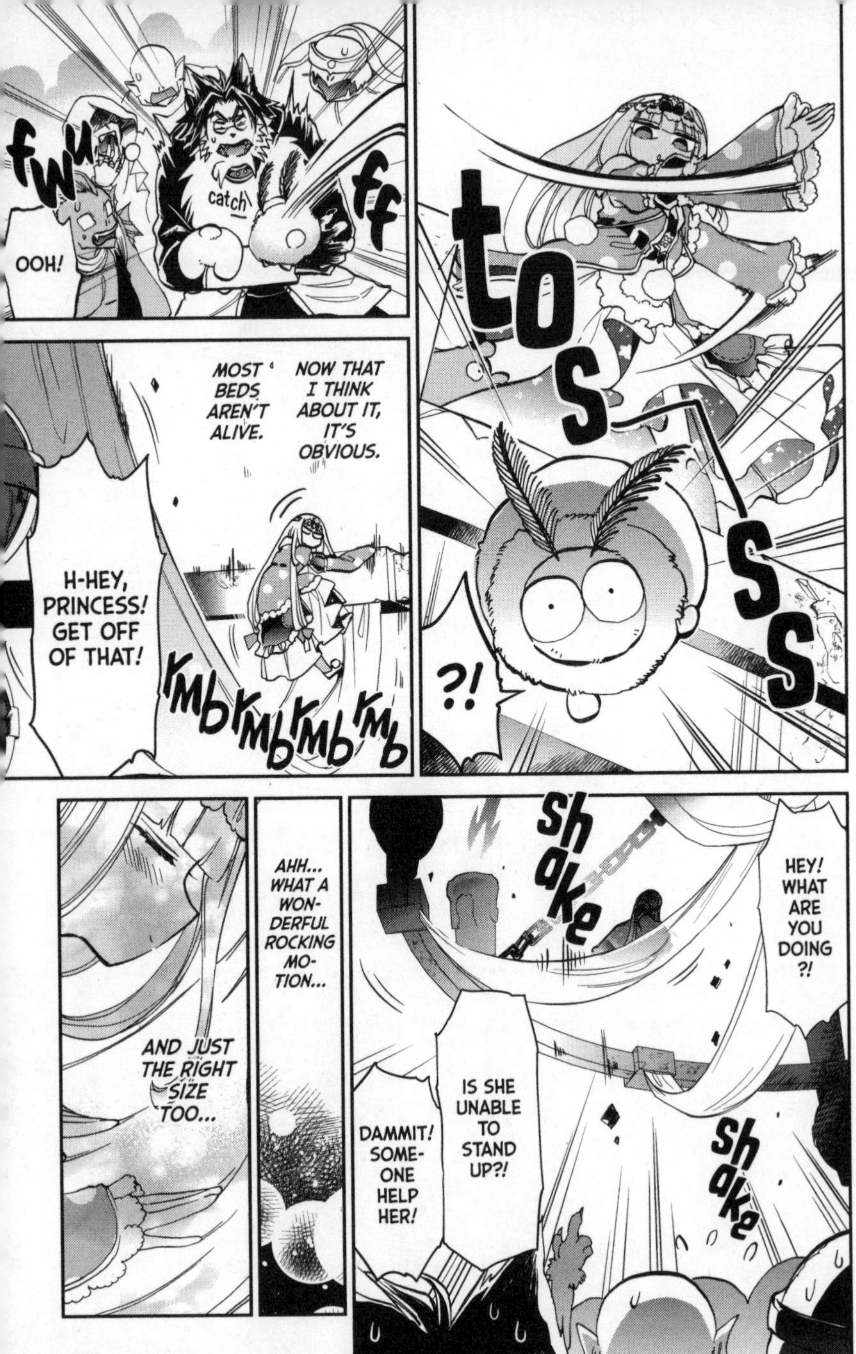
tosss
?!
fwuff
catch
OOH!
NOW THAT I THINK ABOUT IT, IT'S OBVIOUS.
MOST BEDS AREN'T ALIVE.
H-HEY, PRINCESS! GET OFF OF THAT!
rmbrmbrmbrmb
shake
HEY! WHAT ARE YOU DOING?!
IS SHE UNABLE TO STAND UP?!
DAMMIT! SOMEONE HELP HER!
shake
AHH... WHAT A WONDERFUL ROCKING MOTION...
AND JUST THE RIGHT SIZE TOO...

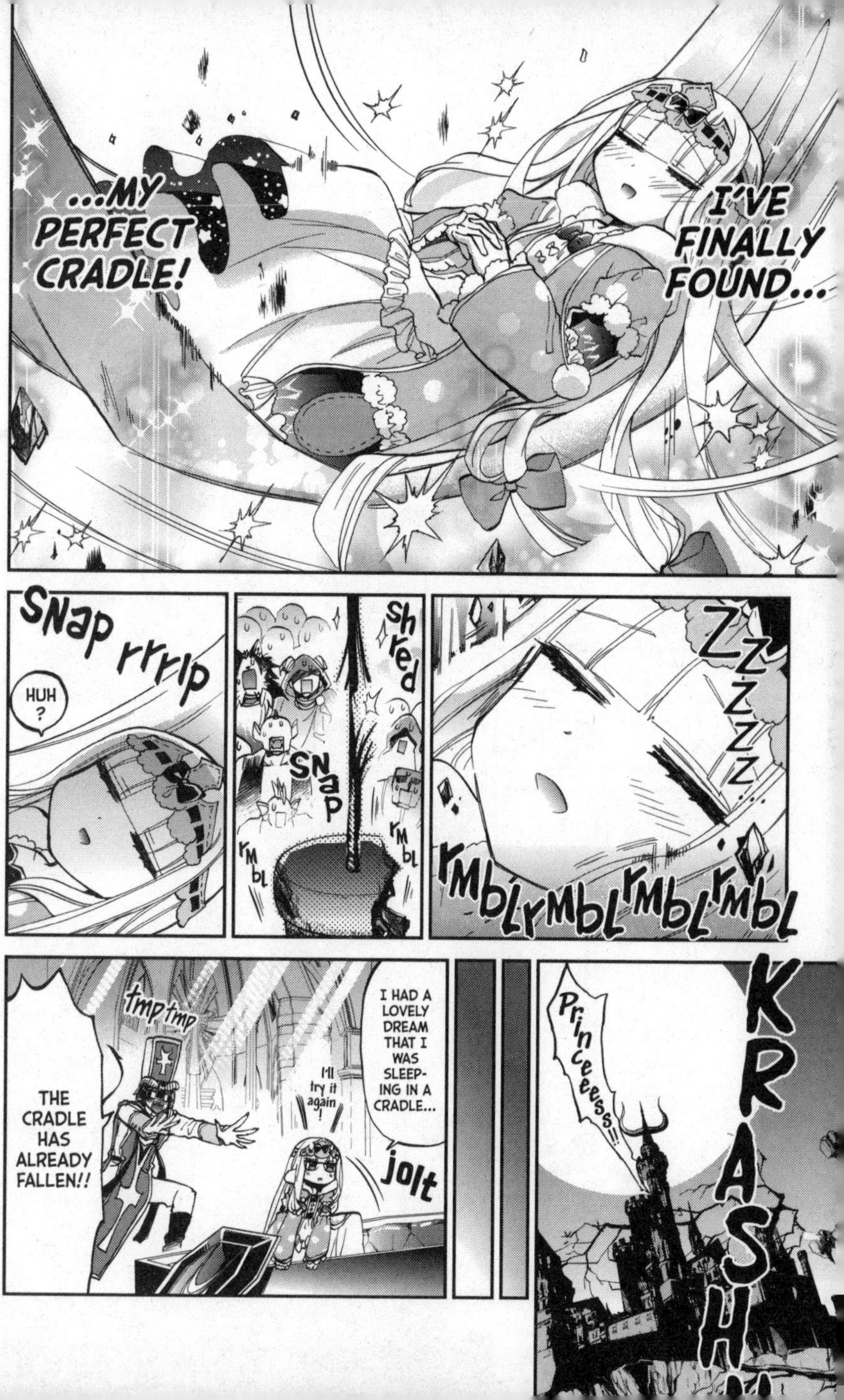
I'VE FINALLY FOUND...
...MY PERFECT CRADLE!
ZZZZZ...
rmbl rmbl rmbl rmbl
shred
SNAP
rmbl
rmbl
SNAP rrrip
HUH?
KRASH
Princeeess!!
I HAD A LOVELY DREAM THAT I WAS SLEEPING IN A CRADLE...
jolt
I'll try it again!
tmp tmp
THE CRADLE HAS ALREADY FALLEN!!

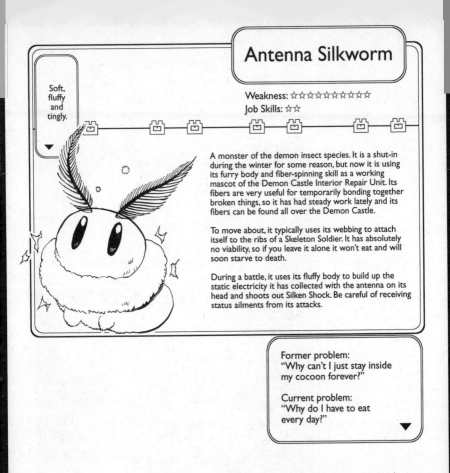

Antenna Silkworm

Soft, fluffy and tingly.

Weakness: ☆☆☆☆☆☆☆☆☆☆☆

Job Skills: ☆☆

A monster of the demon insect species. It is a shut-in during the winter for some reason, but now it is using its furry body and fiber-spinning skill as a working mascot of the Demon Castle Interior Repair Unit. Its fibers are very useful for temporarily bonding together broken things, so it has had steady work lately and its fibers can be found all over the Demon Castle.

To move about, it typically uses its webbing to attach itself to the ribs of a Skeleton Soldier. It has absolutely no viability, so if you leave it alone it won't eat and will soon starve to death.

During a battle, it uses its fluffy body to build up the static electricity it has collected with the antenna on its head and shoots out Silken Shock. Be careful of receiving status ailments from its attacks.

Former problem:
"Why can't I just stay inside my cocoon forever?"

Current problem:
"Why do I have to eat every day?"

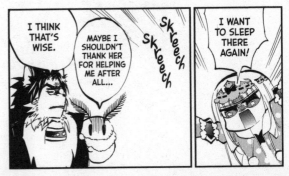

I WANT TO SLEEP THERE AGAIN!
Skreech
Skreech
MAYBE I SHOULDN'T THANK HER FOR HELPING ME AFTER ALL...
I THINK THAT'S WISE.

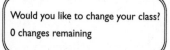

Would you like to change your class?
0 changes remaining

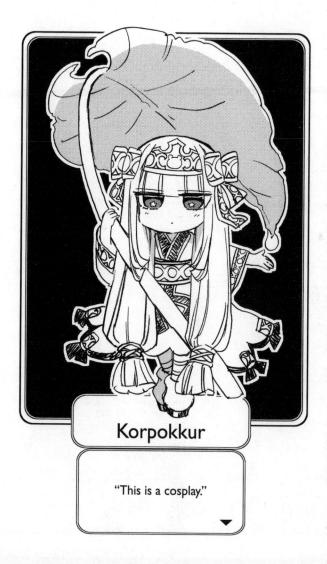

Korpokkur

"This is a cosplay."

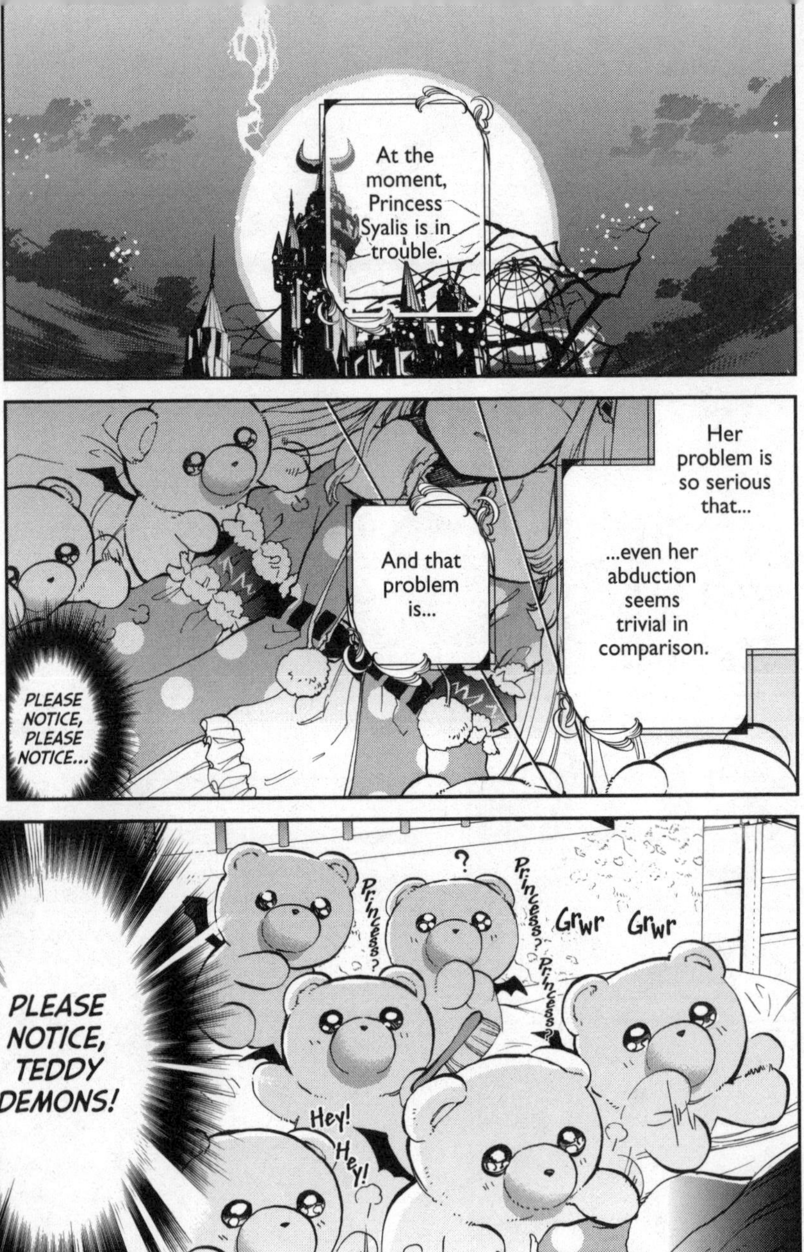
At the moment, Princess Syalis is in trouble.
Her problem is so serious that...
...even her abduction seems trivial in comparison.
And that problem is...
PLEASE NOTICE, PLEASE NOTICE...
Grwr Grwr
Princess?
Princess?
?
Princess?
PLEASE NOTICE, TEDDY DEMONS!
Hey! Hey!

26th Night: Demon Castle Paralysis

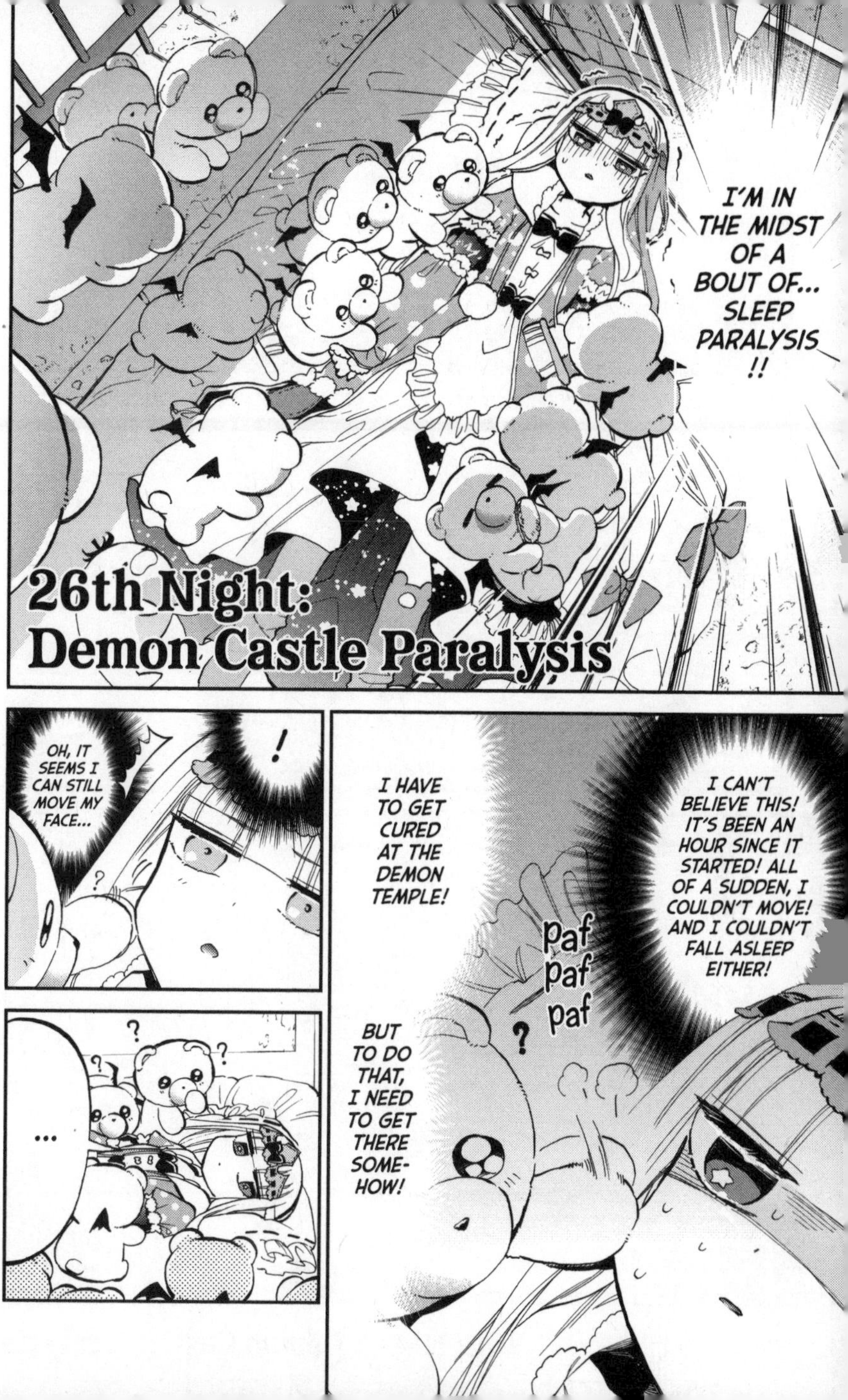
I'M IN THE MIDST OF A BOUT OF... SLEEP PARALYSIS !!
26th Night: Demon Castle Paralysis
I CAN'T BELIEVE THIS! IT'S BEEN AN HOUR SINCE IT STARTED! ALL OF A SUDDEN, I COULDN'T MOVE! AND I COULDN'T FALL ASLEEP EITHER!
I HAVE TO GET CURED AT THE DEMON TEMPLE!
paf paf paf
?
BUT TO DO THAT, I NEED TO GET THERE SOMEHOW!
OH, IT SEEMS I CAN STILL MOVE MY FACE...
!
?
?
?
?
...

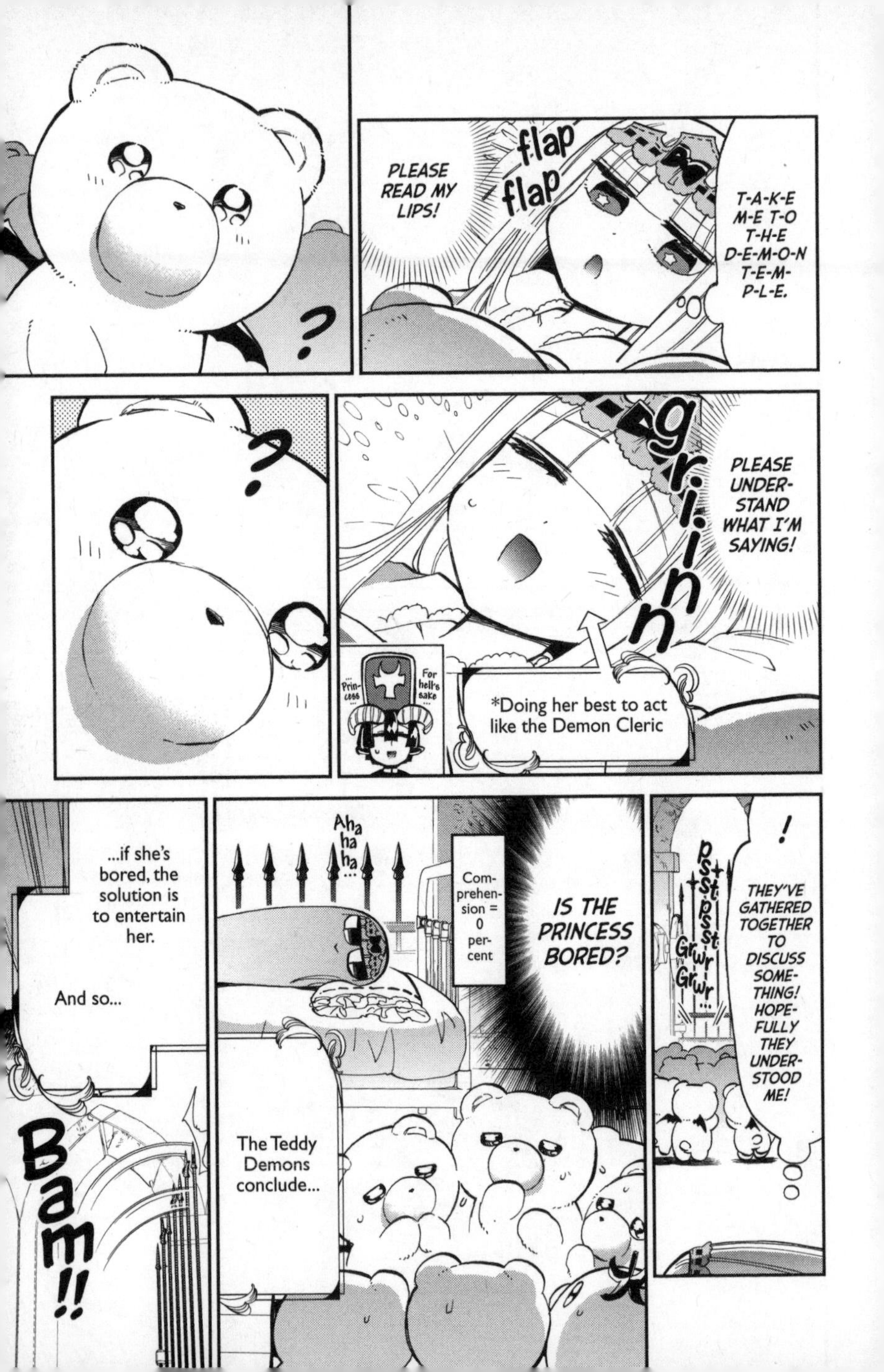
T-A-K-E M-E T-O T-H-E D-E-M-O-N T-E-M-P-L-E.
flap flap
PLEASE READ MY LIPS!
?
PLEASE UNDER-STAND WHAT I'M SAYING!
grinnn
*Doing her best to act like the Demon Cleric
For hell's sake
...Princess...
?
!
THEY'VE GATHERED TOGETHER TO DISCUSS SOME-THING! HOPE-FULLY THEY UNDER-STOOD ME!
pstpstpst
Grwr Grwr...
IS THE PRINCESS BORED?
Com-prehen-sion = 0 per-cent
Ahahahaha...
The Teddy Demons conclude...
...if she's bored, the solution is to entertain her.
And so...
Bam!!

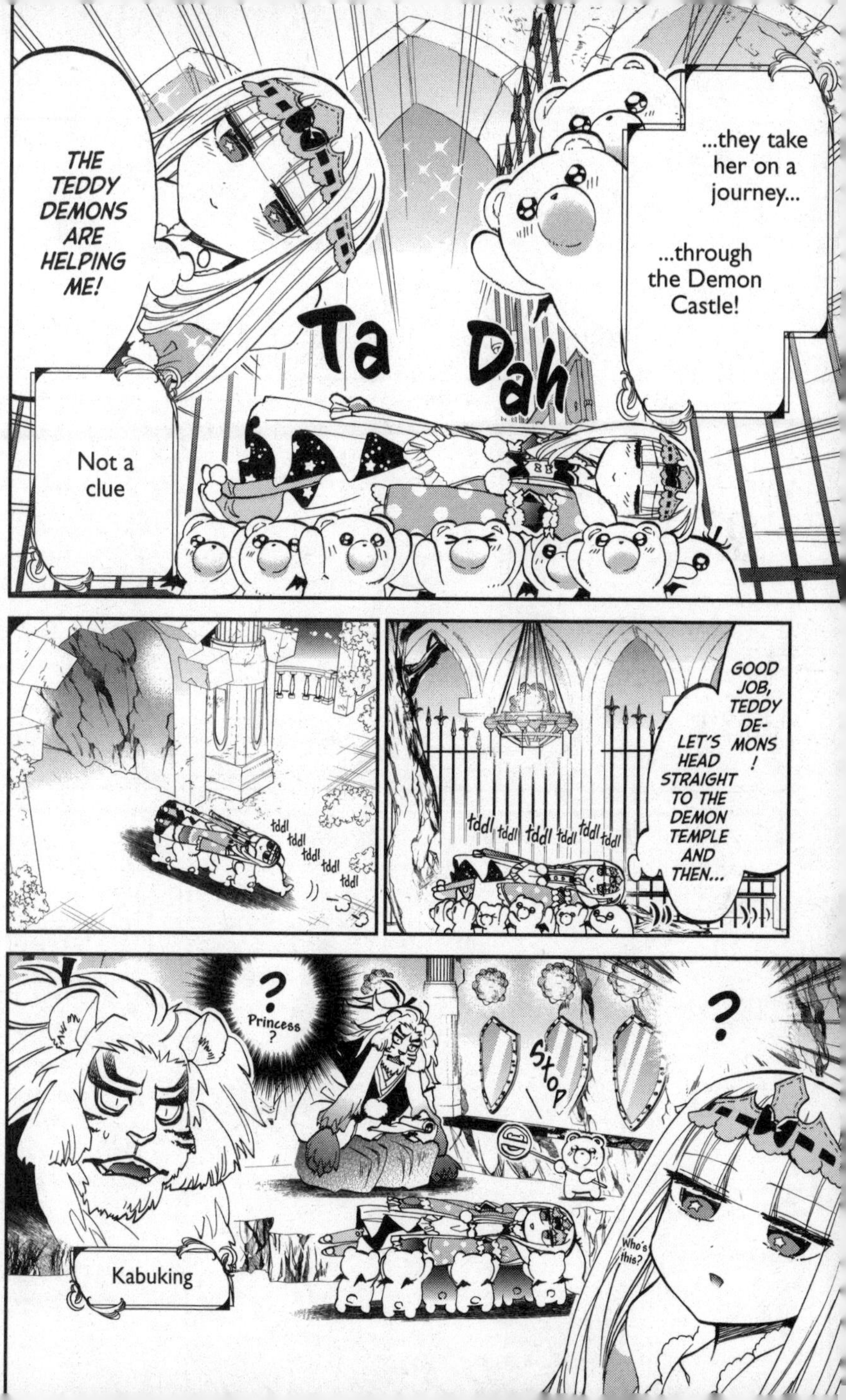
...they take her on a journey...
...through the Demon Castle!
THE TEDDY DEMONS ARE HELPING ME!
Ta Dah
Not a clue
tddl tddl tddl tddl tddl tddl
GOOD JOB, TEDDY DEMONS!
LET'S HEAD STRAIGHT TO THE DEMON TEMPLE AND THEN...
tddl tddl tddl tddl tddl
?
Stop
Who's this?
?
Princess ?
Kabuking

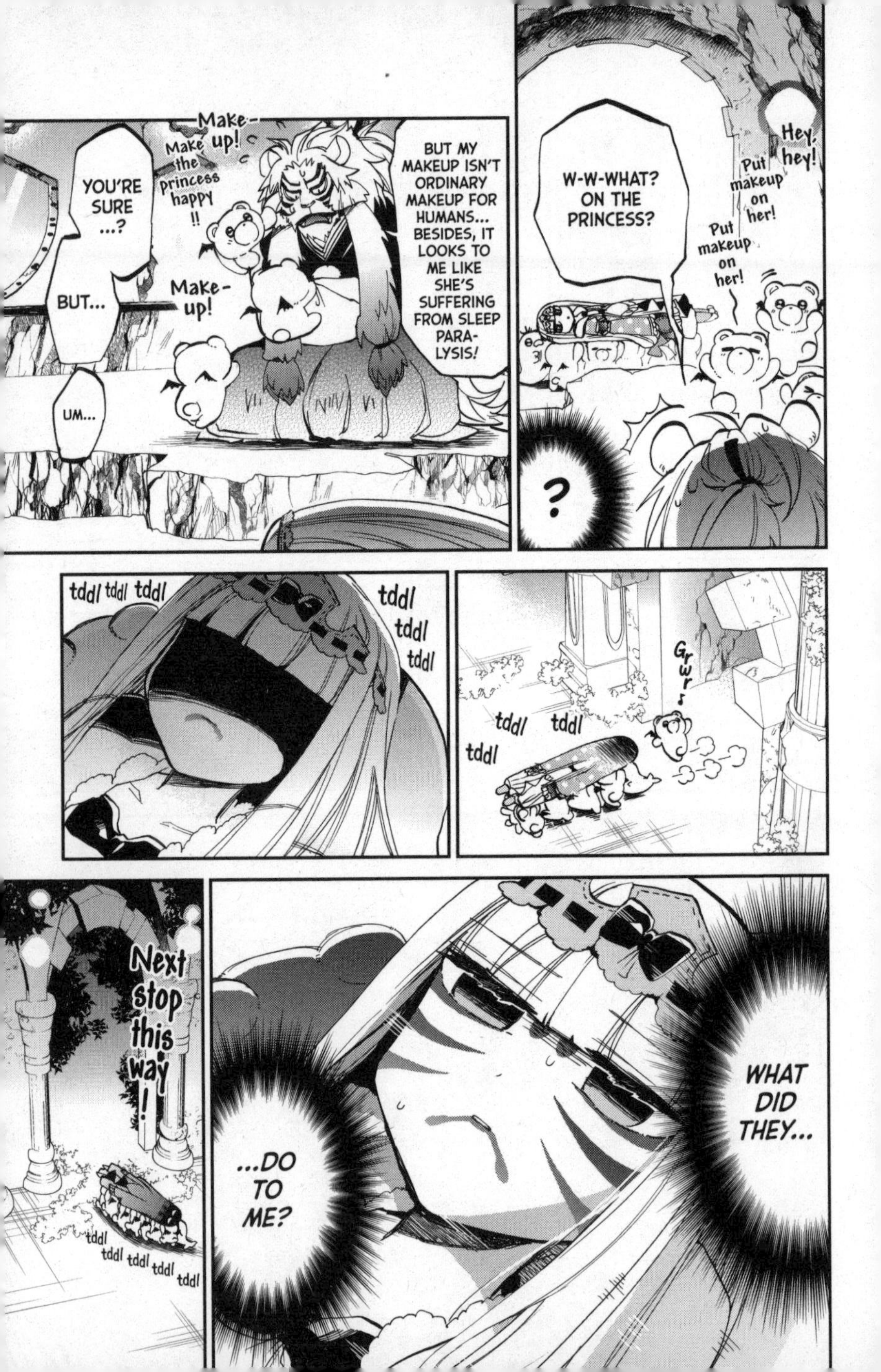
Hey, hey!
Put makeup on her!
W-W-WHAT? ON THE PRINCESS?
Put makeup on her!
?
BUT MY MAKEUP ISN'T ORDINARY MAKEUP FOR HUMANS... BESIDES, IT LOOKS TO ME LIKE SHE'S SUFFERING FROM SLEEP PARA-LYSIS!
Make-
Make up! Make the princess happy!!
YOU'RE SURE ...?
Make-up!
BUT...
UM...
Grwr
tddl tddl tddl
tddl tddl tddl
tddl tddl tddl
WHAT DID THEY...
...DO TO ME?
Next stop this way!
tddl tddl tddl tddl tddl

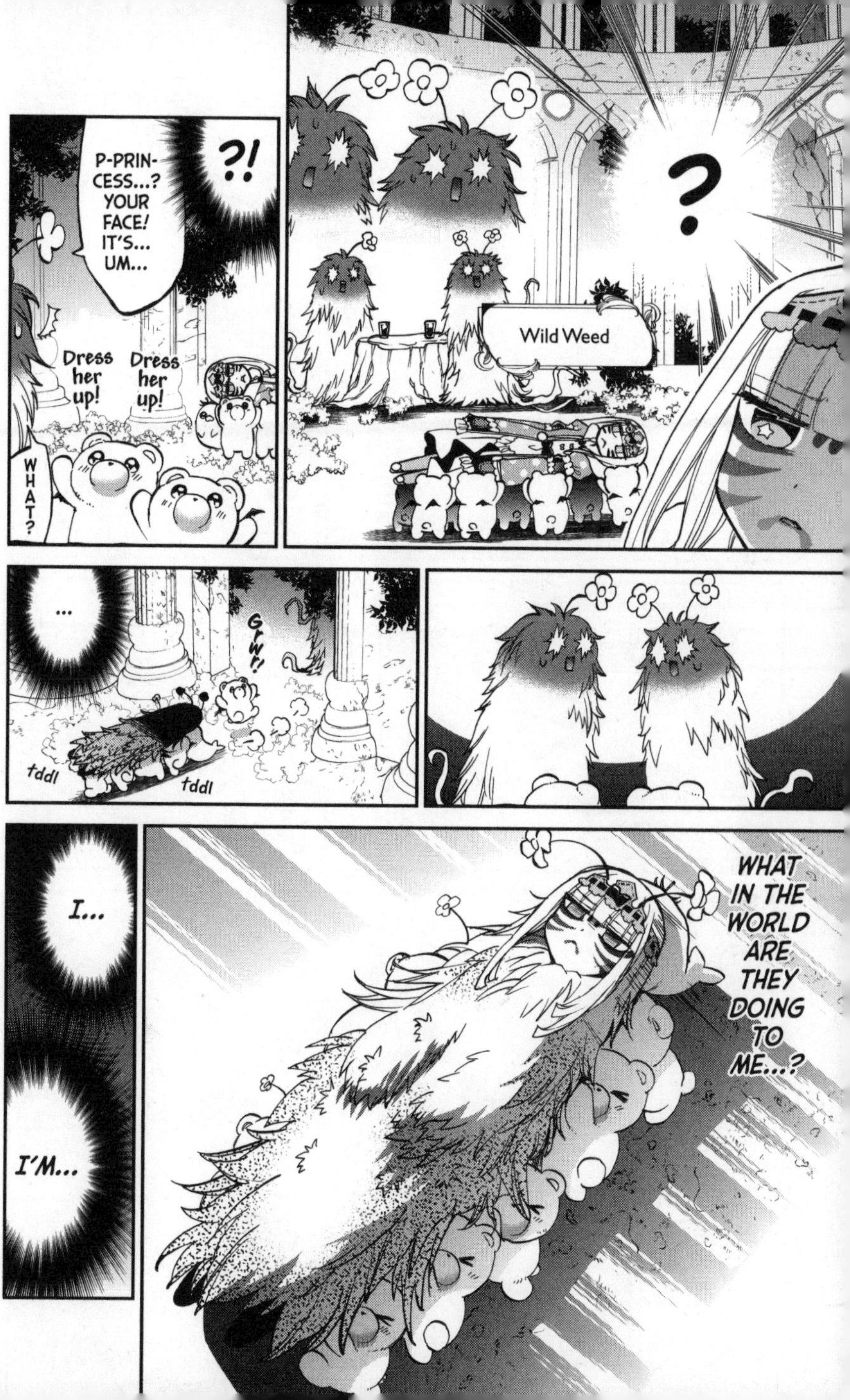
?
Wild Weed
?!
P-PRINCESS...? YOUR FACE! IT'S... UM...
Dress her up!
Dress her up!
WHAT?
...
Grwr!
tddl
tddl
WHAT IN THE WORLD ARE THEY DOING TO ME...?
I...
I'M...

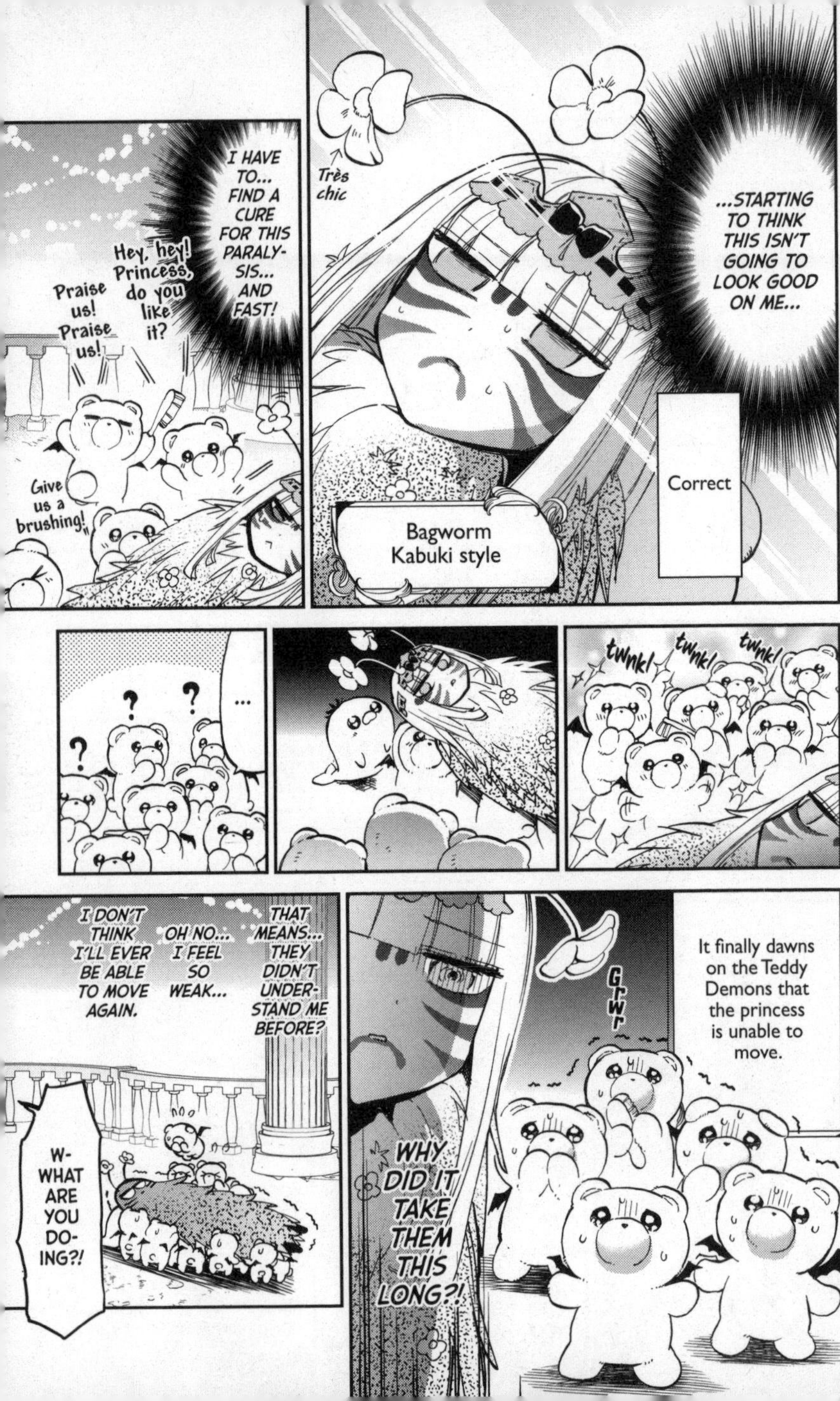
...STARTING TO THINK THIS ISN'T GOING TO LOOK GOOD ON ME...
Très chic
Correct
Bagworm Kabuki style
I HAVE TO... FIND A CURE FOR THIS PARALYSIS... AND FAST!
Hey, hey! Princess, do you like it?
Praise us! Praise us!
Give us a brushing!
twnkl
twnkl
twnkl
...
It finally dawns on the Teddy Demons that the princess is unable to move.
Grwr
WHY DID IT TAKE THEM THIS LONG?!
THAT MEANS... THEY DIDN'T UNDERSTAND ME BEFORE?
OH NO... I FEEL SO WEAK...
I DON'T THINK I'LL EVER BE ABLE TO MOVE AGAIN.
W-WHAT ARE YOU DOING?!

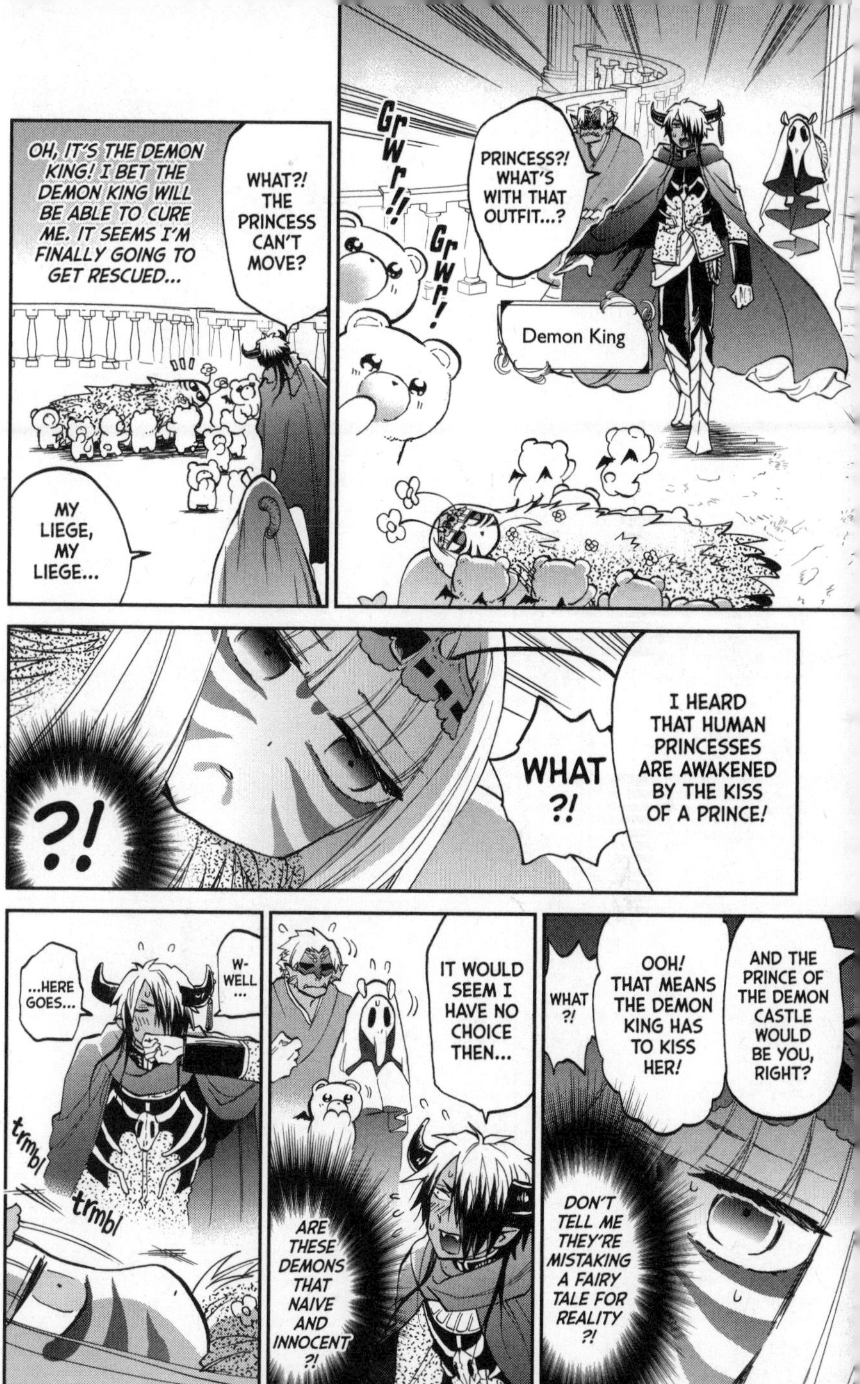
PRINCESS?! WHAT'S WITH THAT OUTFIT...?
Grwr!!
Grwr!
Demon King
WHAT?! THE PRINCESS CAN'T MOVE?
OH, IT'S THE DEMON KING! I BET THE DEMON KING WILL BE ABLE TO CURE ME. IT SEEMS I'M FINALLY GOING TO GET RESCUED...
MY LIEGE, MY LIEGE...
I HEARD THAT HUMAN PRINCESSES ARE AWAKENED BY THE KISS OF A PRINCE!
WHAT ?!
?!
AND THE PRINCE OF THE DEMON CASTLE WOULD BE YOU, RIGHT?
OOH! THAT MEANS THE DEMON KING HAS TO KISS HER!
WHAT ?!
DON'T TELL ME THEY'RE MISTAKING A FAIRY TALE FOR REALITY ?!
IT WOULD SEEM I HAVE NO CHOICE THEN...
ARE THESE DEMONS THAT NAIVE AND INNOCENT ?!
W-WELL ...
...HERE GOES...
trmbl
trmbl

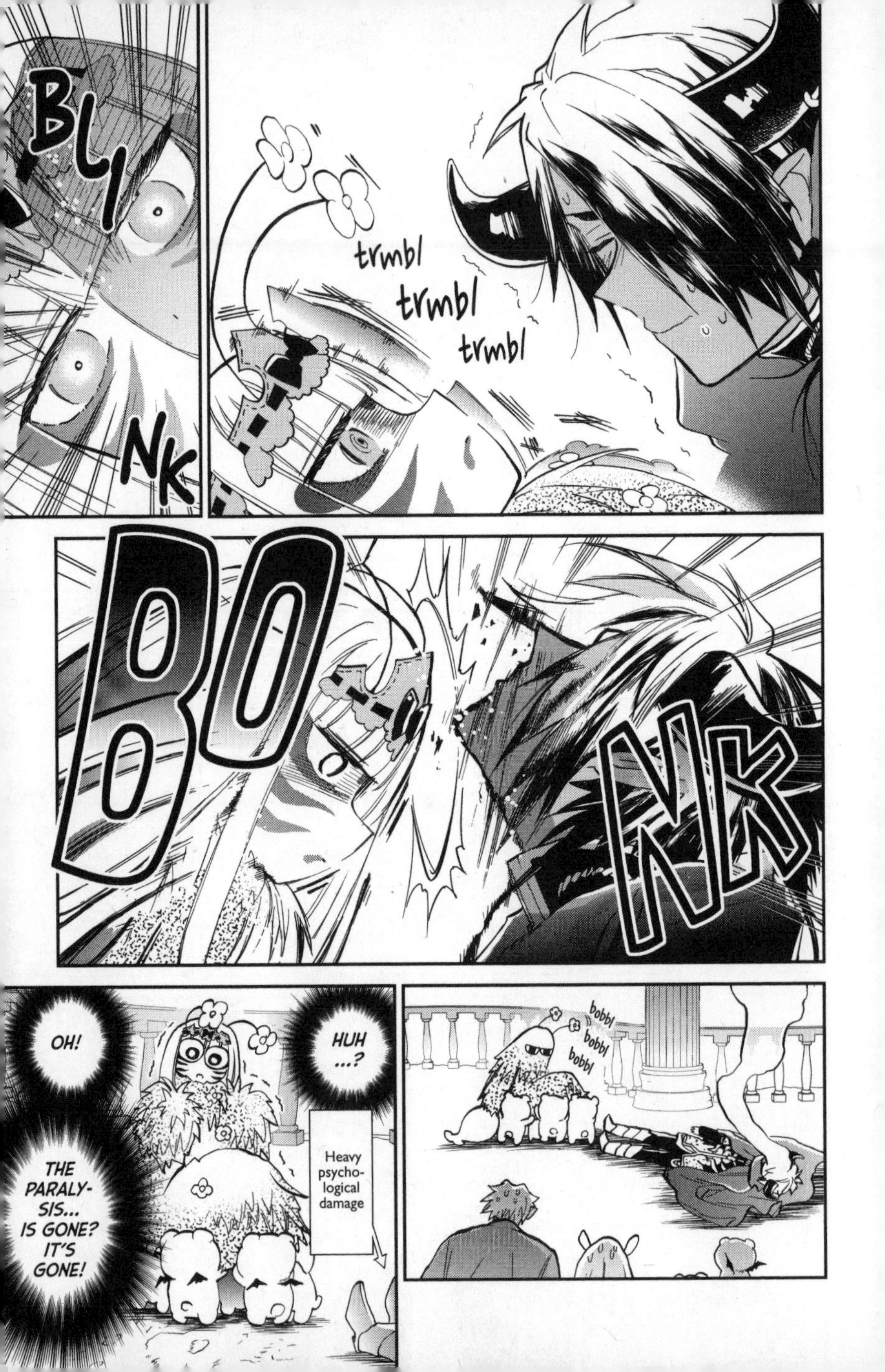
trmbl
trmbl
trmbl
BLI
NK
BOO
NK
bobbl
bobbl
bobbl
HUH ...?
OH!
Heavy psycho-logical damage
THE PARALY-SIS... IS GONE? IT'S GONE!

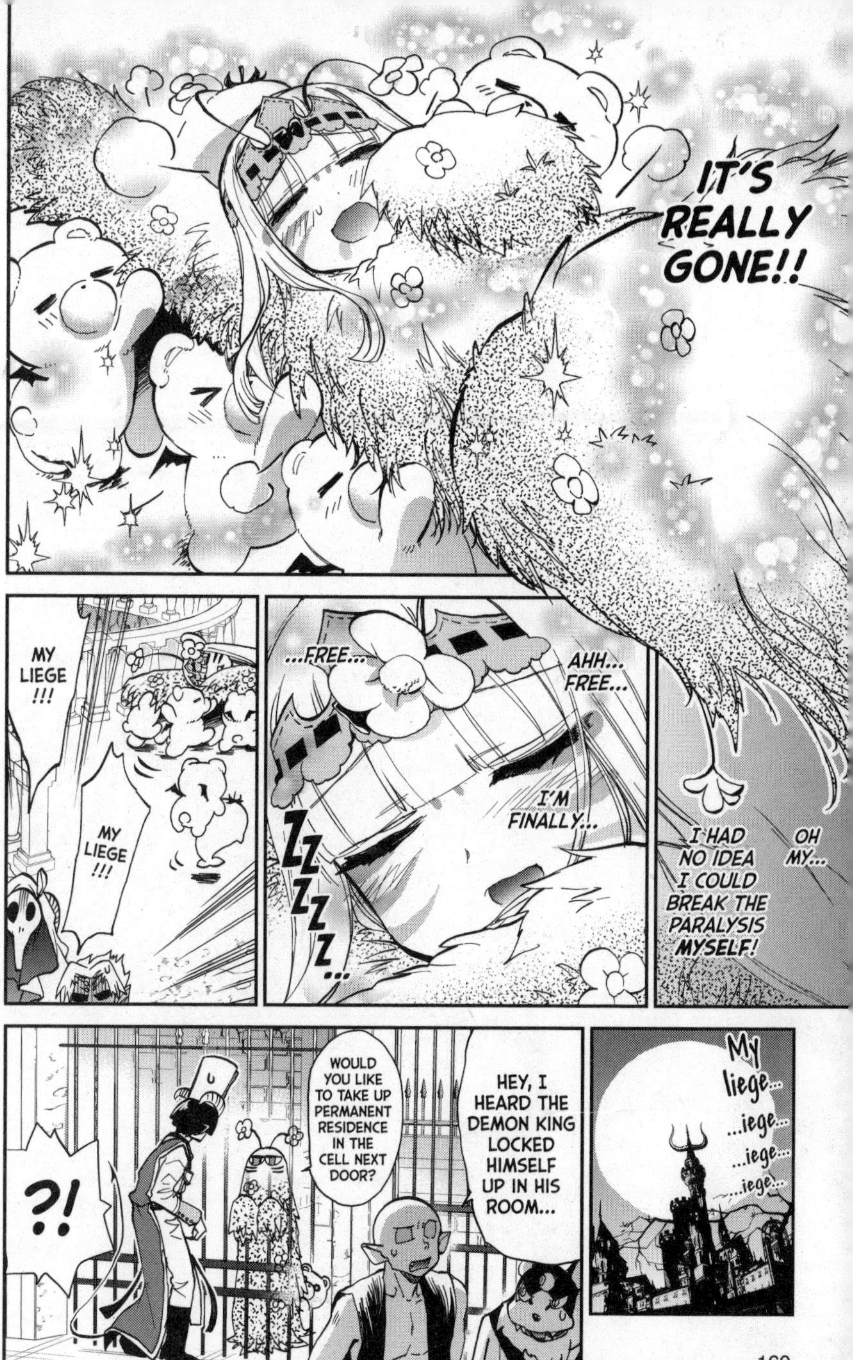
IT'S REALLY GONE!!
OH MY...
I HAD NO IDEA I COULD BREAK THE PARALYSIS MYSELF!
AHH... FREE...
...FREE...
I'M FINALLY...
ZZZZZ...
MY LIEGE!!!
MY LIEGE!!!
My liege...
...iege...
...iege...
...iege...
HEY, I HEARD THE DEMON KING LOCKED HIMSELF UP IN HIS ROOM...
WOULD YOU LIKE TO TAKE UP PERMANENT RESIDENCE IN THE CELL NEXT DOOR?
?!

Demon Castle Route Selection

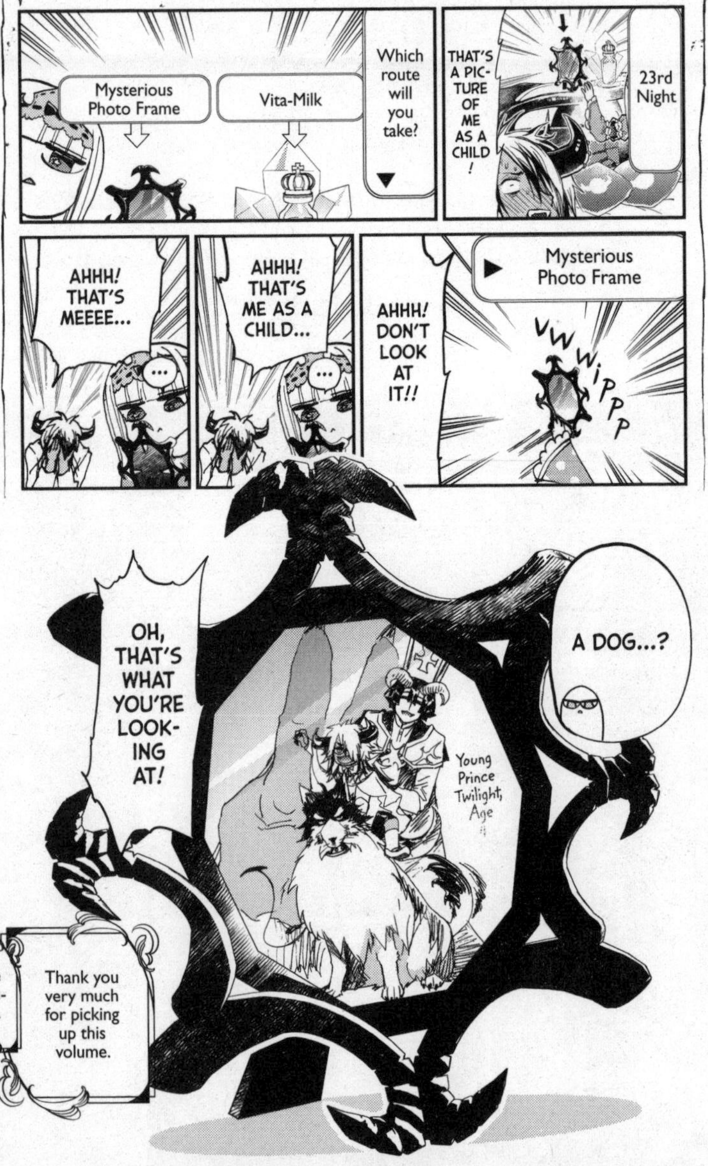
23rd Night
THAT'S A PICTURE OF ME AS A CHILD!
Which route will you take?
Vita-Milk
Mysterious Photo Frame
Mysterious Photo Frame
AHHH! DON'T LOOK AT IT!!
VWWWIPPP
AHHH! THAT'S ME AS A CHILD...
...
AHHH! THAT'S MEEEE...
...
A DOG...?
OH, THAT'S WHAT YOU'RE LOOKING AT!
Young Prince Twilight, Age 4
Thank you very much for picking up this volume.
To be continued...

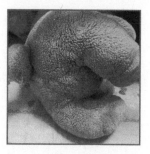

Hello, Kumanomata here. This is *Sleepy Princess in the Demon Castle* volume 2. Thank you for reading. Princess Syalis is sucking away all my sleep time.

— KAGIJI KUMANOMATA

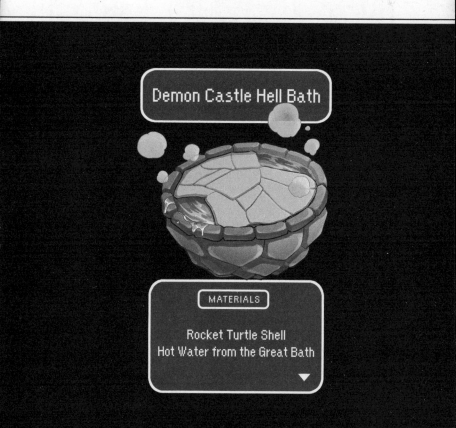

Demon Castle Hell Bath

MATERIALS

Rocket Turtle Shell
Hot Water from the Great Bath

▼

Those who lurk beneath the cover...

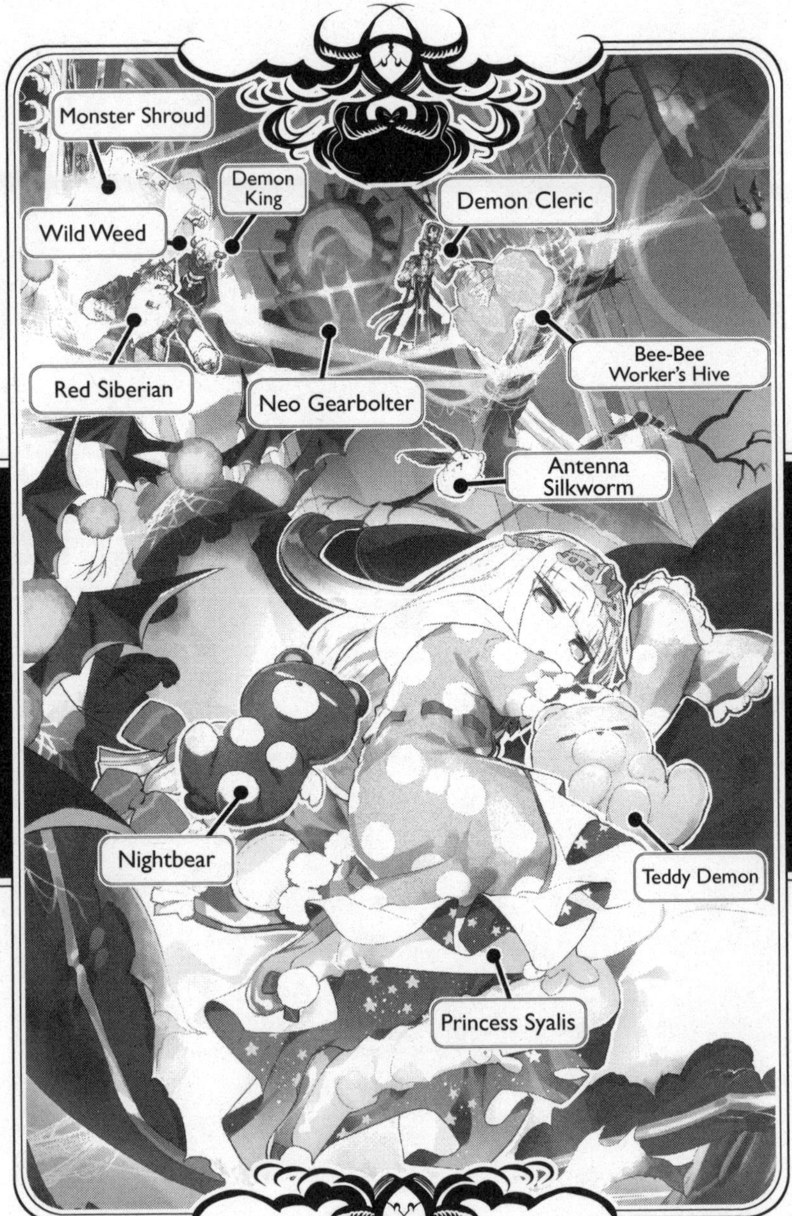
Monster Shroud
Demon King
Demon Cleric
Wild Weed
Bee-Bee Worker's Hive
Red Siberian
Neo Gearbolter
Antenna Silkworm
Nightbear
Teddy Demon
Princess Syalis

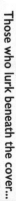

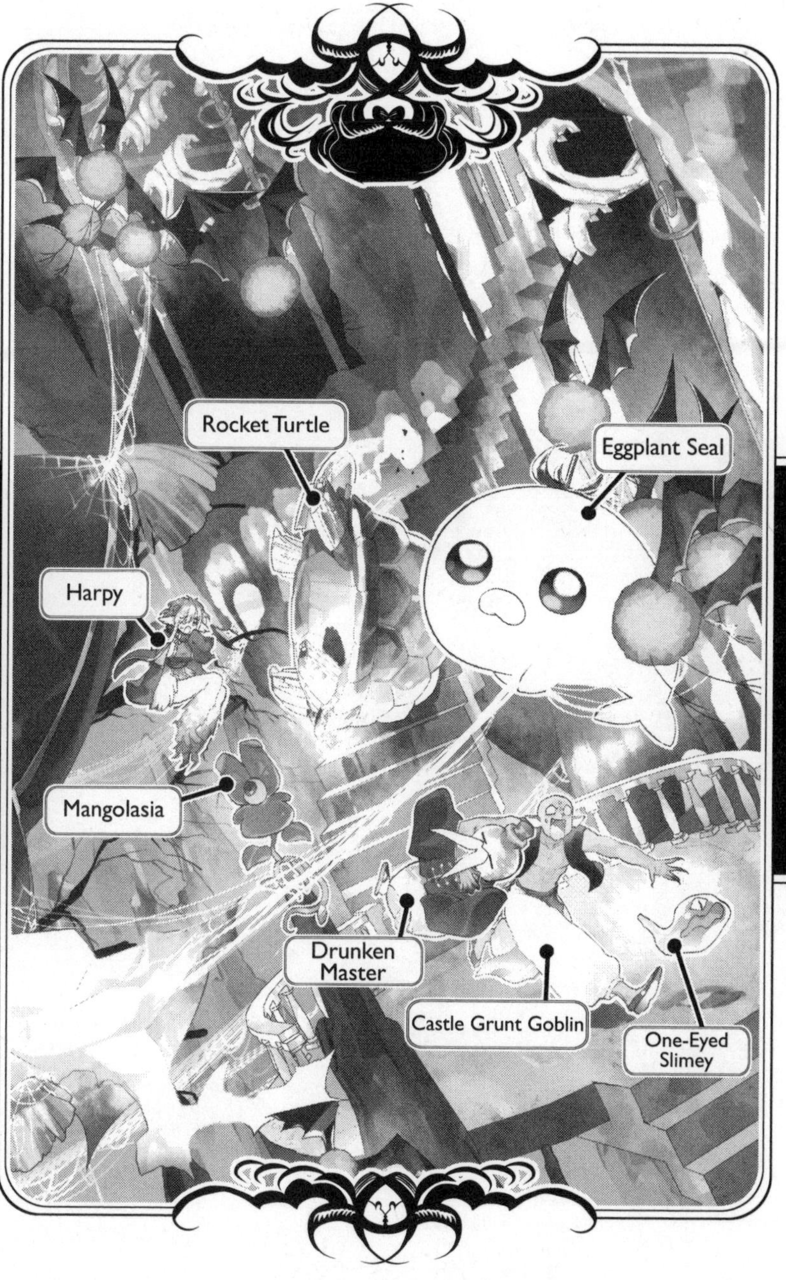
Rocket Turtle
Eggplant Seal
Harpy
Mangolasia
Drunken Master
Castle Grunt Goblin
One-Eyed Slimey

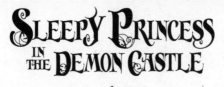

SLEEPY PRINCESS
IN THE DEMON CASTLE
2

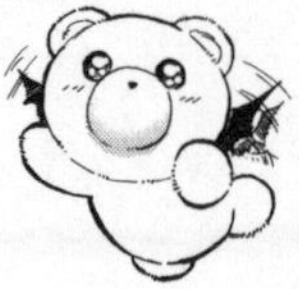

Shonen Sunday Edition

STORY AND ART BY
KAGIJI KUMANOMATA

MAOUJO DE OYASUMI Vol. 2
by Kagiji KUMANOMATA
© 2016 Kagiji KUMANOMATA
All rights reserved.
Original Japanese edition published by SHOGAKUKAN.
English translation rights in the United States of America, Canada,
the United Kingdom, Ireland, Australia and New Zealand arranged
with SHOGAKUKAN.

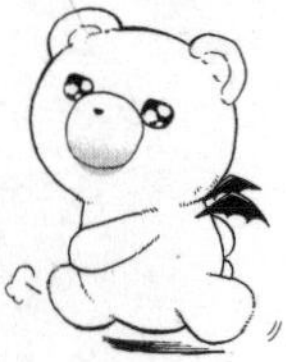

TRANSLATION **TETSUICHIRO MIYAKI**

ENGLISH ADAPTATION **ANNETTE ROMAN**

TOUCH-UP ART & LETTERING **SUSAN DAIGLE-LEACH**

COVER & INTERIOR DESIGN **ALICE LEWIS**

EDITOR **ANNETTE ROMAN**

Printed in the U.S.A.

Published by VIZ Media, LLC
P.O. Box 77010
San Francisco, CA 94107

10 9 8 7 6 5 4 3 2
First printing, August 2018
Second printing, September 2022

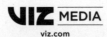

viz.com   shonensunday.com

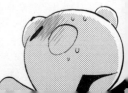

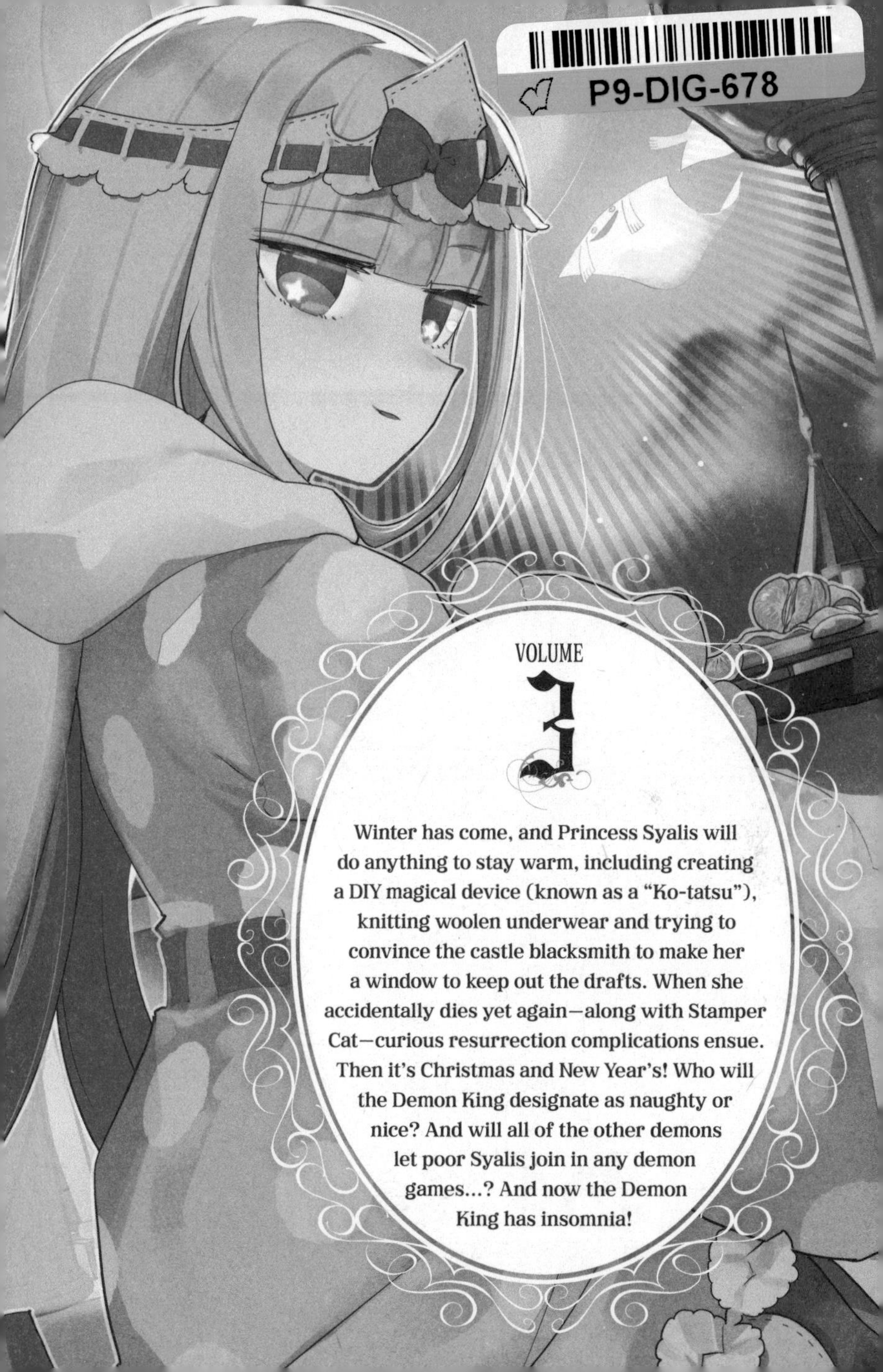

VOLUME

3

Winter has come, and Princess Syalis will do anything to stay warm, including creating a DIY magical device (known as a "Ko-tatsu"), knitting woolen underwear and trying to convince the castle blacksmith to make her a window to keep out the drafts. When she accidentally dies yet again—along with Stamper Cat—curious resurrection complications ensue. Then it's Christmas and New Year's! Who will the Demon King designate as naughty or nice? And will all of the other demons let poor Syalis join in any demon games...? And now the Demon King has insomnia!